Tel Hesi

Tell Jerishe
Jaffa
Fejja
Giv'atayim

Gezer

Emmaus
Jerusalem

Tel Jarmuth

Gibeon
Gibeah

Herodium

Jericho

'Ein Samiya

Kh. Iskander

Heshbon

'Iraq el-Emir

Tell el-Far'a

Hederah

Ein el-Jarba

Hamadiya

el-Husn

Gerasa

Husifah

Japhia

Hammat-Gader

Heptapegon

Bathyra

'En Gev
Hippos
Fiq

Mizra'at Qanef
Deir
'Aziz
Kursi
Eli-'Al
Khasfin

Kh. Daliya

Tell el-Juhadar

Tel Qedesh
'Eynan

Dardara

Hazor
Tel Harashim
'En
Natosh
Kh. Zamimra
Qisrin

Edriya
Dabbura
Dabbiye

GALILEE

UPPER

GOLAN

Surman

er-Rafid

Kh. Zamal

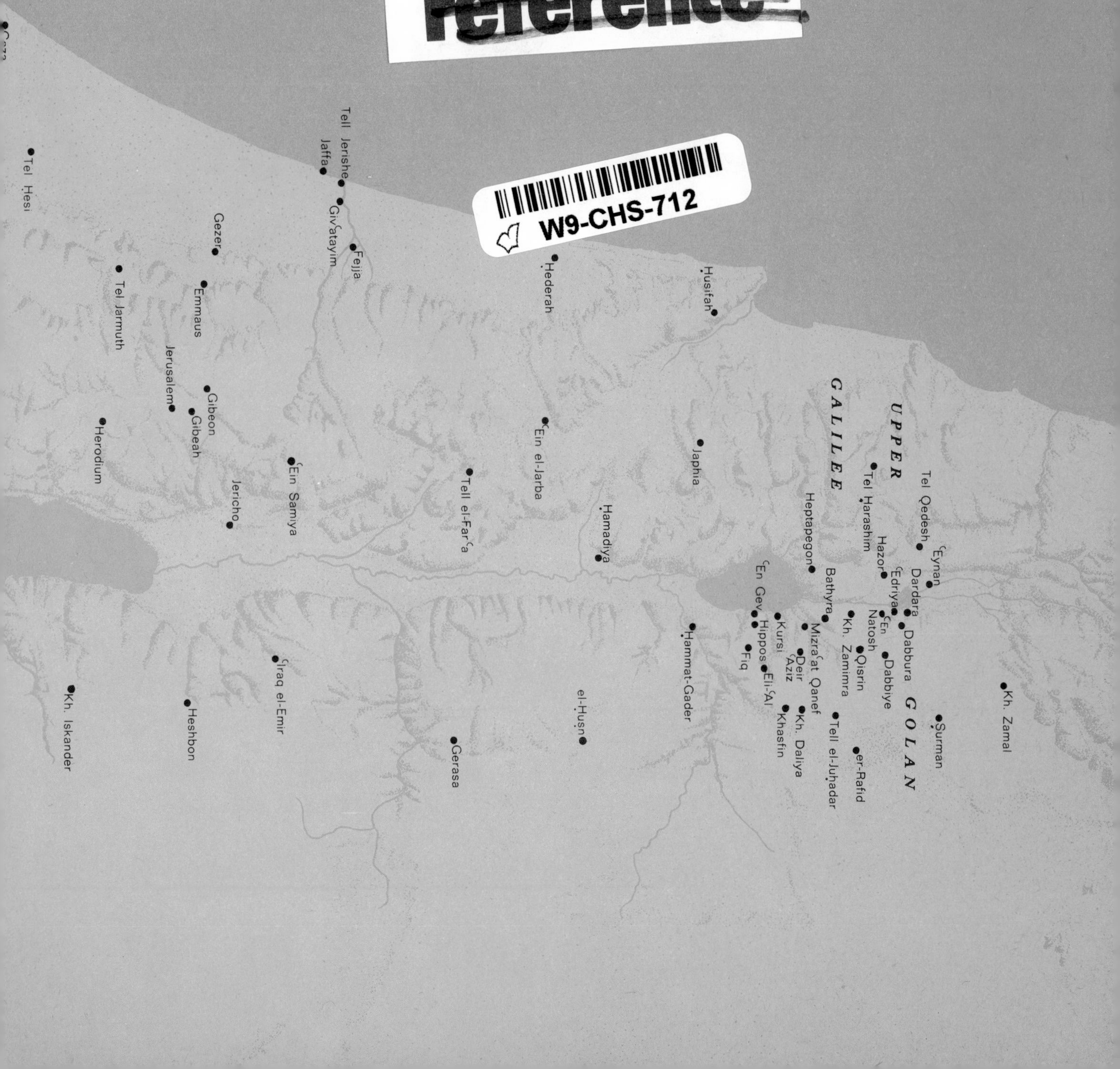

ENCYCLOPEDIA
OF ARCHAEOLOGICAL
EXCAVATIONS
IN THE HOLY LAND

ENCYCLOPEDIA
OF ARCHAEOLOGICAL
EXCAVATIONS
IN THE HOLY LAND

VOLUME II

Editor, English Edition
Michael Avi-Yonah

Prentice-Hall, Inc., Englewood Cliffs, N.J.

LIBRARY OF CONGRESS CATALOGING IN PUBLICATION DATA
MAIN ENTRY UNDER TITLE:
THE ENCYCLOPEDIA OF ARCHAEOLOGICAL EXCAVATIONS IN THE HOLY LAND.
1. Palestine — Antiquities — Dictionaries.
2. Bible — Antiquities — Dictionaries. I. Avi-Yonah,
Michael, 1904–1974 ed.
DS111.A2E5   220.9'3   73–14997
ISBN 0–13–275123–2 (v. 2)

Simultaneously published in Great Britain by
Oxford University Press, London

Printed in Israel by Peli Printing Works Ltd.

CONTRIBUTORS TO THIS VOLUME

PROF. YOHANAN AHARONI, Tel Aviv University — *Upper Galilee*

PROF. RUTH AMIRAN, Israel Museum, Jerusalem — *Tel Ḥesi, Tell Jemmeh*

PROF. SHIMON APPLEBAUM, Tel Aviv University — *Gerasa*

PROF. NAHMAN AVIGAD, Hebrew University, Jerusalem — *Tell Jerishe, Jerusalem*

PROF. MICHAEL AVI-YONAH (deceased), Hebrew University, Jerusalem — *Emmaus, Ḥammat Gader, Heptapegon, Ḥusifah, Jerusalem*

MISS GABRIELLA BACCHI, Tel Aviv University — *Jericho*

DR. DAN BARAG, Hebrew University, Jerusalem — *En-Gedi, Eshtemoa, Japhia*

PROF. OFER BAR-YOSEF, Hebrew University, Jerusalem — *'En Gev, Jerusalem*

DR. AMNON BEN-TOR, Hebrew University, Jerusalem — *Tel Jarmuth*

R. DE VAUX, O. P. (deceased), Ecole Biblique et Archéologique Française, Jerusalem — *Tell el-Far'a (North)*

DR. WILLIAM G. DEVER, W. F. Albright Institute, Jerusalem — *Gezer*

DR. CLAIRE EPSTEIN, Department of Antiquities and Museums, Jerusalem — *Golan, Hippos*

DR. GIDEON FOERSTER, Hebrew University, Jerusalem — *Herodium, Jericho*

PROF. MORDECHAI GICHON, Tel Aviv University — *'En Boqeq*

DR. SIEGFRIED H. HORN, Andrews University, Berrien Springs, Mich. — *Heshbon*

MRS. ḤAYA KAPLAN, Tel Aviv — *Jaffa*

DR. JACOB KAPLAN, Museum of Antiquities, Tel Aviv–Jaffa — *'Ein el-Jarba, Fejja, Giv'atayim, Ḥamadiya, Jaffa*

DAME KATHLEEN M. KENYON, St. Hugh's College, Oxford — *Jericho, Jerusalem*

DR. MOSHE KOCHAVI, Tel Aviv University — *el-Ḥuṣn, Khirbet Iskander*

DR. PAUL W. LAPP (deceased), Pittsburgh Theological Seminary — *'Iraq el-Emir*

PROF. BENJAMIN MAZAR, Hebrew University, Jerusalem — *En-Gedi, 'En Gev, Jerusalem*

PROF. ABRAHAM NEGEV, Hebrew University, Jerusalem — *Eboda, Elusa*

MR. EHUD NETZER, Hebrew University, Jerusalem — *Jericho*

DR. ASHER OVADIAH, Tel Aviv University — *Gaza*

M. JEAN PERROT, French Archaeological Mission, Jerusalem — *'Eynan*

PROF. JAMES B. PRITCHARD, University of Pennsylvania, Philadelphia, Pa. — *Gibeon*

DR. LAWRENCE A. SINCLAIR, Carroll College, Helena, Mont. — *Gibeah*

MR. DAN URMAN, Department of Antiquities and Museums, Jerusalem — *Golan*

DR. GUS W. VAN BEEK, Smithsonian Institution, Washington, D.C. — *Tell Jemmeh*

DR. JOHN E. WORRELL, Hartford Seminary Foundation, Hartford, Conn. — *Tell el-Ḥesi*

PROF. YIGAEL YADIN, Hebrew University, Jerusalem — *Hazor, Ḥederah*

DR. ZEEV YEIVIN, Department of Antiquities and Museums, Jerusalem — *'Ein Samiya*

LIST OF ABBREVIATIONS

Abel, GP. F. M. Abel, Géographie de la Palestine 1–2, Paris 1933–1938

Aharoni, LB. Aharoni, Y: The Land of the Bible, London 1966

Alt, KSch. A. Alt, Kleine Schriften zur Geschichte des Volkes Israel 1–3, München 1953–1959

Avi-Yonah, HL. Avi-Yonah, M.: The Holy Land, Grand Rapids 1966

Benoit et alii, Discoveries 2. P. Benoit — J. T. Milik — R. de Vaux, Discoveries in the Judaean Desert 2 (Les Grottes de Murabba'at), Oxford 1961

Bliss — Macalister, Excavations. F. J. Bliss — R. A. S. Macalister, Excavations in Palestine during the Years 1898–1900, London 1902

Brünnow — Domaszewski, Die Provincia Arabia. R.E. Brünnow — A. V. Domaszewski, Die Provincia Arabia 1–3, Strassburg 1904–1909

Clermont-Ganneau, ARP. C. Clermont-Ganneau, Archaeological Researches in Palestine 1–2, London 1896–1899

Clermont-Ganneau, RAO. C. Clermont-Ganneau, Recueil d'archéologie orientale 1–8, Paris 1888 ss.

Conder-Kitchener, SWP. C. R. Conder–H. H. Kitchener, Survey of Western Palestine, Memoirs 1–3, London 1881–1883

Crowfoot, Early Churches J. W. Crowfoot, Early Churches in Palestine, London 1941

EI. Eretz-Israel, Jerusalem 1950 ff.

Enc. Miqr. Encyclopaedia Biblica, 6 vols, Jerusalem 1955 ff.

Frey, Corpus. J. B. Frey, Corpus Inscriptionum Iudaicarum 2, Roma 1952

Goodenough, Jewish Symbols. E. R. Goodenough, Jewish Symbols in the Greco-Roman Period 1–12, New York 1953–1965

Guérin, Galilée. V. Guérin, Description géographique, historique et archéologique de la Palestine, Galilée, Paris 1868–1880

Guérin, Galilée. V. Guérin, Description géographique historique et archéologique de la Palestine, Judée, Paris 1868–1869

Hill, BMC. G. F. Hill, Catalogue of the Greek Coins in the British Museum, Palestine, London 1914

Klein, Corpus. S. Klein, Jüdisch-palästinisches Corpus Inscriptionum, Wien-Berlin 1920

Kohl-Watzinger, Synagogen. H. Kohl — C. Watzinger, Antike Synagogen in Galilea, Leipzig 1916

Lidzbarski, Ephemeris. M. Lidzbarski, Ephemeris für semitische Epigraphik 1–3, Giessen 1902–1915

Musil, Arabia Petraea. A. Musil, Arabia Petraea 1–3, Wien 1907–1908

Pritchard, ANET. J. B. Pritchard (ed.) Ancient Near Eastern Texts Relating to the Old Testament, Princeton 1950

Robinson, Biblical Researches. E. Robinson, Biblical Researches in Palestine, London 1841

Saller-Bagatti, Town of Nebo. S. J. Saller — B. Bagatti, The Town of Nebo, Jerusalem 1949

Schürer, GJV2. E. Schürer, Geschichte des jüdischen Volkes im Zeitalter Jesu Christi, Leipzig 1907

Sukenik, Ancient Synagogues. E. L. Sukenik, Ancient Synagogues in Palestine and Greece, London 1934

Vincent-Abel, Jérusalem Nouvelle. L. H. Vincent—F. M. Abel, Jérusalem nouvelle 1–2, Paris 1912–1926

Vincent-Steve, Jérusalem. L. H. Vincent — M. A. Steve, Jérusalem de l'Ancien Testament 1–4, Paris 1954–1956

Watzinger, DP. K. Watzinger, Denkmäler Palästinas 1–2, Leipzig 1933–1935

Wilson-Kitchener, Special Papers. Ch. Wilson — H. H. Kitchener, The Survey of Western Palestine, Special Papers, London 1881

AAA	Annals of Archaeology and Anthropology
AASOR	Annual of the American School of Oriental Research
ADAJ	Annual of the Department of Antiquities of Jordan
AJA	American Journal of Archaeology
AJSLL	American Journal of Semitic Languages and Literatures
'Alon	Bulletin of the Israel Department of Antiquities
APEF	Annual of the Palestine Exploration Fund
'Atiqot	Journal of the Israel Department of Antiquities
BA	Biblical Archaeologist
BASOR	Bulletin of the American Schools of Oriental Research
BBSAJ	Bulletin, British School of Archaeology in Jerusalem

BIAL	Bulletin, Institute of Archaeology, London
BIES	Bulletin of the Israel Exploration Society (1951–1962), continuing
BJPES	Bulletin of the Jewish Palestine Exploration Society
BMB	Bulletin du musée de Beyrouth
BPM	Bulletin of the Palestine Museum
BS	Bibliotheca Sacra
BZ	Biblische Zeitschrift
CRAIBL	Comptes-rendus Academie des inscriptions et belles-lettres
HUCA	Hebrew Union College Annual
IEJ	Israel Exploration Journal
ILN	The Illustrated London News
JAOS	Journal of the American Oriental Society
JBL	Journal of Biblical Literature
JCS	Journal of Cuneiform Studies
JEA	Journal of Egyptian Archaeology
JNES	Journal of Near Eastern Studies
JPOS	Journal of the Palestine Oriental Society
JRAI	Journal of the Royal Anthropological Institute
JRAS	Journal of the Royal Asiatic Society
JRS	Journal of Roman Studies
MDOG	Mitteilungen der deutschen orientalischen Gesellschaft
MUSJ	Mélanges de l'Université Saint Joseph de Beyrouth
OLZ	Orientalistische Literaturzeitung
PEFA	Palestine Exploration Fund, Annual
PEFQSt	Palestine Exploration Fund, Quarterly Statement
PEQ	Palestine Exploration Quarterly
PJB	Palästina-Jahrbuch
QDAP	Quarterly of the Department of Antiquities in Palestine
RAr	Revue Archéologique
RB	Revue biblique
RHR	Revue de l'histoire des religions
TLZ	Theologische Literaturzeitung
VT	Vetus Testamentum
Yediot	Continuation of BIES (1962–1968)
ZAW	Zeitschrift für die alttestamentliche Wissenchaft
ZDPV	Zeitschrift des deutschen Palästina-Vereins

EBODA

IDENTIFICATION. Eboda was apparently named for a Nabataean king, whose name has been preserved in the Arabic 'Abdah. The Peutinger map shows Eboda to have been situated on the main Elath–Jerusalem route. The city is also mentioned by Ptolemaeus and by Uranius (a fragment quoted by Stephanus Byzantinus). The identification with Khirbet 'Abdah is certain, in view of the similarity of the ancient and Arabic names and the geographical location. The site lies on the spur of a mountain ridge running from southeast to northwest. At its highest point it is 619 meters above sea level.

HISTORY

Eboda was founded at the end of the fourth or beginning of the third century B.C. as a station on a junction of the caravan routes from Petra and Elath to Gaza. A magnificent temple was constructed there during the reign of Aretas IV (9 B.C.–A.D. 40), and the town became an important center of Nabataean pottery manufacture. The military camp for the camel corps guarding the caravan routes, which stood northeast of the town, may also date from that time. Under Rabel II (A.D. 70–106), agricultural projects were developed in the vicinity as is evidenced by dedicatory inscriptions on libation altars found there.

Eboda was not affected by the annexation of the Nabataean kingdom and the entire Negev into the Provincia Arabia in A.D. 106. The town continued to exist until the first quarter of the second century A.D., at which time it suffered from incursions of Arab tribesmen into the central Negev. Toward the middle of the third century, settlement was revived, part of the new town rising along the southern spur of the city's ridge on the ruins of Nabataean residences. A temple dedicated to the local Zeus (Zeus Obodas) as well as a shrine to Aphrodite were built on the acropolis, apparently on the spot where a former Nabataean sanctuary had once stood. A large catacomb (en-Nuṣrah) was dug into the southwestern slope. Construction in the town went on as late as A.D. 296. It appears that the Roman town continued to exist until it was struck by an earthquake at the beginning of the Byzantine period.

Jerusalem. Aerial view of the Old City, looking east. In the foreground, Jaffa Gate.

Eboda reached the zenith of its development in about the middle of the sixth century. A town composed of caves and houses sprang up along its western slopes, while on the acropolis were built two churches, a monastery, and a fortress. Most of the remnants of agricultural works in the town's vicinity belong to this period. During this period, the town's economy rested, at least in part, on the cultivation of a fine variety of grapes and wine production. In the years 618–620, the Persian invasion probably engulfed Eboda. A small settlement remained for a short time, however, until the city was finally abandoned at the beginning of the Arab conquest.

EXPLORATION

U.J. Seetzen was the first traveler to reach 'Abdah (1807). The town was surveyed by E. H. Palmer and T. Drake in 1870. In the summer of 1902, A. Musil conducted a more detailed survey, and in the winter of 1904, 'Abdah was explored by A. Jaussen, R. Savignac, and L. H. Vincent on behalf of the Jerusalem Ecole Biblique. In 1912, the site was visited by a team headed by C. L. Woolley and T. E. Lawrence on behalf of the Palestine Exploration Fund. T. Wiegand, an officer of the unit for the preservation of monuments *(Denkmalschutzkommando)* attached to the German-Turkish army, came to the area in 1916 and drew a precise sketch of the churches and some architectural details. In 1922, A. Alt published a corpus of the 'Abdah inscriptions known at the time.

The exploratory soundings made at 'Abdah in 1937 by the Colt expedition brought to light the large Byzantine building at the southern end of the town and investigated the southwestern tower of the Byzantine fortress. Extensive excavations were undertaken from May, 1958, until October, 1960, by the National Parks Authority. The 1958 excavations were directed by M. Avi-Yonah, those of 1959–60 by A. Negev.

EXCAVATIONS

A. The Nabataean Period. The results of the excavations point to a possible division of this period into three sub-periods: 1. the third–second centuries B.C.; 2. the time of Aretas IV, 9 B.C.–A.D. 40; 3. the time of Rabel II, A.D. 70–106, to about the middle of the second century.

1. Ceramic and numismatic evidence of this period was uncovered. On the western side of the acropolis and in a dump of the Nabataean town, Rhodian jar handles of an early type were found (dating to 320–280 B.C.). Megarian bowl fragments and Ptolemaic and other coins minted by towns in Asia Minor in the third–second centuries B.C. were also found. No pottery of the first century A.D. was unearthed, and there may be a basis for the assumption that Eboda lay in ruins at the time as a result of the conquest of Gaza by Alexander Jannaeus.

2. The earliest structures found so far at Eboda may be assigned to this phase, 9 B.C.–A.D. 40. The rock of the western spur was leveled. Traces of this leveling are distinguished where the Byzantine pavement was removed in the western section of the acropolis, south of a building annex of the northern church. In order to prepare a suitable building space, the rock was buttressed by high retaining walls on the north (56 meters), west (51 meters), and south (32–58 meters). The western wall was 6 meters high. Rubble and dirt were used to fill the space between the retaining walls and the rock. It was in this fill that the majority of Nabataean and Early Roman potsherds were found.

The acropolis was made accessible by two entranceways. One was built at the eastern extremity of the northern retaining wall, and the other in the southwestern corner. The first entrance is a tower (7 by 7 meters) of large stonework and a ceiling supported by three arches. It had two portals, on the west and on the east. During the Byzantine period, the western portal (7.4 meters wide) was blocked, the eastern narrowed, and the entrance chamber paved with stone. Beneath the pavement level was found a large amount of Nabataean sherds and an inscription dating to Aretas IV. The second entrance, in the southwestern corner of the acropolis, consisted mainly of a courtyard (10 by 6 meters) with roofed wings supported by four pillars. Extending from the eastern porch was a roofed passage of which three arches rested on the eastern wall of the court and on the western wall of the tower standing in the courtyard's northeastern corner. All the arches were overlaid with stone slabs, a few of which still stand in situ. The roofed passage led to the tower (4 by 3.6 meters), which was ascended by means of a spiral staircase winding around a thick pillar. Above the three arches of the passage was a chamber in which was found a treasure trove of

Aerial view of the site.

347

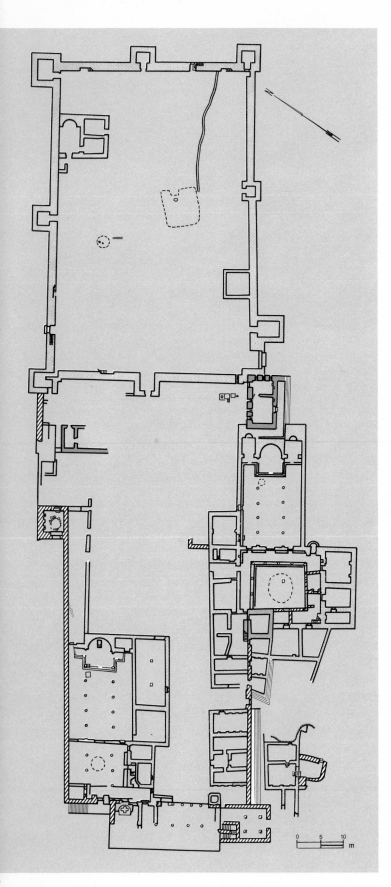

Nabataean pottery, Roman bronze objects (one of which bears a Nabataean inscription), and two Nabataean inscriptions dating to Aretas IV. This entranceway led to the open square above it, atop of which was located a porch.

The open square (23 by 9.4 meters) was constructed by erecting the western retaining wall approximately 9 meters distant from the rock and running parallel to it. Between the rock and the wall parallel partitions were built to buttress the high wall and serve as foundations for the pavement of the square. Save for the retaining wall, virtually nothing has remained in the square from the Nabataean period except column drums and other architectural details that were re-used in later periods. These remains, which include Nabataean capitals and column drums with marks of Nabataean stone dressers, seem to have been piled up during the Byzantine period in the southwestern corner of the square. Similar marks of Nabataean stone dressers were discovered on the eastern row of columns in the porch. All of these fragments may have belonged to the Nabataean shrine erected in this section of the acropolis under Aretas IV. Nabataean

Opposite page: The acropolis, showing Late Roman and Byzantine remains.

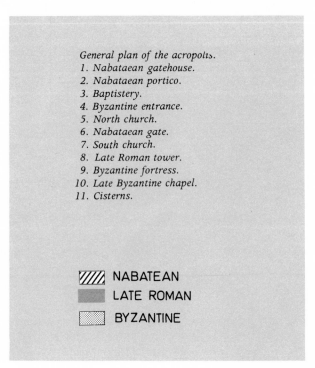

General plan of the acropolis.
1. *Nabataean gatehouse.*
2. *Nabataean portico.*
3. *Baptistery.*
4. *Byzantine entrance.*
5. *North church.*
6. *Nabataean gate.*
7. *South church.*
8. *Late Roman tower.*
9. *Byzantine fortress.*
10. *Late Byzantine chapel.*
11. *Cisterns.*

NABATEAN
LATE ROMAN
BYZANTINE

building fragments were also found embedded in the walls, pavements, and church entrances at Eboda.

A potter's workshop, uncovered east of the Nabataean town, is considered by the excavator to have belonged to the second construction phase. Although it revealed only three kilns, more seem to have existed there. West of the workshop is a courtyard, in a corner of which stands a small pool apparently used for clay levigation.

A room was discovered in the workshop and its northern part excavated. Inside the room is a Π shaped bench, .6 meter high, with each of its sides 4 meters long. Adjacent to the bench is a round pedestal (1 meter in diameter, .9 meter high), apparently used for the emplacement of a potter's wheel, while the bench served for drying the pottery before firing and for cooling it afterward. East of the potter's wheel a kiln was cleared; it is built of rough stone bound with clay (3 meters in diameter, with a wall .5 meter broad and 2.3 meters high). Judging by the coins found there, together with Arretine and Puteolan imported ware, Augustan Italian lamps, and locally produced

Herodian lamps, the potter's workshop may be regarded as having been in operation during the first half of the first century A.D. It has supplied a foundation for the chronology of Nabataean pottery.

3. Evidence for the existence of a settlement at Eboda in the time of Rabel II has been found mainly in two valleys south and west of the town. Two complexes of dammed valleys and several houses were discovered in the valleys. Located near them in each of the valleys are two pairs of large libation altars made of hard limestone. They bear dedicatory inscriptions from the years 18 and 28 of Rabel II. Fragments of two similar altars also have been discovered in the fill of the Byzantine fortress courtyard.

The annexation of the Negev in A.D. 106 did not bring about any change in the history of Nabataean Eboda. This is attested by epigraphic evidence. An inscription dated 107 was found in a cave on the western slope. Another inscription dated 126 was discovered embedded in one of the Byzantine fortress towers. Both are Nabataean inscriptions dealing with constructions erected at Eboda in the

years following upon the Roman annexation of the Nabataean kingdom and the establishment of the Roman province of Arabia.

B. The Late Roman Period. Only a few remains on the acropolis can be ascribed to this period with any certainty. However, several Greek inscriptions of the second half of the third century mention building activities at the site. This indicates that the acropolis was still standing at that time. The whereabouts of the temples of Zeus Obodas (Ζεὺς Ὀβόδας) and Aphrodite, which are mentioned in several inscriptions, are unknown. It is quite possible, however, that the Nabataean temples were repaired in Roman times and adapted to the new needs. In any case, the square gateway of the acropolis was reconstructed with re-used stones, doorposts, and capitals of Nabataean workmanship. Near the gateway were found a lintel and a dedicatory inscription dated to 268 which apparently belonged to the same structure.

Another remnant of this period is the large tower (11 by 6 meters) which has been preserved almost to roof level. The southern church of later date was built adjacent to this structure. The tower itself was probably incorporated into the Byzantine fortress. It original entrance was in the southern wall. The entrance preserved in its northeastern corner dates to the Byzantine period. The interior of the tower is covered with several layers of colored plaster. The outer white coating belongs to the Byzantine period, while the three layers beneath, decorated with geometric patterns, date to the Late Roman period. The tower seems to have belonged to the curtain of defense works erected during the Late Roman period.

One street in the Late Roman residential quarter, situated south of the tower, has been cleared. It ran across the quarter in a north-south direction. The dwellings in this quarter were built around courtyards. Their walls are made of rather small and well-dressed stones.

The tower in the southwest was also cleared. From the inscription above the lintel of the only doorway preserved, that in the northern wall of the tower, it appears that it was erected in 294. This tower is two stories high and apparently served as an observation post. In the lower story a small entrance chamber was found. On the southern side are two doorways. One of them leads to a long, narrow chamber with apertures for illumination and observation high up in the walls. The second opens onto a large hall where three ceiling arches were found in situ. The chambers were coated with a thin white plaster. In the northeastern corner of the hall there is a low entrance leading to a room beneath the staircase of an upper chamber. A doorway in the eastern wall of the entrance chamber leads to the upper story, of which only several stone courses and thresholds of doors have been preserved. From the eastern side of this upper story, stairs led to the observation post.

The finds show that the houses in the Late Roman quarter were still in use at the beginning of the Byzantine period and that their plan then underwent various modifications. Since no Christian remains were found here, it would seem that during the time the churches were constructed — from the sixth century onward — the quarter already lay in ruins. Perhaps this was the result of an earthquake, traces of which are clearly discernible at Eboda.

The burial cave (en-Nuṣrah) discovered in the southwestern slope can be attributed to the Late Roman period. Three Greek inscriptions, one dated to 242, were discovered in the vaulted entranceway and its vicinity. From the inscriptions and the great quantity of pottery found, this layer can be dated to the middle of the third century A.D.

C. The Byzantine Period. Three phases are distinguished in this period, with the demarcation between them occasionally blurred: 1. the fifth and

Burial cave; Late Roman.

beginning of the sixth century A.D.; 2. the mid-sixth century to 619/20; 3. from 620 to the middle or end of the seventh century.

1. The earthquake that apparently damaged the Roman residential quarter and the southern retaining wall of the acropolis occurred near the beginning of this phase. To that period must be attributed the semi-circular buttresses built to consolidate the retaining wall and the southern and eastern walls of the large tower, as well as the new entrance at its northern side. It is also possible that in this phase the northwestern Nabataean entranceway was converted into a Byzantine dwelling.

2. The main structures on the acropolis belong to the second phase, whereas the previous one only laid the groundwork for this, the main Byzantine phase. The acropolis was then divided into two main sections: a fortress in the eastern section; churches, a monastery, and annexes in the western section.

THE FORTRESS. This is a rectangular structure, about .5 acre in area. The walls are 1.6–2 meters thick. The courtyard measures 61 meters from east to west. Its eastern side is 39 meters long, the western one 41 meters. The fortress has nine towers (three to each wall), of unequal size. The towers could be ascended by stairs attached to their walls at some distance from the towers themselves. The main gate (2.7 meters wide) was on the southwestern side of the fortress. Its arch has been preserved. The gate was protected by two towers, the western one belonging to the Late Roman period. On the northwestern side of the fortress is another, smaller gate. On its outer lintel are carved a cross and other Christian symbols. There are also three posterns. One is in the east. Beneath its southern doorpost was discovered a deep, narrow pit whose purpose is unknown. There are two posterns in the west. The one in the middle tower was found blocked with various materials. It appears to have been sealed in haste before the Persian invasion. The other postern, located in the northwestern corner, had been properly blocked with masonry.

Inside the fortress there are only two permanent structures: a chamber (6 by 5.5 meters) attached to the south wall and a chapel in the northeastern corner, constructed during phase 3. In the center of the fortress is a cistern (7 by 7 by 4 meters) with an approximate capacity of 200 cubic meters. Two channels supplied rainwater to the fortress. One channel was in the east and conveyed water collected in the vicinity. The second hugged the outside of the southern wall. Both channels passed underneath the fortress walls. Northwest of the large cistern was found another, smaller cistern (2.4 meters in diameter).

CHURCHES, MONASTERY, AND ANNEXES. West of the fortress is an unpaved square (51 by 40 meters), supported on the northern side by the large Nabataean retaining wall. In its northeastern corner is a large cistern, the measurements of which equal that of the large cistern in the fortress.

THE SOUTHERN CHURCH. In the southern part of the square stands the church named in an inscription the *Martyrium of St. Theodore*. The church is directed east–northeast. Its orientation has been slightly deflected because of its contiguity with the Roman tower. A semi-circular buttress of the western tower wall serves as a prop for the central apse.

The church is of the basilical type, with two rows of seven columns each. The first column in each row is attached to the wall of the central apse, and the last column to the west wall of the church. All the columns stand on square plinths and Attic bases. The bema is raised two steps above the level of the hall. There are three openings in the chancel screen — one in front of the central apse and two leading to small cubicles in front of the prothesis and diaconicon. The side apses are smaller than is

The northern church.

*From top to bottom: Two Byzantine lintels.
Nabataean inscription on the side of a libation altar;
A.D. 98.*

usual. In the hall in front of the southwestern corner of the bema is the circular base (1.25 meters in diameter) of the pulpit (ambo).

The church is paved throughout with limestone flags. Five tombs were discovered in the aisles, two of them twin storied. Another grave was discovered in the prothesis and three in the atrium. The oldest tomb inscription dates to 541, and the latest (above an abbot's tomb) to 618. The atrium is surrounded by colonnades on three sides. In its center is a cistern. Monastic cells are built along its southern, northern, and western sides. The southwestern corner of the atrium verges on a tower which may date to the Late Roman period.

In an annex, a plastered underground treasury vault was found covered by a stone slab with a padlock. It was empty. A group of long, narrow cells built in a westward direction links the southern church to an exedra.

THE NORTHERN CHURCH. This church is apparently older than the southern one. A large quantity of Nabataean stones were used in building the wall and the floor.

The northern church is also slightly deflected from a true easterly direction. It is of the basilical type, with a single apse and only the diaconicon and several rooms attached to it at the southern side. The apse does not face the hall directly, apparently in order to correct the deviation in the orientation of the structure. Set in the apse is a sort of step which served to support a wooden bench for the clergy (synthronon). In its center was a stone pedestal for the bishop's seat. The number and arrangement of the columns are similar to those in the southern church. In the center of the atrium is a cistern with a sump at its base coated with a pink water-resistant plaster. In the course of the excavations scores of pillar drums and capitals from the church were found in the cistern. Apparently they were thrown there at the end of the Byzantine period, when the church was burned and the site turned into a sheepfold. In the rooms at the southern side of the church bronze ritual objects and a marble reliquary were found.

BAPTISMAL FONT. West of the atrium is a narrow lane, 2.5 meters wide. A doorway at its western side leads to a flight of steps. These steps were built during the Byzantine period to allow access to the church square after the destruction of the Nabataean entrance. A second doorway leads from the lane to the baptistery.

Two pillars, whose bases alone have been preserved, supported the roof of the baptistery. The font is cross-shaped (each arm 1.35 meters long) and was built of rubble and clay coated with plaster. The whole was faced on both sides with thin marble slabs. At the bottom of the font is a drainage pipe. Adjoining this font is a smaller one for infant baptisms. The entire structure leans upon the corner of the large northwestern retaining wall of the Nabataean period.

WINE PRESSES. The three wine presses found are similarly constructed. The press near the southern gate of the Byzantine fortress has a square treading area (length of a side 5.7 meters) around which nine cubicles of unequal size are arranged. Their total area is 6–9 square meters. The grapes were stored in baskets in these cubicles prior to the treading process. The cubicles open out onto steep slopes that conveyed the grapes to the treading area .6 meter below their floor level. The treading area was coated with thick plaster and paved with stone flags (now removed). It slopes toward a small, centrally situated sump (.4 by .4 meters). A channel runs along the bottom of this sump beneath the pavement of the treading area toward a container for the newly pressed wine (3 meters in diameter, and preserved to a height of only 1.1 meters). The grape skins would sink to the bottom of the container. The sump is constructed of packed rubble and clay, coated with thick plaster. South of it are storerooms.

HOUSE AND CAVE. The Byzantine town consisted of 350 to 400 residential units of caves and houses arranged terrace-like along the western slope of Eboda hill. One unit is situated 45 meters beneath the acropolis in the lower residential tier. The house and the adjacent cave form one dwelling unit, as is typical of Byzantine Eboda. The complex is entered from the south into an enclosed court (10 by 4.5 meters). A flight of steps in the southern wall of the courtyard led to an attic, which has not been preserved. On the northern side of the courtyard are two halls. The latter were roofed with stone flags laid atop three stone arches, all of which have been preserved. In the western section of the west hall is a pantry (5.7 by 2.25 meters) and a bench attached to the wall. The pantry and the walls of the hall contain niches which apparently served as cupboards.

Two other doorways were found in the courtyard, the northern one having been blocked when the building was destroyed. The southern doorway leads to another room. Along its northern wall was built a sewage drain which extends outside the house. A narrow passage on the west leads to another complex of chambers, constructed at a later date. South of the corridor is a small chamber (2.5 by 2.25 meters) paved with large stones. On the western side of the paving lie small receptacles ending in an inclined gutter which protrudes outside the house wall (lavatory).

To the west of the building are courtyards that are 2.3 meters lower than the building. The walls of these structures are thick and constructed of large, coarsely chiseled stone chunks. Building work indicates a utilitarian approach, without any unnecessary embellishments.

CAVE. The cave is entered through the hall to the north of the interior courtyard. Two chambers (the larger 6 by 12 meters in area), partly built and partly rock cut, link the two parts of the house—cave unit. On the eastern side of the larger hall

The southern church. Tombstone dated A.D. *551.*

lies a rock partition shaped like a demi-arch. On it are drawn in red ocher the figures of Saints George and Theodore and Greek inscriptions. A wide doorway leads eastward to another chamber (approximately 5 by 5 meters) along whose northern and eastern walls low benches have been cut. There are also rock-cut niches higher up. The corners of the room are decorated below the ceiling with carved heads and bunches of grapes, while a cross is carved into the ceiling itself. All rooms have smooth, hollowed-out recesses for lamps and packs. These recesses are painted red.

A doorway in the eastern wall leads to a central hall, 20 centimeters lower than the one in front of it. The walls of the hall have small niches for oil lamps. In the ceiling are cut rows of projections (painted in red) for hanging bunches of fruit and the like. A doorway pierced into the hall's eastern wall leads to another hall (5.5 by 7 meters) with benches cut in the rock on three of its sides. Along the eastern wall of this hall runs a stone bench with two rows of hollows in which jars could have been placed upright. The other benches also appear to have been employed as bases for jars, although they

Plan of the Byzantine bathhouse. 1. Court.
2. Apodyterium. 3. Frigidarium. 4. Tepidarium.
5. Caldarium. 6. Hypocaust. 7. Pool.

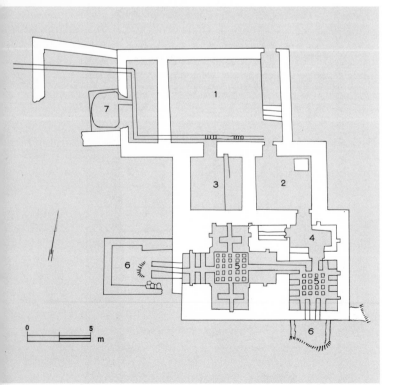

have no hollows in which to stand them up. The passage between the two halls had special arrangements for blocking it when necessary. In such event, the face of the blocked entrance pointing to the western hall could be used as a cupboard. The cave itself seems to have served as a wine cellar, the new wine being strained on the bench of the western hall and then stored in the eastern hall for fermentation.

Additional openings in the northern wall of the central hall lead, on the one side, to a small pantry and, on the other, to rock-hewn bins, probably used for the storage of grain or dried fruits. Earlier surveys suggested that this cave was once part of the Nabataean necropolis, but later excavations indicated that it was not earlier than the Byzantine period and that from the outset it had been hewn to serve as a wine cellar and a storage place.

THE BATHHOUSE. The bathhouse is situated in the plain at the foot of Eboda hill. On its eastern side is a well, 60 meters deep, which supplied the bathhouse with water. North of the bathhouse is a courtyard (19 by 6.3 meters); it was roofed in temporary fashion, as evidenced by the two thinnish pillars in its center. In the northern wall of the bathhouse are two doorways. One leads to a chamber containing a pool coated with water-resistant plaster (4.2 by 4.1 meters wide and 1.35 meters deep). This was apparently the frigidarium. Its ceiling has been completely preserved. The second doorway leads directly to the hot-bath section. From the passage, an opening leads into a small room containing three stone benches, apparently the dressing room, and from here one entered the hypocaust room (4 by 4 meters). The brick ceiling of the latter has not been preserved, but the debris of sixteen pillar bases built of bricks is extant.

Adjacent to the south side of the bathhouse was a brick flue that conveyed the heated air from a furnace. Two flues on the south side and three each on the west and east sides directed the heated air into a network of clay piping, much of which has been preserved intact near the west wall. Two grooves run the entire length of the east wall, opening above the room's vaulted roof and serving as exhausts for excess heat. Small apertures in the ceiling served as windows.

West of the hot room is the tepidarium, which is cross shaped. In its center is the hypocaust,

containing the bases of the twenty brick pillars which supported the ceiling of the installation. The northern, southern, and western arms of the cross contain the bathtubs constructed of brick fragments and water-resistant clay. The bathtubs were heated by means of channels (also cross shaped) connected with the hypocaust. The whole chamber was heated by a furnace situated west of the building and by a channel from the first hypocaust. In the walls surrounding the bathtubs were slits acting as exhausts for the excess steam. The room has a domed roof supported by four spherical pendentives. Part of the dome has been destroyed. It appears to have contained a central aperture for light and ventilation. The water was evacuated from the building by means of a channel, large segments of which were discovered in the courtyard north of the bathhouse. The bathhouse at Eboda is one of the best preserved Byzantine buildings of this type found so far in Palestine.
3. Coming in the wake of the Persian invasion, this phase witnessed a reduction of construction activities. Both churches, as well as the fortress towers, were found filled with ashes and the partially charred beams of the church roofs. The sole edifice in the fortress which shows no traces of the large conflagration is the chapel (10 by 8 meters), built of large dressed stones, most certainly taken from a previous building. The chapel contains two chambers, the northern one having a single apse and two small cubicles on its southern side. Many sherds of jugs, some bearing incisions and Greek inscriptions, were discovered in this structure. The atrium of the southern church and several of its chambers show traces of repairs carried out in this stage. The workmanship is of decidedly inferior quality.   A. NEGEV

BIBLIOGRAPHY

E. H. Palmer, *PEF QSt* (1871), 1–80 • Musil, *Arabia Petraea* 2, 106–51 • A. Jaussen, R. Savignac, H. Vincent, *RB* 13 (1904), 404–24; 14 (1905), 74–89, 235–44 • M. J. Lagrange, *CRAIBL* (1904), 279–98 • C. L. Woolley, T. E. Lawrence, *APEF* 3 (1914), 93–107 • T. Wiegand, *Sinai*, Berlin-Leipzig, 1921, a-1 • A. Negev, *Yediot* 25 (1960/61), 92–93, 129–42; 27 (1962/63), 145–57 (Hebrew); idem, *Archaeology* 14 (1961), 122–30; idem, *Sefer Eilath* (Eighteenth National Convention of the Israel Exploration Society), Jerusalem, 1962/63, 118–48 (Hebrew); idem, *IEJ* 11 (1961), 127–38; 13 (1963), 113–20; 15 (1965), 185–95; idem, *Cities of the Desert*, Tel Aviv, 1966; idem, *PEF QSt* 99 (1966), 89–98; idem, *IEJ* 17 (1967), 46–55; idem, *PEF QSt* 101 (1969), 5–14.

'EIN EL-JARBA

IDENTIFICATION. The Chalcolithic site of 'Ein el-Jarba is located in the southwestern part of the Plain of Esdraelon on the lands of Kibbutz Hazorea, about 100 meters north of the Yokneam–Megiddo road. This area, rich in springs whose waters flow into the Kishon, contains many prehistoric sites. In 1955 during the digging of an east–west drainage channel near 'Ein el-Jarba, fragments of pottery, stone vessels, and flints were brought to the surface. They belong to the Wadi Rabah culture, which was identified by the writer in the 1950's at Wadi Rabah itself, Tel Aviv, Tuleilat Batashi, and other sites. The finds in the channel included fragments of a hole-mouth jar decorated on either side with reliefs of two human figures masked like rams and dancing with their hands upraised.

In July, 1966, excavations directed by J. Kaplan on behalf of the Tel Aviv–Jaffa Museum of Antiquities were carried out in the drainage channel, at the spot where the hole-mouth jar was found. Four strata of settlement were distinguished, all belonging to the Wadi Rabah culture. In stratum I, which was close to the surface, no buildings had survived but only scattered stones. In strata II and III, parts of structures were uncovered. The plan of these structures was of a rectangular room with an adjacent enclosed courtyard. In stratum IV, which was found on virgin soil, two sections of thin walls were discovered. Near one wall was a secondary burial, containing, inter alia, parts of five human skulls and fragments of a large jar. The hole-mouth jar, mentioned above, whose base was found in situ apparently had also been deposited as one of the grave goods in the burial of a group of human bones. A hearth and seven shallow pits dug in the virgin soil were also found. In all four strata small, elliptical-shaped plastered floors were uncovered. These floors had probably been used (after heating) for baking bread made of thin sheets of dough. The existence of these floors in all four strata suggests that the four were close in time.

THE FINDS

The pottery finds included all types of vessels and decoration already known from the excavations at Wadi Rabah and the sites mentioned above. It also included new types of vessels and decoration hitherto unknown in this culture. The black burnish typical of the Wadi Rabah culture is common on bowls and large vessels. Among the various pottery types are jars, hole-mouth jars, pithoi, bowls, lids, incense stands, cornets, and cups, as well as fragments of a jar with a bow rim and the carinated bowls typical of the Wadi Rabah culture. These were also found in stratum VIII at Jericho (excavated by J. Garstang). The two vessels found in level IV at 'Ein el-Jarba probably served as funerary offerings. The hole-mouth jar with the dancing figures and the vessel found near the burial with the skulls are distinctive in form.

Most of the stone finds at 'Ein el-Jarba are made of flint and some of hard stone. Chips and fragments of blades of obsidian were also discovered. Among

Hole-mouth jar with applied relief decoration.

the various implements were the chopping tools—adzes, axes, and picks—cutting tools, scrapers, various awls, borers, and sickle blades. The chopping tools of hard stone have many parallels in Syria, Upper Mesopotamia, and Anatolia. Other stone objects are the weapons—mace heads and oval sling stones—found in all four levels, especially in stratum IV. There are also bone tools and spindle whorls made of rounded and perforated broken pieces of pottery.

DATING

A Carbon-14 test from level IV indicates a date 5690 ± 140 years ago, *i.e.*, 3740 B.C. ± 140 years. Even assuming that 'Ein el-Jarba is not the oldest of the Wadi Rabah settlements, it is hard to conceive that other sites of this culture will be found from before 4000 B.C. This date appears to be the earliest possible limit for this culture.

CONCLUSION

The excavations at 'Ein el-Jarba have added to our knowledge of the Wadi Rabah culture and of the Chalcolithic period in Palestine in general. The parallels between the Wadi Rabah and the Halafian cultures indicate a strong affinity, especially between the forms of the pottery. Just as the Halafian culture was not Neolithic but Chalcolithic (because of the presence of copper objects), so, too, the Wadi Rabah culture is Chalcolithic (in spite of the fact that no copper was found among the objects), as it was derived from the Halafian. The parallels between the Wadi Rabah finds and those from level VIII in Jericho also indicate a close affinity. In Jericho VIII, however, the black burnish and certain forms of decoration are missing. Jericho VIII is hence a later development of this culture, before the Ghassulian infiltration of the country. The Ghassulian entry, which occurred around 3500 B.C., introduced into Palestine new elements in pottery and other cultural features. However, many ceramic elements of the Wadi Rabah culture continued to exist in the Ghassulian civilization either in form or in decoration. The development of the Palestinian Chalcolithic, chronologically, is therefore Wadi Rabah → Jericho VIII → Ghassul.   J. KAPLAN

BIBLIOGRAPHY

J. Kaplan, *IEJ* 8 (1958), 149–60; *idem*, *BASOR* 194 (1969), 2–39.

'EIN SAMIYA and DHAHR MIRZBANEH

IDENTIFICATION. On the border of the hill region and the Jordan Valley to the east of Kafr Malik, an extensive necropolis stretches over an area of about 3 kilometers between Dhahr Mirzbaneh in the north and Khirbet Samiya in the south. The necropolis lies for the most part on the slopes of the Wadis Samiya and Kuheila.

The cemetery contains thousands of burials, most of them dating to the Middle Bronze Age I, with some from the Early Bronze Age and Roman-Byzantine period and a smaller number from the Iron Age I–II and the Hellenistic period. The burials from the Early Bronze Age, Iron Age, Hellenistic, and Roman-Byzantine periods appear to have belonged to a settlement whose remains are located at Khirbet Marjama, between Dhahr Mirzbaneh and Khirbet Samiya. To the west of the latter is the spring of 'Ein Samiya, which still supplies water to nearby Kafr Malik.

EXPLORATION

The site was first investigated in 1907 by D. G. Lyon, then Director of the American Schools of Oriental Research. In 1963, P. W. Lapp excavated in three areas (cemeteries A, B, C). The cemetery was again explored in 1968 by Y. Meshorer. In 1970 a group of tombs were cleared in a rescue excavation under the direction of Z. Yeivin, Archaeological Officer, Judea and Samaria. In all, some 150 tombs have been examined.

EXCAVATIONS

Of the tombs excavated, by far the greatest number belong to the Middle Bronze Age I (Intermediate Bronze Age, in the terminology of Kathleen Kenyon, P. Lapp, and others). The burials were made in similarly constructed shaft tombs. A circular shaft was hewn in the rock to a depth which, in some cases, reached 7 meters, and cuts were made in the shaft to facilitate the descent. At the base of the shaft were one or two burial caves. The mouths of the caves were blocked by flat stones.

This type of tomb was common in all parts of the country, but so far no settlement has been discovered from that time with a sufficiently large population to account for the number of burials found in the necropolis.

The tombs served for more than one burial. The bodies were laid on their backs with no special orientation for the head. Beside the bodies were placed offerings, including pottery, weapons, beads, and other objects.

The tombs can also be differentiated by their accompanying objects — mainly pottery. Some of them contained only small amphoriskoi, others had a somewhat richer assortment of pottery. The repertoire is a limited one: hole-mouth jars with folded ledge handles, amphoriskoi, jars with lug handles, juglets, lamps of the four-pinch type, and teapots. The majority of the finds can be apparently assigned to Family C, according to the classification of Ruth Amiran.

The weapons found in the tombs are also essentially alike and of a limited range. They include daggers with midrib attached to the hilt by means of rivets, spear butts with prominent midribs and curled tangs, and spearheads with metal strips for binding the blade to the shaft. The weapons are made of copper and are common throughout the country in the Middle Bronze Age I.

This cemetery resembles a contemporary burial ground at Bab edh-Dhra' (q.v.) in Transjordan. It, too, apparently belonged to the nomadic tribes which had put an end to the urban civilization of the Early Bronze Age but did not establish large permanent settlements for themselves.

In one of the tombs (Number 204-a), excavated in 1970, a unique goblet was found. The goblet is made of silver sheeting and decorated in repoussé with fine pointed tools. It apparently portrays two scenes of the Creation Epic (Enūma eliš) of Mesopotamia. One scene depicts two figures, dressed in fringed skirts (one of the figures is missing). The figures stand facing each other and hold a band of some kind in one hand (as can be seen in the preserved figure). The other hand is held to the breast. Above the band is a kind of sun disk divided into twelve segments with a human face in the center. Below the band between the figures is a twisting serpent. The second scene depicts a mythological figure with outstretched arms. The upper torso is in the form of a Janus-faced human being. The lower part of the body consists of the two hind parts of beasts, probably oxen. The figure holds a plant in each hand. Facing the plant is an

Left: Silver goblet from Tomb 204-a. Above: Drawing of the scene depicted on the goblet.

upright dragon standing on its tail (the dragon on the left side is missing). Between the legs of the mythological figure is another disk divided into eight segments. The scenes have been interpreted as depicting the victory of Marduk over Tiamat.

In addition to the Middle Bronze Age I tombs, which make up the bulk of the necropolis, there were also, as stated above, tombs from later periods. The Roman-Byzantine tombs were cut into and disturbed the earliest graves. The latter tombs consisted of single burials in rectangular-shaped graves hewn in the rock, *kokhim* burials, and vaulted tombs.

Z. YEIVIN

BIBLIOGRAPHY

D. G. Lyon, *Supplement to AJA* 11 (1907), 42–49; *idem, AJA* 12 (1908), 66–67; *idem, Harvard Theological Review* 1 (1908), 70–96 • W.F. Albright, *AASOR* 4 (1922), 124–33 • P.W. Lapp, *The Dhahr Mirzbaneh Tombs*, New Haven, 1966 • B. Shantur and Y. Labadi, *IEJ* 21 (1971), 73–77 • Z. Yeivin, *ibid.*, 78–81 • Y. Yadin, *ibid.*, 82–85 • R. Grafman, *IEJ* 22 (1972), 47–49 • W.G. Dever, *ibid.*, 95–112.

ELUSA

IDENTIFICATION. Elusa, a town in the Negev about 20 kilometers (12.4 miles) southwest of Beersheba, was founded in the Hellenistic period and continued to exist until the beginning of the Early Arab period. Its ancient name has been retained in the Arabic name el-Khalusa. In his *Geography* (V. 15, 57) Ptolemaeus mentions Ἔλουσα as one of the settlements in Idumaea west of the Jordan. The city appears on the Peutinger road map 71 Roman miles from Jerusalem and 24 Roman miles from Eboda. On the Madeba map it is shown as a large settlement east of Φωθις and south of Ιεθορ. The Hebrew name Ḥaluṣa is found in the Jerusalem Targum of Genesis 16:7, where it is appended to the name "Shur" as a kind of explanation or description. In the Greek-Arabic papyri of Nessana, the name appears in the form el-Khaluṣ. The Arabic name el-Khaluṣ is mentioned in a fifteenth-century document.

EXPLORATION

The site was discovered and identified by E. Robinson in 1838 during the course of his investigation of the area. An expedition organized by the Ecole Biblique, the Dominican archaeological school in Jerusalem, in which A. Jaussen, A. Savignac, and L.H. Vincent took part, explored Elusa in 1905 and uncovered some Byzantine and pre-Byzantine tombstones. The first attempts to prepare a plan of the city's remains were made in 1914 by C.L. Woolley and T.E. Lawrence and in 1917 by the German scholar T. Wiegand. J.H. Iliffe, who inspected the site in 1933, was the first to find there Nabataean and Greek black-glazed pottery (apparently Hellenistic). The first exploratory excavation was organized in 1938 by the Colt expedition under the direction of T.J. Colin Baly.

HISTORY

Elusa is one of the settlements founded in the Negev in the third century B.C. by the Nabataeans, as we may learn from the Rhodian stamped jar handles, and from the Hellenistic pottery, which is similar to that uncovered at Petra, Eboda, and Nessana. A pottery lamp, now at the Rockefeller Museum, Jerusalem (as yet unpublished), has also been assigned to this period. It bears an inscription which some scholars have regarded as Hebrew. In the opinion of G.E. Kirk, this attests to commercial relations between Elusa and the Hasmonaean kingdom. It seems that at that period Elusa was a station on the main caravan route from Petra by way of Eboda and Elusa to Gaza.

The archaic Nabataean inscription, which mentions the name of Aretas "king of NBTW" (Nabatu) and is assumed to refer to Aretas II in the publication of the inscription, discloses that a Nabataean settlement existed in Elusa at the beginning of the first

Left: Nabataean inscription in honor of King Aretas (probably Aretas II). Right: Lamp with Nabataean inscription.

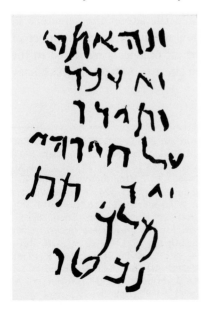

century B.C. Recent paleographic research has assigned this inscription to an earlier date, *i.e.*, to the first half of the second century B.C. This is the earliest Nabataean inscription found in Palestine and one of the oldest in that script. The Nabataean pottery found at Elusa indicates that the Nabataean settlement also existed there in the days of Aretas IV (9 B.C.–A.D. 40).

Elusa enjoyed its greatest prosperity in the Late Roman period and became the chief city in the western part of the Provincia Arabia. The earliest testimony to this effect are two letters from the years 356 and 359 written by Libanius, an inhabitant of Antioch. The Peutinger map also shows the name of the city. Several sources attest to the existence at Elusa of a community of idol worshippers and a small community of Christians, dwelling side by side in the fifth century. The bishops of the city took part in the Councils of Ephesus (431) and Chalcedon (451). In his book *The Life of Hilarion*, Hieronymus relates that a shrine to Venus was located at Elusa and that a Christian community dwelt there at the same time. These facts are also stated in the *Life* of Saint Nilus, who lived at Elusa at that time. In the lists of Hierocles of the sixth century and those of Georgius Cyprius of the seventh century, Elusa is referred to as one of the cities of Palestina Tertia. Stephanus Byzantinus informs us that the city was at first in Arabia but that in his day it belonged to Palestina Tertia. Two tombstones from the years 426 and 426/27 uncovered in the course of the surveys provide no definite information as to whether they belonged to Christian burials. No other definite proof of Christianity occurs at Elusa before 519.

In the sixth century, Theodosius (about 530) stated that Elusa was three stations distant from Jerusalem and seven stations from Aila. Antonius of Placentia described Ailah (also written Elual, Eluaha), which seems to be Elusa, as situated "at the beginning of the desert that stretched to Sinai" and in this connection mentions the name of the bishop who held this seat. In many of the Nessana Papyri, especially in the military archives of the period between 505 and 596, Elusa is referred to as the capital of the country of Nessana. A papyrus of 605, from the church archives, also mentions Elusa as the capital of the district. The latest of the archaeological remains on the site is a tombstone from the year 603.

Elusa retained its status as a district city in the Arab period. The archives of Georgias, the son of Patricius of Nessana, contain bilingual documents from the years 675 to 689, written in Greek and Arabic. In their superscriptions occurs the recurrent notation: "To the men of Nestan [Nessana] in the province of Gaza, in the district of el-Khaluṣ [Elusa]."

EXCAVATIONS

Many stones were removed from the ruins of Elusa for the building of Gaza. In the course of generations the site was extensively damaged. The plan of the site made by C. L. Woolley and T. E. Lawrence furnished little information beyond the fact that the city was surrounded by an irregular wall with three gates on the north and one on the east. A well was found in the south of the city, near the edge of the valley. Colt's expedition confined itself to a limited inspection of the area and the dumps around it. The excavators were able to distinguish pottery vessels from the Hellenistic to the Arab period. Further investigation of the rubble proved that the city reached the height of its prosperity in the third and fourth centuries. Trial digs also located the site of the cemetery in the Hellenistic period and uncovered a number of tombstones, the earliest of which are dated to the year 426/27 and the latest to 544–603.   A. NEGEV

BIBLIOGRAPHY

Robinson, *Biblical Researches*, 201–02 • E.H. Palmer, *PEF QSt* (1870), 35 • Musil, *Arabia Petraea* 2, *Edom*, Wien, 1907, 202–03 • A. Jaussen et al., *RB* 14 (1905), 253–57 • F.M. Abel, *RB* 18 (1909), 89–166 • E. Huntington, *Palestine and Its Transformations*, London, 1911, 121, 124 • C.L. Woolley and T.E. Lawrence, *The Wilderness of Zin* (*APEF* 3 [1914–16]), 4, 30–31, 108–10, 138–43 • T. Wiegand, *Sinai*, Berlin-Leipzig, 1920, a-1 • A. Alt, *Die griechischen Inschriften der Palaestina Tertia*, Berlin-Leipzig, 1921, 26–31 • J.H. Iliffe, *QDAP* 3 (1934), 132–34 • T.J. Colin Baly, *QDAP* 8 (1938), 159 • G.E. Kirk, *PEQ* (1941), 62 • C.J. Kraemer, Jr., *Excavations at Nessana* 3, Princeton, 1958, *passim* • A. Negev, *Qadmoniot* 7 (1974), 94–97 (Hebrew).

Byzantine lintel.

'Ein Samiya. Silver goblet; MBA.

EMMAUS

IDENTIFICATION. Emmaus, a city in Judea, is situated at the eastern end of the Aijalon Valley, at the junction of the Shephelah and the mountains. The name of the city has persisted in the name of the Arab village 'Imwas (map reference 148149). Emmaus (Greek Ἐμμαοῦς, Ἀμμαοῦς) occupies an important strategic position on the road that ascends from the west to Jerusalem.

HISTORY

Emmaus is first mentioned in I Maccabees (3:40, 57; 4:3) as the place where the armies of the Seleucid kingdom encamped in their third campaign against Judas Maccabaeus, and where they were defeated and their camp captured. In the middle of the first century B.C., Emmaus was the capital of one of the toparchies of Judea. The Roman commander Casius sold its inhabitants into slavery and in 4 B.C., after Herod's death, it became the center of an insurrection led by the shepherd Athronges. In retaliation, Varus, the proconsul of Syria, set fire to the city. Several tombstones found there bearing the names of Roman soldiers indicate that the Fifth Legion was encamped in the city during the First Revolt, as is stated by Josephus (*War* IV, 444–45). Emmaus was still in existence in the days of Rabbi Akiba. During the war of Bar Kokhba the garrison of Petra was stationed there. In the Talmud, the town is referred to as a major site of the Shephelah (Palestinian Talmud, *Shevi'it* 8, 9, 38d) and as a seat of the Samaritans (Palestinian Talmud, *Abodah Zarah* 85, 44d). In the third century A.D., Emmaus was granted city rights by the Emperor Heliogabalus (222–48) and named Nicopolis. In the Byzantine period, its vicinity was made unsafe by the "brigand" Cyriacus at the head of a Jewish and Samaritan band. Samaritan inscriptions were discovered on the site, among them a bilingual inscription in Greek and Samaritan. After the Arab conquest in 639, Emmaus was struck by a plague which claimed thousands of lives. During the Crusades, a garrison of Knights Templars was stationed there.

It is certain that the city of Emmaus-Nicopolis was situated close to 'Imwas near Latrun, on the Tel Aviv–Jerusalem road. Scholars differ, however, as to whether this is the Emmaus mentioned in the New Testament (Luke 24:13), 60 (according to some versions 160) stadia from Jerusalem where, according to the Gospels, Jesus appeared to two of his disciples after his resurrection. Some scholars take this latter Emmaus to be Abu Ghosh or Moza west of Jerusalem or Qubeibah northwest of it.

EXCAVATIONS

Remains found at the site called el-Keniseh, south of the city, attracted the attention of explorers as early as 1875. In 1882, J. B. Guillemot started excavations there, but the main work was carried out by the Dominican fathers L. H. Vincent and F. M. Abel in 1924, 1925, and 1927.

The excavators were able to distinguish the remains of five structures:

1. Recesses hewn out of the rock and foundations of walls (about .8 meter thick) which they assigned to the second and first centuries B.C.

2. The remains of a Roman villa of the second century A.D., a square structure (18 by 17 meters) comprising a long room at its northern extremity and a 7 square meter room (or courtyard) in its northeastern part. A long courtyard surrounded by porticoes runs along the northern side of the building, to which the excavators assigned also the mosaic floors with flower and guilloche borders. The field of the mosaic was composed of a pattern of circles and octagons combining into squares and lozenges filled with various kinds of guilloche motifs. In the octagons extant are portrayed a lion devouring a bull, a panther tearing a gazelle, and birds perched on lotus flowers. One of the circles contains an inscription that mentions "the other brothers Pelagius and Thomas," which led the excavators to assign it, together with the adjacent mosaics, to a Christian church of the third century.

3. A third-century Christian basilica (46.4 by 24.4 meters) divided into a nave and two aisles by two rows of thirteen columns each. In the eastern side, the basilica ended in three apses. There are no traces of a narthex. The remains of two layers of mosaic pavements have been preserved in the western part.

4. Beyond an intermediate hall (5.8 meters wide) there is a parallel structure made up of two parts: a basilica (18 by 10 meters) with two rows of six columns each, and behind it a baptistery supported by four columns. In the baptistery, a trefoil-shaped, stone baptismal font was found and, beside it, a

smaller baptismal font for children. Near the baptistery is a deep well. The excavators dated the basilica and baptistery to the sixth century. In the baptistery were found the remains of mosaics with geometric motifs and a fragment decorated with floral borders with intertwining tendrils, as well as part of an inscription which mentions an *episcopus* and the laying of the mosaic. Another inscription, in which a certain Johanan and the laying of a mosaic are mentioned, was found near the eastern extremity of the southern aisle of the basilica.

5. The best-preserved remains are those of a twelfth-century Crusader church built in the prevailing Romanesque style. The central Byzantine apse of the church was re-used by the Crusaders as the apse of their own church, with the addition of a vaulted hall measuring 23 by 10.25 meters. The main entrance to the hall was in the west, and two side entrances were made in the vault in front of the apse. As was usual in that period, the roof of the hall rested on four pointed arches with voussoirs supported by pillars attached to the wall of the hall (1.5 meters thick). On the western facade of the Crusader church, two free-standing pillars supported a porch in front of the main entrance to the hall. Among the smaller finds were fragments of inscriptions, one of which was bilingual: Greek, "God is One," and Samaritan, "Blessed be His name forever." Also found were fragments of the sculpture of an eagle, estimated to have been about 1 meter high, the remains of a Byzantine oil press, and numerous architectural fragments. Except for several Arab and Hellenistic-Herodian potsherds, the excavators did not record any ceramic finds from the various periods of construction.

REVIEW AND EVALUATION

J. W. Crowfoot has already observed that the dates suggested by the excavators are unacceptable, at least those assigned to the mosaic floors and the large basilica. The excavators themselves were obliged to admit that the style of the mosaics and their inscriptions could not be reconciled with their proposed date, since the mosaic fragment dated to the second century would also fit the third-century building. However, the large church cannot be dated to the third century, a period when Christianity was a prohibited and persecuted religion and its adherents were compelled to worship in private houses (as we know was the case at Dura Europos). The church plan with a triple apse

Above: Capital with Samaritan inscription. Below: Detail of mosaic from the Roman villa, depicting a panther tearing a gazelle, birds on lotus flowers, and various guilloche motifs.

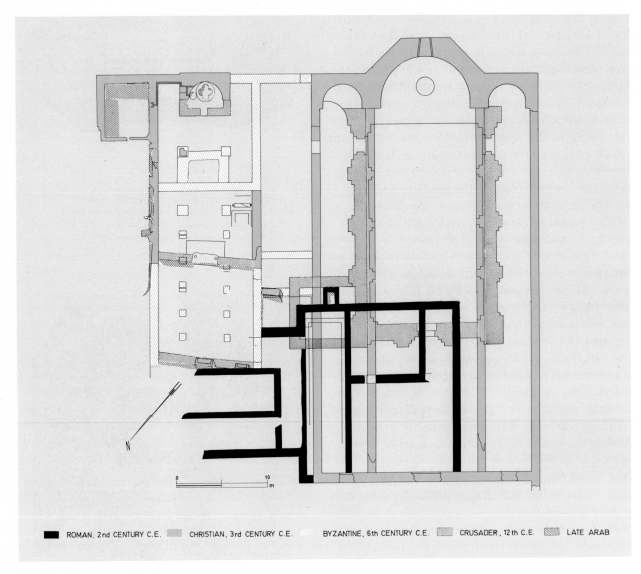

ROMAN, 2nd CENTURY C.E.　　CHRISTIAN, 3rd CENTURY C.E.　　BYZANTINE, 6th CENTURY C.E.　　CRUSADER, 12th C.E.　　LATE ARAB

Church and baptistery; plan.

appears for the first time in this country in the days of Theodosius II. It became prevalent in the first half of the fifth century (Gethsemane, St. Stephen), especially in the Negev (St. Theodore in Eboda, St. George at Subeita, etc.). The main church cannot be separated from the baptistery. Auxiliary structures such as these are found at many sites, as, for example, at Subeita and Mount Nebo. The mosaics, assigned to the second century, are similar in many details to those of the fifth-century church at Heptapegon (q.v.) and even more so to those at Mahattat el-'Urj near Beth Govrin (see Marisa Beth Govrin), which are presumably of the sixth century. In any case, they have nothing in common with the Roman mosaics. At the time the excava-

tions were completed, there was much less information concerning the dating of mosaics than is at our disposal at present. It is difficult to establish dates in the absence of strata, pottery, or coins and in the presence of the many disturbances caused by subsequent building. It seems, nevertheless, that on the foundation of the Constantinian villa (building 2), a church was erected in the fifth century (building 3). The additions to the church and the floors date to the sixth century (building 4).

M. Avi-Yonah

BIBLIOGRAPHY

L. H. Vincent–F. M. Abel, *Emmaüs, sa basilique et son histoire*, Paris, 1932 • Crowfoot, *Early Churches*, 71, 125.

'EN BOQEQ

IDENTIFICATION. The oasis of 'En Boqeq (map reference 185067) on the Dead Sea shore was maintained by two perennial springs, 'En Boqeq (216,000 cubic meters per annum) and 'En Noith 17,500 cubic meters per annum). The springs irrigated the fields in the delta of Naḥal Boqeq, as well as the terraces beneath the Boqeq ascent, leading toward the Judean highlands. Archaeological evidence shows that palm trees, as well as aromatic and pharmaceutical plants, were grown on the site.

HISTORY

To the best of our knowledge, the first phase of occupation at 'En Boqeq belongs to the Herodian period, although it is highly probable that the tower, which was incorporated in th Herodian installation, dates back to Alexander Jannaeus. In the Herodian period, pharmaceutical plants were intensively cultivated here. The oasis was destroyed during the war of A.D. 66–73, perhaps in the course of one of the raids by the Zealots based on Masada (Josephus, *War* IV, 405). Settlement was permanently reestablished only during the second half of the fourth century A.D., when 'En Boqeq was made into the eastern flank fortification of the main zone of defense of the Limes Palaestinae. During the fifth century, it became a *limitanean* establishment (*i.e.*, a settlement of the Byzantine agricultural frontier militia). It was destroyed during the Persian conquest in 614, and later rebuilt. It is probably mentioned under the name "Tetrapyrgion" and was finally destroyed during the Arab conquest.

EXCAVATIONS

'En Boqeq (Qaṣr Umm Baghgheq) was visited in 1853 by F. de Saulcy. The first general survey was made in 1931 by F. Frank and was followed in 1958 by a survey of the *castellum* by M. Gichon and in 1966 by S. Appelbaum's survey of the agricultural remains. Excavations were begun in 1967 by Gichon for the Unit of Frontier Studies of the Classics Department of Tel Aviv University and were continued intermittently until 1972.

The excavations comprised the Herodian factory, the Boqeq aqueduct and cisterns, the *castellum*, the Noith nymphaeum, aqueduct, and bathhouse(?), the agricultural remains, and the cemetery.

The Herodian Factory. This is a square building of 20 by 20 meters. The walls, 80 centimeters thick, were built in two faces of roughly dressed stones with a rubble-and-mortar core. Inside, three major phases of occupation with a haphazard re-occupation prior to the final abandon have been observed. Phase 1 was Herodian, possibly destroyed during the uprisings following Herod's death (Josephus, *Antiquities* XVII, 269–85). Phase 2 can be assigned to the first procurators, when the area became an imperial estate. Phase 3 belongs to the time of Agrippa I and was destroyed and rebuilt (phase 4) during the later procurators. During the three major phases, few substantial changes occurred in

The courtyard and barracks against the north wall of the castellum.

Counterclockwise, both pages: Southern facade of the castellum *with gate and two corner towers. View of the courtyard of the* castellum, *from the east. Ashlars in corner of the southeastern* tower. Looking through the northwestern tower to the western wall. Ceiling of the northeastern tower with wooden beams in situ. Plan of the *castellum. Plan of the officina.*

the interior plans. All the rooms were arranged around a central courtyard. The main (?) entrance from the south gave access to an anteroom with plastered benches, from which a door on the left led into a storeroom. On the right was a partly covered work room, in which various operations (including drying, crushing, pressing, and boiling) were carried out. The thinness, as well as the relative weakness of the plaster covering the basin and working platform, attest to the fragility of the raw materials used (plant leaves, buds, petals, resins, etc.). A passage led from the anteroom into the courtyard past a staircase ascending to the roof. Walls jutting into this passage from west and east created five working compounds, some of them furnished with fireplaces and ovens. Of these, the southeastern one was the main distilling plant, with a reservoir for the raw material, a fireplace for pre-heating, a grinding platter, a vat, and upper and lower distilling ovens. Two rooms (10 by 3.75 meters) occupied the space to the west and east of the courtyard. The former preserved a heavy plaster coating. Its plastered floor slopes from its northern edge 3.5 meters down toward a 15-

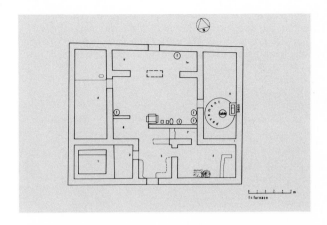

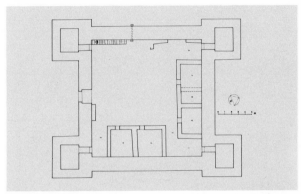

Both pages, counterclockwise: Map of the site. Juglet of the Herodian period. Silver plaque from the castellum with relief decorations on both sides. Denarii of Hadrian found on the eye sockets of a body buried in the farm. Papyrus fragment with a list of debtors and creditors, dating from the sixth–seventh centuries A.D.

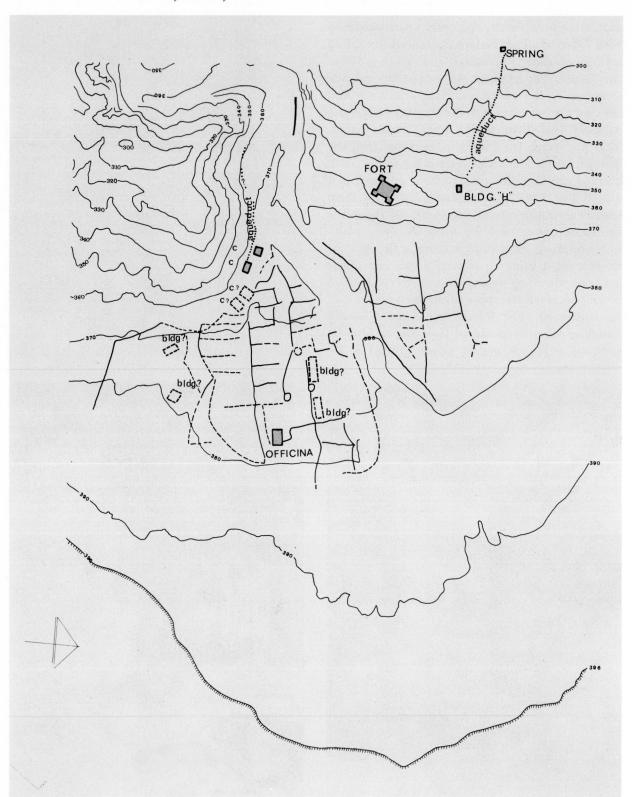

centimeter-high barrier. This was the crushing or treading floor. The liquefied or pulverized substance prepared was collected in a sunken pit (55 by 35 by 50 centimeters) at the southeastern corner. The east room was used for a different industrial process centered around a working table set upon a flagstone floor. This table was replaced in the third phase by a small pressing device.

Security was provided by the earlier tower, the double walls of which were 1.2 meters wide. It stood 1.3 meters above ground. To strengthen the tower further, there was no entrance from the ground-floor level.

The Castellum. This is a square building (20 by 20 meters) with four towers (6 by 6 meters) projecting from its corners. The curtain walls, about 1.9 meters wide, still stand up to a height of 6 meters. Their mode of construction was similar to that of the Herodian factory, but of more massive masonry. Corners, doorways, apertures, etc., were built of ashlar. The single arched entrance gave access to a central courtyard, onto which rooms opened along the eastern and northern curtain walls. The west side was occupied by wooden sheds. This arrangement remained unchanged throughout the four phases of occupation: phase 1, about 360–400; phase 2, Anastasius to Justinian; phase 3, second half of the sixth century to the Persian invasion (614); phase 4, 629–35. The original building may have been connected with the Arab wars in the time of Valens. The first destruction could have been due to the Arab inroads of the early fifth century. The second destruction may have been the result of the border wars of the Ghassanians or Lakhmids in the time of Justinian.

Fireplaces in all the barrack rooms indicate an occupation during the second phase by a regular force of up to seventy men. During the third phase, the *castellum* served as a base for the *limitanean* farmers settled around it. The great amount of broken glass vessels found in some of the rooms demonstrate that these chambers were turned into stores for the finished products of the pharmaceutical industry then revived.

The rooms and towers had roofs carried by wooden beams. Access to the towers was made difficult for hostile intruders by narrow and low doors (.7 by 1.65 meters). Moreover, the roof above the entrance passage was pierced for attack from above, and the upper story(s) could be entered only by

means of detachable wooden ladders. All the tower entrances have early examples of low relieving arches with small lunettes above their lintels.

In order to set the structure firmly upon the sloping gravel hill that served as its base, the foundations of the eastern side were built to a depth of 2 meters beneath the first floor. The rooms were filled with gravel crammed between the floors like layers of beaten earth.

The blocking of the gate with a wall of stones, hasty patching of the inside of the west wall, and the erection of a narrow staircase from the courtyard toward the platform of the southwestern tower all point to hasty preparations on the eve of the Muslim invasion.

Water and Irrigation Works. 1. The waters of 'En Boqeq were carried in an aqueduct 1 kilometer long to a series of square cisterns in the oasis. The channel, built of plaster round a stone core, was laid beneath a retaining wall on the southern slope of the canyon. A branch, bridging the valley at its last bent, provided for the area of the *castellum*. The cisterns measured 12 by 11.65 by 3.54 meters and 16.6 by 10.3 by 3.2 meters, respectively. They were built of large blocks, covered with several coats of plaster, keyed with crowfeet or potsherds. 2. The waters of 'En Boqeq gushed forth from a small nymphaeum of 3 by 3 meters (without annexes) and were carried down the slope of 35 degrees for about 200 meters, toward the bathhouse (?) by an aqueduct constructed largely of well-cut stone links, U-shaped in section. These were covered by roughly rounded slabs of local limonite. Because of their therapeutic qualities, the Noith waters probably served for both bathing and drinking before their waste was channeled out for irrigation from the bathhouse (not yet cleared).

Agricultural Remains. At 'En Boqeq a series of field enclosures, field partition walls, and terraces are preserved. All were built of local unhewn stones, in dry courses. To forestall grazing cattle, there was no passageway into the enclosures, only rough stone steps jutting out at various places from both sides of the wall faces.   M. GICHON

BIBLIOGRAPHY

F. de Saulcy, *Narrative of a Journey around the Dead Sea*, London, 1857, 252–62 • F. Frank, *ZDPV* 57 (1934), 191 ff. • M. Gichon, *Bonner Jhrb.* 171 (1971), 386–406; idem, "'En Boqeq, Preliminary Report on the First Campaign," *Proceed. of the 8th Congress of Roman Frontier Studies*, Durham, 1973.

EN-GEDI

IDENTIFICATION AND HISTORY. En-Gedi is an oasis on the western shore of the Dead Sea. En-Gedi (Engaddi in Greek and Roman sources and 'Ein Jidi in Arabic) is the name of the perennial spring that flows from a height of 200 meters above the Dead Sea. In the cycle of stories about David's flight from Saul, the desert area in the vicinity of the spring is called the "wilderness of En-Gedi" (I Samuel 24:1–2). The enclosed camps at the top of the mountains appear as the "strong holds of En-Gedi" (I Samuel 23:29). En-Gedi is mentioned in the list of the cities of Judah among those in the wilderness (Joshua 15:62). In a late biblical source, it was somewhat arbitrarily identified with Hazazon-Tamar (II Chronicles 20:2). The site is also mentioned in the Song of Songs (1:14) in connection with its vineyards, and in Ezekiel (47:10). Various references to En-Gedi are found in sources from the Second Temple and the Roman and Byzantine periods. Josephus lists it among the cities of the toparchies of Judah (*War* III, 55) and relates that the Sicarii raided it during the First Revolt (*ibid.* IV, 492). Pliny reports its destruction in the same war. From documents discovered in the Cave of the Letters in Naḥal Ḥever, it can be deduced that, during the period preceding the Second Revolt, En-Gedi was a Jewish village that had become the property of the emperor, and a Roman garrison was stationed there. In the time of Bar Kokhba, En-Gedi was one of the administrative and military centers of the Prince of Israel. The Church Fathers attest in their writings to the existence of a settlement at En-Gedi in the Roman-Byzantine period. Eusebius (*Onomasticon* 86:18) describes it as a very large Jewish village. According to the sources, En-Gedi was renowned for its excellent dates and crops of balsam-producing plants.

EXCAVATIONS

In 1949, a small expedition headed by B. Mazar (with the participation of A. Reifenberg and Trude Dothan) began a series of surveys and excavations in the oasis of En-Gedi. Trial soundings in Tel Goren (Tell el-Jurn), a narrow hillock in the southwest of the plain near Naḥal 'Arugot, established that from the end of Iron Age onward this had been one of the main centers of settlement in the oasis. On the western slope of the mound were discovered the remains of a solid tower, built of rough stones, which the excavators ascribed to the Hellenistic period. The investigation of the building remains, the terraces on the slopes of the hill, and the aqueducts leading from the spring to reservoirs in the plain has shown that from the Hellenistic to the Byzantine period an efficient system of agriculture and advanced techniques for collecting water for irrigation had been developed. The combination of a tropical climate and an abundant water supply enabled the inhabitants of En-Gedi to develop an advanced irrigation system for the cultivation of the soil, especially for the balsam plants for which En-Gedi became famous. The settlement was apparently administered by a central authority which dealt with the construction of terraces, aqueducts, and the network of strongholds and watch towers. A second survey was carried out under the direction of Y. Aharoni, and a third under J. Naveh. Archaeological excavations were carried out at En-Gedi on behalf of the Hebrew University and the Israel Exploration Society. In the first two seasons (1961–62) the excavations were directed by B. Mazar, I. Dunayevsky, and Trude Dothan, and in the following three seasons (1964–65) by B. Mazar and I. Dunayevsky.

The Chalcolithic Enclosure. During the surveys conducted by Y. Aharoni and J. Naveh in En-Gedi in 1956–57, a building complex was discovered on a hill terrace above the spring of En-Gedi, some 150 meters north of it. A trial excavation carried out by J. Naveh showed that this was a public building from the Chalcolithic period. During the second season systematic excavations on the spot uncovered a sacred enclosure, the various structures of which were outstanding in their plan and architecture. The solid stone walls were preserved to a considerable height. The building complex comprised a main building in the north and a smaller building in the east. In the enclosure wall north of the smaller building, was a gate leading to Naḥal David, and to the south was another gateway from which there was a descent to the spring of En-Gedi. A stone enclosure wall, built in sections, linked the buildings into one unit. In the center of the enclosed courtyard, surrounded by the buildings and the enclosure wall, is a circular structure (diameter about 3 meters) built of small

stones, which probably served a cultic purpose. The main building in the northern part of the enclosure (about 20 meters long) is a broad-house structure, with its entrance in the middle of the long wall on the south side. The door of this structure, as well as the doors of the smaller building and of the gateway, opened inside. This is shown by the stone sills of the doors, all of which have hinge holes to the left of the entrance. Along the wall opposite the entrance of the main structure,

Chalcolithic enclosure; plan and view.

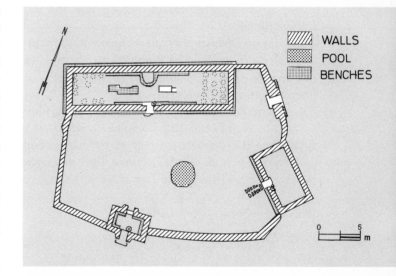

was a hoof-shaped niche surrounded by a stone fence. It probably served as an altar, as may be seen from remains of animal bones, fragments of pottery, and an accumulation of ashes. The clay statuette of a bull laden with a pair of churns was also found there. On both sides of the entrance and of the hoof-shaped niche stood stone benches. Of special interest are the groups of small pits sunk into the floor near both short walls of the building. Inside these pits were remains of burned bones, horns, pottery, and many ashes.

The smaller building is also a broad house. Its floor is coated with light-colored plaster. A stone-paved path in the center of its long wall led into the courtyard.

The gateway consists of a square room with benches built along its walls. The room has two entrances, one in the outer wall and one in the inner wall opening onto the courtyard.

There is no evidence of different stages of building or repairs of this building complex. It seems that it is to be dated in its entirety to the same short and limited period. All the pottery finds belong to types characteristic of the late stage of the Ghas-

sulian: small bowls, cornets, and cups. They also have parallels in the late pottery of the Beersheba culture and of various sites in the Judean Desert. No domestic ware was found in the enclosure, nor have any remains of dwelling houses of the Chalcolithic period been discovered up to now. It seems, therefore, that this enclosure was solely a cult place, perhaps even the central sanctuary for the inhabitants of the region. In its character and plan it resembles the Chalcolithic sanctuary discovered in stratum XIX at Megiddo (q.v.). The enclosure at En-Gedi was not destroyed but was abandoned, and when the last worshipers left the place, they apparently took the cult furniture with them.

Tel Goren. During the five seasons, the excavations were concentrated mainly on Tel Goren, the most prominent site in the oasis. It appeared that even the first settlers had not limited themselves to the small summit of this narrow and elongated hill but had already found it necessary to terrace its rather steep slopes and build on the terraces. In later periods the settlement expanded and spread over extensive areas in the plain between Naḥal David and Naḥal 'Arugot. Five occupation levels

Chalcolithic enclosure, looking southeast.

can be distinguished at Tel Goren. The following strata were found (from bottom to top):

V. End of the Iron Age (about 630–582 B.C.).

IV. Persian Period (fifth to fourth century B.C.).

III. Hellenistic Period (mainly the Hasmonaean period from Alexander Jannaeus to the death of Herod, 103–4 B.C.).

II. Early Roman Period (mainly the time of the Herodian dynasty, 4 B.C.–A.D. 68).

I. Roman and Byzantine Periods (second to sixth centuries A.D.).

STRATUM V. The earliest settlement at Tel Goren was built on the top of the hill and on the terraces on its slopes. On the southern slope, the remains cleared consisted mostly of courtyards with adjoining buildings. The numerous finds made here under the brick debris and a layer of ashes included large pottery vessels (pithoi) shaped like barrels or vats and with their bases sunk into the ground. In one of the courtyards was uncovered a row of seven such pithoi set close together. Around them was an abundance of pottery vessels, such as jars, bowls, cooking pots, jugs, juglets, decanters, lamps, etc., as well as a basalt mortar, perforated clay balls, and

lumps of bitumen. The majority of the vessels belong to types characteristic of the second half of the seventh century B.C. and the beginning of the sixth century B.C. To this period also belong the buildings on a wide terrace in the middle of the northern slope of the mound. These structures had a uniform plan. They consisted of a courtyard with two interconnected small rooms along one side. Stairs leading up from the street on the lower terrace gave access to these houses.

Along this street were discovered a group of installations, including ovens. Pithoi, similar to those found on the southern slope, pottery, as well as metal and bone objects were found in one of the courtyards. The excavators assumed that these structures were used for some special industry, most probably for the production of perfume. En-Gedi was known as a center for the cultivation of perfume producing plants, especially the balsam (opobalsamum). It can be assumed that the workshops processing such costly products were concentrated at Tel Goren and that the local growers and perfume workers were employed in the royal service. A gloss of Rabbi Joseph on Jeremiah 52:16

Tel Goren: In the foreground, building 236 (Herodian); behind it, building 234 (Persian).

Both pages, counterclockwise: Stratum V, corner of room with pottery barrels. Plan of IA house. Pottery plaque with applied reliefs of a man and animals; end of IA. Stamp and impression: lṭbšlm; stratum V; end of IA. Stamp and impression: l'ryhw 'zryhw; stratum V; end of IA.

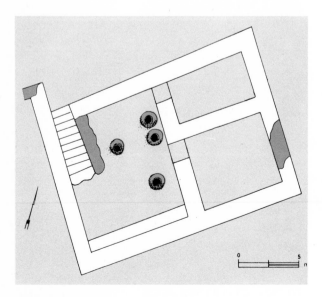

"But Nebuzar-adan...left certain of the poor of the land to be vinedressers and husbandmen" states that these were the "balsam gatherers from En-Gedi to Ramtha" (in the southern Jordan Valley —Babylonian Talmud, *Shabbat* 26a).

Individual finds included a seal impression on a jar handle, showing a double-winged symbol and an inscription in ancient Hebrew which can be read *lnr', lnrt, lmrt,* or *lmr'.* The last reading ("Belonging to Mr' ") could refer to the Aramaic royal title *mar'* ("lord," "sovereign"), possibly an allusion to Nebuchadnezzar, king of Babylonia. Another find was a small square seal with the Hebrew inscription which can perhaps be read *L'ryhw 'azryhw* ("Belonging to 'Uriyahu [son of] 'Azaryahu"). A larger stamp made of limestone bears the name "Tobshalom." Near the name is a design resembling the plan of the building in which the seal was found. Another find was a fragment of a store jar inscribed *Lptyhw* ("Belonging to Putiyah"). Numerous jar handles with rosette stamps were also discovered. One jar handle was found with the seal impression of the double-winged symbol above which are the words *Lmlkh* ("Belonging to the king") and *zyp* (Ziph). Beside the seal are incised concentric circles, made with a compass. Also found was a jar handle stamped with the figure of a horse.

Other finds were stone weights, each marked with the sign representing the shekel with the numerals "one," "four," or "eight." In a building on the northern slope (where the stamp of Tobshalom was found) was a pot covered with a lamp. Inside it was a hoard of silver ingots of various shapes, which must have served as a form of currency. In various buildings, silver jewelry, such as rings, beads, and earrings, were discovered. Although these finds can be dated with certainty to the end of the kingdom of Judah, there remain doubts regarding the dating of a potsherd which has no parallel in Palestinian ceramics. Pieces of clay were applied to the vessel in a horizontal row and then stamped with various impressions, three of which are identifiable. One shows a bearded man sitting on a chair in a hut (?), his right hand resting on his knee and the left one near his face and holding some object. Another impression shows a ram with projecting antlers. The third consists of the remains of a mask (or a lion's head?).

This early settlement was completely destroyed by

a conflagration, perhaps in the year 23 of the reign of Nebuchadnezzar (582/81 B.C.). See also Jeremiah 52:30; Josephus, *Antiquities* X, 181.

STRATUM IV. During the Persian period the settlement covered the top of the hill and its slopes. Toward the north, it extended considerably beyond the area of the earlier stratum. The structures of stratum IV are impressive in their size and strength. Of special interest is the large building situated on the north slope of the mound. It was unearthed under a thick layer of accumulated silt and building debris. Many pottery fragments were found there, the sherds having rolled down from the terraces on the slope. Most of the pottery is characteristic of the Persian period. It includes a jar handle with a seal impression of a roaring lion, handles with *Yhwd, Yhd,* and *Yh* seal impressions, Attic ware, and sherds decorated with triangular wedge-shaped and reed impressions. A small part of the pottery finds belong to types typical of stratum V.

The plan of the large building and the finds discovered there indicate that this was a large dwelling, in part two-storied. The walls, floors, and probably also the ceilings were covered with a thick coat of plaster. Trunks of palm trees were used for the construction of the roof and other purposes. The building covers an area of about 550 square meters and contains twenty-three rooms, enclosed courtyards, and storerooms of various sizes. From the study of the building and the finds (among which was Attic pottery), it can be concluded that this large house was erected in its entirety in the first half of the fifth century B.C. and was destroyed in about 400 B.C. or at the beginning of the fourth century B.C. The western "wing" of the building was restored subsequently for dwelling purposes, perhaps by the inhabitants who had remained at En-Gedi after its destruction. It continued to be in use for about fifty years more.

Among the finds in this building was a conical chalcedony seal of the type common in Babylonia from the seventh to fifth centuries B.C. Another seal of the same type was discovered on the southern slope of the mound. Other finds included two pendants of opaque-colored glass, one in the form of the head of a woman wearing earrings and the other the head of a bearded man, as well as fragments of a rhyton (drinking horn) decorated with

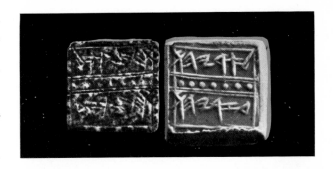

the relief of a crouching lioness. The pottery found on the floors and in the rubble is generally of the type common in the Persian period. Attic ware is abundant. Of special interest is the rich collection of potsherds from the Persian period, found under a layer of ashes in a room in the northern part of the building near the main entrance. The epigraphic material includes two Aramaic ostraca and jar handles with *Yhwd* and *Yh* seal impressions.

West and east of the large building and south of it on the rising slope, other structures were uncovered. These were dwelling houses that were separated by narrow lanes. On the southern slope of Tel Goren, part of another large building was cleared, and a few building remains were excavated on the western slope.

STRATUM III. A few coins from the time of the Ptolemies and the Seleucids and Early Hellenistic potsherds are evidence of settlement in the oasis in the period of the Diadochi. The palm plantations existing at En-Gedi in this period are also referred to in Sirach 24:14: "I was exalted, like a palm tree in En-Gedi." In the Hasmonaean period the site flourished again, especially in the time of Alexander Jannaeus and his successors. This is evidenced by numerous coins of Jannaeus collected throughout the area of the oasis, as well as by the finds from the cave tombs in Naḥal David and especially by the citadel on the summit of Tel Goren.

The remains of the defense system of this citadel (stratum III) were uncovered on the top of the mound, along its southern, northern, and western slopes. The citadel consisted of two parts. The western, smaller section was built on a trapezoidal plan. Its walls are 1.2 to 1.4 meters wide, and at its western extremity there is a rectangular tower. The eastern section has the form of a large rectangle (width of the walls 1.7–2 meters), with a rectangular tower in the southern part. The whole area of the citadel covered about 3,500 square meters. The finds which can be attributed to stratum III are not numerous. Most of them can be ascribed to the Late Hasmonaean period. It can be assumed that the citadel was destroyed during the Parthian invasion and in the war of the last Hasmonaeans against Herod.

STRATUM II. A strong citadel was uncovered in this stratum. Its remains, including walls built of large rough stones about 2 meters thick, were cleared on the top of the mound, along the southern, western, and northern slopes of Tel Goren. Of special interest is the tower at the western extremity of the mound, separated from the west wall of the citadel by a narrow passage. The tower is a solid rectangular structure (14 by 7 meters) enclosing two rooms and two narrow cells. The building technique is similar to that of the citadel wall. Details of the plan of the tower were elucidated in the first two seasons of excavation. The dating of the citadel and of the tower has now been established by the results of the later excavations at En-Gedi, by a new assessment of the finds from the tower, and by a comparison with the pottery from Qumran and Masada. Stratum II at Tel Goren is

thus to be dated to the time of Herod's successors, although the beginning of the stratum may date to an earlier period. The two buildings were destroyed by fire, probably during the First Revolt.

A large building discovered on the northern slope of Tel Goren, north of the large Persian building (which was described above), belongs to the same period. The building consists of a spacious courtyard enclosed by a stone wall. It contained several rooms on its north and west sides. Especially interesting are several ovens set in a row along the southern wall of the courtyard. Near one oven was a large Herodian lamp, sealed with a plug and containing a hoard of 139 coins struck in the sixth year of Agrippa I, in the fourteenth year of Claudius, and in the fifth year of Nero. Two phases of building can be distinguished in the rooms. This building may have originally been a public one and only later converted into a private dwelling. The beginning of the later phase is dated by coins of Agrippa I and the date of its destruction by coins from the second year of the First Revolt found in the ash layer. A few remains found in the same area date from a period immediately following the destruction of the building.

STRATUM I. The remains of this stratum at Tel Goren from the Roman-Byzantine period indicate that no permanent settlement existed at that time on the site. The structures were temporary ones and the terraces were used for agriculture. It appears that at this period as in the preceding ones—at least from the Herodian period onward—the

center of the settlement at En-Gedi had moved to the plain east and northeast of Tel Goren, between Naḥal David and Naḥal 'Arugot.

The Bathhouse. In its last three seasons the expedition cleared a bathhouse from the Roman period, situated in the center of the plateau between Naḥal David and Naḥal 'Arugot, about 200 meters west of the shore of the Dead Sea. The building is long and narrow (40 by 50 meters). Its chambers form one continuous row, aligned from north to south —a rather unusual manner of construction, which may suggest that it was perhaps part of a larger complex. Visitors entered the bath at its northern extremity, where a vestibule was discovered. After dipping their feet in a small basin, the visitors proceeded to the two dressing rooms. South of these was the actual bath consisting of three units: frigidarium (cold room), tepidarium (warm room), and caldarium (hot room). South of the caldarium was the heating room with the furnace. The purpose of another room is not quite clear. The entire

Both pages, counterclockwise: From the Persian period: Sherds with impressed decorations. Jar handle with Yhd impression. Sherd with molded decoration. Babylonian seal showing priest praying before the emblems of Marduk.

frigidarium was paved with carved building stones taken from an earlier building, which included eleven Doric capitals. West of the frigidarium was a square plastered pool, reached through a large opening and by descending two steps. The floors of the tepidarium and caldarium have been destroyed, but the underground rooms with the installations of heating channels are preserved, as is a channel covered with pottery tiles. Through it, the heated air passed from the furnace to the caldarium and from there to the heating channels.

The bath dates from the period between the destruction of the Second Temple and the revolt of Bar Kokhba. The dating was established by the pottery, the fragments of glass vessels, and the coins, especially a group of six bronze coins hidden in a hollow of a door frame. The oldest of the coins dates from the time of Titus, and the latest were minted in the first year of Hadrian. For the construction of the bath numerous architectural elements were re-used: Doric capitals, ashlars, door and window frames. Some of these were decorated in relief. These stones were presumably taken from an important Herodian structure that had stood nearby and had been destroyed during the First Revolt. After the destruction of the bath, part of it was apparently temporarily converted into dwellings (in the time of Bar Kokhba?).

From the Roman-Byzantine period there were only a few building remains extant. In a sounding made in the northwestern corner of the bath, a structure was uncovered containing two adjoining pools. The southern and larger of these was reached by descending a flight of steps. This building was perhaps a *miqve* (ritual bath). On the basis of the pottery and the coins, which are dated to the period between the reign of Agrippa I and the second year of the First Revolt, it is possible to ascribe this lower structure to the time before the destruction of the Second Temple.

The Buildings Near the Spring. In the second season of excavation, the solid, deep stone foundations of the square tower east of the spring of En-Gedi were unearthed. It had already been explored in previous surveys. It could be established with certainty that the foundations were contemporary with stratum V at Tel Goren and should be dated to the second half of the seventh and beginning of the sixth century B.C. The so-called circular structure was also cleared about 40 meters northeast of the

spring. This structure was found to be a limekiln of the Roman-Byzantine period. To the same period belongs a construction built of ashlar discovered on the slopes of the ridge near the road leading from the spring to Tel Goren.   B. MAZAR

The Synagogue. The ruins of En-Gedi of the Late Roman and Byzantine periods (third to sixth centuries A.D.) were identified during the surveys of Y. Aharoni and J. Naveh in the area northeast of Tel Goren. In 1966, the remains of a mosaic pavement were discovered there. An expedition sponsored by the Institute of Archaeology of the Hebrew University, the Department of Antiquities, and the Israel Exploration Society (with the participation of the En-Gedi Field School) excavated at the site during three seasons (1970–72). The expedition was directed by D. Barag, assisted by Y. Porat and E. Netzer. Three strata were cleared, the third being divided into two phases.

STRATUM I contained disturbed occupation remains from different periods between the eighth century A.D. and the present. The latest synagogue, which was found in STRATUM II (second half of the fifth and first half of the sixth century A.D.), was a stone structure about 12.5 meters wide, 13.5 meters long on the east side and 16 meters long on the west side. It was divided into a nave and two side aisles and had a short aisle with stepped benches at its southern end. The synagogue had an additional small room in its southwest corner and another room, entered from the east aisle, in the northeast. Three entrances in the west wall led into the synagogue. In front of the three entrances, along the western side of the building, was a narthex, 4 meters wide and paved with white mosaics. The narthex had two entrances, one at the south and one at the north. Near the southern entrance were the remains of the *kiyor,* the basin for washing the hands and feet of worshipers. Near it were found a large stone bowl and a two-handled pottery jar standing on a concave stone base.

The semi-circular niche of the Ark of the Law was situated in front of the northern wall, the one facing Jerusalem. To its right was a stepped seat for the head of the community (?), the so-called Seat of Moses. In front of the Ark of the Law was a podium (bema), approximately 4 by 2 meters, surrounded by screens. Between the niche and the northern wall was a rectangular structure (1.5 by

3.25 meters) which was used for storage. In it were found scorched manuscripts, large quantities of coins, a bronze beaker, glass and pottery lamps, and other objects.

The mosaic pavement of the bema was decorated with a bird inside a small circular medallion. Three small seven-branched candlesticks (menorahs) were uncovered in the mosaic pavement in front of the bema. In the center of the mosaic pavement of the nave is a circular medallion inside a lozenge and a square. Two pairs of birds are depicted in the medallion, and in each corner of the square are a pair of peacocks holding a bunch of grapes.

The mosaic pavement of the western aisle contains five inscriptions in Hebrew and Aramaic. The first inscription quotes I Chronicles 1:1–4. The second inscription lists the names of the twelve signs of the zodiac, the twelve months of the year starting with Nissan, and then mentions the three patriarchs, the three companions of Daniel, and ends with "Peace on Israel." The third inscription, in Aramaic, mentions three donors and includes curses on those who commit certain sins (*e.g.*, cause dissension in the community, pass on to the Gentiles malicious information, or reveal the secrets of the town). The fourth inscription, also in Aramaic (a later addition), mentions the donors who built the "great steps," perhaps the stairs leading up to the galleries. A fifth inscription in Aramaic is a blessing on all the people of the town who renovated the synagogue and mentions also the hazan (a synagogue official). The blessing on the entire population indicates that in the fifth century the population of En-Gedi consisted almost entirely of Jews.

The absence of figural representations (such as zodiacs or biblical scenes) points up the difference between this community and those situated closer to the Hellenized urban centers.

The synagogue was destroyed by a conflagration in the early part of the reign of Justinian. A seven-branched menorah, cast in bronze, was found in the debris close to the Ark of the Law.

Below the synagogue of stratum II were discovered the remains of an earlier synagogue, of STRATUM III-A (late second–early third century A.D.). It was a rectangular building of about 10 by 15.5 meters,

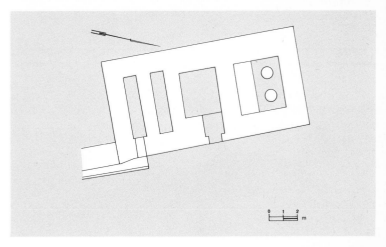

From top to bottom: General view of Tel Goren, from the northwest; on the right, tower from the Hasmonaean period. Wall of Hasmonaean tower. Plan of the tower.

with two entrances in the northern wall. This building had a white mosaic floor with a black rectangular frame (8 by 3 meters) and three squares (1.4 by 1.4 meters). The southern square bears a large swastika turning to the left.

In STRATUM III–B, the building underwent extensive changes. The central entrance in the northern wall was blocked and turned into a niche for the Ark of the Law. On its eastern side was constructed the stepped seat (Seat of Moses), and stepped benches were added at the southern end of the synagogue. The inner space was divided by columns into a nave and two aisles (one in the east and one in the south). Three (?) entrances were opened on the west side of the building, and in front of the entrances a portico was constructed.

Streets and dwellings of stratum II were uncovered north and west of the synagogue. North of the synagogue, a two-room house was excavated, which possibly served as the guest house of the community. All over the settlement traces of the final conflagration were found. Below the remains of stratum III were found remains of a settlement that date from the last generations before the destruction of the Second Temple.   D. BARAG

BIBLIOGRAPHY

B. Mazar, *Archaeology* 16 (1963), 99–107 • B. Mazar–I. Dunayevsky, *IEJ* 14 (1964), 121–30; 17 (1967), 133–43 • B. Mazar–T. Dothan–I. Dunayevsky, *'Atiqot* (English series) 5 (1966) • D. Ussishkin, *BA* 34 (1971), 23–39 • A. Kempinski, *IEJ* 22 (1972), 10–15.

Bottom, left: The Roman bathhouse situated on the plateau between Naḥal David and Naḥal 'Arugot. Below: Two carved architectural fragments re-used in the bathhouse.

'EN GEV

PREHISTORIC SITES

Excavations. During the survey made by D. Ben-Ami of Kibbutz 'En Gev on the eastern side of the Sea of Galilee, the sites of 'En Gev I and IV were discovered on a hill adjacent to the kibbutz on a flank of the Golan Plateau, about .5 kilometer east of the shore. An expedition under the auspices of the Israel Academy of Sciences and Humanities, directed by M. Stekelis and O. Bar-Yosef, excavated there during the summers of 1963–64. The main excavation took place at the site of 'En Gev I, where a human skeleton was found. Additional test pits were opened in 1965 and 1967–68 in 'En Gev II, III, and IV.

'En Gev I. The excavation uncovered six layers, numbered 1 through 6. The stratigraphy was based on the succession of floors on which large concentrations of flints and bones were exposed. The configurations of the layers suggest a hut dug into the slope of the hill, so that its eastern side is higher than its western. The floor was a kind of shallow basin enclosed on the east and probably open to the west, as the westward elevations of the site (except for the lowest layers, 4–6) suffered from later erosion. The infilling of the floors of the hut indicates a rapid accumulation of sand from the slope between each period of occupation. In layer 4, a hearth with white ash was uncovered. Near the hearth were a basalt mortar and two pestles, one of which was broken. On a paved area at the southern edge of the pit, several horn cores were found. Some large bones were laid on a paved area inside the dwelling pit.

In the center of the pit in layer 3, a female skeleton lying on its right side was found buried in a shallow grave. The legs were drawn up, the left hand was resting on the thigh, slightly bent, and touching the left leg. The skull, lying on several stones, was crushed. Large bones of animals were found around the skull. On the basis of its position it may be assumed that the burial took place toward the end of the occupancy of layer 3.

The lithic industry defines the material culture of 'En Gev I as Kebaran. It is characterized by obliquely truncated, backed bladelets. Other characteristics are the Falita points which relate this culture to other Kebaran sites in Syria and Lebanon, scrapers, burins, denticulates, and several picks. The bone tools are burnishers made of *Oryx* horn cores.

The numerous kitchen remains include bones of gazelle, Nubian ibex, fallow deer, roe deer, bovids, wild cat, wolf, common red fox, as well as several birds and mollusks from a nearby spring.

'En Gev II. This site was found across the gully, about 30 meters south of 'En Gev I, on the same topographic elevation (between 150 and 160 meters below sea level). Technologically and typologically, the material culture is the same as in 'En Gev I.

'En Gev III. 'En Gev III is located 25 meters further west of site II. A cross-section of this site showed the same type of pit-dwelling construction as was seen in 'En Gev I. The flint industry, however, is somewhat different, as it also includes a few rectangles. This indicates a trend toward geometrization, *i.e.*, the transition from Kebaran to Geometric Kebaran.

'En Gev IV. 'En Gev IV is located on the northern edge of the same hill as the other sites. The industry, found within a small sounding of 2 by 1 meters made in 1968, was characterized by the use of the micro-burin technique. The products of this technique amount to 50 or 60 percent of the total assemblage of the five layers uncovered. The tools are mainly end scrapers on blades with some on flakes, and a few burins. The microliths are generally obliquely truncated or micro-gravette points. The geometric microliths include scalene and isosceles triangles and several lunates, all of which are products of the micro-burin technique. Also found were many notched tools and denticulates, some of which were made on large blades or thick flakes, and a few burins. The microliths are gener-typological grounds, seems to be later than the industries of the other sites.

The fauna includes horses, wild boar which did not appear at the other sites, gazelle, some bovids, roe deer, fallow deer, rabbits, wolf, wild cat, some birds, turtles, and vertebrae of fish (from the Sea of Galilee).

Summary. The descending locations of the sites from I to IV probably indicates the regression of the lake as well as the gradual freshening of its water, as testified by the existence of fish remains in site IV. The Kebaran hunters, living in small and probably familial huts on this hill, were provided with abundant game and wild cereals from their immediate environment: the valley beside the lake and on the escarpment of the plateau of the Golan Heights. The evolution of the tool kit is seen by the typological modifications of the microliths, from non-geometric to a fully geometric type. Such a development is parallel to other Kebaran and Geometric Kebaran sites in other areas of Palestine.

O. BAR-YOSEF

HISTORIC PERIODS. Situated on the narrow plain on the eastern shore of the Sea of Galilee (in Arabic: Khirbet el-Asheq), this site is today occupied by Kibbutz 'En Gev.

The remains found here attest to a continuous occupation from the tenth to the second centuries B.C. The site rises only a few meters above the plain and has none of the typical characteristics of an ancient mound. It is evident that its inhabitants were content to forgo the natural protection afforded by a hill and to build their settlement on the coast, along the road that ran from Beth-Shean to the fords of the Jordan and then followed the eastern coast of the Sea of Galilee as far as the environs of 'En Gev, whence it went up to Hippos and Aphek (Fiq) and continued north to Damascus.

Exploration. In 1961 an expedition on behalf of the Department of Antiquities and the Hebrew University made exploratory soundings at the end of September and at the beginning of December, in all, eleven days. The expedition was led by B. Mazar, A. Biran, I. Dunayevsky, and M. Dothan, assisted by volunteers from the Absalom Foundation and from kibbutzim of the Jordan Valley. The mound was found to be about 250 meters long and 120 meters wide.

The plan of the ancient city reflects the topography. It was divided into two sections. The southern one was a residential area surrounded by a wall, while

the northern section, built on an elevation about 3 meters high, was a citadel. The trial sounding in the south (area I) sought to trace the fortifications and determine the stratigraphy of the settlement. That in the north (areas II–III) was intended to ascertain the nature of the citadel.

Excavations. The trial trench dug in area I established clearly that the earliest city (stratum 5) had been built on level ground and that the elevated mound is nothing but the accumulation of occupational levels. All the layers throughout the excavated area were horizontal, which made it relatively simple to establish the stratigraphy.

The five strata uncovered in area I provided numerous indications of the cultural continuity of the settlement in the Iron Age, from the tenth to the eighth centuries B.C. No remains of other periods were uncovered in this area. To stratum 5, which represents the earliest settlement on the site, is assigned the foundation (1.85 meters thick), built of

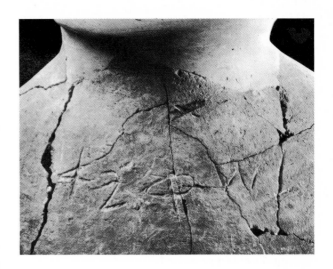

Counterclockwise, both pages: Incense shovel; stratum 3. Carved orthostat. Incense stand; stratum 3. Store jar with inscription: "Belonging to SQY" (see enlarged detail above); stratum 2.

medium-sized rough stones on which once stood a brick wall. When this wall went out of use, it was replaced by a casemate line (stratum 4), whose two walls, the southern or exterior wall (1.75 meters thick and preserved to a height of .9 meter), and the northern one (1.15 meters thick and preserved to a height of .45 meter), were built of large, undressed stones with a fill of smaller stones between them. The space between the two walls (1.4 meters) is paved with flagstones. This casemate wall is of the type common in the country during Solomon's reign, and it is similar to the walls at Megiddo V-A–IV-B and Hazor X–IX. The need for such a massive wall was dictated by the topography of the area —an almost level plain for which strong defenses were necessary.

Few building remains were uncovered in strata 4 and 5. In stratum 5 were found the remains of a house, separated from the nearby city wall by a street (5.5 meters wide). The plan of the house could not be established. No remains of building were found in stratum 4, since most of the excavation in the trial trench reached down only to stratum 3. The few potsherds found in the two strata (which included fragments of brightly burnished Cyprian-Phoenician vessels), are to be assigned to the tenth century B.C.

In stratum 3, it is evident that after the destruction

of the earlier city new settlers erected a town on its ruins with an altogether different character. In the building of the walls they used the foundations of the outer casemate wall, while the inner wall went out of use. The new wall of stratum 3 was buttressed on the outside with additional structures, apparently at regular intervals, and hence it consisted of sections alternately thin (1.75 meters) and broad (3.15 meters) on the plan of "offsets and insets," common in the ninth century (Megiddo IV-A, Hazor VIII). A glacis was added, consisting of a stone revetment supported by the remains of the wall of stratum 5.

Most of the area north of the wall was occupied by a single building separated by only a narrow alley from the wall. The building evidently consisted of a courtyard surrounded by rooms on two or three sides. In one room, which was completely paved with large flagstones, the excavators unearthed a wealth of finds, including ritual libation and incense vessels, such as a clay incense burner, a stone incense spoon, a small funnel of bronze, as well as decorated pottery vessels. All this may indicate that the room served the cultic needs of a family, similar to the cultic room in House 2081 at Megiddo (stratum V-A–IV-B). North of this room was a courtyard sparsely paved with stones. It had a silo attached to its wall. Within the courtyard were found several vessels, including a store jar with an Aramaic inscription incised on its shoulder: "belonging to Shaqiah [the "cupbearer"]." On paleographical grounds, the inscription can be assigned to no later than the middle of the ninth century B.C. *Shaqiah* is evidently the Aramaic equivalent of the Hebrew *mashqeh*, "cupbearer," perhaps the title of a high official in the Aramaean kingdom.

Of the many clay vessels found in stratum 3, the majority are typical of pottery from sites in northern and central Palestine of the ninth century B.C. Some of the pottery, however, was imported, especially from the Aramaean portions of Syria.

The structures of stratum 2 were built over the ruined buildings of stratum 3 after the latter had been burned to the ground. They were constructed according to the same plan. The wall of stratum 3, however, continued to be used in stratum 2. It appears that these two strata belong to one historical-cultural period and that after the destruction of city 3 the same inhabitants built it anew, albeit with some changes. The thick wall, which in

stratum 3 separated the house from the courtyard on the north, was replaced by a wall consisting of a row of pilasters built of flat stones arranged one upon the other with the spaces between them filled with mud brick. The pottery of stratum 2 also did not differ to any marked degree from that of stratum 3.

The settlement of stratum 2 was also destroyed by fire, but this time the destruction was complete. The settlement that followed in stratum 1 was of an altogether different character. On the ruins of stratum 2, the excavators found a public building of generous dimensions, built of stone walls (1.1 meters thick), which may have served some military purpose or as a storehouse protected by heavy walls. Judging from the pottery, stratum 1 is to be assigned to no later than the eighth century B.C. (The table at the end of this article gives estimated dates of the strata from top to bottom.)

At the northeastern tip of the mound, at the spot where the citadel stood, two exploratory soundings were made: a small pit in area II and a somewhat larger excavation nearby (area III). These soundings revealed the nature of the citadel and its stratigraphy. It is quite certain that the dimensions of the citadel were about 60 square meters. The wall of the citadel uncovered in area II (1.35 meters thick and preserved to a height of 4.15 meters) was built of large, undressed stones within and without, with a fill of smaller stones. Since the wall was built directly on virgin soil, a fill of earth was heaped up on both its sides to a height of 3 meters. On this fill was laid the earth floor of the citadel. It seems that the builders of the citadel had raised the level of the floor so that the fortress would dominate the entire area.

In area III, four strata were distinguished. Stratum 4* is represented by a layer of earth which rises to a height of 1.35 meters above virgin soil. In it were found remains of furnaces, many potsherds, and a considerable amount of charred matter. This stratum, which preceded the citadel, was also found in area II, where a pavement of large stones laid on virgin soil was uncovered.

To stratum 3* are to be assigned remains of the citadel, which was built on a high fill. The thick stone walls that surrounded the fortress were built on virgin soil 1.4 meters below the level of the floor. The southern limit of the fill was marked by a heavy brick wall. To the south, the space between the virgin soil and the floor of the citadel was used to build a basement divided into rectangular rooms, two of which were uncovered. The rooms were found filled with earth and sherds. In one room, the excavators found large, flat, well-dressed flagstones, which evidently had faced the lower part of the citadel walls and had fallen into the cellar when the ceiling collapsed.

About 10 meters south of area III, a section of a stone wall could be seen. Judging from its construction and direction, it was evidently the southern wall of the citadel and marks the limit of the cellar rooms in the south.

Stratum 2* is represented by two stone walls built at right angles to one another. The earth floor of this stratum is about .5 meter higher than the top of the walls of stratum 3*.

In stratum 1* were also found two stone walls built at right angles to each other and a rough stone pavement about .5 meter above the level of the floor of stratum 2*. The pottery of this stratum does not differ from that of stratum 2* and belongs to the Iron Age II-C.

The dates of the strata range from the beginning of the United Monarchy (the beginning of the tenth century) to the campaign of Tiglath-pileser III (733/732 B.C.). The table at the bottom of the page presents a tentative synchronization of the strata in areas I with those of areas II–III and their approximate dates.

An additional sounding was made near a building used by the fishermen of the kibbutz (area IV). There two basalt orthostats, one of them decorated with a relief of a palm tree, were found about twenty years ago. The uppermost stratum in this area could be assigned to the Hellenistic period and the lower strata parallel those of areas I and II–III. Persian and Hellenistic vessels and sherds were also found in trenches and ditches dug on the summit of the mound and in the vicinity.

B. MAZAR

BIBLIOGRAPHY

B. Mazar, A. Biran, M. Dothan, I. Dunayevsky, *IEJ* 14 (1964), 1–49 • M. Stekelis and O. Bar-Yosef, *L'Anthropologie* 69 (1965), 176–83 • M. Stekelis, O. Bar-Yosef, and E. Tchernov, *Yediot* 30 (1966), 5–21 (Hebrew).

AREA I	AREAS II–III	PERIOD (ALL DATES ARE B.C. AND APPROXIMATE)	FORTIFICATIONS
1	1* 2*	790–733/32; Joash and Jeroboam II, to the campaign of Tiglath-pileser III against Damascus	Unfortified city
2	3*	838–790; Hazael and Ben-hadad III, to the campaigns of Joash against Aram	
3		886–838; Ben-hadad I and II (the Omrid dynasty in Israel) to the campaign of Shalmaneser III in northern Transjordan	Citadel and walls with "offsets and insets"
4		945–886; the middle of Solomon's reign to the campaign of Ben-hadad I	Citadel and casemate wall
5	4*	990–945; David and the first part of Solomon's reign	Solid wall

ESHTEMOA

IDENTIFICATION AND HISTORY. Eshtemoa was a town in the territory of Judah (Joshua 15:50) that was granted to the Levites (Joshua 21:14; I Chronicles 6:57). David sent part of the spoils taken in his campaign against the Amalekites to the elders of the city (I Samuel 30:28). According to Eusebius "a very large Jewish village" existed there as late as the fourth century A.D. (*Onomasticon* 26:11; 86:20). The site has been identified with the Arab village of es-Samu' in the southern Judean hills, about 14 kilometers (8.5 miles) southwest of Hebron.

Building stones decorated with menorahs and other motifs, re-used in the village, were discovered by various explorers in the second half of the nineteenth and beginning of the twentieth century.

These finds led to the assumption that a synagogue had once existed here. In 1934, L.A. Mayer and A. Reifenberg succeeded in locating the ruins of the synagogue, and in the winter of 1935–36 they undertook an exploratory excavation on behalf of the Hebrew University. From 1936 to 1968, these remains decayed considerably and their poor condition necessitated salvage excavations and a partial restoration. These were carried out in 1969–70 by Z. Yeivin, Archaeological Officer, Judea and Samaria.

EXCAVATIONS AND FINDS

The synagogue stood on an elevation in the southern part of the village. It was built in the form of a broad house (13.3 by 21.3 meters). All four walls of the building have been preserved. A section of the western wall still stands about 8.5 meters high. The walls were built of dressed stone, laid in some sections in headers and stretchers. On the short sides —*i.e.*, on the east and west—the walls are about

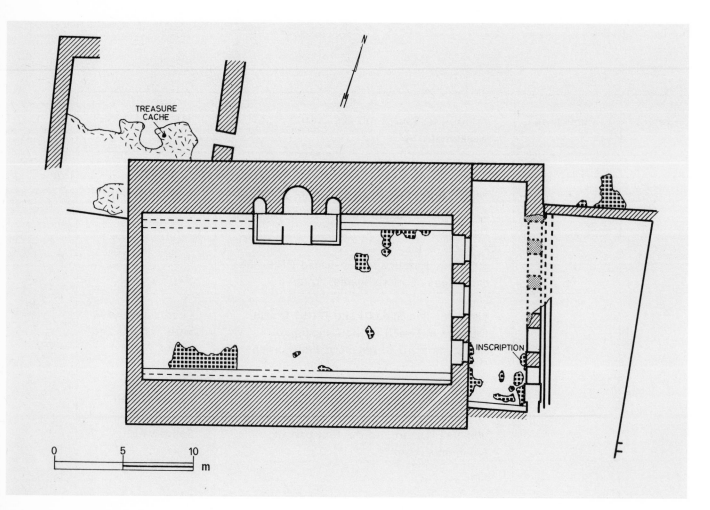

TREASURE CACHE

INSCRIPTION

0   5   10
m

1.2–1.5 meters wide. The northern and southern walls, however, are 3–3.5 meters wide, since the weight of the roof rested on them. The facade of the structure (situated on its narrow side) faces east and has three openings, the central one being broader than the side ones. In front of the facade is a portico (4.1 meters wide). Its roof rested on two pillars at the corners and four columns set on square bases. On its southern side is a bench. The portico was paved with a mosaic floor. Fragments of the mosaic preserved in its southern part include a multicolored tree and a dedicatory inscription in Aramaic. The inscription mentions L'azar the priest and his sons who donated one tremissis (third of a gold denarius). East of the portico is a piazza paved with large flagstones, which antedates the synagogue. Two stairs along the eastern side of the portico connect it with the piazza.

The synagogue consisted of one large hall. In the center of its long north wall, which faces Jerusalem, was the space for the Ark of the Law. It consisted of three circular niches, which were built at a height of 2.1 meters above the floor. This determines the character of the building as a broad house. In the central niche, which is larger and deeper than the side niches, were probably kept the scrolls of the Scriptures. The side niches apparently held menorahs. The niches were reached by means of stairs, probably made of wood. A podium (bema) approximately 5.5 by 2 meters was built on the floor of the synagogue in front of the Ark of the Law. It had a circular niche in its center. West of the niche was an inscription in Hebrew characters that has not yet been deciphered satisfactorily. (S. Klein assumed it to be part of the prayer of the Eighteen Benedictions.) We cannot know whether this unusual bema niche served for the reading of the Scriptures or whether it was meant to receive the Seat of Moses. (The stones of the lower niche and the inscription disappeared in the period between 1936 and 1967.) Stepped benches were built along the southern and northern walls on both sides of the bema. The small sections of the mosaic floor of the synagogue that were preserved are decorated with geometric and floral ornaments.

A large room, apparently contemporary with the synagogue, abuts its northwestern corner. Below its floor was revealed a treasure of about 25 kilograms of silver jewelry and ingots. It was found in

Opposite page: Plan of the synagogue. Below: Relief of menorah. Bottom: Western wall of the synagogue, from the outside.

five pottery jugs, one of them bearing an inscription in red paint in Paleo-Hebrew script reading "five." Y. Yadin has suggested that each jug contained five manes (*i.e.,* 500 shekels of about 10 grams). It has also been suggested that this treasure may be connected with the booty sent by David to Eshtemoa (I Samuel 30:26–28).

The carved building stones discovered in the synagogue and re-used in the Arab village, and which must have been used — at least in part, if not all — in the construction of the synagogue, bear the same type of ornaments found in the synagogues of the third and fourth centuries in the Galilee and in the Jewish necropolis at Beth She'arim. Unlike these places, however, no figurative representations were discovered at Eshtemoa. The synagogue was probably built in the fourth century A.D., and it existed until the end of the Byzantine period. In the medieval period, a mihrab was added to the southern wall and the site was converted into a mosque. A local legend attributes the construction of this mosque to Saladin.   D. BARAG

BIBLIOGRAPHY

S. Klein, *History of the Jewish Settlement in Israel*, Tel Aviv, 1935, 302 ff. (Hebrew) • L. A. Mayer–A. Reifenberg, *JPOS* 19 (1939–40), 314–26, pls. XXIII–XXX and plan; *idem, BJPES* 10 (1943), 10–11 (Hebrew) • A.L. Sukenik, *Kedem* 1 (1942), 64–65 (Hebrew) • Goodenough, *Jewish Symbols* 1, 232–36 • Z. Yeivin, *RB* 77 (1970), 401–03, pl. XXIV; *idem, Qadmoniot* 5 (1972), 43–46 (Hebrew); *idem, IEJ* 21 (1971) 174–75.

Opposite page, top: Benches along the north wall of the synagogue. Bottom: Bema of the synagogue. Below: Lintel with relief of menorah, from the synagogue.

'EYNAN

THE SITE AND ITS EXPLORATION. 'Eynan is situated in the Ḥuleh Basin, about 100 meters west of the Rosh Pinna–Metulla road, near the spring of Mallaḥa. The site is 72 meters above sea level and only a few meters above the old Ḥuleh Lake. It was discovered in 1954 during the draining of the Ḥuleh swamps. The site covers an area of 2,000 square meters, 2–3 meters deep and throughout contains remains of the Natufian culture.

Three Natufian levels have been excavated, all consisting of a brown earth deposit overlying a deposit of red clay with pebble inclusions. The red clay deposit contained a few rolled Middle Paleolithic artifacts.

Excavations were conducted at 'Eynan in 1955 and 1956 under the direction of J. Perrot, with the participation of the Centre National de la Recherche Scientifique and the Israel Department of Antiquities and, in 1959 and 1961, the American Philosophical Society and the Wenner-Gren Foundation for Anthropological Research. An area of about 175 square meters was excavated.

THE STRUCTURES

The structures discovered are dwelling pits rather than real houses. The pits were dug into the slope, and a stone wall was erected against the walls of the pit to retain the earth. The dwellings are circular and of various sizes, the earlier ones larger than the later ones. Near the center of these structures there was generally a fireplace surrounded by rough stones.

Numerous silos and pits were noted inside the layers of the fill of structure 62 (layer II–III). In level 3 of layer II one of the most unusual structures at 'Eynan was discovered. This is a circular pit, rather shallow (.4 meter deep), with a diameter of 5 meters, the walls not stonelined but coated with hard plaster. The plaster coating was very carefully smoothed and the interior still bore traces of red color. It also covered the rim of the pit, forming a kind of brim inclined outward over a width of .7 meter. The plaster-coated area is bounded by rough, oblong stones forming a circle (diameter 6.5 meters) on the floor of the dwelling. The floor is made of large, flat stones, very carefully arranged. To the northeast there is a square

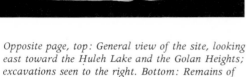

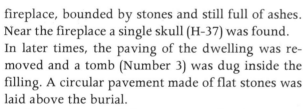

Opposite page, top: General view of the site, looking east toward the Huleh Lake and the Golan Heights; excavations seen to the right. Bottom: Remains of round stone dwellings with hearth, basins, and other installations. Above: Pebbles incised with likenesses of human heads.

fireplace, bounded by stones and still full of ashes. Near the fireplace a single skull (H-37) was found.

In later times, the paving of the dwelling was removed and a tomb (Number 3) was dug inside the filling. A circular pavement made of flat stones was laid above the burial.

In the structures of the uppermost level a similar general plan can be discerned, but they are of smaller diameter (3.5–4 meters). In contrast to the previous structures, which as a rule were entered from the north, the entrance to one of the later structures is from the southwest.

In these buildings, small installations were found, sort of stone troughs, perhaps belonging to the fireplaces. One of them seems to have been partly vaulted. Similar stone "troughs" are also found above the layer of small angular stones.

THE PITS

The stratigraphical study of the site was made difficult by the pits or basins dug into all the lower layers. Their diameters are 1.5 meters on the average and their depth reaches .8 meter. The openings of the pits are narrow and in some cases cannot be clearly recognized. As a rule, the pits contained bones and appear to have been dug for burial purposes. Other pits, the walls of which are coated with whitish plaster, were probably used for water or food storage.

THE BURIALS

Two kinds of burials can be distinguished at 'Eynan:

1. **Collective burials.** These graves served for secondary burials and as a rule were not very deep. In one circular pit were gathered the skulls and part of the bones of several individuals. Pits 25, 28, and 64 contained five, six, and three skulls, respectively. A large, flat stone generally covered the bones and marked the burial. Many tombs contained pieces of red ocher. In pit 25 there were also three gazelle horns.

2. **Individual burials.** In these graves, the skeleton is buried complete, usually in the foetal position. The body was probably brought into this position by sewing it in a hide. It seems that no importance was attached to the direction in which the bodies were buried; they were placed on their back or on a side, or even in a sitting position. In pit 18, two skeletons were found lying face to face.

Both pages, counterclockwise: House no. 26 with hearth in the center. Skeleton of infant with necklace of shells. Skeletons buried under a dwelling; first period of occupation. Skeleton found between strata I and II.

Only rarely were these burials accompanied by offerings, but a flint dagger near skull H-82 should be mentioned here. Skeleton H-23, which was buried under skeleton H-19, was adorned with a string made of dentalia, mother-of-pearl, and gazelle bones.

Physical Description of the Burials. The study of the remains of the more than eighty individuals discovered in 'Eynan has yet to be completed. In the opinion of Denise Ferembach, they belong to a type characterized by a skull with a large cranial capacity, generally of very oblong shape, high or relatively high, and, when seen from above, showing an egglike contour. The stature of the human remains of 'Eynan is average to tall. From this type descended the European-African man, which is distinguished from the contemporary Proto-Mediterranean type.

Stone Artifacts. Most of the stone artifacts are made of basalt, only a few of limestone. They are very numerous, more than three hundred objects having been collected. In the opinion of Ephrat Yeivin, who examined them, there are no typological changes between the various layers.

Small basalt implements were found, as were large mortars and pestles made by striking and smoothing. A large bowl is decorated beneath the rim with geometrical motifs in relief. Other vessels have incised decorations of lines or dots or a motif of U-shaped designs.

Other finds include flat grinders, grinding stones, querns, polishing implements, other grinding implements, whetstones with a groove, hammers, and fish-net sinkers. Of special interest are small disks, flat or with a small cup mark in the center, made of limestone or basalt, showing traces of red ocher. The stone ornaments also include ovoid-shaped beads, not incised but with a groove all round.

Bone implements. The complex of bone implements includes points, needles with eyes, a double fish hook, a sickle of the Kebaran type (its haft broken), a spatula, and beads.

Art. A human face was found incised with a flint point on a calcite pebble, the natural form of which probably inspired the artist. A similar depiction appears on a flat pebble. A small limestone figurine was also found. The head is missing, the arms are reduced to simple protrusions, the hips are marked by an incised line, and incisions on the back side probably represent the hair.

FAUNA

The fauna was studied by P. Ducos. Among ungulate animals the following should be mentioned: *Equus sp., Bos taurus cf. primogenius, Bos t. cf. brachyceros, Cervus elaphus, Dama mesopotamica, Capreolus capreolus, Gazella dorcas, Gazella gazella(?), Capra nubiana(?), Sus scrofa.*

Other species that were identified include hyena, fox, hare, small carnivores, rodents, and numerous species of birds and fish. Mollusks and tortoises of the species existing today around Lake Ḥuleh were also found.

The frequency of the species found is as follows: deer 31 percent, gazelles 42 percent, pigs 16 percent, *Bos t. brachyceros* 5 percent, others 6 percent. No evidence of domestication was found on the site.

CONCLUSION

'Eynan is an open-air site with built shelters and installations, such as ditches, basins, lodgings, etc., suggesting, at the very least, a temporary residence. The presence of a cemetery indicates a prolonged occupation, which may also be deduced from the number and thickness of the archaeological layers. The heavy basalt equipment was not meant to be transported. The analysis that can be made of the food resources allows us to determine that there was no necessity for seasonal migrations of the whole population. It seems that 'Eynan can be reasonably considered a permanent site.

If our estimate of the extent of the site is correct (2,000 square meters, based on test trenches and surface collection), and if the habitation density was constant throughout the entire site, 'Eynan then could have comprised from two hundred to three hundred inhabitants.

Our image of this site and of the life of the population hardly corresponds, at first glance, with the classical Natufian of the Carmel Caves or of Judea. A preliminary analysis of the lithic assemblages and a comparison with the Carmel Caves reveal clear differences. Is this the same culture? What is the relationship between 'Eynan and the Natufian of the caves?

The most striking feature at 'Eynan is the constructions, the existence of "houses," which are doubtless the most ancient known (at this time) in the Near East and which appear in a context where one hardly expected to find them. Actually it is not a question of a new and isolated fact; Dorothy Garrod had already noted a wall several meters long on the terrace of el-Wad. Other walls, whose construction technique is similar to that of the 'Eynan walls, were excavated by M. Stekelis on a terrace of the cave of Naḥal Oren in the Carmel,

Plan of part of the Natufian village showing the burials.

Burial no. 3, covered with stone slabs laid in a circle.

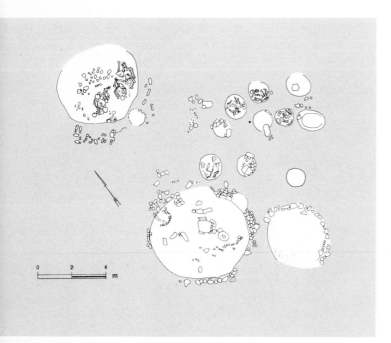

where they are associated with an industry described by the excavator as Natufian. These walls, of a sinuous outline, retain the earth of the terrace and maintain a series of blocks in front of the cave.

A small quantity of geometric microliths characterizes the 'Eynan lithic assemblages, as these pieces hardly represent 15 percent of the tools, although they may reach more than 75 percent in the cave sites. Bilateral retouch (Helwan retouch), considered characteristic of the Natufian, is rare at 'Eynan. The tools seem archaic and lead us to the conclusion that the 'Eynan Natufian is quite old. The local assemblages appear a continuation of the Upper Paleolithic, and it seems more and more probable that the origins of the Natufian are to be sought on the spot. This aspect of the Natufian should not deceive us, however. It also contains trihedral picks, like those of el-Wad, as well as tools on large flakes with simple powerful cutting edges, which appear to be the prototypes of the *tranchets* typical of the following period at Jericho (pre-pottery Neolithic A) and at Naḥal Oren (level 2). The industry of 'Eynan thus differs proportionally from that of the caves, but the specific stock of tools is the same. The variations are quantitative and may reflect different life styles: the Natufian of the caves and of Judea may represent groups whose dominant activity was hunting, whereas the Natufian at 'Eynan was concerned with a wider variety of food quest activities.

The differences between the flint tools of these two types of Natufians cannot mask the cultural and ethnic affinities and homogeneity evident when comparisons are made between all of the equipment — bone tools, grinders, mortars, funerary customs, etc. El-Wad, Kebara, Naḥal Oren, 'Irq el-Ahmar, and 'Eynan are all aspects of a single culture, lasting a millennium and perhaps more.

J. PERROT

BIBLIOGRAPHY

J. Perrot, *Antiquity and Survival* 2 (1967), 91–110; *idem, Year Book of the American Philosophical Society* (1960), 543–46; *idem, IEJ* 10 (1960), 14–22, 257–58 • D. Ferembach, *Comptes-rendus du 6e Congrès Intern. des Sc. Anthrop. et Ethnol. Musée de l'Homme,* Paris, 1960, 587–91; *idem, L'Anthropologie* 65 (1961), 46–66 • J. Perrot, *Year Book of the American Philosophical Society* (1962), 604–07; *idem, L'Anthropologie* 70 (1966), 437–83 • M.C. Cauvin, *ibid.,* 484–94 • M. Lechevallier and J. Perrot, *IEJ* 23 (1973), 107, 239.

EL-FAR'A, TELL, North

IDENTIFICATION AND HISTORY. Tell el-Far'a (in the north, as distinct from the southern site, which is also called Tel Sharuhen, q.v.) lies 11 kilometers (7 miles) northeast of Shechem, on the Nablus–Tubas road. The mound stands near the source of the Far'a brook, which flows down to the Jordan. It is situated on a rocky ridge sloping in a southwest–northeast direction. Two springs, 'Ain Far'a to the north and 'Ain Daleib to the south, supply the site with ample water. The fertile valley of Wadi Far'a is the main thoroughfare between the Jordan Valley and the western mountain district. The French School of Archaeology in Jerusalem (Ecole Biblique) conducted nine seasons of excavations at the site (1946–60), under the direction of R. de Vaux.

Various scholars have attempted to identify the site with a biblical town. K. Budde, G. Dalman, and A. Alt considered it to be the Ofrah of Abiezer. F. M. Abel suggested Beth-Barah (Judges 7:24), and W. F. Albright identified it with Tirzah. The latter view has been borne out by the excavations and is accepted today by most scholars.

This identification is based upon the following considerations: Tell el-Far'a is situated in the territory of Manasseh, which included Tirzah. In the biblical account of the daughters of Zelophehad (Numbers 26:33, 36:10–11; Joshua 17:3), Tirzah and Hoglah are mentioned together, and the Samaria Ostraca enable us to locate Hoglah not far from Tell el-Far'a. Moreover, the archaeological finds at Tell el-Far'a agree with the biblical history of Tirzah. In the beginning, Tirzah was a Canaanite town (like Tell el-Far'a). The stratum attributed to the Late Bronze Age shows signs of destruction, which can be regarded as the result of the Israelite conquest. Tirzah as capital of the Kingdom of Israel corresponds to stratum III of Tell el-Far'a. This level was devastated during the Omrid capture of the town subsequent to Zimri's seizure of power (about 885 B.C.). The fortress in the northwestern corner may be the king's castle mentioned in I Kings 16:15–18 which Zimri himself set on fire and in which he met his death. Omri was able to rebuild Tirzah and to set up his residence there only at the end of a four-year struggle with his rival, Tibni.

The foundations sunk into level III probably belong to his structures. However, after two years Omri transferred the capital to Samaria (cf. I Kings 16:23–24). This explains why there are buildings in the area that were never completed. The royal household and the military and state officials left Tirzah, undoubtedly followed by the artisans and merchants. It is quite possible that the town was completely abandoned for some time. This would explain the paucity of the interim stratum constructed apparently after a short period of settlement. As the Northern Kingdom flourished under Joash and Jeroboam II, Tirzah, too, enjoyed a measure of prosperity. It is from this town that Menahem launched his attack upon Samaria (II Kings 15:14). Stratum II represents this era with its magnificent structures and administrative headquarters. As some have suggested, these may have served Menahem, if indeed he held sway at Tirzah. During the Assyrian invasion of the Northern Kingdom, the town was captured. The destruction in stratum II dates from that time.

EXCAVATIONS, NEOLITHIC PERIOD

According to all indications, the first settlement on the site was very small and poor. It dates to the pre-pottery stage of the Neolithic. Excavations revealed several limestone floors and hearths on virgin soil, as well as flint and basalt implements. This culture is similar to the pre-pottery Neolithic at Jericho in its second phase (PPN-B).

CHALCOLITHIC PERIOD

During the fourth millennium B.C., the settlement grew. Of the two strata attributable to this period, the earlier can be defined as Middle Chalcolithic, for want of a more precise subdivision of the Palestinian Chalcolithic. Typical of this phase are flint and basalt implements, whose closest parallels come from Sha'ar ha-Golan. Bone objects are extremely rare.

The pottery is handmade with white or pink clay that underwent an incomplete firing process. The common ornamentation consists of raised, incised, or impressed bands. Painted decoration is rare. Although there is a certain resemblance between this ware and that of Ghassul, the closest parallels are to be found in the pit dwellings at Beth-Shean XVIII and in stratum VIII (the so-called Garstang

En-Gedi. Main mosaic pavement of the synagogue, looking north.

layer of Jericho) — defined by Kathleen Kenyon as phase B of the pottery Neolithic.

In a cave situated on the southern slope of the mound were discovered pottery fragments of another type. Some of them are identical with sherds found at Ḥorvat Beer Matar and other sites in the Beersheba region. Tell el-Far'a thus shows evidence of a phenomenon characteristic of Palestinian Chalcolithic: communities of people belonging to different ethnic and cultural groups existing side by side and even intermingling.

LATE CHALCOLITHIC PERIOD

The main innovations in the tools of this period are the appearance of fan-like scrapers made of flint flakes, Canaanite "blades," and the increased use of bone implements. Pottery at this stage can be clearly distinguished from that of the preceding phase, the clay being different and most of the forms new. The most common decorations are bands, decorated either with finger indentations or crescent-shaped impressions made by nails or reeds. These differ decidedly from the decorated bands of the Middle Chalcolithic. Two groups of pottery are of particular interest: the red-burnished and the gray-burnished wares, which are also found in the lower strata at Beth-Shean, Megiddo, 'Afula, Beth-Yeraḥ, in the two upper strata at Mezer, and in several tombs at Jericho.

These strata, attributed to the Middle and Late Chalcolithic, contained no buildings. Circular pits served as dwellings (2–4.5 meters in diameter, up to .8 meter deep), above which were erected walls made of mud mixed with rubble. The same is true of the Neolithic pottery phase at Jericho (strata A–B, of which B is parallel to the Middle Chalcolithic stratum at Tell el-Far'a) and the lower strata at Beth-Shean, Beth-Yeraḥ, 'Afula, Shechem, and other sites.

No Middle Chalcolithic tombs were encountered, but two Late Chalcolithic burial sites were found, one at the southern side of the mound, toward Wadi 'Ein Daleib, and the second at an appreciable distance north of the mound. A third burial ground may have been located east of the mound, where a single grave was investigated. These are large mass-burial tombs hewn out of the soft chalk rock with flint tools. Inasmuch as bones did not keep well in the soil of the area, and the southern burial site had been re-used in the Middle and Late Bronze Ages, it was impossible to ascertain the position in which

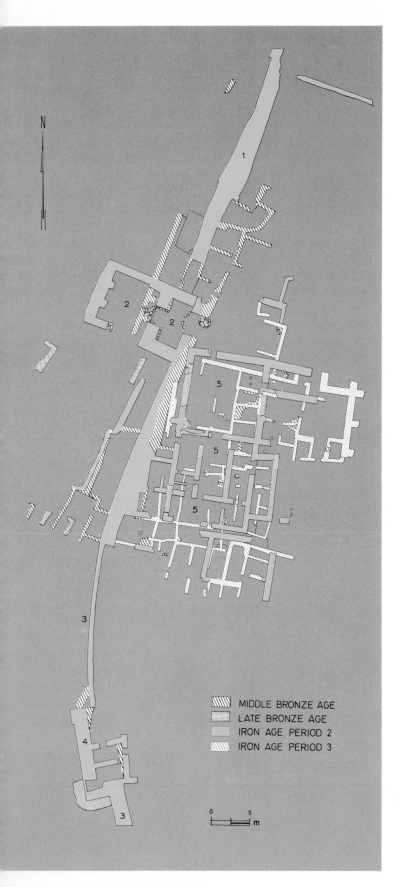

MIDDLE BRONZE AGE
LATE BRONZE AGE
IRON AGE PERIOD 2
IRON AGE PERIOD 3

0   5
m

the bodies were buried. These tombs, however, produced the richest pottery hoard of the Late Chalcolithic period.

EARLY BRONZE AGE

As early as the beginning of the period, the mound presented a greatly altered picture of settlement. The Chalcolithic remains were leveled and the first buildings erected. These were rectangular structures with two rows of stones as foundations and mud-brick walls of which very few have been preserved. Parallel to the axis or width of the room were stone slabs on which stood the wooden pillars supporting the roof. Some rooms had low benches placed along the walls. Six successive phases of settlement were distinguished in these houses. Two other buildings, differing from ordinary private dwellings, were excavated, but their character could not be determined.

From the very first phase, the town contained a temple with an open hall, oriented to the east, and a sanctuary with benches around the walls. This temple continued in use, with some modifications, until the end of the third phase.

In addition, two potter's workshops and a two-story kiln were found. A horizontal, perforated partition divided the furnace from the baking compartment. This was the first kiln found in this country of a type that continued in use until the Roman period.

Urbanization is already apparent in the first settlement in the area. The buildings stand along clearly outlined streets, one of which was 2 meters wide. Several streets had drains.

Somewhat later, the town was surrounded with a wall. In phase 1, this wall was built of mud brick on three stone courses, which served as a foundation. On the west side of the town, the wall continues in a straight line over a distance of 125 meters. It includes several towers incorporated into it and a few others abutting it. The southern part of the mound faces the sheer drop of Wadi 'Ein Daleib, a natural defense which made a wall on this side unnecessary. To the north, it was impossible to

Plan of the western part of the city. 1. The second EBA wall re-used in the IA. 2. MBA gate re-used in the IA. 3. MBA inner wall re-used in the IA. 4. MBA or LBA tower. 5. Houses, workshops, and administrative buildings; IA II.

determine the extent of the walled area, as this section of the wall was destroyed. During phase 3, the fortifications were rebuilt and moved slightly southward. The newly built wall is of solid stone erected on the ruins of the wall of phase 2. At that time, a stone wall with a rampart in front of it was added to the existing western brick wall, thereby doubling the width of the wall on that side. An earthen glacis was attached to the rampart somewhat later. Toward the end of phase 5, a section of the western wall collapsed inside the town, and after the wall was hastily repaired a new residential level was built on top of the fallen bricks.

The most important part of this wall is the fortified western gate, which dates to phase 1, *i.e.,* to the beginning of the Early Bronze Age. A passageway (4 meters at its widest point, gradually narrowing to 2.5 meters) passes between two mud-brick towers set on stone foundations. The brick masonry has been preserved to a height of 4 meters. After the gateway had been reduced to ruins, a new gate was built at a higher level on debris blocking the entrance, with steps leading to it from the outside. The steps were of beaten earth supported by a frame of tree trunks. During the next phase, the passageway between the towers mentioned above was blocked off by a thick wall. It is clear that this was done for reasons of security, since the town was still settled and it is reasonable to assume that at least one other (as yet not discovered) gate existed at the time. The wall was finally reconstructed, and a new passageway was opened above the blocking wall, level with the raised layers inside the town.

These remains attest to a developed urbanization and are radically different from the Chalcolithic remains. Tell el-Far'a, which in its beginnings was no more than a large conglomeration of huts, was suddenly transformed into a fortified town. This drastic change did not come about as a result of local development. Rather, it testifies to the settlement in the town of a new influx of people who had knowledge of building with stone and, especially, with bricks and who were accustomed to an urban way of life. This migration marks the beginning of the Early Bronze Age in Canaan. Ceramic evidence collected from the six well-stratified residential levels clearly attests to the origin of this culture as different from the Chalcolithic and to its internal unity. Although the pottery repertory underwent no striking changes between the various levels, when viewed in their entirety a certain development is immediately recognizable. Levels 1 and 2 fit into the framework of the Early Bronze Age I-B, according to the accepted subdivision (I-A contemporary, at least for a short time, with the Late Chalcolithic). Level 3 represents a transition stage. Level 4–6 are datable to Early Bronze Age II. No remains were discovered that could be assigned with certainty to the Early Bronze Age III, nor were there found any sherds of the Khirbet Kerak type —the hallmark of that period. No burial site of the period came to light, although two graves of the Chalcolithic period were re-used in the Early Bronze Age II.

The settlement at Tell el-Far'a was apparently abandoned about 2500 B.C., the site lying desolate for approximately six hundred years. The end of the third millennium is marked by a decline in urban civilization in Canaan. This phenomenon may be explained by the penetration of the semi-nomadic Amorites, although Tell el-Far'a's early destruction must certainly be sought in other specific causes.

MIDDLE BRONZE AGE

No remains were uncovered from the Middle Bronze Age I. The site was resettled only during the early part of Middle Bronze Age II. The new settlement was quite small and poor. The new inhabitants re-used the wall of the Early Bronze Age, reconstructing it in a slipshod manner. Their houses were scattered over the area and the dead were buried in empty spaces inside the wall. Several floor levels were distinguished in the houses, whose walls were rebuilt several times following a slightly different layout. The pottery of this period is similar to that discovered at Tell Beit Mirsim (strata F–G, possibly also E) and to the corresponding stratum at Rosh ha-'Ayin. The finds seem to indicate an extended period of settlement.

Still later, in about 1700 B.C., the population of the site increased, and the town was encircled by a new wall. On the western side, the wall was erected on top of the ruins of the Early Bronze Age wall, while in the north it was built along the line of the second (stone) wall of the Early Bronze Age. However, in turning southward, it excluded the entire eastern section of the earlier town. A large stone pile in the northwestern corner is almost certainly the remains of foundations of a demolished citadel.

North of the Early Bronze Age gate, a new gate was built in the west wall. This is a direct-entrance gateway with frontal defenses. It is subdivided into several successive chambers. Sometime later an earthen glacis, supported by a smooth wall, was added to the town fortification. Inside the town, in front of the gate, stood a basin built of stone slabs, probably serving a ritual need.

The southwestern quarter is particularly well preserved with workshops and storerooms, all attached to the wall. A subterranean temple containing traces of three successive levels was also discovered. This temple remained in use throughout the Middle Bronze Age II-A–B. In the shrine and sacrificial pit were animal bones. It appears that suckling pigs were sacrificed to the local deity. Many infant graves were unearthed beneath the house floors. The bodies were interred inside large jars which included two or three small jars as offerings. During this period, however, older children and adults were buried outside the town. Several graves had been dug in the eastern, abandoned portion of the earlier town, and the southern Chalcolithic cemetery was restored to use. The cemetery yielded a large collection of pottery dating from the final years of Middle Bronze Age II, but these finds do not contribute much to what was already known of the period.

LATE BRONZE AGE

Strata of this period are not well preserved. Its structures present a shoddy appearance. It is possible to detect a few places where the wall was repaired or additions were made to it, but a reconstruction of the town plan is impossible. One structure, broader than usual, consists of a large sanctuary with two rows of pillars. In front of it is a hall and behind it an elevated holy-of-holies, ascended by means of steps. A silvered-bronze figurine of a goddess was found inside. The plan of this temple resembles that of the two small sanctuaries at Beth-Shean, which are dated to the eleventh-tenth centuries B.C. but retain the traditional style of Late Bronze Age temple construction. It is noteworthy that this temple was erected on the site of its Middle Bronze Age predecessor. Repeated use of sanctified areas was typical of all ancient cities.

Tombs are fewer in this period than in the Middle Bronze Age, although the same sites were employed. Infants were interred in jars placed beneath the house floors, whereas adults were buried either outside the town or in former Chalcolithic tombs. Judging by the pottery found in the graves and in the strata of the mound — Cypriot and Mycenaean imported wares — it may be assumed that the Late Bronze Age settlement existed at least until the end of the fourteenth century B.C., but it is quite possible that the settlement continued into the thirteenth century.

IRON AGE (ISRAELITE PERIOD)

Several layers date to this period, some of them in a good state of preservation.

EBA gate; plan and proposed reconstruction.

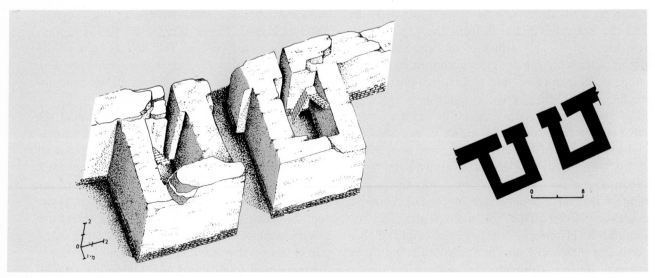

Stratum III. Above the ruins of the Late Bronze Age town are the clear remains of a building complex, in which several walls of the preceding period were re-used. Structures built according to an identical plan line parallel streets or blind alleys. These are four-room houses, each of whose entrances leads to a rectangular courtyard enclosed by chambers on three sides — two long rooms on either side and a short one at its rear. Construction is uniform. Walls are one-stone wide and have practically no foundations. In many houses, the side chambers are separated from the courtyard by merely a row of pillars between which were partitions made of small stones. Many of the side chambers are paved, but not a single courtyard.

The fortified gatehouse of the Israelite city dated to the Middle and Late Bronze Ages. It continued in use, but the level of the outer threshold was raised and that of the inner threshold altered. Excavation revealed a large rectangular basin hewn out of a single stone and a square stone pedestal in front of the gate in line with its axis. On the pedestal was a pillar, apparently a *massebah,* which was also used in a later period (stratum I). Both the *massebah* and the basin are undoubtedly remnants of a gate temple, and it appears that during the Israelite period they continued to build on the same spot according to the custom of the Middle Bronze Age. Thus, we can witness here the survival of Canaanite ritual practices, abhorred by the prophets of Israel.

It is difficult to ascertain the outer defense works

Bottom, left: EBA I house. Bottom, right: Pottery kiln; EBA. Top, right: Paved street in stratum 2. To the right, temple of stratum 1. EBA city wall in the foreground.

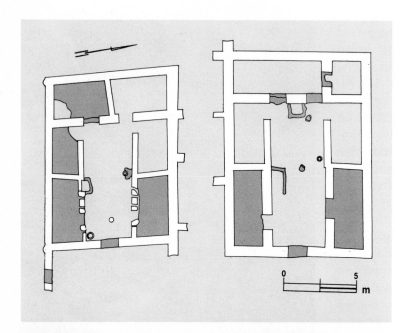

Counterclockwise: Plans of houses of the eighth century B.C.: On the right, no. 327; on the left, no. 328; ☐ walls ▨ floors and installations. Sewage drain beneath city gate; MBA. Silver-plated bronze figurine; LBA.

of the city at that period, as the upper strata of the mound have been eroded by the weather. In any case, it is clear that the line of the Middle Bronze Age wall was preserved and that the citadel in the northwest continued to be used. This was defended by a ditch, which separated it from the rest of the town.

The settlement in this stratum existed for a long period of time. Houses were repaired and restored virtually without any alteration of plan. One or two steps were built at courtyard entrances, as the street level rose faster than the court level. Because the town was not troubled then by external foes, it is possible to establish the date for the final level of the settlement solely on the basis of sherds discovered in private houses. These date to the tenth century and the beginning of the ninth century B.C. The dating is supported by the find of several conical seals typical of this period, and by a small pottery model of a temple, similar to those found in Cyprus, Megiddo, and Transjordan.

Unfinished Structures. The town of stratum III suffered destruction (perhaps at the time of Omri's conquest of Tirzah), and among its debris were discovered foundations of more imposing structures. These finds came to light in only one definite section of the site. In laying the foundations of these buildings, no early walls were used. The most clearly defined complex of these structures contains a courtyard with three rooms around it, two set length-wise and one room breadth-wise. Along one side of this building was an adjoining hall with a wide entrance and semi-attached pillars along the side walls. The masonry is of better workmanship than in stratum III. Walls are wide and constructed of a gravel-filled core faced on both sides with masonry. The corners are well built and connected by occasional cross-stones set in the manner usual in the palace at Samaria.

These walls are situated on top of the floors of the previous stratum so that their thresholds are very high and somewhat above the debris of the adjacent stratum III walls, which had not been cleared. The conclusion to be drawn is that these are no more than foundations. There are several other indications that the walls were never completed, in particular the fact that there is no "living" level attributable to them but only foundation trenches filled with debris taken from stratum III. As previously stated, the buildings left incomplete may

have resulted from Omri's transfer of the capital to Samaria.

Interim Stratum. Tell el-Far'a apparently was deserted for some time. The resettled area was limited, and, aside from the incomplete structures, the sole remains are walls revealed in several places. Since the wall foundations are higher than the stratum III structures and lower than those of stratum II, this can be termed an interim stratum. The sherds in the stratum date to the ninth century B.C.

Stratum II. This is a much better defined level. A bench was built along the walls in the inner chamber of the citadel gate. This bench was probably reserved for the town elders "sitting in the gate." In front of the gate, above the stone basin of stratum III, another basin, made of stone slabs, was installed, and the *massebah* quite likely stood by its side.

South of the gate stood a large structure which abutted the wall and served as the residence of the local ruler and as the administrative headquarters. A long chamber was found filled with jars.

Well-built houses were uncovered, which were constructed according to a plan similar to that of stratum III but somewhat larger and of superior construction. Walls are better placed and have carefully dressed facings on both sides with well-joined corners. These are the homes of the wealthy, which were once separated from the quarter of the

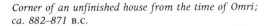

Corner of an unfinished house from the time of Omri; ca. 882–871 B.C.

poor by a long, straight wall. The latter quarter contained small, densely built, makeshift dwellings. In contrast with the uniformity of the tenth-century residences, this great difference between the dwellings of the poor and of the wealthy in stratum II conforms with what we know of the development of Israelite society at the time.

The pottery of stratum II can be dated mainly to the eighth century B.C. This stratum bears the traces of a complete devastation, undoubtedly the result of the Assyrian onslaught against the Israelite towns prior to the siege of Samaria. The date of the destruction of stratum II is therefore fixed at about 723 B.C.

Stratum I. This stratum has extremely poor remains. It has been unearthed only in a part of the excavation. One section of the mound had been eroded and other sections had been disturbed by agricultural work. After the Assyrian conquest, the town walls were breached, the gateway was blocked, and a nearby opening served as the entrance. Tell el-Far'a became an open city.

Notwithstanding all this, the gate temple survived, and the *massebah* was found inside a square enclosure. The residence underwent some modifications, secondary partitions being installed. Extant houses were of inferior construction. The pottery discovered there is, however, of great interest. It includes, inter alia, Assyrian bowls of the type found at Samaria, Dothan, and in the Assyrian fortress at Tell Jemmeh. This ware is identical with the pottery encountered recently at Nimrud, in the palace of Sargon II. It thus seems likely that the place was settled by an Assyrian garrison or civilian settlers.

The town declined quickly and appears to have been completely abandoned close to the year 600 B.C. Only isolated finds are attributable to the Hellenistic-Roman period. An Arab cemetery of the thirteenth–fourteenth centuries has disturbed strata I–II in a section of the mound.   R. DE VAUX

BIBLIOGRAPHY

Preliminary excavation reports: R. de Vaux–A. M. Steve, *RB* 54 (1947), 394–433, 573–89; 55 (1948), 544–80; 56 (1949), 102–38 • R. de Vaux, *RB* 58 (1951), 393–430, 566–90; 59 (1952), 551–83; 62 (1955), 541–89; 64 (1957), 552–80; 68 (1961), 557–92; 69 (1962), 212–53.
Also, J. Gray *PEQ* (1952), 11–13 • R. de Vaux, *PEQ* (1956), 125–40; idem, *Von Ugarit nach Qumran (Festschrift Otto Eissfeldt)*, Beihefte *ZAW* 77 (1958), 250–65 • C. Picard, *RAr* (1958) A, 91–93 • U. Joachims, *ZDPV* 76 (1960), 73–96.

FEJJA

IDENTIFICATION. The ruins of the Arab village of Fejja, today within the municipal boundaries of Petaḥ-Tiqvah, are located about 5 kilometers (3 miles) from the mound of Aphek (Ras el-'Ein). The name "Fejja" recalls the Greek name of the Hellenistic site, Pegai (Πηγαί), meaning "The Springs." Pegai is mentioned for the first time in 259 B.C., in the Zenon Papyri, as a frontier post, probably between Idumaea and Samaria. It seems that, for topographical reasons, and especially because of the lack of springs at Pegai, this post was actually located at Tel Aphek and not at the former site. In mishnaic sources two places are mentioned — Mei-Pigah ("Waters of Pigah" in Mishnah *Parah* 8:6) and Pigah (Mishnah *Terumot* 1:15). In the Mishnah Aphek is usually known as Antipatris, a city founded by Herod. Possibly the whole neighborhood of Aphek was called "The Springs" from the Hellenistic period onward. This would explain the persistence of the name in such a remote settlement. The writer carried out an archaeological survey in Fejja in 1951 and later excavated there on a small scale.

EXPLORATION

The survey showed that the Arab village was built on formerly uninhabited land. Ancient remains, however, were found some dozen meters north of the village. The remains were found scattered through three areas, all in the same vicinity. Area A, the closest to the ruins of the village, was made up of whitish-gray earth that contained a great number of Middle Bronze Age II and Persian sherds. Area B extended over a strip of grayish earth, northwest of area A and parallel to the Lod–Petaḥ-Tiqvah road. The ground in this area was covered with small fieldstones and many sherds from the Persian period and Iron Age II. In area C, about 100 meters northeast of area A, there were a number of structures, the remnants of a wine industry: wine presses and wine cellars sunk into the ground.

EXCAVATIONS

In November–December, 1963, the writer carried out trial excavations in areas A and B, assisted by R. Cohen. In area A, five short trenches were dug 2 by 3 meters each. In trench A1, two levels of settlement were revealed but no building remains. The upper level dated from Middle Bronze Age II-B–C and the lower one, which was built on virgin soil, from Middle Bronze Age II-A. Trench A2 yielded similar finds with the addition of a single potsherd (bow rim) belonging to the Wadi Rabah culture and two Ghassulian potsherds. A number of Iron Age II sherds were also found, and on the surface, near trench A1, lay a coin of Alexander Jannaeus.

In trench B, a 60 centimeter thick layer dating from the Persian period was followed by two Middle Bronze Age strata, the first belonging to Middle Bronze Age II-B–C and the second (built on virgin soil) to Middle Bronze Age II-A.

In trench C, immediately below the surface, a Roman level of settlement was uncovered. It contained, inter alia, a Roman coin from the first century A.D. Below the Roman stratum was a Middle Bronze Age II-B–C level of settlement, containing two sections of mud-brick walls. On the floor by these walls were sherds of juglets and jars of Middle Bronze Age II-B–C. Below this stratum was a Middle Bronze Age II-A level founded on virgin soil. In the upper part of this level, the foundations of a stone wall were uncovered.

Trench D was apparently outside the ancient zone of area A. The top layer yielded only a throwout of mixed Persian and Middle Bronze Age pottery fragments. The earth beneath this mixed layer was sandy and in it were discovered, inter alia, fragments of a basalt bowl whose rim was decorated on the interior with incised hatched triangles typical of the Chalcolithic period.

Area C contained remains of wine presses and cellars for the wine industry, all dating to the Roman period. The remnants of three different installations were uncovered. Number 1 was for the most part in ruins, with only a part of the mosaic-paved treading floor remaining. Number 2 was also almost completely damaged, save for part of a round winery pit, with a mosaic floor paved in a pattern of circles. Number 3 was almost completely preserved. A section of the treading floor and the entire square winery pit were cleared. The floor of the pit was paved with mosaics. A lead pipe was found running from the treading floor to the pit.

CONCLUSION

The presence on the site of a potsherd from the Wadi Rabah culture, of Ghassulian pottery, and of fragments of a Ghassulian basalt bowl provides evidence that remains of settlements belonging to these periods are buried nearby. Investigations in the trenches showed that the site was established and reached its height of development chiefly during the two phases of the Middle Bronze Age II-A and II-B–C, from which time also building remains were found. The settlement at Fejja at that period was doubtless connected with the mother settlement of Tel Aphek, which was first excavated in the 1930's by J. Ory. The extent of the settlement in the Iron Age II was not examined, but it appears to have been limited. In contrast, the Persian stratum (apparently fifth century B.C.) revealed extensive settlement. The lack of Hellenistic remains is not surprising, as has been pointed out above. It was only in the first century A.D. that settlement was renewed to continue throughout the Roman-Byzantine period.   J. KAPLAN

Round winery pit (no. 2); Roman period.

GALILEE, UPPER

No archaeological excavations have as yet been conducted in the mountains of Upper Galilee, but surveys and two trial excavations have thrown light on the history of the occupation of the region in the biblical period. Several sites have been examined in surveys on behalf of various archaeological schools, in particular those of A. Alt, W. F. Albright, and J. Garstang. In 1950, Ruth Amiran explored Tel Rosh (Khirbet Tell e-Ruweisah), and in 1951–53, Y. Aharoni made a comprehensive archaeological survey, including trial excavations at Tel Qedesh and Tel Ḥarashim (Khirbet et-Teleil), both archaeologists working on behalf of the Department of Antiquities and of the Israel Exploration Society.

THE TRIAL EXCAVATIONS. TEL QEDESH

Situated about 10 kilometers (6 miles) northwest of Hazor (map reference 199279), this is the largest of the mounds of Upper Galilee, occupying an area of 90–100 dunams. It dominates a fertile valley and stands about 400 meters above sea level. At its foot there is an abundant spring. This site has been identified with the biblical Kedesh, a Canaanite town, which later became one of the fortified cities of Naphtali (Joshua 12:22, 19:37). It is also mentioned in the lists of the Cities of Refuge and of the Levites (Joshua 20:7, 21:32; I Chronicles 6:61). Tiglath-pileser III conquered the city in 733/32 B.C. (II Kings 15:29). The usual identification of this site with Kedesh-Naphtali, the native town of Barak son of Abinoam (Judges 4:6) is to be rejected. (Kedesh-Naphtali should probably be identified with Khirbet Qedish, east of the Jabneel Valley in Lower Galilee.)

The trial excavation was carried out on the northwestern slope of the mound, where the highway cuts into the foot of the hill. A section of an early brick wall was cleared there. On the steep, terraced slope a trench, 17 meters long and 1.25 meters wide, was excavated. The layers reach a thickness of about 11 meters and show the following stratigraphy:

PERIOD	APPROXIMATE THICKNESS OF THE LAYER
Arab	3.00 m
Hellenistic	.75 m
Iron Age I–II and Late Bronze Age	.75 m
Middle Bronze Age	1.25 m
Early Bronze Age	5.25 m

Although it is not certain that the measurements obtained in the above small section correspond to the rest of the mound, most of the layers are probably represented in their correct proportion. Especially numerous and thick are the occupation layers from Early Bronze Age I–III in which were found much red-slip burnished ware, many vessels with combed decoration, a few sherds with band slip, and pottery of the Khirbet Kerak type. The brick wall, which is more than 5 meters thick, should probably be assigned to the Early Bronze Age II. From the Middle Bronze Age I were, among other finds, fragments of "teapots," which have been found also at Hazor. On the whole, the Middle Bronze Age is well represented. In contrast to this, little was found from the Late Bronze and Iron Ages, although sporadic potsherds are evidence of a continuity in the occupation of the site. It can be assumed, however, that pottery remains of these periods are scarce because occupation during the time may have been confined mainly to the eastern part of the mound, which has not been excavated.

TEL ḤARASHIM (Khirbet et-Teleil)

The ruins of this site are situated on a peak which

KH. MISHEIRIFA
KH. ADAR
KH. ADMIT
'ABDON
YOQRAT
MI'ILYA
T. ROSH
GATH
T. HARASHIM
ACCHO
NAHEF
KEDESH
T. el-KHIRBEH
HAZOR
GUSH HALAV
KH. BEERSHEBA
KINNERET

▲ CANAANITE–ISRAELITE SITES
■ CANAANITE MOUNDS
● ISRAELITE MOUNDS
— AREA SURVEYED
--- BOUNDARY OF MOUNTAINS

0 5 10 km

dominates the mountainous area south of Peqi'in (map reference 18142636). They indicate the existence of a typical Iron Age settlement in the region. The ruins extend over 5–6 dunams and today form several terraces of cultivated and sown fields. In the trial excavation, carried out in the northwestern corner of the mound on an area of about 7 by 10 meters, the following four occupation layers were uncovered:

Stratum IV (Middle Bronze Age I), revealed a dwelling cave, the ceiling of which had collapsed. The pottery found in this level is simple and coarse, and includes a large pithos, an envelope ledge handle, and numerous sherds with rope and combed decoration and herringbone patterns.

Stratum III dates from the early phase of the Iron Age. The main structure cleared is a chamber (6.25 by 5.25 meters) which served as a bronze foundry. Stone shelves were found near three of the walls, and near the fourth wall were the remains of a large kiln. The entrance was in the southwestern corner. To the left of it, near the western shelf, there stood a stove made of the upper part of a big jar turned upside down. On the stove were found fragments of a cooking pot. On and near the shelves stood various stone bowls, as well as a clay smelting furnace and two horn-shaped casting ladles. The pottery finds include large storage jars with thickened rims, a ridge at the base of the neck, and decorations incised or in relief on the body. Similar jars have been found in stratum XII at Hazor (about twelfth century B.C.), and a vessel which is the archetype of such jars was discovered in the Late Bronze Age strata at Hazor. Cooking pots found here are also similar to those of Hazor XII, which, in turn, are of the same style as the Bronze Age cooking pots but with a longer folded rim. There is no doubt that these vessels in Hazor and in the small settlements in Galilee were connected with the new Israelite settlers. It is also evident that they were produced in the new centers of settlement in imitation of the Canaanite ware produced in the neighboring towns.

Stratum II, the following settlement, was erected after a certain pause. To this level belong two parallel walls (each 1.25 meters wide) with straight partitions between them, probably part of a casemate wall. Two building phases, both of the Iron Age II, were distinguished in this level.

Stratum I, the upper layer, contained Persian and

Opposite page: Survey map. Below: Tel Harashim; selection of pottery from the beginning of IA I. Bottom: Tel Harashim; plan of a workshop from the beginning of IA, with section of a casemate wall above it.

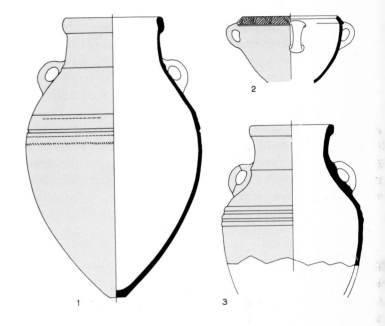

1   2   3

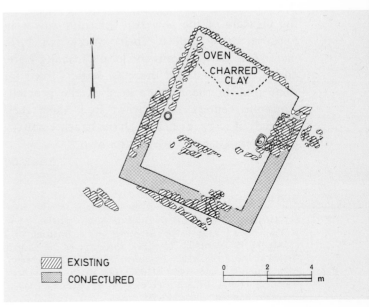

OVEN
CHARRED CLAY

N

EXISTING
CONJECTURED

0 2 4
m

Hellenistic pottery, including Rhodian stamped jar handles, but no building remains.

THE SURVEY

Besides Tel Qedesh, four other mounds first settled in the Early Bronze Age have been discovered so far in Upper Galilee. The occupation periods of these mounds are roughly similar to those of Tel Qedesh. The sites are Gush Halav (el-Jish), Tell el-Khirbeh, Tel Rosh, and Tel Yoqrat (Iqrit). All five, including Tel Qedesh, are situated near the Israel-Lebanon border, north of the Mount Meron massif. They are evidence of the existence of a dense and well-developed Bronze Age occupation in the northern parts of Upper Galilee.

In the central part of Upper Galilee, a continuous survey has been carried out. The northern part of the survey network includes Tel Rosh and Tel Yoqrat, which were occupied, as has been mentioned above, in the Bronze and Iron Ages as well as during later periods.

In the southern part of the surveyed area, no city mound was found. Only the ruins of fifteen small settlements were discovered there, the finds of which are similar to those of Tel Ḥarashim. Most of these settlements contained pottery from the beginning of the Iron Age, indicating that this mountainous area was densely populated precisely during this early period, whereas only nine sites were found in the area from the Roman and Byzantine periods. The Iron Age settlements, therefore, were undoubtedly established by the new Israelite settlers, who had probably been pushed into these rugged mountain areas under the pressure of the powerful Canaanite towns in northern Upper Galilee. Their pottery, which, as mentioned above, recalls the local Canaanite ware, attests to the fact that the new settlers lived for some time in the neighborhood of the previous Canaanite centers and learned from them their methods of work, even though the Israelite pottery has certain characteristics of its own.

Y. AHARONI

BIBLIOGRAPHY

J. Garstang, *Joshua-Judges*, London, 1931, *passim* • R. Amiran, *EI* 2 (1953), 117 ff. (Hebrew) • Y. Aharoni, *EI* 4 (1956), 56 ff. (Hebrew); idem, *The Settlement of the Hebrew Tribes in Northern Galilee*, Jerusalem, 1957, 34–38 (Hebrew); idem, *Antiquity and Survival* 2 (1957), 142–50 • M. Kochavi, *Yediot* 27 (1963), 165–72 (Hebrew) • Y. Aharoni, *Land of the Bible*, London, 1967, 219–20.

GAZA

HISTORY. A city on the southern coastal plain, in Hebrew, 'Azzah (עזה); in Greek, Gaza (Γάζα). Gaza served as the base of Egyptian operations in Canaan. It was occupied by Thutmose III (about 1469 B.C.). In Egyptian reliefs, it is called "the [town] of Canaan." Gaza is also mentioned in the el-Amarna and Taanach tablets as an Egyptian administrative center. The city was allotted to the tribe of Judah (Joshua 15:47; Judges 1:18), but it remained in the possession of the Canaanites until the beginning of the twelfth century B.C. At that time, it became the southernmost city of the Philistine Pentapolis (Joshua 13:3, I Samuel 6:17; Jeremiah 25:20). The famous Philistine temple of Dagon was located there.

In 734 B.C., the Assyrian king Tiglath-pileser III captured Gaza, but it remained a Philistine city, and the short-lived conquest of Hezekiah (II Kings 18:8) did not alter its status. Pharaoh Necho II occupied Gaza briefly in 609 B.C. Under the Per-

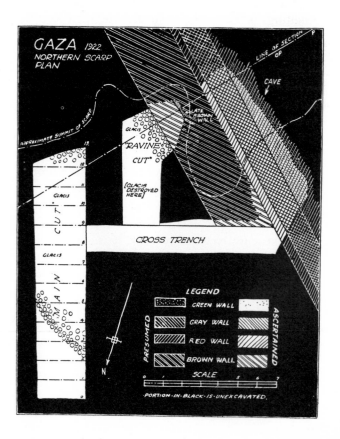

sians, Gaza became an important royal fortress. It is called Kadytis by Herodotus (II, 159). In 332 B.C. it was the only city in Palestine to oppose Alexander the Great, who besieged it and sold its people into slavery.

In the Hellenistic period, Gaza was the outpost of the Ptolemies until its capture by Antiochus III in 198 B.C. The city was attacked by Jonathan the Hasmonaean in 145 B.C. (I Maccabees 11:61–62) but was taken only by Alexander Jannaeus in 96 B.C. after a long siege. The "desert Gaza" (ἔρημος Γάζα) in the New Testament (Acts 8:26), which is the city proper, was so called because of its destruction by Jannaeus. It was restored by Pompey and rebuilt by Gabinius in 57 B.C. King Herod held it for a short time. After his death the city was under the Roman proconsul of Syria.

Gaza flourished under Roman rule. A famous school of rhetoric was established there, as well as magnificent temples, such as those of Zeus, Helios, Aphrodite, Apollo, Athene, and the local Tyche. The largest of the sanctuaries was that of Marnas (a Cretan deity), the main god of the city, to whom it was fanatically devoted. Marnas' name also appears on the coins of the city, and worship of him continued even under Christian rule. Only in the fifth century A.D. was the temple of Marnas and those of the other deities destroyed, and Christianity became the ruling religion.

From the fifth century A.D., Gaza was a prominent city in the Byzantine world. Many famous scholars taught in its school of rhetoric. The most important of these was Procopius of Gaza (born at the end of the fifth century).

Jews settled in Gaza during the Roman and Byzantine periods. On the Madeba map, Gaza is shown as a large city with colonnaded streets crossing its center and a large basilica in the middle, probably the church erected over the temple of Marnas. The New City (Neapolis) was the harbor and was known as Maiumas Neapolis. It was named Constantia from the fourth century A.D. onward. Its fair (panegyris) was one of the three main fairs in Roman Palestine.

In a great battle fought near Gaza in 635, the Muslims vanquished the Byzantine army. The city itself fell soon afterward. It remained the seat of the governor of the Negev, as is known from the Nessana Papyri. The Jewish and Samaritan communities flourished under Arab rule.

Opposite page: Northern scarp plan; 1922 excavations. Below: Northern scarp plan, west face; 1922 excavations. Bottom: Northern scarp plan, section OP; 1922 excavations.

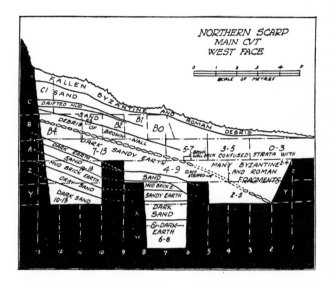

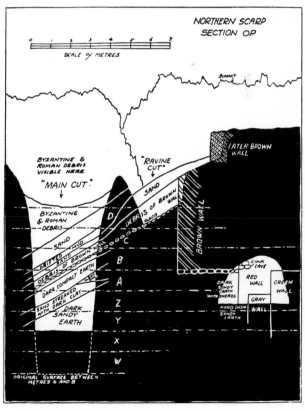

Both pages, counterclockwise: Fragmentary marble chancel screen. Industrial installation and street to its left, looking southwest. Mosaic of David playing the harp, in nave of synagogue; before excavation. Fragment of chancel screen with incised menorah, lulab, and shofar; from the synagogue (Goodenough 3, fig. 583).

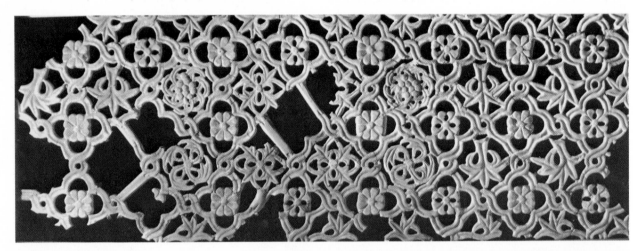

King Baldwin I of Jerusalem occupied Gaza, which was known in the Crusader period as Gadres. From the time of Baldwin III (1152) it was a Templar stronghold. In 1170 it fell to Saladin. Under Mameluke rule Gaza was the capital of a district *(mamlaka)* embracing the whole coastal plain up to 'Atlit. The city continued to flourish under Ottoman rule.

EXCAVATIONS

Tell Ḥarube or Tell of Gaza is the site of ancient Gaza. It is situated about 5 kilometers (3 miles) from the seashore in the northeastern part of the present city. Its location corresponds with the description of Arrian (II, 26, 1). The Roman city was extended up to the seashore. In the Middle Ages, the city of Gaza occupied the same location.

The mound was partly excavated by W. J. Phythian-Adams on behalf of the Palestine Exploration Fund toward the end of 1922. The results of the excavations were published in the *PEF QSt*, 1923. Three trenches (Main Cut, Cross Trench, and Ravine Cut) were dug without any connection between them. Five brick city walls were discovered and marked Brown, Red, Gray, and Green walls. Also found was a rude stone "skin deep" glacis, which ran obliquely into the mound and apparently abutted upon some portion of the main (Brown) wall. The associated pottery showed, however, that the glacis belonged to a decadent period in the city's Philistine history, a period which seemed to the excavator to have closed with a disaster and, at least on part of the site, to have ended in desolation and perhaps total abandonment.

The archaeological results disclosed the absence of any Greek remains of importance in the present mound of Gaza. A change came only in the Roman era, when old Gaza once again sprang into prominence and the Greek city on the coast apparently disappeared.

In his attempt to assign approximate dates to the five brick walls discovered, Phythian-Adams arrived at the following conclusions: The late Brown wall is the uppermost and latest wall of the city. The glacis and the very strong Brown wall represent the period of Alexander the Great (332 B.C.). The Red wall goes back at least to the fifth or sixth centuries B.C. or even earlier to the days of Pharaoh Necho (609–593 B.C.), who apparently inflicted severe damage upon the town (Jeremiah 47:1). The Gray and Green walls, therefore, may date back to the middle of the second millennium or to the arrival of the Philistines. According to the excavator, it was impossible to find any datable pottery relating to these ancient walls, and their chronology was estimated by comparison with the depth of the Late Bronze Age fragments in the Main cut.

In the trenches, Phythian-Adams found various ceramic types, including pottery from the Late Bronze Age (Cypriot base-ring ware, white slip wishbone-handle bowls, and part of a pointed juglet), Early Iron Age (Philistine) and Iron Age II pottery (pebble-burnished ware). The upper debris consisted of a mixture of glazed Arab fragments, masses of Roman and Byzantine sherds, some Hellenistic sherds, and numerous fragments of glass from those periods.

The Area of the Ancient Synagogue. In 1965, a mosaic pavement was discovered on the seashore of Gaza, about 300 meters south of the present harbor. The Egyptian Department of Antiquities conducted excavations there, and a brief note was published on the results. A rescue excavation was carried out at the site in August–September, 1967, under the direction of A. Ovadiah, on behalf of the Israel Department of Antiquities and Museums, and with the cooperation of the Gaza Military Government.

The excavations were concentrated in two areas: in the synagogue and in the industrial installations immediately west of it.

Of the synagogue, only the mosaic pavement has survived, and even this only in part. The remains, however, point to a large building with an east–west orientation. It measures about 30 by 26 meters. The building consisted of a wide nave and two narrow aisles on each side, making five halls altogether, and thus differing from the Palestinian synagogues of the same period. These halls were apparently separated by rows of columns. The location of these columns can be reconstructed from the archaeological evidence. In the western wall there were probably three entrances: a central one leading to the nave and two side entrances leading to the inner northern and southern aisles. In the southern wall there was an additional entrance. On the east side of the building was an apse (reconstructed), 3 meters in depth, which was used for the Ark of the Law.

The nave was originally paved in mosaics, though later it was almost entirely repaved with large

marble slabs, few of which remain. The surviving section of the central panel, on its western-most side, depicts King David as Orpheus, dressed in Byzantine royal garments and playing a lyre. Above the instrument is the Hebrew legend דויד — "David." Around the king are a lion cub, a giraffe, and a snake, all listening to the music. The whole is surrounded by a border of geometric patterns.

In the southern-most aisle, the mosaic pavement is better preserved. It has a floral motif, forming medallions in which are enclosed various animals. A geometric border surrounds the whole. This mosaic is very similar to those of the Ma'on (Nirim) synagogue and the Shellal church, which are also of the sixth century A.D. Thus, it can be assumed that the pavements at these three sites, which are all in the Gaza region, were made in one and the same workshop. In one of the medallions of the Gaza mosaic is a Greek inscription commemorating the names of the donors ("Menahem and Yeshua, the sons of the late Isses [Jesse], wood merchants") and the date (A.D. 508/9, according to the era of Gaza).

Chancel screens and other finds from the area of the synagogue add support to the assumption that this large building, with its colorful mosaic pavement, was indeed an ancient Jewish synagogue. Other indications are the typical Jewish names in the Greek inscriptions, the term "holy place" that appears in the mosaic inscription, the figure of King David and his name written in the square Hebrew script, and the east–west orientation of the building. The synagogue seems to have belonged to Maritime Gaza — Constantia Maiumas Neapolis. Evidence for the end of the synagogue is provided by pottery lamps from the end of the Byzantine period (late sixth–early seventh century A.D.). Such types continue just into the Early Arab period. Thus, the synagogue was probably destroyed shortly after the Arab conquest.

To the west of the synagogue, and on a level lower by about 2.5 meters, there came to light a well-preserved industrial complex, probably a dye works. This complex, which spreads over 250–300 square meters, is surrounded by a mud wall built on a stone foundation. It consists of two rooms, an eastern one with four large reservoirs and two smaller ones, and a western room with two large

Mosaic pavement in southern aisle of synagogue, looking east.

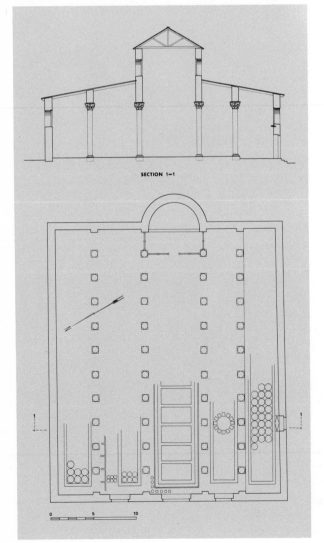

SECTION 1—1

0   5   10

Both pages, top row left to right; from the mosaics of the synagogue: Lioness suckling her cub. Zebra. Tigress. Giraffe. Bottom row, left to right: Plan and section of the synagogue, reconstruction. Drawing of relief of a menorah enclosed by a wreath and a bilingual inscription in Hebrew and Greek: "Hananiah son of Jacob"; on a column in the Great Mosque (Goodenough 3, fig. 584). From the synagogue, the dedication in Greek.

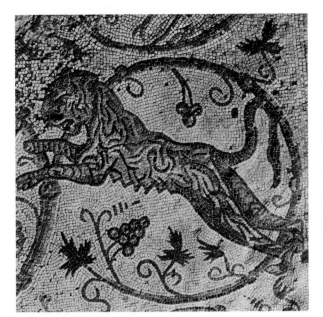

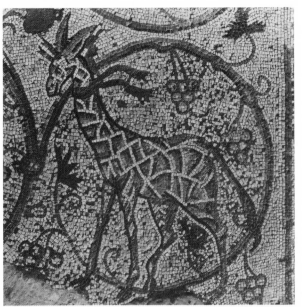

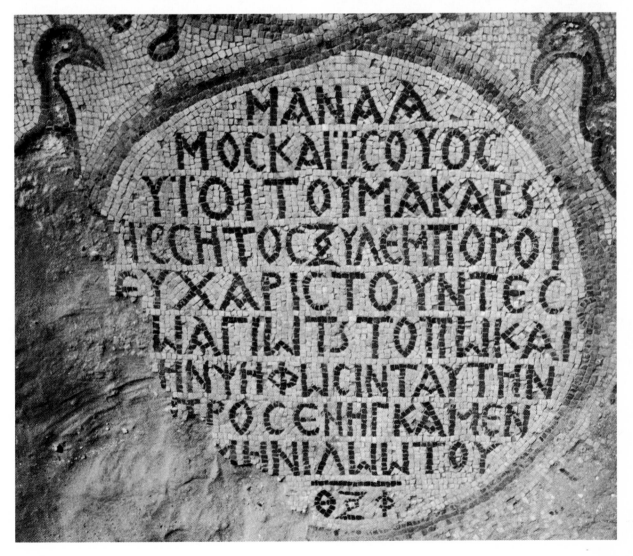

MANAA
MOCKAIICOYOC
YIOITOYMAKAP-
ICCHTOCEYLEMTOPOI
EYXAPICTOYNTEC
NAГIWITBTOПWKAI
HNYHΦICNTAYTHN
TPOCENHГKAMEN
UINIΛIWNTOY
ΘZΦ

reservoirs. Three round limestone basins found here had probably been used to grind the dyes. Remains of charred wood and ashes indicate that the building had had a wooden roof which collapsed when the structure was destroyed by fire.

East of the dye works is a mud-paved street, about 3 meters wide, running north-south. On the far side of this street, a house was partly excavated (for it runs beneath the floor of the synagogue). The house, street, and dye works are all contemporary and appear to be some seventy to a hundred years older than the synagogue.

Byzantine Churches and the Great Mosque. According to Christian sources, churches were built at Gaza, mainly in the days of the Empress Eudoxia. A graphic account of the construction of the church of Eudoxia—the Eudoxiana—is presented by the deacon Mark (*Life of Porphyry,* by Mark the Deacon, ed. G. F. Hill, Oxford, 1913). The Eudoxiana was erected on the site of the large and famous pagan temple, the Marneum. The Church was designed and erected by the architect Rufinus, who was brought by Porphyry from Antioch. As far as we can tell from the records, its construction may have taken from five to ten years. It was said to be greater than all the churches of the time. Indeed it was criticized as being too large for the congregation. The church was completed in about A.D. 408. No trace of it has been found. A second church at Gaza was that of Saint Sergius, but it, too,

unfortunately has not been discovered. This church is dated to the sixth century and its mosaics are described at length by Choricius (translated by R. W. Hamilton, *PEF QSt,* 1930, 181 ff.). The founder of the church was a governor named Stephen. Choricius also describes the mosaics of a third church at Gaza, that of Saint Stephen. They included the figure of the founder holding a model of the church, the figure of Saint John the Baptist, etc. No evidence of this church has been found so far.

The Great Mosque at Gaza (Djami el-Kebir) is located in the center of the city. The building was originally a twelfth century Crusader cathedral dedicated to Saint John the Baptist. The Crusader church was located on the probable site of the Eudoxiana. The building itself was completely preserved, and only a few changes were made. To this day the decorated, magnificent façade of the Crusader church with its arched entrances is visible. The church was a basilical building and contained rows of double columns, one above the other. On the western side was an external wing. On the southern and southeastern sides the building was enlarged and a mihrab was added. The minaret was built on the eastern side, probably on the site of the bell tower.

The streets and lanes of the marketplace that lead to the Great Mosque are erected according to the Mameluke style of the fourteenth to sixteenth centuries. Around the Great Mosque are scattered some granite columns, which probably originated from Roman and Byzantine buildings.

Sporadic Finds and Remains. Evidence of a considerable Jewish population during the Byzantine period at Gaza is also provided by a relief of a seven-branched menorah, a shofar, a lulab, an ethrog, and a bilingual inscription in Hebrew and Greek ("Ḥananiah, son of Jacob"), which appears on a column now in the Great Mosque of Gaza. This column must have originally come from a synagogue. A Greek inscription engraved on a synagogue chancel screen was also found at Gaza. It mentions Jacob, son of Eleazar, who "renovated the structure of the apse of this holy place together with its screen from the ground up." Also found was a fragment of a marble slab from a synagogue

Left: Facade of the Great Mosque, originally the Church of St. John the Baptist, built in the twelfth century. Opposite page: Eastern entrance to the marketplace, possibly dating to the Mameluke period.

screen on which was carved a primitive and simple menorah, with a shofar and a lulab. Other discoveries include small fragments of inscriptions.

Judging from these sporadic finds and the synagogue discovered on the seashore, it can be concluded that at least two synagogues existed at Gaza during the talmudic period.

A colossal statue of Zeus from Gaza is exhibited in the Archaeological Museum of Istanbul. It is the largest known statue of Zeus of the Roman period (second century A.D.).   A. OVADIAH

BIBLIOGRAPHY

M. A. Mayer, *A History of the City of Gaza*, New York, 1907 • W. J. Phythian-Adams, *PEF QSt* (1923), 11–36 • S. Klein, S. Assaf, and L. A. Mayer (eds.), *Sefer ha-Yishuv*, 2 vols., 1939–44 (Hebrew) • Goodenough, *Jewish Symbols* 1, 223; 3, figs. 583–84 • J. Braslavski (Braslavi), *Le-Heqer Arsenu — 'Avar u-Seridim*, Tel Aviv, 1954, index (Hebrew); *idem, Mi-Resu'at 'Azzah ad Yam Suf*, Tel Aviv, 1957 (Hebrew) • G. Downey, *Gaza in the Early Sixth Century*, Norman, 1963 • M. Avi-Yonah, *Yediot* 30 (1966), 221–23 (Hebrew) • A. Ovadiah, *Qadmoniot* 1 (1968), 124–27 (Hebrew); *idem, IEJ* 19 (1969), 193–98.

GERASA

IDENTIFICATION. Gerasa (Greek Γέρασα), a Greek city of Gilead, now Jarash, 36.5 kilometers (22 miles) north of 'Amman. Its identification is based on the similarity of the present Arab name to the ancient one and on several inscriptions found there mentioning its inhabitants as τῶν πρότερον Γερασηνῶν. According to inscriptions and coins of the Roman period, the city's name was "the city of the Antiochenes on the River Chrysorhoas, formerly [of] the people of Gerasa, holy and sacrosanct (ἄσυλος)."

The site is close to the Aila–Damascus route. It stands on the border of the desert and the sown in the hill country, between the Jordan Valley and the Arabian desert, 570 meters above sea level. It lies on the banks of the River Chrysorhoas (Wadi Jarash), which crosses the city from north to south. To the east is a rich spring, 'Ein Qeruan. The city was founded at the place where the valley widens. It is surrounded by broad stretches of arable and pasture land and woodland. To the west of the valley, the land rises gradually to the point on which a synagogue was built in antiquity.

The southern hill, on which stood the temple of Zeus, was apparently the original nucleus of the Hellenistic settlement. The fortified enceinte seen today appears to belong to the Roman-Byzantine city, which extended on both sides of the River Chrysorhoas. The wall, 3,456 meters in length, encloses an elliptical area of 840 dunams. It dates to the Flavian period.

HISTORY

L. Harding was the first to discover Stone Age sites near Gerasa. Diana Kirkbride published details of these in 1952–58. Implements of Acheulean-Levalloisian type were found on the hill east of the triumphal arch. Remains of the Neolithic period (animal bones, arrowheads, points, chisels, scrapers, denticulated blades, awls, etc.) were also found. N. Glueck noted evidence of settlement in the area from the Early Bronze Age onward: a walled enclosure on a hill 200 meters from the northeast corner of Gerasa contained pottery from Early Bronze Age I to Middle Bronze Age I. He also found an Israelite (Iron Age) settlement on the hill north of the city overlooking the Valley of Birketein.

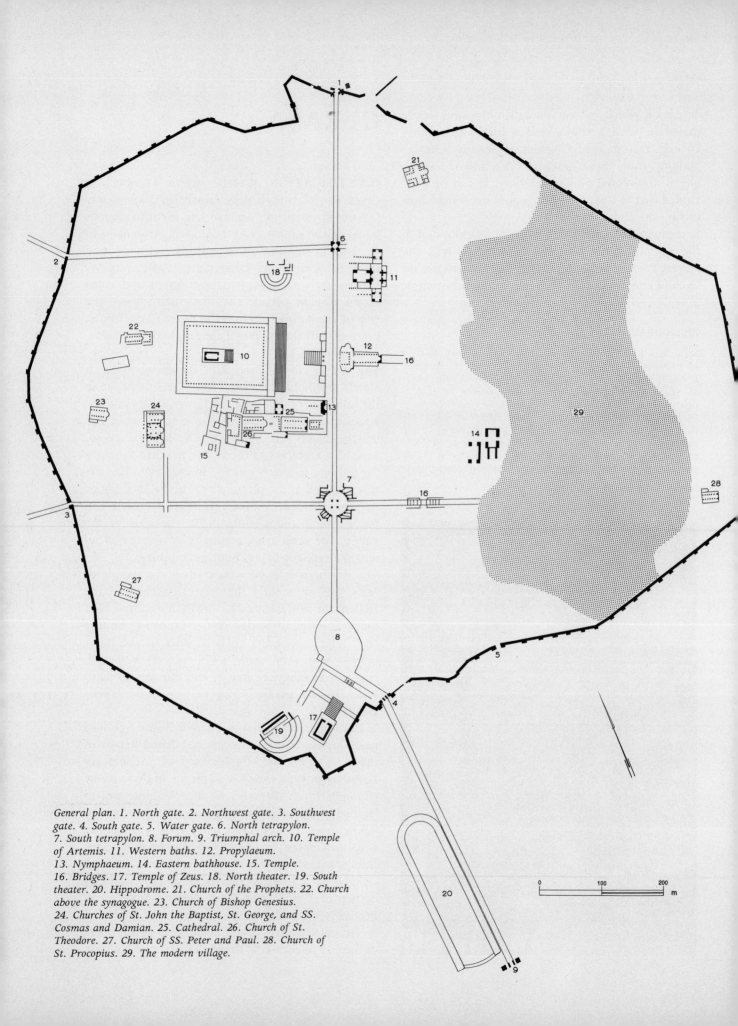

General plan. 1. North gate. 2. Northwest gate. 3. Southwest
gate. 4. South gate. 5. Water gate. 6. North tetrapylon.
7. South tetrapylon. 8. Forum. 9. Triumphal arch. 10. Temple
of Artemis. 11. Western baths. 12. Propylaeum.
13. Nymphaeum. 14. Eastern bathhouse. 15. Temple.
16. Bridges. 17. Temple of Zeus. 18. North theater. 19. South
theater. 20. Hippodrome. 21. Church of the Prophets. 22. Church
above the synagogue. 23. Church of Bishop Genesius.
24. Churches of St. John the Baptist, St. George, and SS.
Cosmas and Damian. 25. Cathedral. 26. Church of St.
Theodore. 27. Church of SS. Peter and Paul. 28. Church of
St. Procopius. 29. The modern village.

A Greek tradition held that Alexander the Great founded the Hellenistic city for his veterans (γέροντες). According to another tradition, when Alexander captured the city all the younger men were killed and only the elderly survived, hence the city's name. More trustworthy is the fact preserved by an inscription of the Roman period (published by C. B. Welles in Kraeling's excavation report), according to which a statue of Perdiccas, Alexander's general and after his death regent of the kingdom, was set up at Gerasa. It may perhaps be concluded from this that Perdiccas was regarded as the founder of the Hellenistic settlement. A Roman inscription (Welles, Number 78) discloses that a group of Macedonians were among its first inhabitants. The city was subsequently known as Antioch, as in 200 B.C. Transjordan had passed to the Seleucid dynasty, and the new name was bestowed in honor of Antiochus III or IV.

Gerasa was an important link in the chain of

fortified towns erected by the Hellenistic kings against the desert tribes. Archaeological evidence of the Hellenistic city is very scanty. On the southern hill, where the temple of Zeus was built (it is referred to in the first century B.C.), Rhodian stamped jar handles of the period 210–180 B.C. have been found. It may be assumed that the cult of Zeus long preceded the Roman period, as the city received the titles of ἱερὰ καὶ ἄσυλος ("holy and sacrosanct") and therefore enjoyed certain privileges. In Alexander Jannaeus' reign, Zeno and Theodorus, the tyrants of Philadelphia ('Amman), deposited part of their treasure in the temple of Zeus at Gerasa. Hence in their time the city was in their hands. Jannaeus (102–76 B.C.) captured Gerasa in the last years of his reign and died while besieging Ragaba within Gerasene territory. The city remained under Jewish rule until 63 B.C.

In the Roman period, it reckoned by the Pompeian era, hence it is to be assumed that Pompey took

General view of the south theater; first century A.D.

Gerasa from the Jews and that it became a member of the Decapolis (Confederation of Ten Cities). This association and the signs of Nabataean influence at Gerasa attest to its connection with the trade routes between southern Arabia, Damascus, Phoenicia, and Judea.

Gerasa enjoyed a period of rising prosperity in the Roman period. During the First Jewish revolt (A.D. 66–74), friendly relations prevailed between Gerasa and the local Jews, who went unscathed. Most scholars, therefore, consider that the Gerasa captured by the Romans before the siege of Jerusalem (Josephus, *War* IV, 487–88) was not the Transjordan town (cf. also the presence of non-Jewish refugees in Gerasa at that time — inscriptions Welles, Numbers 5 and 6). Architectural fragments attributed to a synagogue and found in the fill of Hadrian's arch to the south of the city are perhaps evidence that the Jewish community left the city during the Revolt, but it may equally have suffered in Trajan's time — cf. inscriptions Numbers 56 and 57 dedicated to Trajan in 115. A Trajanic inscription appears to show that Gerasa was included in the Province of Syria, but Ptolemy's information, dated to the mid-second century (V, 74, 18) and prior to 162, indicates that at some unknown date Gerasa had been transferred to the Province of Arabia. According to milestones, it was already part of that province in 111/12. Signs of Nabataean influence in the city are coins (mostly of Aretas IV, 9 B.C.–A.D. 40), a Nabataean inscription, and cults of the "Arab God" as well as of Pacidas and Dionysus (Dushara).

The Nabataean influence disappeared with the establishment of the Provincia Arabia (A.D. 105/6).

The first indication of renewed prosperity at Gerasa under Roman rule is the new temple dedicated to Zeus (A.D. 22/23–23/24 — Welles, Numbers 2 and 3). There was an increase in the number of Roman coins from the reign of Claudius to the second half of the first century. From 75 to 76, a new street plan was laid out using the cardo as its main axis (Welles, Number 50). The city wall was begun at the same time. The south theater existed by Domitian's time (Welles, Numbers 45 and 46), and in the Flavian period the first temple of Artemis was adorned and the temple of Hera built in the place later occupied by the cathedral. A new phase of development began under Trajan with the building of the north gate. Among its causes was the inclusion of the city in the province of Arabia, when new roads were built (Welles, Numbers 252–57). The triumphal arch and the new south gate were erected during Hadrian's stay in A.D. 129/30 (Welles, Numbers 30, 44, 58). The south and central sectors of the colonnades of the cardo were probably built under Hadrian and Antoninus Pius. The splendid propylaea of the temples of Hera and Artemis were built contemporarily. The temple of Artemis was rebuilt, its magnificently impressive approach to the east erected, and the focus of Gerasa was thus transferred northward. Under M. Aurelius (A.D. 163), the north theater was added (Welles, Number 65), and the west baths were built in the second half of the second century.

Inscriptions add information on the city's economy and the composition of its population in the second and third centuries, recording guilds of weavers (Welles, Number 190) and potters (Welles, Number 79). In this context should be mentioned the Trajanic figurines and lamps found south of the Circassian village, attesting to a local workshop. One citizen performed the duties of Phoenicarch (Welles, Number 188), indicating that Gerasa had trade links with the cities of Phoenicia. Gerasa began to strike its own coins under Hadrian and continued to do so down to the reign of Alexander Severus. The coins usually bear the figure of Artemis, the Tyche of the city, or the figure of Tyche with that of Caesar. Tyche and the river god of the Chrysorhoas appear together under L. Verus. The city's name of Antioch and its titles are recorded in inscriptions from the time of Verus. In

Both pages, counterclockwise: Head of Aesculapius; second century A.D. Temple of Zeus, rebuilt in A.D. 161–166. Colonnaded street and nymphaeum; A.D. 191. Coin of Gerasa; second century A.D.

the third century, Gerasa received the status of a Roman colony (Welles, Numbers 179 and 191). The festival theater (Welles, Number 153) and the northern tetrapylon were erected under the Severi, while Temple C was already in ruins. Gerasa began to decline in the mid-third century, when the city ceased to mint its own coins. It revived under Diocletian. The south tetrapylon was surrounded with shops, and fourth-century coins became numerous. Yet, written sources record almost nothing of the city until the fifth century A.D.

Representatives of Gerasa took part in church councils as early as 359. In the mid-fifth century, the city's fortifications were repaired. Its first church was erected in about 400. The Church of the Apostles was built in 464 and building activity increased, the Church of Saint Theodore with its annexes being erected in 496, reflecting the expansion of the ecclesiastical bureaucracy. The Church of Procopius dates to 562, and the rest of the churches of Gerasa were also built in the sixth century, until the year 611. Other public buildings were enlarged contemporarily. The plans of the churches of Gerasa in general resemble those of the churches of Palestine and Constantinople. They possess raised platforms with altars and a schola cantorum enclosed by chancel screens. The bishop's throne stood within an apse with a semi-circular bench for the priests on both sides. Semi-domes decorated with glass tesserae are numerous, but the narthex is rare at Gerasa. Colored mosaic floors become frequent from the fourth century, chiefly in the churches, and include in their decorative repertoire human figures, birds, animals, objects, plant and geometric motifs. Unique are the portraits of donors and the pictures of Egyptian walled cities in the Churches of Saint John and Saints Peter and Paul. All human figures, however, were deliberately effaced, apparently in the eighth century after the iconoclastic legislation of the Muslims. The mosaics are in the classical style. By the sixth century, however, the artists of Gerasa had achieved an independent style, and they belong to a school common to Palestine and Syria, which also influenced early Islamic art.

The coins, of which a great number have been found, date down to Justin II (565–78), but by then many buildings in the city were already in ruins, many of the streets had become blind alleys, and the water system was in a state of neglect. In 614–28, the city was captured by the Persians, and it fell into Muslim hands in 635. Coins testify that settlement continued until 774, the business center reverting to the southern tetrapylon. Poor buildings were erected, which disfigure the forum. Most of the churches were still in use in the eighth century, but meanwhile the capital of the Caliphs had been transferred to Baghdad, and a series of earthquakes afflicted the city, all hastening its ruin. In the ninth century, Gerasa was still a mixed Greco-Arab settlement. In the eleventh century, the temple of Artemis was a temporary fort. Baldwin III destroyed the walls of the town in 1122. William of Tyre found the place deserted.

The city's territory extended as far west as Ragaba. On the north it included Enganna ('Ein Jann, cf. inscription Number 71), Eglon, Erga, and Samta. Rihab to the east was not in its territory. In the east the boundary passed near the highway from Philadelphia to Bostra, and in the south close to, but somewhat to the south of the Jabbok River.

EXPLORATION

Gerasa was first discovered in 1806 by U. J. Seetzen. It was subsequently visited by J. L. Burkhardt (1812) and J. Buckingham (1816). Conditions of visiting improved with the settlement of a Circassian community in 1878, and between 1891 and 1902 Gerasa was explored by G. Schumacher, R. Brünnow, and J. Germer-Durand. In 1902, a German expedition under O. Puchstein investigated the ruins. Excavation and conservation work were begun by G. Horsfield under the auspices of the British Mandatory Government in 1925. The first finds uncovered were the court of the temple of Zeus, the nymphaeum, the propylaeum of the temple of Artemis, and the main street or cardo. Work continued until 1931 under P. A. Ritchie, A. G. Buchanan, and G. Horsfield. Meanwhile, systematic excavation directed by J. W. Crowfoot had begun in 1928 under the auspices of the British School of Archaeology in Jerusalem and Yale University. In 1930, the American Schools of Oriental Research replaced the British School, and direction was assumed by C. S. Fisher. N. Glueck continued the work in 1933–34, and from 1937–40 the clearing of the forum in the south of the city proceeded under L. Harding. From 1953–56, the restoration of the southern theater began, under the supervision of T. Canan and Diana Kirkbride, but the work was not completed.

PLAN AND BUILDINGS

The city wall is of uniform construction and possesses 101 towers spaced at intervals of 17–22 meters. There are five gates: the north and south gates, two gates in the west wall (connected with cross streets), and the water gate whence the River Chrysorhoas issues southeastward. The cardo, the main street of the city, crossed the city from north to south, west of the Chrysorhoas, and constituted the axis of the street system, which is roughly Hippodamian (*i.e.*, on the checkerboard plan). Two of the east–west streets (decumani) are known: one on the south, crossing the cardo at the southern tetrapylon, continues east to cross the river by means of a bridge; the other, on the north, meets the cardo on the west at the northern tetrapylon. The cardo led to the forum in the south. The principal buildings will be described in order from south to north, first the Roman structures (Numbers 1–16), then the Byzantine churches (Numbers 17–23).

1. **The Triumphal Arch,** uncovered in 1931, stood 400 meters south of the city. It was dated by an inscription to A.D. 130, when Hadrian visited Gerasa. It has a main gate and a subsidiary passage on each side. Both facades have four Corinthian columns carrying an architrave and pediment. Between the columns are niches. A passage passed from side to side over the main gate, showing that the structure was originally designed to be a gate in the city wall south of its existing line. However, this extension was never carried out. Later on, pavilions were built abutting the sides of the arch.

2. **The Hippodrome,** or chariot racetrack, was excavated in 1933 northwest of the triumphal arch, parallel with the Roman road leading to Philadelphia. Its interior length was 244 meters, and it could have held 15,000 spectators. On its south end were ten compartments from which the chariots started. The excavators differed on the date of construction. One view held that it was erected in the second or third century and never used for races, another, that it was built in the first century A.D.

3. **The Temple of Zeus Olympius** is situated on the city's southern hill. Cave dwellings had previously existed in the area, and two successive temples were erected over them, the first between A.D. 22 and 43. The temple is surrounded by a large court enclosed by a wall. East of this was another court, and the two enclosures extended over three terraces. The shrine stood on the westerly terrace. The temple was rebuilt in A.D. 161–66 as a peripteral structure with 8 by 12 columns.

4. **The Forum** is a broad ellipse surrounded by a portico of Ionic columns open to the southeast. Its excavation was begun in 1931. The court was built at the beginning of the first century A.D. From the fourth century onward, dwellings were erected in its colonnades. In the sixth century the forum was in ruins, although an Arab settlement existed there until the eighth century.

5. **The South Theater,** situated west of the temple of Zeus, was excavated in 1925–31. The lower auditorium (*ima cavea*) was divided into four segments (*cunei*) and the upper (*summa cavea*) into eight. The theater held some 3,000 spectators. Four exits (*vomitoria*) issued from the gangway (*praecinctio*), and a passage (*parodos*) led into the orchestra on each flank. The facade (*scena frons*) behind the stage had two stories and three doors, the central one placed in a niche. The stage front had an inscription from the time of Domitian (Welles, Number 51), but the building was built earlier, in the first century. Another inscription (Welles, Number 52) records the erection of a statue of Nike in the theater to commemorate the Roman victory over the Jews (A.D. 66–74).

6. **The South Tetrapylon.** The south and middle sectors of the cardo were lined on both sides with Corinthian colonnades, while the sector north of the northern decumanus, or main east–west street, was lined with an Ionic colonnade. The Corinthian colonnades are generally considered to belong to a phase in which the city was replanned in the mid-second century A.D. The south tetrapylon, uncovered in 1931, stands where the southern decumanus crosses the cardo. It is situated in a circular piazza and is composed of four pedestals, each carrying four Corinthian columns bearing baldachins. Its position indicates that it was probably erected in the mid-second century, along with the Corinthian colonnades that form part of the same plan. The piazza was completely surrounded by an ornamental facade of columns, behind which shops were built at the beginning of the fourth century. These were still used as dwellings in the Arab period.

7. **The North Tetrapylon** stands at the intersection

ΑΛΕΞΑΝΑΡΙΑ

of the cardo and the north decumanus. It is a circle inscribed in a square, with four gates. This tetrapylon was built under the Severi.

8. **The Eastern Baths** are situated at the edge of the Circassian village east of the cardo. They have not been explored.

9. **Temple C** was the smallest temple found in the city. The facade faced southeast and was surrounded by a court with porticoes. The prostyle *naos* is small, opening into an exedra at the rear. There was a vaulted chamber beneath the podium. The excavators believed that this building was a ἡρῶον or hero's monument, but L. H. Vincent defined it as a Nabataean temenos. The building belongs to the first half of the second century A.D.

10. **The Nymphaeum** (ornamental public fountain), situated north of a lane west of the cardo, is the most resplendent of the ornamental buildings of Gerasa. It faces east and consists of a facade of two stories and a central apse, with niches and a Corinthian colonnade along its length. The first story is crowned by an architrave and the upper by pediments, the whole being topped by a semi-dome. In front of it is a pool and a portico. The nymphaeum was built in A.D. 191.

11. **The Temenos and Temple of Artemis** are north of the Byzantine Cathedral (see below, Number 19). The area of the temenos is 34 dunams. Its excavation began in 1928 but was not completed. The building complex begins east of the Chrysorhoas, as an approach crossing the river on a bridge and ending with a triple gate. From here, a Corinthian colonnade continues to a trapezoidal court flanked by exedrae opening onto the cardo. (The portico was converted into a basilical church in about 565. The apse was situated at the triple gate, while the trapezoidal court became the atrium of the church.) West of the cardo rises a natural terrace, the slopes of which are retained by a great wall, with an entrance in the center, in the form of a portico with steps leading to a triple gate. The exterior portico was flanked by shops. Beyond the entrance, a magnificent stairway ascended to the outer court. Another portico, also fronted by steps, bounded the court on the temple side and gave access to an inner court (124 by 88 meters) surrounded by colonnades, chambers, and a strong outer wall. The temple, standing on a podium reached by steps from the east, was peripteral, with 11 by 6 columns. Its facade was pseudodipteral in

Both pages, counterclockwise: Church of St. John the
Baptist; mosaic depiction of the city of Alexandria.
Church of St. John the Baptist; mosaic pavement
in the northwestern exedra. Church of SS. Cosmas
and Damian; detail of mosaic pavement in the nave.
Plan of church complex of St. John the Baptist,
St. George, and SS. Cosmas and Damian. Christian
glass cup (note cross at left); Byzantine.

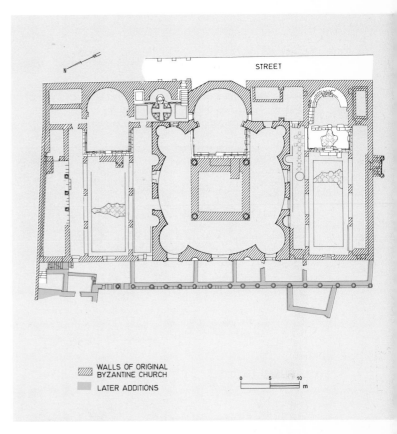

WALLS OF ORIGINAL
BYZANTINE CHURCH

LATER ADDITIONS

Below: Synagogue inscription in mosaic pavement.
Bottom: Part of the mosaic pavement of the synagogue showing animals entering Noah's ark.

Corinthian style. The entrance to the *naos* was between antas. The podium contained basements. The building and its annexes were erected around A.D. 150.

12. **The North Theater,** situated northeast of the Temenos of Artemis and south of the north decumanus, has not yet been excavated or properly investigated. It is smaller than the south theater. Its *cavea* faces north. Colonnaded entrances are found behind the *scena frons* at its flanks. The upper *cavea* has eight *cunei*, and the lower four, reached by four entrances. The theater was built between A.D. 162 and 166 (Welles, Number 65).

13. **The Western Baths** lie between the north tetrapylon and the Chrysorhoas, their entrances being from the east into the frigidarium. On the west is the domed caldarium, and to the south and north are smaller halls. The building has additional flanking halls north and south of the frigidarium, with ceilings supported by piers. The plan is paralleled at Timgad and Cyrene, hence the building is probably to be dated in the second half of the second century A.D. Noteworthy are the arches at the corners of the domed hall, which rest on pendentives—one of the oldest known examples of this architectural device.

14. **The North Gate** of the city was built in A.D. 115, replacing an earlier entrance. It had a single passageway flanked by pavilions of two stories of the Corinthian order. Two trapezoidal bastions were added to its north front in the Byzantine or Arab period.

15. **The Festival Theater.** Ancient structures and tombs exist to the north of the town near the Roman road to Pella, including a temple of Nemesis of the Antonine period. One kilometer north of the gate is the pool of Birketein, and west of it is the festival theater, linked to the pool by colonnades, the whole forming an amusement area for the celebration of the festival of Maiumas, a Syrian festival probably in honor of Artemis, celebrated every three years by water sports and dramatic spectacles. (According to inscription Number 279, the festival was still held in the sixth century A.D.) The theater accommodated some thousand spectators. The auditorium faces east and is divided into four *cunei*. There is no building behind the *scena frons*. The theater was built in the Severan period (Welles, Numbers 153, 197, 198). North of it stood the temple of Zeus Epicarpius and the tomb of the centurion Germanus, built in the Antonine period.

16. **The Cemetery.** Various remains of villas are to be found south of the city. The cemetery of Gerasa extended all around the city. Aboveground, sepulchral structures are seen chiefly along the road running north from the city. West of the hippodrome, twelve rock-cut tombs, dating mainly to the second–fifth centuries A.D., were uncovered in 1930. Most of the finds were of the third century.

17. **The Church of Saints Peter and Paul** in the southwest quarter of the city was exposed in 1929. On its northwest corner was a small chapel attached to it end on. The first church was a basilica with three apses and an Ionic atrium at its west end. Judging from its mosaics and plan it was erected about A.D. 540. The **Mortuary Church** was a simple hall terminating in an apse that opened on the south into a burial cave evidently built at the end of the sixth century A.D.

18. **The Church of Procopius,** which stands at the end of the south decumanus in the southeast of the city, was excavated in 1928. It is of basilical type with three internal apses, a nave, and aisles. On its northwest side stood a chapel. The church was built in A.D. 526/27.

19. **The Cathedral of Gerasa** and its associated buildings were constructed north of the south decumanus, at right angles to the cardo and to the west of it. The buildings are placed on four terraces rising westward. Their excavation was begun in 1928. The approach from the cardo was by a monumental colonnade and by steps built in the second century and repaired in the fourth. This structure, in its original plan, dates to the Antonine period, and a temple apparently occupied the second terrace in the first century. West of the cathedral, on its second terrace, stood the **Fountain Court,** where a Christian festival was held on the anniversary of the marriage of Cana (John 2:1). Inscriptions found here indicate that the festival originated in a cult of Dionysus-Dushara, the Nabataean god of wine. The third terrace was occupied by the **Church of Saint Theodore.** On the fourth terrace, north of the Fountain Court, were the **Baths of Flaccus,** and to the west was the **Clergy House.** Southwest of the Church of Saint Theodore stood Temple C (see above, Number 9), and to the north of it was a residential quarter built in the fourth century A.D. over burial caves of the first century B.C. The quarter expanded in the fifth century and existed till the seventh.

The cathedral is a basilica with an internal polygonal apse and a chapel to the southwest, the Fountain Court to the east being its atrium. The oldest church known in Gerasa, it appears to have been built about A.D. 400. The Church of Saint Theodore was erected to the west of the Fountain Court between A.D. 494 and 496, and to its west was a rhomboid-shaped atrium. The hall is surrounded by various annexes, a chapel, baptistery, etc. The church contains magnificent mosaic pavements. The Baths of Flaccus were built in A.D. 454/55 and renovated in A.D. 584. Their rooms, which are relatively small, are ranged about two courts. The Clergy House, erected in a third-century street, was divided in its first phase into two suites, that on the northwest apparently serving to accommodate a person of high rank. Additional rooms were later built onto the house.

20. **The Churches of Saint John the Baptist, Saint George** (on the south), and **Saints Cosmas and Damian** are situated west of the Church of Saint Theodore, in one line with it. The three churches actually comprise one structure, *i.e.*, a central church with a lateral church on either wing. All three face the west with a narrow atrium in front of each. The Church of Saint John was built in A.D. 531 and is circular, with four exedrae opening from it to each point of the compass. The apse is on the east with the chancel in front of it. The dome is supported by four columns. The plan resembles the Cathedral of Bostra (A.D. 512/13). The

two flanking churches are identical basilicas with apses in their east walls. Saint George's was built in 529, Saints Cosmas and Damian's in 533. All three buildings were damaged by earthquakes. Only Saint George's continued in use in the eighth century. It was excavated in 1929.

21. **The Church of Bishop Genesius,** uncovered in 1929 to the west of the three churches described above, was erected in 611. It is a basilica with an exterior apse and a chapel on the southwest.

22. **The ''Synagogue Church,''** revealed in 1929, was built in A.D. 530/31 west of the Temenos of Artemis on a higher point. The court of the church was on the west side, and the atrium was built to the east in the third or fourth century. The remains of a synagogue were found beneath the church. Its entrance was on the east, whereas the church erected on its foundations was entered from the west. Beneath its apse was the narthex of the synagogue with a mosaic floor depicting animals entering Noah's ark. From the narthex, three doors opened onto the synagogue hall, which was divided into a nave and aisles by two rows of columns, four in each row. In the west part of the floor of the nave was an inscription recording the names of the three donors, reading: ''Peace on all Israel, *amen, amen, selah;* Phineas bar Baruch, Jose bar Samuel and J(u)dan bar Hezekiah.'' The eastern floor dates to the fourth or fifth century. The westerly floor was sixth century in style.

23. **The Church of the Prophets, Apostles, and Martyrs** was built in the north of the city, east of the Chrysorhoas, and dedicated in A.D. 464/65. It was examined, incompletely, in 1929. The church is unusual in its cruciform plan. Each of its arms possesses a nave and aisles, and the angles of the cross are occupied by rooms. The central area of the cross was supported at the corners by tall Corinthian columns. The chancel is placed in the apse and nave of the eastern arm. The plan has parallels at Salona and Ephesus.   S. APPLEBAUM

BIBLIOGRAPHY

C. H. Kraeling, ed., *Gerasa, City of the Decapolis*, New Haven, 1938 • N. Glueck, *BASOR* 75 (1939), 22–30 • C. H. Kraeling, *BASOR* 83 (1941), 7–14 • A. Detweiler, *BASOR* 87 (1942), 10–17 • J. Iliffe, *QDAP* 11 (1944), 1–26 • G. L. Harding, *PEQ* (1949), 12–20 • D. Kirkbride, *Bull. Arch. Institute London* 1 (1958), 9–20; idem, *ADAJ* 4–5 (1960), 123–27 • M. Avi-Yonah, *The Holy Land*, Grand Rapids, Michigan, 1966, index.

GEZER

IDENTIFICATION. Ancient Gezer has been located at Tell Jezer (or Tell el-Jazari), a 30-acre mound 8 kilometers (5 miles) south–southeast of Ramleh (map reference 14251407), since C. Clermont-Ganneau first made the identification in 1871. Just two years later, he discovered the first of the famous boundary inscriptions in the vicinity of the mound, reading ''the boundary of Gezer'' in an archaizing Hebrew script of the Herodian period, confirming the identification (see below). Gezer is situated on the last of the foothills of the Judean Range, where it slopes down to meet the northern Shephelah. Although it lies only about 225 meters above sea level, the hilltop is nearly cut off from the surrounding terrain and thus commands almost a 360-degree view, with an especially impressive sweep across the coastal plain from beyond Ashdod to the southwest nearly to the Carmel promontory. (It is possible that the name ''Gezer'' derives from the Semitic root גזר ''to cut, divide''). In fact, Gezer guards one of the most important crossroads in the country, where the trunk road leading to Jerusalem and sites in the hills branches off from the *via maris* at the approach of the Valley of Aijalon. In addition to its strategic location, Gezer possesses strong springs just at the base of the mound and fertile fields in the nearby valleys. It is no wonder that it was occupied almost continuously from the Late Chalcolithic period through to the Roman-Byzantine period, or that in the Bronze Age it had already become one of the dozen or so most important sites in Palestine.

HISTORY

It is in Egyptian sources that the references to Gezer are the most numerous and important. The earliest mention of the site is in an inscription of Thutmose III (about 1490–1436 B.C.) on the walls of the great Temple of Amon at Karnak, where a scene commemorating this pharaoh's victories on his first campaign to Asia in 1468 B.C. portrays bound captives from Gezer. A short inscription of Thutmose IV (about 1410–1402 B.C.) in his mortuary temple at Thebes makes reference to Hurrian captives from a city, the name of which is broken but is almost certainly Gezer. During the tumultuous Amarna period in the fourteenth century B.C., Gezer figures prominently among Palestinian city-states under nominal Egyptian rule. In the corpus of the el-Amarna letters are ten letters from three different kings of Gezer. Perhaps the best-known Egyptian reference to Gezer is that of Merneptah (about 1220 B.C.) in his "Israel" stele, where it is claimed that Israel has been destroyed and Gezer seized. The conquest of Gezer is also celebrated in another inscription of this pharaoh, found at Amada.

Literary references from Mesopotamia are understandably scarce, since the dominant influence in the earlier periods came from the other direction. A relief of Tiglath-pileser III (about 745–728 B.C.), found on the walls of his palace at Nimrud, depicts the siege and capture of a city called *Ga-az-ru*. This is undoubtedly Gezer in Palestine, and the background would be the campaign of the Assyrian monarch in Philistia in 734–733 B.C.

References to Gezer in the Bible itself are not as numerous as one might expect. However, that simply reflects the reality that, on the one hand, Gezer had already passed the peak of its power by the Iron Age and that, on the other hand, it lay on the periphery of Israel's effective control until rather late in the biblical period. In the period of the Conquest it is recorded that the Israelites under Joshua met a coalition of Canaanite kings near Gezer in the famous Battle of Makkedah, in the Valley of Aijalon. Although Horam the King of Gezer was killed, the text does not say specifically that Gezer itself was captured (Joshua 10:33, 12:12). Later, according to several passages, "Gezer and its pasture lands" was allotted to the tribe of Joseph (or "Ephraim," cf. Joshua 16:3, 10; Judges 1:29; I Chronicles 6:67, 7:28). However, the footnote that the Israelites "did not drive out the Canaanites, who dwelt in Gezer" makes it clear that the Israelite claim was more imaginary than real. Gezer was also set aside as a Levitical city (Joshua 21:21), but again it is unlikely that it was actually settled by Israelites. The same ambiguity is reflected in several references to David's campaigns against the Philistines, where Gezer is usually regarded as in the buffer-zone between Philistia and Israel, although it is implied that it was actually the farthest outpost of Philistine influence (II Samuel 5:25; I Chronicles 14:16, 20:4). The most significant biblical reference to Gezer — and now

Plan of excavations.

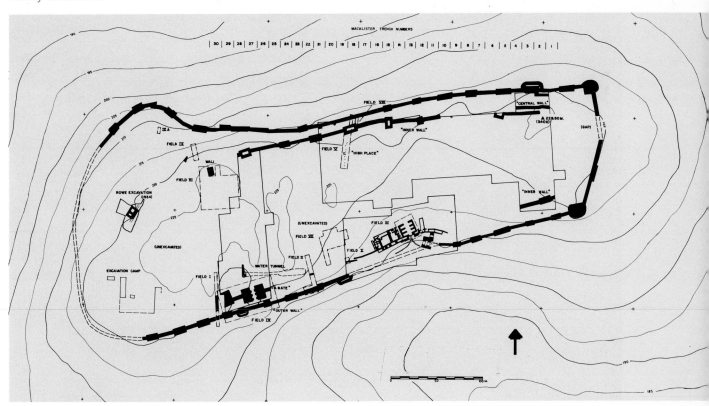

Both pages, counterclockwise: Four middle stelae (out of row of ten) and "basin" on "high place"; MBA II-C. Macalister's "South Gate"; MBA II-C, ca. 1650–1600 B.C., as re-excavated by Hebrew Union College; note mudbrick superstructure. Macalister's "Inner Wall," ca. 1600 B.C.; note glacis, or plastered ramp, in section at left. Macalister's "Outer Wall" dating to the LBA and apparently re-used throughout IA and Hasmonaean period. Row of stelae on "high place"; MBA II-C.

confirmed as the most reliable historically — is I Kings 9:15–17, where it is recorded that the city was finally ceded to Solomon when the pharaoh presented it as a dowry in giving his daughter to the Israelite king in marriage. Thereafter, Solomon fortified Gezer, along with Jerusalem, Megiddo, and Hazor.

There are no further references until post-biblical literature, when Gezer appears to have played a rather significant role in the Maccabean Wars. The Seleucid general Bacchides fortified Gezer (by then known as Gazara) along with a number of other Judean cities (I Maccabees 9:52). In 142 B.C., Simon Maccabaeus besieged Gezer and took it, after which he refortified it and then built himself a residence there (*ibid.* 13:43–48). His son, John Hyrcanus, made his headquarters at Gezer when he became commander of the Jewish armies the next year (*ibid.* 13:53).

LITERARY REMAINS FROM GEZER

Gezer has produced only a few inscriptions, although relatively speaking it is one of the richer

sites in Palestine for epigraphic materials. The earliest is a potsherd reading *klb* (or "Caleb") in pictographic characters of the Proto-Sinaitic script and belonging in all probability to the seventeenth–sixteenth centuries B.C. A fragment of a cuneiform tablet was dated by R. A. S. Macalister to the Assyrian period, but has been shown by W. F. Albright to belong to the Amarna Age. It mentions a nearby site of "Kiddimu" (Tell Ras Abu Hamid?), where apparently an Egyptian commander is demanding that the King of Gezer present himself. The well-known Gezer Calendar from the Solomonic era, one of the earliest Hebrew inscriptions, is a schoolboy's exercise tablet, giving a mnemonic ditty for the seasons of the agricultural year. Two cuneiform tablets found in the early excavations belong to the period of the Assyrian conquest and dismemberment of Israel. These tablets are legal contracts from the mid-seventh century B.C. and bear Hebrew and numerous Assyrian names. Slightly later in date are several royal stamped jar handles from these excavations, belonging possibly to the

*From cave 10A. Below: Pottery sarcophagus in situ;
LBA I. Bottom: Plan of LBA I burial level. Opposite
page: One of the latest burials in the passageway;
ca. 1400 B.C.*

reign of Josiah (about 640–609 B.C.) when Gezer had become part of the Kingdom of Judah. A Greek graffito in the vicinity of the re-used Solomonic city gate, if properly deciphered, reflects the disgust of one citizen, Pamphras, at the Maccabean take-over, for it reads something like "To blazes with Simon's palace!" The boundary inscriptions, from the last period in Gezer's history in the Roman era, of which eight are now known, have already been mentioned.

EXCAVATIONS

R. A. S. Macalister, 1902-09. The first excavations at Gezer were conducted between 1902 and 1909 by R. A. S. Macalister for the Palestine Exploration Fund, and the findings were published in three substantial volumes in 1912 as *The Excavation of Gezer*. These excavations were the largest yet undertaken by the fund or anyone else in Palestine, not surpassed in size or importance until the Germans began at Jericho and the Americans at Samaria in 1908. At Gezer, Macalister worked alone except for an Egyptian foreman, employing up to two hundred

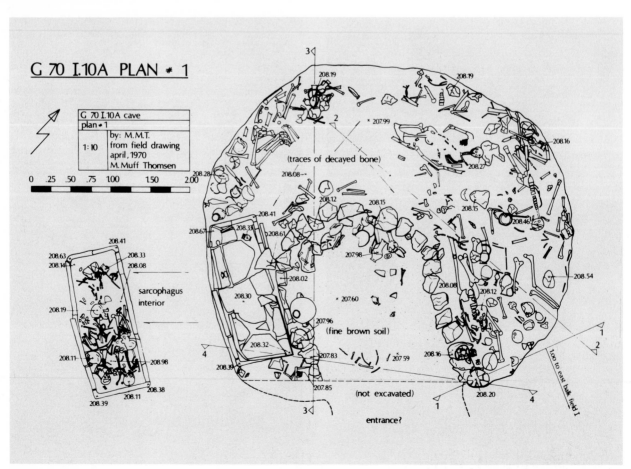

laborers from the village of Abu Shusheh and working year round in the field, interrupted only by occasional winter storms, outbreaks of cholera, and troubles with his Turkish excavation permit or his Arab workmen.

Macalister began at the eastern end of the mound with a series of trenches, each about 10 meters wide, running the entire width of the mound. He dug each trench down to bedrock (as deep as 13 meters in some places). Then, proceeding to the next trench, he dumped the debris into the trench he had just completed, intending, as he put it, "to turn over the whole mound." Although his notion of stratification was primitive — even judged by the standards of the day — he was able to recognize as many as nine strata (cf. the twenty-six strata of the Hebrew Union College excavations). His failure to provide trained staff meant that he inevitably lost control of the mass of excavated material and he was unable to correlate his strata as he moved from one trench to the next.

Consequently, in the Preface to the final publica-tion he admitted that he had been forced to give up his original intention "to follow the natural division of the remains into epochs and culture levels," since "the complexity of the stratification of the mound itself made it difficult to carry through the work of description in the form proposed." Thus, he combined his architectural remains into six large plans in Volume III, each of which purports to represent a coherent stratum but is actually a composite of elements several centuries apart, thus making neither architectural nor stratigraphic sense. (Even basic surveying was neglected. No elevations appear on the plans, there are errors and inconsistencies of 10 meters or more when plans are compared, and even compass bearings are off.) The pottery was grouped according to seven general periods, some covering as much as eight hundred years: Pre-Semitic, First through Fourth Semitic, Hellenistic, and Roman-Byzantine. The remaining material was published by categories rather than by chronological periods — all the burials together, all the domestic architecture, all the cult objects,

all the metal and lithic objects — and scarcely a single item can be related to the general strata, let alone to specific buildings. As Macalister rationalized it, "The exact spot in the mound where any ordinary object chanced to lie is not generally of great importance." The tragedy of Macalister's excavation at Gezer was that a mass of rich material was torn from context and published in such a way as to make it virtually useless for reconstructing the history of the site.

A. Rowe, 1934. What was to have been the beginning of a second series of excavations was sponsored at Gezer by the Palestine Exploration Fund in the summer of 1934 under the direction of A. Rowe. He opened an area just west of the acropolis, which both Macalister and he were unable to touch because of the Muslim cemetery and the shrine of the *weli*. However, bedrock was reached in a short time, and the excavations were abandoned. The only significant exposure, apart from an Early Bronze Age cave, was a Middle Bronze Age tower which probably belongs to the Inner Wall (see below).

Hebrew Union College, 1964-73. G. E. Wright had attempted a history of Gezer in 1937, but he was forced by the inadequacy of the published material to confine himself to an article on the earliest period. In 1964, Wright initiated a new ten-year project at Gezer, sponsored by the Hebrew Union College Biblical and Archaeological School (later the Nelson Glueck School of Biblical Archaeology) in Jerusalem and supported chiefly by grants from the Smithsonian Institution in Washington, with some assistance from the Harvard Semitic Museum. The project was directed in 1964–65 by Wright (thereafter, he was Adviser), from 1966 through 1971 by W. G. Dever, and in 1972–73 by J. D. Seger. H. D. Lance was Associate Director, and Glueck was Adviser from 1964 through 1971. A professional staff of thirty was joined each season by some one hundred student volunteers.

STRATIGRAPHY

The following brief reconstruction uses the latest excavations as a framework, but it incorporates the earlier excavations as well as the literary sources where these can be utilized.

THE CHALCOLITHIC PERIOD

The earliest occupation in stratum XXVI is represented by Macalister's Cream Ware, which was found in crevices in the bedrock and was evidently deposited by primitive camp sites. More of the material was recovered in the latest excavations in phase 14 of field I, again from hearths and thin deposits on the surface of the bedrock. Both the ceramic and the lithic industries are similar to those of the Ghassul-Beersheba horizon and are to be dated toward the end of the Chalcolithic period, about the thirty-third century B.C.

THE EARLY BRONZE AGE

The beginning of the Early Bronze Age is fairly well represented, although domestic occupation was not substantial, and there is no evidence that the site was fortified at this time. (Macalister's Central Wall. attributed to his First Semitic period, is almost certainly nothing more than an element of the complex Middle Bronze Age ramparts.) Most of the Early Bronze Age material published by Macalister (mixed in his Pre-Semitic and First Semitic periods) came from the Troglodyte Dwellings — caves in bedrock which were initially used for habitation and storage and were later re-used as burial places. The recent excavations cleared another one of these enlarged and modified caves in the rock, from which came a variety of store jars filled with grain, some stone vessels, and several grindstones and other implements. The grain yielded a Carbon-14 date of 3040 ± 110 B.C., which tends to confirm the relative placement of this occupational phase at Gezer and elsewhere (De Vaux's Early Bronze I-A, Wright's Early Bronze I-B, Kenyon's Proto-Urban A–B) immediately following Late Chalcolithic but preceding the development of the earliest fortifications. In addition to the cave-dwellings and burials, a few straggling house walls of phase 13 in field I and slight remains just above bedrock in fields V and VI give evidence of the beginnings of more substantial settlement, which we may designate stratum XXV (about 3200–2950 B.C.).

The Early Bronze Age II (about 2950–2600 B.C.) is represented by rather meager evidence, principally from phases 12–11 in field I and phase 4 in field V, with their unimpressive domestic constructions. There are at least two building periods (strata XXIV–XXIII), and if most of the elements of the town plan of Macalister's First Semitic belong here, as seems likely, occupation may well have spread over most of the mound. However, the pottery and small objects of this period from the latest excavations were scant and rather poor, as they were from Macalister's excavations. (Most of the pottery from his First Semitic seems to have been Early Bronze Age I, even allowing for his tendency to publish only whole vessels from the tombs, which are indeed early, cf. above.) Further evidence for the relative obscurity of Gezer in the Early Bronze Age II is the fact that among the large, strategically located sites known from this period, it is the only one which remained unfortified (cf. the massive city walls at Tell el-Far'a, Megiddo, Taanach, Ai, Jericho, Arad, etc.).

Whether the site was destroyed or simply deserted, occupation seems to have come to an end by Early Bronze Age III-A at the latest, for apart from one doubtful tomb placed by Wright in Early Bronze Age III (cave 16-I) and a single Khirbet Kerak sherd, there is no clear Early Bronze Age III material from either the early or the more recent excavations. The gap in occupation continues throughout Early Bronze Age IV and Middle Bronze Age I and into Middle Bronze Age II-A, although one may note a few sherds from Macalister's publication (cf., for instance, tomb 27-I, last used in Middle Bronze Age I, and possibly also the original cutting of tomb 1). In field I, an erosion layer of rubble and occupational debris containing pottery and small objects was washed down the slope from higher on the mound, accumulating to a depth of some 1.5 meters during this gap (stratum XXII, about the twenty-sixth–nineteenth centuries B.C.).

THE MIDDLE BRONZE AGE

It was in the Middle Bronze Age II that Gezer enjoyed its greatest expansion and prosperity, with the main developments already underway by the end of Middle Bronze Age II-A (stratum XXI, about 1800 B.C.). Although the city was not yet fortified, fairly elaborate domestic installations were found in phase 9-C of field VI on the acropolis. Houses and courtyards were well planned and constructed, with fine plaster floors. Rock-hewn cisterns were filled by runoff water carried from catchment areas by plastered and stone-capped drains. A partly subterranean granary was extremely well built, with substantial stone foundations, a mud-brick superstructure, and walls and floors sealed against moisture and rodents by a coat of plaster up to 15 centimeters thick. The pottery of stratum XXI was transitional Middle Bronze Age II-A to early Middle Bronze Age II-B. The finer vessels, especially from three infant burials, were of delicate eggshell ware turned on a fast wheel, either painted or red-slipped and beautifully burnished. These finds complemented those of Macalister from several tombs, including a cist tomb with typical Middle Bronze Age II-A pottery (tomb 30-III). A Twelfth-Dynasty statuette bearing the name "Heqab" probably also belongs to this (or the succeeding) period.

Gezer reached the zenith of its power in the Middle Bronze Age III-B–C period. To this phase (strata XIX–XVIII) belong the first fortifications of the city. Macalister traced the Inner Wall for nearly 400 meters, one third of the way around the mound. Eight rectangular towers were located by Macalister and one by Rowe in 1934, so the wall may have had twenty-five or more such towers. The only known gate is Macalister's South Gate, a typical three-entryway Middle Bronze Age city gate, re-excavated in the modern excavations as field IV. On the west, it is flanked by tower 5017, 15.6 meters in width and the largest single-phase defense work known in the country.

The wall itself was constructed of large, roughly dressed stones, some of them almost cyclopean, with a mud-brick superstructure. It averaged 4 meters in width and is still preserved as much as 4.5 meters in height. It was set into a deep foundation trench reaching almost down to bedrock. It was this trench, when excavated in field I of the recent excavations, that provided a date for the construction of the wall. Macalister had assigned the Inner Wall to his First Semitic period (Early Bronze Age I–II), but renewed investigation with modern methods proved that the foundation trench was cut from phase 9 surfaces and that the latest pottery in the trench was contemporary. Two clear phases, both in Middle Bronze Age II-C, have been discerned in the connector wall between tower 5017 and the South Gate, as well as in the gate itself. Thus the date of the initial construction must be placed early in the Middle Bronze Age II-C, in the mid-seventeenth century B.C. (somewhat earlier than the date of about 1600 B.C. suggested in preliminary reports). The suggestion of several rather complex phases of fortification within the Middle Bronze Age II-C is supported by the observation that tower 5017 and the first connector wall were certainly free standing for a short while before the glacis (and the second connector wall) was added in the last phase. The latter was made up of alternating, closely packed fills of debris

Below, left: Kohl tube of limestone with monkey figures, from cave 10A. Right: Egyptian glass vessel from cave 10A. Bottom: Solomonic gate, looking south-southeast; note large drain running through street.

from the mound and freshly quarried chalk, topped with a thick plaster coating. It sloped up for about 10 meters at an angle of 30 degrees, leveling off in places to form a horizontal platform some 3–4 meters wide before abutting the Inner Wall. Its height above ground level was about 5 meters.

Another piece of monumental architecture belonging to this period (strata XIX–XVIII) is the famous High Place discovered by Macalister. It consists of a row of ten monoliths, some over 3 meters high, erected in a north–south line just inside the Inner Wall in the north-central area of the mound. To the west of the alignment is a large stone block, perhaps a basin or a socket for a now-missing monolith. The surface over the area is plastered and is surrounded by a low stone curb wall. Macalister dated the main installation to his Second Semitic period (Middle Bronze–Late Bronze Ages) and compared it with later biblical "high places," interpreting the stelae as typical Canaanite 'asherôth and construing burial jars in the vicinity (now known

Below: Philistine house; plan. Bottom, left: Looking through Solomonic city gate; IA and Hellenistic streets in section in foreground and Solomonic ashlar masonry at threshold at rear. Right: Solomonic gate, plan.

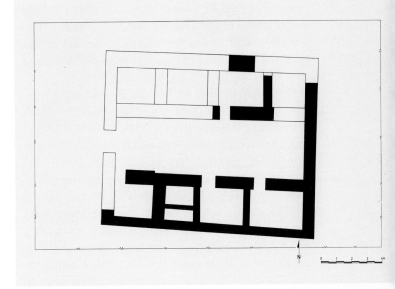

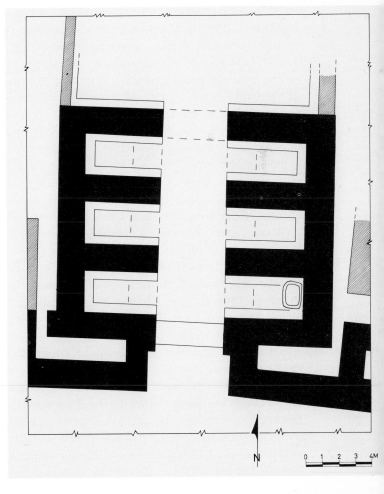

to be earlier) as evidence for child sacrifice. While most of Macalister's theories must now be discarded as fanciful, renewed investigation of the High Place in 1968 (field V) demonstrated that it was constructed in Middle Bronze Age II-C, with a possible re-use phase in the Late Bronze Age. A cultic interpretation still seems best, perhaps in connection with the covenant renewal ceremony of a tribal or city-state league (cf. Exodus 24:1–11).

Domestic structures of Middle Bronze Age II-B–C (strata XIX–XVIII) show continuity with the Middle Bronze Age II-A levels, especially in field VI, where an unbroken sequence extends from Middle Bronze Age II-A/B through late Middle Bronze Age II-C. (Elsewhere there may be a brief gap in mid-Middle Bronze Age II-B.) There is little to distinguish this occupation anywhere, except for a series of infant jar burials and some unusual ovens situated in courtyards. These ovens are made of the necks and shoulders of large store jars set upside down into the floors flush with the surface. However, the prosperity and artistic development of the period is attested to by several rich tombs of Middle Bronze Age II-C found by Macalister, especially tomb 28-II with its alabasters, scarabs, and gold jewelry.

The Middle Bronze Age II strata were brought to an end by a destruction which left a meter or more of burned bricks in every field investigated. Along the inner face of the city wall, just to the west of the South Gate, was found a row of hovels and storerooms containing quantities of grain-filled store jars and other vessels, crushed under an accumulation of burned beams, ashes, fallen mud bricks, and collapse from the wall. Imported Monochrome, local Bichrome, and Chocolate wares, as well as other transitional Middle Bronze–Late Bronze Age pottery, all suggest a date as late as possible for this destruction. Provisionally, it may be correlated with the first campaign of Thutmose III in about 1468 B.C., which is when this pharaoh claims to have destroyed Gezer (see above).

THE LATE BRONZE AGE

Apart from a few hints in Macalister's material, the Late Bronze Age I-A (early fifteenth century B.C.) is scarcely represented, so a partial desertion may have taken place following the Thutmose III destruction. Stratum VII of Late Bronze Age I-B (late fifteenth century B.C.) is also poorly known, except for cave I.10A of field I, cut into the bedrock outside the Inner Wall. Most of the several dozen

burials deposited in the lower level of this cave during a generation or so show signs of advanced arthritis, probably from stoop labor, which may be an indication of the hardships of life during this period. However, imported Cypriot pottery, Egyptian glass, alabaster and ivory vessels, and a unique terra-cotta sarcophagus of Mycenaean inspiration, all indicate international trade, even in this era. It is clear that the Inner Wall was for the most part too badly damaged to be repaired, and it seems equally clear that construction of the Outer Wall that replaced it would not have been undertaken in this period of decline. Thus, Gezer was essentially unfortified (or at least undefended) for a brief period in the mid–late fifteenth century B.C. The raid of Thutmose IV (see above) may have occurred at this time.

A renascence got underway with the beginning of Late Bronze Age II-A (about fourteenth century B.C.), undoubtedly associated with the well-known el-Amarna period, when Palestine was under Egyptian domination. Stratum XVI, which should provide the context for the several el-Amarna letters from Gezer (see above), was exposed extensively only in field VI (phase 7), where unfortunately it had been almost entirely disturbed by later pits. There are slight remains of phase 6 in field I, and cave I.10A contains a few burials of this period in the upper level, above a silt deposit. Elements of the plan of Macalister's Third Semitic period probably belong here (particularly the large palace-like complex of his stratum III-a, built over the Inner Wall in the north end of trenches 27–28). In field VI, mere hints were preserved of what must once have been an impressive material culture. House walls were as much as 2 meters in width and exceptionally well constructed. Thick plaster surfaces ran across floors and outdoor courtyards and sealed stone-capped drains. Among the small objects were quantities of Egyptian imports, especially fragments of el-Amarna glass, glass beads, faience pendants, scarabs, fragments of gold foil, and a statuette base bearing the name of "Sobek-nefru-ankh" or the like. Local objects included a clay crucible for copper smelting and a perfectly preserved bronze serpent about 15 centimeters long. (Cf. also illustrations on pages 433 and 436 for burials and small objects of Late Bronze Age II found by Macalister.)

To this period, in all likelihood, belongs the construction and first-phase use of the Outer Wall, which Macalister traced for some 1,100 meters, or four-fifths of the way around the perimeter of the mound (attributed to his Third Semitic period or roughly our Late Bronze Age). It supplanted the ruined Middle Bronze Age Inner Wall, following a line farther down the slopes and enclosing perhaps one fourth more area, particularly on the northwest (where the lower city has never been investigated). In most places, the wall was set into a deep trench reaching to bedrock and destroying the earlier glacis. It averaged 4 meters in width and is still preserved as much as 4.5 meters high. A rather crude glacis was added to the exterior. (See illustrations on pages 431 and 440. The towers and bastions belong to later phases, as shown below.) The gateway has not been located, but it almost certainly lies below the Solomonic Gate on the south slopes (field III). If our date is correct, this city wall is unique in being the country's only defense system *originally* constructed in the Late Bronze Age and not re-used from an earlier period.

It has been suggested that the Water Tunnel may have been dug in this period, but the shaft was cut off from its context by Macalister and cannot now be dated. (It may belong instead, like those at Hazor, Megiddo, and Gibeon, to the Iron Age II.) A keyhole-shaped flight of steps and a round shaft about 7 meters deep led to a sloping tunnel some 45 meters long, reaching ground water in an enlarged cavern at the end of the tunnel.

The Late Bronze Age II-B (about thirteenth century B.C.) may have witnessed something of a decline at Gezer, as elsewhere in the post-Amarna age. No large-scale destruction had taken place at the end of stratum XVI, but some disturbance may be evident in the fact that in both fields I and VI almost no element of the architecture survived to be re-used in stratum XV, and the rather unimpressive buildings which succeeded were built on a new orientation. The ceramic repertoire of stratum XV was limited, with degenerate platter bowls, carinated bowls, kraters, juglets, and cooking pots all marking the end of a long tradition going back to the Middle Bronze Age. Imported wares virtually ceased, and among the local wares only the painted pottery showed any vitality. Kraters were decorated with crude stick figures or occasionally with geometric designs, and the series of palm-and-zigzag-panel bowls begins here (especially in the

lamp-and-bowl deposits — cf. below).

The end of stratum XV presents a problem. In field II, domestic occupation (phase 13) was interrupted by a destruction that left quantities of smashed pottery and other objects lying about a heavily burned courtyard. This may have been a localized destruction, however, for in field I, phase 4 with Philistine pottery succeeds phase 5 after a brief, distinct gap, but there are no signs of destruction. The clearest evidence was obtained from field VI, where an interlude *preceding* the introduction of Philistine pottery was marked by extensive digging of pits for stone robbing and disposal of refuse (the post-6 phase), although there were virtually no other signs of human activity. Taken together, the evidence suggests a partial hiatus in occupation at the very end of the thirteenth and the beginning of the twelfth century B.C., which we may designate stratum XIV, perhaps a post-destruction period. It would be tempting to relate this to the destruction claimed by Pharaoh Merneptah, about 1220 B.C. (see above; cf. also among Macalister's finds, a pectoral bearing the cartouche of Merneptah). That would explain the curious fact that nowhere did the excavations encounter a real destruction accompanying the arrival of the Philistines, or Sea Peoples, in the early twelfth century B.C. The site may have already been partially destroyed and deserted. An alternative would be to attribute the disturbance to an Israelite destruction and brief occupation, but the literary tradition (see above) is explicit that Gezer was not taken in the conquest.

THE IRON AGE

1. **The Philistine Period.** The Philistine period at Gezer is especially well attested, with strata XIII–XI all belonging to this horizon. On the acropolis, phase 5, with its several sub-phases, is characteristic of the energetic but stormy cultural history of the era. Although there is continuity in basic architectural elements, and certainly in the typical painted pottery, no less than three major destructions are evident. In the first, sometime in the early twelfth century B.C., a large public granary was destroyed and then rebuilt (phase 5-E–D). After the second destruction in the mid-twelfth century B.C., it was abandoned, and the adjacent threshing floor was converted into an area of fine private houses. Two courtyard houses on the upper terrace have been excavated. Both were destroyed by fire toward the end of the twelfth century B.C., then rebuilt,

GEZER

destroyed again, and finally rebuilt very poorly before being abandoned (phase 5-C–A). Elsewhere, in fields I and II, two or three Philistine phases are also evident, though with less dramatic demarcations. Macalister's tombs 9 Upper, 58 Upper, and 59 Upper may all be ascribed to this period.

The pottery of this horizon, particularly in the twelfth century B.C., is a mixture of local traditions of degenerate Late Bronze Age, plus the sudden appearance of the characteristic Philistine Bichrome wares. Among the former are the lamp-and-bowl deposits found under the floors of houses and near the foundation of houses in both Macalister's and the latest excavations (from stratum XV through XII), in which one of the bowls is often of the palm-and-zigzag-panel design known from earlier levels at Gezer and from Fosse Temple III at Lachish. The distinctively Philistine painted wares are relatively scarce, and they decline in both number and quality toward the end of the period.

In both fields II and VI, two ephemeral post-Philistine/pre-Solomonic phases were discerned, strata X–IX. In particular, these phases were marked by a distinctive pottery which was no longer painted but was merely treated with an unburnished, thin red slip, especially on small bowls. The architecture succeeded that of the Philistine strata but was much poorer. Everywhere they were investigated, these levels came to an end in a violent destruction, which may be correlated with the campaigns of the Egyptian pharaoh who according to I Kings 9:15–17 had "taken Gezer and burnt it with fire" before ceding it to Solomon, probably around 950 B.C. (cf. above). (It has been suggested that this pharaoh was Siamun, of the ill-fated Twenty-First Dynasty, but this is uncertain on present evidence.)

2. **The Israelite Period.** The first Israelite level is stratum VIII, to which belongs Macalister's Maccabean Castle. This structure, only partially excavated, was first recognized by Y. Yadin as a typical Solomonic four-entryway city gate, almost identical to those previously published from Megiddo and Hazor. The recent excavations in field III have fully confirmed the date and have filled in many details concerning the plan and construction. The gate was exceptionally well built, with foundations in

Field I, during 1965 campaign. Roman wall in foreground and LBA walls in background.

the guardrooms going some 2 meters below the surface and with fine ashlar masonry at the jambs. Plastered benches ran around the three walls of each of the inner chambers, a feature considered so essential that each time floor levels were raised these benches were also raised and replastered. Roofs over these inner chambers are indicated by a plastered downspout drain at the rear corner of the gate structure. Shortly after its construction about the mid-tenth century B.C. (phase 6), the gate was altered by the raising of the street level and the addition of a large drain, over a meter wide, running down the middle of the street and under the threshold (phase 5).

The casemate wall connected with the gate has been investigated in field II, and it is also Solomonic in date. In all probability, the towers of ashlar masonry, which Macalister demonstrated were an addition to the Outer Wall, are of this period. If so, this would mean that Solomon simply repaired and re-used the Late Bronze Age fortifications wherever possible, adding his own distinctive type of city wall and gateway only in the area where we conjecture that the ruined Late Bronze Age gate had been situated.

The domestic architecture of stratum VIII was unimpressive, indicating perhaps that Gezer under Solomonic control was little more than a token administrative center. In field VI, large ashlars identical to those in the gate were found in secondary usage in a citadel wall of about the Assyrian period — virtually all that survives here of the post-Philistine period — so it is possible that there was a Solomonic fortress or palace on the acropolis. No tombs were found in the recent excavations, but tombs 84–85 Middle, 96, and 138 of Macalister's excavations have good late tenth-century material. The pottery is typical of the period, with the red-slipped wares of the previous period now hand burnished. Among the small objects, one may note a small limestone incense altar inscribed with a stick figure who resembles the Canaanite storm god Ba'al, with an uplifted arm grasping a bundle of lightning bolts.

A destruction, particularly heavy in the vicinity of the gateway, brought stratum VIII to an end in the late tenth century B.C. This was probably the work of Shishak about 924 B.C., as part of his well-known raid in Palestine.

Macalister's arbitrary selection and publication of

441

Below: Philistine stirrup jug. Bottom: Gezer calendar; tenth century B.C. Opposite page: One of the boundary inscriptions found south and southeast of the mound; top line: "The boundary of Gezer," bottom line: "Alkios"; end first/beginning second century A.D.

the material of the Iron Age II (mixed in his Fourth Semitic period) had led most scholars, including Albright, to assume that the site was virtually abandoned in the ninth–seventh centuries B.C. However, Macalister's tombs 28, 31, 84–85 Upper, and 142 certainly belong to Iron Age II, and the "gap" has been closed by strata VII–V of the recent excavations. Nevertheless, it is evident that occupation was rather sparse, and the site seems to have declined in importance following the Shishak destruction (cf. above on the infrequent literary references). The total accumulation during strata VII–V was no more than 1–1.5 meters, and even that has been almost completely eroded in fields I and VI.

In stratum VII (ninth century B.C.), the Solomonic gate was rebuilt as a three-entryway gate, identical to that of Megiddo IV-A. This gate survived until stratum VI was destroyed, probably by Tiglath-pileser III in the Assyrian campaigns of 734/33 B.C. (see above). Domestic levels were also brought to an end, these in a conflagration that has left dramatic evidence in field II.

Stratum V (late eighth–seventh century B.C.) was of little importance, except that it provides a context for Macalister's Neo-Assyrian tablets and the royal stamped jar handles (see above). Although little evidence survives, the gate apparently was converted at this time into a two-entryway gate like that of Megiddo III. Shortly after, it was destroyed so badly — probably in the Babylonian invasion of 587/86 B.C. — that it was never rebuilt as a chambered gate. In fields II and VIII, stratum V domestic levels were found badly destroyed. In the casemate of the city wall in field II, there was found a quantity of smashed pottery, some of the sherds marked by firebrands, and a spill of calcined limestone. In field VII, a great collapse of burned mud brick had fallen into a storeroom, sealing in a row of early sixth century B.C. store jars leaning against a wall.

THE PERSIAN, HELLENISTIC, AND ROMAN PERIODS

There is a gap following the end of stratum V, which stratum IV of the Persian period (fifth–fourth centuries B.C.) only partially fills. As J. Iliffe has shown, Macalister's Philistine Tombs, with their rich deposits of silver vessels, belong here. The recent excavations produced very scant material, although typical Persian pottery was found in small quantities in stratum IV. Otherwise, only a few pits and some flimsy walls of the period survive. However, two phases (3-A–B in field II) can be discerned.

Strata III–II are Hellenistic, spanning the third and nearly all of the second centuries B.C. but representing for the most part the Maccabean era, as the literary sources lead one to expect (see above). From the Ptolemaic period, to which stratum III seems to belong, there is little material from the recent excavations, although Macalister's *Yehud* and *Yerushalayim* stamp impressions attest to occupation. Somewhat later, the gate in field III was rebuilt here (phase 2, the slanting building of Macalister), perhaps by the Syrian general Bacchides. For the Hasmonaean period, a fairly extensive exposure in fields II and VII has produced several fine courtyard houses. From the ruins of the last phase came a coin of Demetrius II (about 144 B.C.). In fills beneath the floors was a coin of Antiochus VII (about 138–129 B.C.). Rhodian jar handles, lead weights, and a mass of iron tools were also found. The gate of field III was rather hastily repaired, the threshold being narrowed nearly a meter, and only parts of the interior structure re-used (Macalister's Maccabean Castle). It seems certain that the Outer Wall was retrenched and re-used, Macalister's semi-circular bastions being added around the towers at this time.

With the destruction of stratum II sometime toward the end of the second century B.C., Gezer's long history as an important city in Palestine came to a virtual end.

Stratum I belongs to about the Herodian era (late first century B.C.–first century A.D.), as shown by material from both the earlier and the more recent excavations. The site proper was virtually deserted, and most of the known material comes from Macalister's *kokhim* tombs in the vicinity. (However,

later Roman material in some of these tombs indicates continued occupation in the second–third centuries A.D.). On the mound, a large wall crowning the slope in field II appears to have been a boundary wall rather than a defense wall, and the domestic remains (phase 1) suggest little more than hovels or sheepfolds. The well-known boundary inscriptions, found in an arc some distance from the mound (see above), are further evidence that in the Herodian period Gezer was no longer an independent city but merely part of a large private estate, thinly occupied and no longer of consequence. The owner or administrator, whose Greek name "Alkios" is given on the inscriptions, may have been Jewish, but that is uncertain. Macalister's Syrian Bath probably belongs to this period.

THE BYZANTINE AND LATER PERIODS

The only later material consists of tombs excavated by Macalister, most of which are Byzantine (fourth–sixth centuries A.D.), and faint traces of occupation in the vicinity of the mound. Two coins attributed to Khosrau II (about A.D. 614–628 in Palestine) attest to the era of the Persian conquest in the seventh century A.D. Gezer was identified by Clermont-Ganneau with Mont Gisart of the Crusaders, but this identification is without supporting evidence. A few coins and some vessels of the Mameluke period in re-used Byzantine tombs are evidence of an occupation in the thirteenth century A.D. A small *weli* (or shrine of a holy man) was built on the acropolis in the sixteenth century A.D. but is now destroyed, as is the modern village of Abu Shusheh on the west slopes, which was founded in the late eighteenth or early nineteenth century. Nearby, Kibbutz Gezer perpetuates the name.

W. G. DEVER

Clermont-Ganneau, *ARP* 2, 224–75 • R.A.S. Macalister, *The Excavation of Gezer*, London, 1912, Vols. I–III • A. Rowe, *PEQ* (1935), 19–33 • G.E. Wright, *PEQ* (1937), 67–78 • W.F. Albright, *BASOR* 92 (1943), 28–30 • R. Amiran, *IEJ* 5 (1955), 24–45 • Y. Yadin, *IEJ* 8 (1958), 80–86 • J.A. Callaway, *PEQ* (1962), 104–17 • W.G. Dever, *BA* 30 (1967), 47–62 • H.D. Lance, *ibid.*, 34–47 • J.F. Ross, *ibid.*, 62–70 • W.G. Dever, *BA* 32 (1969), 71–78; *idem, Qadmoniot* 3 (1970), 57–62 (Hebrew) • W.G. Dever, H.D. Lance, G.E. Wright, *Gezer I. Preliminary Report of the 1964–66 Seasons*, Jerusalem, 1970 • W.G. Dever, H.D. Lance, et al., *BA* 34 (1971), 94–132 • J.D. Seger, *Qadmoniot* 5 (1972), 15–18 (Hebrew) • W.G. Dever, *PEQ* (1973 — in press) • W.G. Dever, H.D. Lance, R.G. Bullard, D.P. Cole, J.D. Seger, *Gezer II, Preliminary Report of the 1967–70 Seasons, Fields I and II*, Jerusalem, 1974.

GIBEAH

HISTORY. Gibeah, Gibeah of Benjamin, Gibeah of Saul was the center of the territory of the tribe of Benjamin during the period of the Judges and the royal residence during the reign of Saul. The town has several appellations in the Bible (see Judges 20:4, 14, 19; I Chronicles 11:31). In some cases, the names Geba and Gibeah are confused.

During its first period of settlement, Gibeah was apparently the capital of the Benjaminites, located on the main road leading from Judah and Jerusalem to Mount Ephraim (Judges 19:11–13). The destruction of the town by burning is the subject of a story in Judges 19–20. Saul lived there before he rose to royal rank (I Samuel 10:26, 11:4). Although the grave of his father Kish was in Zela (II Samuel 21:14), the lands of his family were probably near Gibeah. The genealogy of Saul, as preserved in I Chronicles 8:29 ff., speaks of Gibeon as the place of origin of Saul's family. This may be true, but we know that after the victory of Saul and Jonathan over the Philistines, Gibeah became the king's residence. It was then renamed Gibeah of Saul (I Samuel 15:34 ff.).

One of David's warriors came from this town: "Ittai the son of Ribai out of Gibeah of the children of Benjamin" (II Samuel 23:29; I Chronicles 11:31). According to I Chronicles 12:3, Shemaah of Gibeah was among those who came to David in Ziklag from among Saul's kinsmen. Michaiah, the daughter of Uriel, who was the mother of Abijah, king of Judah, was from Gibeah (II Chronicles 13:2).

The abandonment of Gibeah is mentioned in the description of the putative route of the Assyrian's invasion from the north (Isaiah 10:29). There is little information about Gibeah from later periods. Josephus (*War* V, 51) mentions a village named Gibeah of Saul about 30 furlongs north of Jerusalem, near which Titus camped the night before he attacked Jerusalem.

THE SITE

The modern name of the ancient site of Gibeah is Tell el-Fûl, located at a height of about 840 meters near the Jerusalem–Nablus road, about 5 kilometers (3 miles) north of Jerusalem. This mound was one of the first sites excavated in Palestine. In May, 1868, C. Warren sent a group of laborers to dig trenches on the north and south sides of the mound and a small pit on the summit. These early soundings had little or no archaeological value for the subsequent excavators of the mound.

EXCAVATIONS

The American Schools of Oriental Research carried out excavations at Tell el-Fûl in 1922–23 and 1933 under the direction of W. F. Albright, and in 1964 jointly with the Pittsburgh Theological Seminary under the direction of P. Lapp, assisted by J. Kelso. Albright concentrated in two areas, the hillock on top of the mound, where an ancient fortress once stood, and the eastern edge of the mound, once occupied by an ancient village.

Lapp extended the areas previously excavated and uncovered a part of the western edge of the summit north of the fortress tower. His finds confirmed the latest stratigraphic analysis, differing only at several points with the interpretation of the earlier excavators. Five periods of occupation were uncovered:

Period I	(Pre-Fortress)	12th century B.C., ending about 1100 or a little later
Period II-A	(Fortress I)	11th century B.C.
Period II-B	(Fortress II)	late 11th century B.C.
Period III-A	(Fortress III-A)	late 8th–7th century B.C.
Period III-B	(Fortress III-B)	7th–early 6th century B.C.
Period IV-A	(Fortress IV-A)	late 6th–5th century B.C.
Period IV-B	(Fortress IV-B)	3rd–2nd century B.C.
Period V		1st century B.C.–1st century A.D.

The earliest occupation of the mound seems to have been in the Middle Bronze Age, as indicated by potsherds from this period and a mace-head. This minor settlement, from which no building remains were uncovered, antedates Period I.

It was definitely established that the Iron Age town was founded about the twelfth century B.C., presumably by the Benjaminites. Only fragmentary masonry remains of the first period were uncovered in the fortress and eastern area. This town was destroyed, probably at the hands of the Israelites, as described in Judges 19–20.

Large roughly dressed stones laid in irregular

courses characterize the construction of the first fortress. Only the southwest corner tower and parts of the adjacent casemate walls were preserved. The fortress was a rectangle with casemate walls and reinforcing towers, presumably one in each corner. Some casemates were filled with earth and stones while others were used for storage, having doorways into the fortress. A possible reconstruction of the fortress would place its length at about 52 meters, its width 35 meters, and the preserved area of the tower about 13 by 9 meters. It seems probable that Saul built fortress I, but it has been suggested by A. Alt and B. Mazar that it was one of a series of Philistine fortresses built to control the principal trade routes and was later occupied by Saul (fortress II). Our original conclusion that fortress I was built by Saul and that David may possibly have repaired it (fortress II) following the original plan must now be reconsidered. The stone masonry from the second fortress shows improved workmanship in comparison with the previous one. In the fortress proper an iron plow tip came to light. This and a similar plow tip from Beth-Shemesh can be considered as the earliest known iron objects of Israelite date.

Lapp found a 3-meter section of wall north of the fortress tower which he assigned to this period. The wall is not in line with the outer fortress wall, which is strange, but Lapp argued that since he found no casemate wall in this area, we therefore must abandon the idea that Saul's fortress had such a wall. The evidence for his argument does not seem to be sufficient to invalidate Albright's archaeological finds and interpretation.

In the third period, a completely new and much smaller fortress was erected. The new construction may be described as a frontier fortress and watch tower *(migdal)*. This fortress was built on and around the southwest tower of the original citadel of the previous period, and well-built revetments protected its outer walls. The first phase (III-A) built in the late eighth century B.C. was probably destroyed during the Assyrian attack on Jerusalem in 701 B.C. None of the pottery from the period requires a date before the seventh century B.C., but the situation under Hezekiah demanded a fortification on the summit of Gibeah. A rebuilding and occupation in the seventh century B.C. (III-B) is indicated by the handles of jars bearing the royal stamps of the kingdom of Judah (the flying-scroll

Top: Southern tower room. Bottom: Casemate wall of the seventh century B.C., built above the southwestern corner of the citadel. Plastered basins of the Hellenistic period are built inside a casemate.

type and the rosette design). Lapp assigned to this period a casemate wall uncovered along the western edge of the summit which was bonded into the north face of the tower revetment. The full extent of the wall is not known. The Chaldeans probably brought this phase to an end in 597 or 587 B.C.

After a short period during which the site was abandoned, the mound was reoccupied in the late sixth century B.C. (IV-A). The fortress was reconstructed on a plan similar to III, and a small village occupied the eastern slope of the mound.

J.B. Pritchard has pointed out (in a private communication to W.F. Albright) that the small pits hewn out of the rock under the latest (Roman) occupation are identical in shape and size with the wine pits he discovered at Gibeon. Albright confirmed the similarity between the pits at the two sites. Both date to the Persian period.

The only tombs thus far discovered at the site were found at the southern base of the mound and can be dated to this period (IV-A). A gap certainly exists between IV-A and IV-B, and nearly all of the pottery from IV-B dates to the third–second centuries B.C. Three bronze coins, all of Ptolemy Philadelphus, prove a third-century date for part of the period which extends into the second century B.C. There seems to be evidence that the mound was occupied during the Maccabean period, but more precise pottery data are needed in order to determine the number of phases in IV-B and their dates. The latest floor levels of the house complex on the eastern slope of the mound and the houses built around the side of the then ruined fortress represent the last period of occupation of the mound. This occupation belongs to the Hellenistic-Roman period, now usually called Early Roman. The village seems to have been destroyed by Titus, who encamped near it the last night before he reached Jerusalem in A.D. 70.   L. A. SINCLAIR

BIBLIOGRAPHY

Warren's excavations: Conder-Kitchener, *SWP* 3, 158–60 • V. Guerin, *Description de la Palestine, Samarie* 1, 188 ff.
Albright's excavations: W.F. Albright, "Excavations and Results of Tell el-Fûl (Gibeah of Saul)" *AASOR* 4 (1924); idem, *BASOR* 52 (1933), 6–12 • L.A. Sinclair, *AASOR* 34/35 (1960), 1–52; idem, *BA* 27 (1964), 52–64.
Lapp's excavation: P. W. Lapp, *BA* 28 (1965), 2–10; idem, *Festschrift für Kurt Galling*, Tübingen, 1970, 179–97.
General: A. Alt, *KSch* 2, 31, n. 1; 3, 259 • K. Galling, *Biblisches Reallexikon* (Handbuch zum Alten Testament), Tubingen, 1937, 193 • B. Mazar, *Enc. Miqr.* 2, 412–16 (Hebrew).

GIBEON

IDENTIFICATION. In 1838, E. Robinson visited the village of el-Jib, 9 kilometers (5.5 miles) north of Jerusalem, and identified it as the site of biblical Gibeon. This identification, which had been proposed previously by F. F. von Troilo (1666) and by R. Pococke (1738), was generally accepted until 1926, when A. Alt opposed it on the grounds of information preserved in the *Onomasticon* of Eusebius. The discovery at el-Jib (during the excavations of 1956, 1957, and 1959) of thirty-one jar handles inscribed with the name *gb'n* has now confirmed the identification of Gibeon with el-Jib.

HISTORY

Gibeon is first mentioned in the account of the Conquest in Joshua 9. The inhabitants of the enclave of the cities of Gibeon, Chephirah, Beeroth, and Kiriath-Jearim obtained by deception a covenant of peace from Joshua, and the Gibeonites, later, upon the discovery of the ruse, were sentenced to become "hewers of wood and drawers of water" (Joshua 9:21, 23, 27). When Gibeon was attacked by the Amorite king Adoni-zedek for its defection to Joshua, the Israelites responded by making a forced march from Gilgal and driving the Amorite forces down the way of Beth-Horon, miraculously aided by the hailstones and the sun standing still upon Gibeon (*ibid.* 10:1–14). The "pool of Gibeon" was the scene of the contest between the young men of Abner and those of Joab (II Samuel 2:12–17), in which twelve men from each group were thrust through with the swords of their opponents. It was at the "great stone which is in Gibeon" (*ibid.* 20:8) that Joab slew Amasa and left him in the highway wallowing in his blood. Seven sons of Saul were executed "at Gibeon on the mountain of the Lord" (*ibid.* 21:1–11). This was done in order to end a three-year famine thought to have been sent in retribution for Saul's slaying of the Gibeonites in violation of the ancient covenant. According to I Kings 3:4–5, Solomon made sacrifices and had his famous dream at the High Place in Gibeon. In II Chronicles 1:3, 13, it is asserted that the tent of the meeting was at Gibeon, and in I Chronicles 16:39 and 21:29, it is said that the tabernacle and the altar of burnt offering were there. Gibeon appears in the Karnak list as one of the cities taken by

Shishak in the second half of the tenth century B.C. The city is mentioned as the home of Hananiah, the false prophet (Jeremiah 28:1); and "the great waters that are in Gibeon" are mentioned as the place where Johanan met Ishmael and the Judeans whom he had seized at Mizpah (*ibid.* 41:12). The men of Gibeon are said to have assisted in the rebuilding of the wall of Jerusalem (Nehemiah 3:7–8). Josephus relates that Cestius pitched his camp at Gibeon on his march to Jerusalem in October of A.D. 66 (*War* II, 515–516).

EXPLORATION AND EXCAVATION

In 1889, the rock-cut tunnel leading from the spring of the village into the hill was explored and a rough plan was published by C. Schick. An Iron Age tomb was discovered in 1950 and published by A. Dajani. The first major excavation was undertaken in 1956 by an expedition sponsored by the University Museum of the University of Pennsylvania and by the Church Divinity School of the Pacific, with the cooperation of the American Schools of Oriental Research, under the direction of J.B. Pritchard. Subsequent excavations were carried out under the same direction and the sponsorship of the University Museum during the seasons of 1957, 1959, 1960, and 1962.

RESULTS OF EXCAVATIONS

1. **The Water System.** Two systems for providing the inhabitants of the walled city with spring water in time of siege were constructed during the Iron Age. The first is a cylindrical cutting into the live rock, 11.3 meters in diameter and 10.8 meters deep. A spiral staircase was cut along the north and east sides of the pool. At the bottom, the stairway continues downward into a tunnel to provide access to a water chamber which lies 13.6 meters below the floor of the pool. By means of this spiral staircase of seventy-nine steps, the inhabitants of the city had access to fresh water lying 24.4 meters below the level of the city. This construction, which had involved the quarrying and removal of approximately three thousand tons of limestone, may have been the "pool of Gibeon" mentioned in II Samuel 2:13. The second device for obtaining water in time of siege is the stepped tunnel which leads from inside

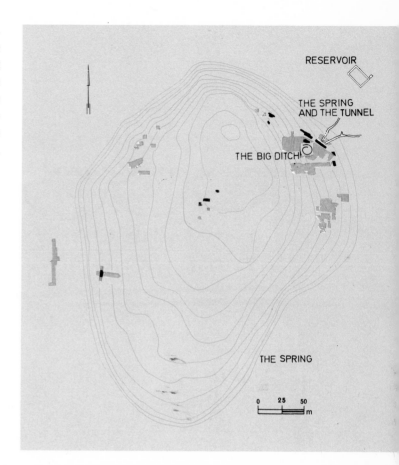

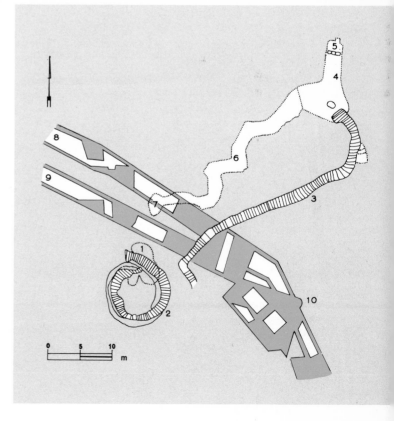

Top: General plan of the site. Bottom: The city wall and water system. 1. Water chamber. 2. Spiral staircase. 3. Stepped tunnel. 4. Room of the spring. 5. Outer entrance. 6. The "feeding" tunnel. 7. The spring. 8. Late wall. 9. Early wall. 10. Tower.

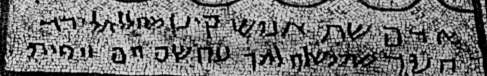

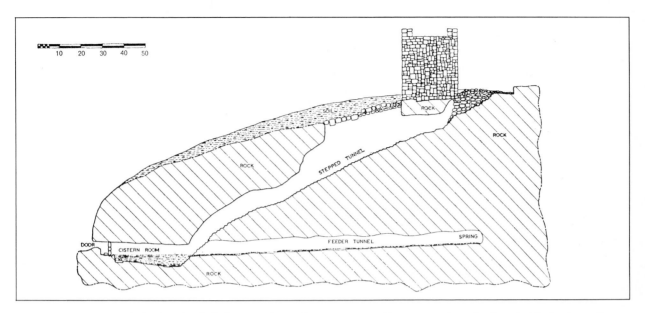

Section of eastern side of hill through which the stepped tunnel was cut to provide access to the spring from inside the city wall.

the city wall to the spring of the village. The construction of this passageway of ninety-three steps through the hill was made later in the Iron Age, perhaps at a time when the flow of water into the water chamber of the pool was inadequate.

2. **The Winery.** Gibeon was a center for the production and export of wine in the eighth and seventh centuries B.C. In the course of the excavations of 1959 and 1960, sixty-three rock-cut cellars were found for the storage of wine at a constant temperature of 18 degrees Centigrade (65 degrees Fahrenheit). The cellars are bottle shaped and average 2.2 meters in depth and 2 meters in diameter at the bottom. The opening at the top averages .67 meter in diameter. In the same area there were found wine presses carved from the rock, channels for conducting the grape juice into fermentation tanks, and settling basins. The jars in which the wine was stored within the cellars had a capacity of 9 3/4 gallons. It is estimated that the sixty-three cellars would have provided storage space for jars containing 25,000 gallons of wine.

Smaller jars with inscribed handles were used for the export of wine produced at Gibeon. The standard formula for the inscriptions on the handles is *gb'n gdr* and one of the following proper names: *ḥnnyhw nr', 'zryhw, 'mryhw*. The proper names of *dml'* and *šb'l* also appear in a slightly different

En-Gedi. Mosaic inscription in western aisle of synagogue.

formula. In the same context with the inscribed jar handles, stoppers and a funnel for filling the jars were found.

3. **Tombs.** During the 1960 season of excavations, eighteen shaft tombs which had been cut into the soft limestone of the west side of the hill were found. Although the tombs had been cut in the Middle Bronze Age I, they had been re-used in the Middle Bronze Age II and in the Late Bronze Age. In the area of the winery on the top of the mound, a Roman tomb which had been cut from more ancient wine cellars was found. This underground chamber, with steps leading down to the doorway, had eleven loculi for burials in the floor and arcosolia cut into the wall which could accommodate four more burials. A painted mural with bas-relief of stucco indicates a date of around A.D. 300 for the construction of the tomb.

SUMMARY

The site was occupied extensively in the Early Bronze Age I. The Middle Bronze Age I is represented only by pottery and other artifacts found in the tombs on the west side of the mound. In the Middle Bronze Age II, however, there was an occupation on the site and the Middle Bronze Age I tombs were re-used. Late Bronze Age pottery has thus far been found only in tombs, of which eight have been found to have been used in this period. During the early part of the Iron Age I, a massive city wall, 3.2 to 3.4 meters in width, was built

Both pages, counterclockwise: Section of the stepped tunnel leading from the city to the spring. The pool with spiral staircase leading down to the water chamber. View of the winery. Inscribed jar handle: gib'n gdr. Bowl; MBA II-B.

around the scarp of the natural hill, and the great pool was cut into the rock to provide a protected access to the water table of the hill. The city apparently reached a peak of prosperity during the Iron Age II, when buildings covered most of the enclosed area and the Gibeonites engaged in producing and trading in wine on a large scale. It was during this prosperous period that the tunnel was cut from the city to the spring. There is but scant evidence for occupation from the end of the sixth century until the beginning of the first century B.C. Evidence of considerable building, including stepped baths and water conduits, has been found from the Roman period, when the city stood without a protecting wall.   J. B. PRITCHARD

BIBLIOGRAPHY

C. Schick, *PEF QSt* (1890), 23 • Robinson, *Biblical Researches* 1, 455 • A. Alt, *PJb* 22 (1926), 11–12; 25 (1929), 14 ff.; *idem, ZDPV* 69 (1953), 1 ff. • J. Simons, *Handbook for the Study of Egyptian Topographical Lists Relating to Western Asia*, Leyden, 1937, 215 • A. Dajani, *ADAJ* 2 (1953), 66–74, pls. 9–10; 3 (1956), figs. 19–22.

Preliminary reports: *University Museum Bulletin* 21 (1957), 3–26; 22 (1958), 13–24 • *Expedition* 2 (1959), 17–25; 3 (1961), 2–9 • *BA* 19 (1956), 66–75; 23 (1960), 2–6 • *Supplement to VT* 7 (1960), 1–12.

General account of four seasons: J.B. Pritchard, *Gibeon: Where the Sun Stood Still*, Princeton, 1962.

Final publications in *Museum Monographs*, University of Pennsylvania: J.B. Pritchard, *Hebrew Inscriptions and Stamps from Gibeon*, 1959; *idem, The Water System at Gibeon*, 1961; *idem, The Bronze Age Cemetery at Gibeon; idem, Winery, Defenses and Soundings at Gibeon*, 1964.

Discussions: F. M. Cross, *BASOR* 168 (1962), 18–23 • A. Demsky, *ibid.* 202 (1971), 16–23.

GIV'ATAYIM

IDENTIFICATION. The city of Giv'atayim is situated in a range of *kurkar* hills which rise 79 meters above sea level. The top of the hill overlooks all of the Ono Valley and the Shephelah toward Gezer in the south and Rosh ha-'Ayin in the northeast.

In the slopes of the ridge, burial caves of the Chalcolithic period have been found. Inside the caves were ossuaries of baked clay containing human bones. The ossuaries were shaped like long houses and most of them had vaulted roofs. In the caves in the northeast part of the ridge, two additional levels of burials were found, dating from the Early Bronze Age I-A and I-B and overlying the Chalcolithic finds.

EXCAVATIONS

In 1964 and 1965 Ḥaya and J. Kaplan excavated four burial caves on behalf of the Giv'atayim Municipality. In cave 1, which measures 3 meters in diameter, only the floor could be cleared, as the walls and ceiling had been destroyed. Fragments of pottery ossuaries, offering vessels, and human bones were found on the floor. Among the finds was a pottery figurine of a donkey carrying two sacks. In the debris above the Chalcolithic finds were remains of the Early Bronze Age I.

Cave 2, measuring about 7.5 by 5.5 meters, was for the most part preserved, together with its ceiling. The cave was entered on the east side by means of steps hewn into the rock. Near the bottom step, to its left, was a column cut into the rock to support the roof. The cave had three levels of different-colored earth containing human burials and offering vessels. In the top level (I) were human skeletons, each one marked by stones placed around it. In level II, burials of ashes and charred bones were found, the bodies having been cremated and only their remains interred. The bottom level (III) belonged to the Chalcolithic period. Burials in ossuaries and offering gifts, most of them broken, were found here in situ. Near the ossuaries or inside them were human bones. In several places, the ossuaries had been damaged by the burials of level I, which had penetrated into the graves of level III. The cave was originally dug in the Chalcolithic period when the pottery ossuaries were placed in it. In Early Bronze Age I, the cave was again used for burials

451

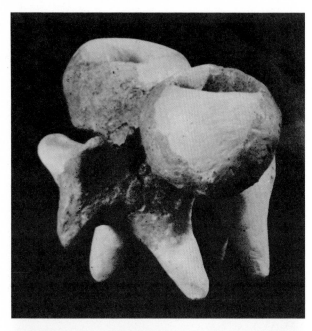

and the settlers followed the burial practices common in the various phases of this period.

Cave 3 is very similar to cave 2, but larger, with dimensions about 8 by 8 m. Here, too, a stepped entrance and a column supporting the roof were found. This cave also contained two Early Bronze Age levels but no level with burials in ossuaries. Those remains, however, were found in a pit in the floor to the left of the entrance steps. Several fragments of pottery ossuaries, two complete incense burners, and jugs of the Chalcolithic period were found. Aside from that isolated find, the entire floor was covered with the ashes of charred bones, offering vessels, as well as a large number of carnelian beads and several other ornaments. All over the southern part of the walls and ceiling of the cave were signs of a great fire. Both areas were black from soot and red from the intensity of the fire. Even the carnelian beads had turned white from the fire. In this cave, the ashes and human bones were found in situ after they had been burned but before burial. It appears that before the settlers of Early Bronze Age I-A turned the cave into a crematory, they cleared the cave of the ossuaries, together with the bones and offering vessels, and placed them outside it. This crematory cave is similar to the one excavated by R.A.S. Macalister at Gezer.

In plan, cave 4 resembles caves 2 and 3, but it is of smaller dimensions and not as deep. It also contained a stepped entrance, a column to support the roof, and fragments of ossuaries and offering vessels of the Chalcolithic period. It appears that this cave was not used in the Chalcolithic period, but that the settlers of Early Bronze Age I threw the contents of cave 3 into it. In the narrow area between caves 3 and 4, a pillar was found hewn into the *kurkar*, part of it projecting above the surface that had been leveled by the Chalcolithic settlers. The pillar served as a mark for the group of graves around it, and it may have been this feature that led the people of the Early Bronze Age to rediscover the burial caves, which they found ready-made for their use.

J. KAPLAN

BIBLIOGRAPHY

Varda Sussman and Sara Ben-Arieh, 'Atiqot 3 (1966), 27–39 (Hebrew).

From top to bottom: Pottery figurine of donkey carrying baskets. Miniature pottery churn; Chalcolithic period. Funerary offering vessels; Chalcolithic period.

GOLAN

IDENTIFICATION. The high basalt-strewn plateau of the Golan bordering the Jordan Valley on the east, from the foothills of the Hermon to the Yarmuk Valley at the southern end of the Sea of Galilee, is pitted with small extinct volcanoes and suitable mainly for grazing. Throughout the centuries, its physical features have to a large extent determined the pattern of settlement, since the very nature of its terrain not only prevented easy access and movement but also restricted its water supply to that of springs and streams. Since it is essentially a fringe area, little is known of the history of the Golan inhabitants.

EXCAVATIONS

Archaeological excavations (chiefly salvage operations) have been made only on a limited scale. Information regarding the Golan thus derives mainly from surface investigations, the most important of which were made by G. Schumacher in the 1880's. He published the results in *The Jaulan,* and partly in *Across the Jordan.* His subsequent surveys prior to and toward the end of World War I were published in the contemporary issues of the *ZDPV.* Schumacher also prepared a detailed map of the Golan. While he did not conduct excavations in the true sense of the word, he documented, described, and made scale drawings of the large number of buildings and architectural details he encountered during the course of his journeys throughout the area. Most of these were from the Roman or Byzantine periods. He also recorded the existence of hundreds of dolmens, many of which he described and drew. The information collated by Schumacher constitutes a basic source of knowledge of the area. After 1967, an archaeological survey was undertaken, and many new sites were discovered.

PRE-ROMAN PERIODS

The overall picture of the periods revealed tied in well with what is known from biblical and extra-biblical sources during the second and early first millennia B.C., especially concerning the lands of Maachah and Geshur whose territories corresponded roughly to the northern and southern Golan. In the middle of the second millennium, settlement became denser. Nevertheless, there is a conspicuous absence of large mounds with a continuity of occupational strata, such as are found west of the Jordan. For the most part, the increase in the number of sites reflects the existence of small towns with adjacent villages, indicating a changed economy with the emphasis on agriculture rather than stock breeding. At the time of the rise of the Aramaean empire in the eleventh century B.C., Maachah in the north and Geshur in the south were independent kingdoms within the Aramaean sphere of influence, although Geshur, allied by marriage with David, did not join the league of Aramaean city-states. The inference is that in the Golan at that time there were a number of petty princes established in fortified cities with a hinterland in which there lived a sizable population. However, it was not until the Roman and more especially the Byzantine period that there was any large-scale development of the Golan. This development was due to the construction of a network of excellent roads, many of which can still be distinguished while the course of others has continued in use to the present day. At that time, all possible sources of water were utilized and, when necessary, conveyed to important centers (see Hippos).

Our knowledge of the earliest human presence in the region is still extremely limited. Most of the evidence to date comes from the north (in the area extending from the foot of the Hermon Range southward toward Kuneitra). Here, Lower, Middle, and Upper Paleolithic flints (including handaxes, choppers, and Micoquian tools) occur on the surface in recognizable concentrations rather than in true sites, whereas in the south only two such concentrations have been identified so far. A gap in the cultural continuity follows, and only from the beginning of the fourth millennium B.C. are there indications of a settled population. A large Early Chalcolithic pre-Ghassulian site is known to have been situated on the north bank of the Yarmuk River, not far from its outflow into the Jordan Valley. The settlement of this valley, however, should be regarded as part of the penetration of the river valleys rather than of the Golan proper. The site is characterized by house remains and a wealth of sherds, flints, and stone artifacts. Recent excavations have revealed a Chalcolithic settlement on the high plateau of central and southern Golan from the second half of the fourth millennium. A series of sporadically situated house complexes were found indicating a population engaged in agriculture and stock breeding, perhaps seasonally. The pottery, which is related to that of Chalcolithic sites in other parts of the country, appears to belong to a regional type and is distinctive in its red ware (made from the local volcanic clay), range of forms, and rope pattern in a rich variety of decorative motifs not previously encountered. There were also basalt vessels and tools. Of particular interest are basalt pillar-form house-god figures set up in houses or courtyards to ensure the well-being of men and flocks. Elsewhere in the Golan, the period is represented for the most part by a small number of Late Chalcolithic sherds (including those of churns) and by occasional finds of flint tools.

Throughout the third and early second millennia B.C., the population of the Golan appears to have been essentially nomadic and semi-nomadic in character. It consisted of tribal groups who appropriated lands for grazing and erected huge enclosures surrounded by massive dry-stone basalt walls within whose protective confines could be gathered men, women, children, and livestock. Such enclosures have been found in northern, central, and southern Golan. In most cases, they were adapted to and exploited the natural features of their position. Not infrequently they were situated high up on an elevated tongue of land that descended steeply on two or three sides to rugged valleys below, the area within being divided by a series of one-course walls, probably for cattle pens or sheep-folds. In one instance, at Rujm Hiri, the enclosure is circular in plan with a maximum diameter of 156 meters. This site is situated on the upper plateau and built in the form of four massive, concentric ring walls, with smaller radial walls dividing the inner space. Although none of the enclosures has been excavated, the earliest sherds found on the surface date to the Early Bronze Age. Characteristic of this type of structure is the Lawieh Enclosure, situated high above the eastern shore of the Sea of Galilee, in which a wealth of Early Bronze Age II pottery lies strewn over the surface. It is possible that all these enclosures date to the Early Bronze Age. On the other hand, since it would appear that nomads constituted the population of the Golan at least until the Middle Bronze Age II, it may well be that not all the enclosures are contemporary, but rather that they were erected successively by new groups reaching the region throughout the centuries. Thus, the Golan enclosures may be considered as a concomitant of a specific way of life rather than as characteristic of a specific period. This is borne out by a small fortified Middle Bronze Age I site, situated in a strategic position in the Wadi Samakh (a wide valley through which there is easy access to the southern Golan Heights). The nature of this site is essentially the same as that of the larger enclosures discussed above. It is surrounded by an outer defense wall with gateway and has an inner "acropolis," likewise walled in on the vulnerable west side, while the enclosed area below is divided up by haphazard one-course walls, indicating cattle stockades. Lower down the slope is a strongpoint utilizing the natural rock formation.

Recent excavation has shown that it was in the Middle Bronze Age I that different types of dolmens, located in various dolmen fields, were erected. The earliest material found on the floors of their chambers is associated with secondary burials and consists of typical Middle Bronze Age I vessels and metal artifacts. The assemblages from the dolmens have distinctly northern affinities with parallels in shaft tombs in Palestine, as well as at contemporary Syrian sites (especially weapons and pins). Dolmens and shaft tombs were built by nomadic groups having a related material culture and similar burial customs. The erection of the dolmen of huge basalt boulders and the cutting of the shaft tomb in the rock necessitated great physical effort, organization, and skill. This reflects the importance attached to the preparation of a final resting place for the

Pottery head of harnessed animal; Early Chalcolithic period.

dead. It was doubtless the geological features of the Golan — and probably of the eastern hinterland beyond — that dictated the actual form of the tomb. Once these nomadic groups reached regions where softer rock was to be found, the nature of the tomb chamber changed, but not the beliefs as expressed in the burial rites. In this connection it should be noted that in the southern Golan, where chalky strata occur below the basalt, Middle Bronze Age I shaft tombs are found.

In the Middle Bronze Age II, most of the sites were located in this same southern sector of the Golan (especially on the valley slopes east of the Sea of Galilee and above the Ruqqad River in the southeast). Some thirty sites have been recorded, many of them small and often protected by a chain of strategically placed forts, the latter not infrequently utilizing naturally defensible hilltops. In the vicinity of the settlements are numerous small springs which gush out through the veins of white limestone found below the basalt cover of the high plateau. The presence of the softer rock also made possible the storage of water in cisterns, which could not be cut into the laval basalt. There appears to be a direct connection between the concentra-

tion of Middle Bronze Age II sites in the south and the physical conditions that facilitated permanent settlement. The pottery from these sites is easily distinguishable, and while exhibiting many Middle Bronze Age II features, it is characterized by traits that are typical of the north (such as are found also at Hazor and Tell Mardik in inland Syria). Middle Bronze Age II artifacts have also been found in one or two dolmens re-used as tombs in later periods.

In contrast, the remains of the subsequent Late Bronze Age are few and far between, being restricted to no more than some half a dozen sites, again mostly in the south. However, the picture may be far from complete in view of the occurrence of isolated Late Bronze Age artifacts — including Cypriot imports — in excavated dolmens. The general absence of Late Bronze Age material is also surprising because it is to this region that reference is made in the el-Amarna letters (EA 256), in which the land of Garu and a number of its cities are named in a suitable geographical context. It has been plausibly suggested by B. Mazar that this is a scribal error for the land of Geshur.

In the Iron Age there was a reflorescence, particularly marked in the south. Most of the sites with

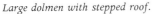

Large dolmen with stepped roof.

evidence of Iron Age occupation had previously been settled during the Middle Bronze Age. It is significant that at nearly all sites sherds from both Iron Age I and II have been found. Of special interest is the discovery of the head of a lion which originally formed part of a basalt orthostat, and which on stylistic grounds can be dated to the ninth century B.C. This was found — albeit not in situ — at a fortified site known as Masharfawi, situated in a strategic position at the entrance of one of the valleys leading up to the high plateau above the Sea of Galilee. For all its provincial execution, the lion was probably one of a pair of orthostats placed at the entrance to the citadel of a petty local prince in emulation of contemporary usage farther north. Its importance lies in the implied existence of a fortified city, the seat of a local princeling, at the entrance to one of the approaches to the Golan. Its position was further strengthened by a small Iron Age fort or stronghold on the edge of the lake below, which also guarded the road running around the eastern shore. Thus despite the relative paucity of presently available evidence relating to a region that was sufficiently important to be of political weight in the power alliances of the time, the broken lion orthostat provides corroboration of what is known from biblical sources. This is further borne out by the neighboring Iron Age fortified citadel of 'En Gev (q.v.). Between the two sites, each guarding the entrance to a valley through which the high plateau could be reached, lies the wide Wadi Samakh (see above). Its entrance is defended by a natural hill, upon which can be seen the remains of fortifications and a profusion of Iron Age I sherds. These three positions, together with sites such as Tell ed-Duweir at the entrance to the Yarmuk Valley and a stronghold situated on the promontory above, which is further strengthened by a small fort on the slope below, indicate a line of strategic strong-points dating to the Iron Age. Evidently there was a well-organized defense system and, by inference, a strong political entity, according well with what is known of the region from the sources. Thus, it is perhaps all the more surprising that so far no evidence has come to light to fill out the picture of what is known from the north of the kingdom of Maachah during this same period. Almost nothing is known of the Persian period, either from written sources or archaeological investigations.

Mention must be made of a distinctive type of pottery, known as Golan Ware, found in several small sites in the north of the Golan. No convincing corroborating evidence is yet available for dating this pottery. Should such evidence come to light, it may add considerably to the present knowledge of the Golan in pre-Roman times.   CLAIRE EPSTEIN

HELLENISTIC TO OTTOMAN PERIODS

History. Little is known of the history of the Golan from the beginning of the Hellenistic to the end of the Second Temple period. Most of our information comes from Josephus. At the beginning of the Hellenistic period, under the Ptolemies, the Golan was an independent administrative unit called Gaulanitis (Γαυλανῖτις), with the rank of hyparchy. Its territory apparently excluded parts of northern and southern Golan. The former belonged to Phoenicia, and the latter to Galaaditis, the district of Gilead. The Seleucids incorporated the whole of the Golan into the eparchy of Gilead. During the Hasmonaean revolt, the inhabitants of the Golan persecuted the local Jews, and Judas Maccabaeus went to their aid during his campaign to Transjordan in 163 B.C. Large areas of Transjordan, including the Golan, were taken by Alexander Jannaeus in 83–80 B.C. Jannaeus seems to have converted most of its inhabitants to Judaism and thus greatly increased the Jewish population in the region.

With the arrival of the Roman forces in Palestine in 64 B.C., Pompey gave all of the Golan to Ptolemy, the son of Menneus, ruler of the Itureans. In 20 B.C., the Emperor Augustus granted the Golan to Herod, who developed the area. The Golan witnessed one of its most flourishing periods during Herod's reign. Up to the time of the First War with Rome, the Golan and its adjacent regions remained in the domain of Herod's heirs. From 4 B.C. to A.D. 34, his third son Philip ruled over all the area, except for the city territories of Hippos and Gadara, which were separated from it. Philip rebuilt and enlarged the city of Paneas and made it his capital. When he died without leaving an heir, his kingdom, including the Golan, was annexed to the Province of Syria. In A.D. 37, the area was restored to the Herodian dynasty, Herod's grandson Agrippa I receiving it from the Emperor Caligula. After Agrippa's death in A.D. 44, it reverted to direct Roman rule but was returned to Agrippa II in A.D. 53. With the outbreak of the First War with Rome, the

Golan became a battlefield between the rebelling Jews and the Roman forces. The climax of the battles is represented by the heroic stand of the city of Gamala (identified in 1968 with the ridge near the village of Deir Kruḥ — map reference 219256) during a siege of seven months. The fall of Gamala on the 25th of Tishri 67 also marks the destruction of the long-lived Jewish settlement in the Golan. After the death of Agrippa II, the southern Golan was annexed to the Provincia Judea, and the northern Golan was annexed to Syria.

The history of the Golan in the period between the two wars with Rome is obscure. It apparently contained a small population with a Jewish minority. After the suppression of the Bar Kokhba Revolt, a large number of Jews from the Coastal Plain and from Judea came to settle in the area, and from this time up to the revolt against Gallus Caesar (351–52) there was a flourishing Jewish community in the Golan which apparently enjoyed municipal rights and internal autonomy. The Jewish settlement was especially prosperous in the days of the Patriarch Judah I, who leased many estates in the area from his friend the Emperor Caracalla. The archaeological finds indicate that the Golan, especially the southern part and the Butayḥa Valley, was one of the most important Jewish centers during the third and fourth centuries A.D. It continued to exist until the Arab conquest. Its remains were still mentioned in the Middle Ages. Most of the Jewish archaeological remains in the Golan date from the end of the second century to the first half of the fourth century (see below for ancient synagogues in the Golan).

Our knowledge of the Golan from the Arab conquest to the Turkish period is very scanty. The French Rabbi Shmuel ben Shimson, who visited Palestine in 1210, mentions a Jewish community in the village of Naveh. In the middle of the fourteenth century, Eshtori ha-Parḥi also refers to a Jewish community there and at "Yehudah" (Yahudiyya — map reference 21622605). The region seems to have been almost completely deserted up to the middle of the nineteenth century.

Exploration. The first explorers were U. J. Seetzen (1806), J. L. Burckhardt (1810), and J. Buckingham (1816). L. Oliphant, who visited the Golan in 1879, gave the first detailed description of the remains, including those of ancient synagogues. A comprehensive archaeological survey was undertaken by G. Schumacher in 1884. In 1905, the synagogues of Umm el-Qanatir and al-Dikke were investigated by H. Kohl and C. Watzinger.

A new survey of the Golan lasted from October, 1967, to March, 1968, under the direction of Claire Epstein and S. Gutman on behalf of the Israel Archaeological Survey Society. The survey discovered sites from the following periods: eleven Hellenistic, forty-five Roman, fifty Roman-Byzantine, seventy-six Byzantine, twelve Arab, fifteen medieval. Further surveys (as yet unpublished) were carried out by the same team in the latter half of 1968. From April, 1968, to May 1972, D. Urman, on behalf of the Department of Antiquities and the Survey Society, conducted surveys and salvage excavations throughout the area.

Excavations. Only excavations and soundings made since 1968 will be discussed here. The sites are arranged in alphabetical order (see also the articles Ḥammat Gader and Synagogues, the latter for Umm el-Qanatir and al-Dikke).

EL-JUḤADAR, TELL. An ancient site built on a volcanic hill, about 5 kilometers (3 miles) southwest of the Rafid intersection (map reference 23022595). A survey headed by S. Gutman found ancient buildings with stone roofs, caves with built entrances, and building remains and potsherds from the Early Bronze Age, the Roman-Byzantine and Arab periods, and the Middle Ages.

In November–December, 1968, and July–September, 1969, two excavation seasons were conducted on the site by D. Urman. The area excavated was along the lower slopes of the southwestern side of the mound. The earliest material uncovered was terra sigillata ware of the first century A.D. Since an area of only 250 dunams along the lower slopes was examined, there is no definite proof that the mound does not contain remains of earlier settlements as well. Four occupational strata were discovered. Stratum I belongs to a small settlement from the twelfth–thirteenth centuries A.D. The nearby Khan Juḥadar is apparently contemporary with it. Stratum II belongs to a settlement of the seventh–eighth centuries A.D. that re-used the buildings of the Byzantine period, at which time the site was densely populated (stratum III). The site reached its zenith both in size and prosperity at the end of the third and first half of the fourth century A.D. (stratum IV). This settlement was probably destroyed during the revolt against Gallus

From Tell el-Juḥadar, top to bottom: Rooms of stratum III. House of stratum IV. Rooms of stratum III.

Caesar (A.D. 351). In this stratum two large dwelling units were uncovered (one measuring 195 square meters, the other about 400 square meters) and a section of a stepped street. The houses, built of ashlar and rubble, were roofed with long basalt slabs. One of the rooms had a roof of ornamented ceramic tiles which were marked with numbers. The roof had fallen onto the floor and was preserved almost intact. In another room was found a tombstone in secondary use with an inscription in Greek: "Be of good cheer, Antonia. [Died] aged 27." At the time of the destruction of this stratum, which was built on virgin soil, the houses were looted, and the robbers scattered many bronze coins on the floors of rooms in which they had found hoards of silver. These coins date the destruction to the time of the revolt against Gallus.

KHASFIN (perhaps identical with the Chaspho or Caspin of I Maccabees 5:26; II Maccabees 12:13). North of the village of Ramat Magshimim. In 1967–68, the Israel Archaeological Survey Society discovered many remains there, including intact buildings roofed with basalt slabs from the Byzantine period, remains of a mosaic pavement, and numerous architectural fragments, some of which came from a church. In a survey carried out by the Archaeological Officer for the Golan in 1969, many new discoveries were made including architectural fragments with Greek inscriptions. During salvage work of the Department of Antiquities in February, 1972, the remains of a large church were examined in the western part of the site by D. Urman and S. Bar-Lev. The church has a basilical plan with three external apses. The southern and central apses were cleared, as were parts of the chancel screen, the schola cantorum, and the beginning of two rows of columns. Mosaic pavements were uncovered in the intercolumnar spaces, the southern aisle, and the nave. The church was 11 meters wide and had rooms attached to it on the southern side. Of particular interest was the mosaic pavement of the southern aisle. Its entire width and 7.2 meters of its length were cleared. The mosaic was surrounded by a border of interlacing rhombuses in various shades of red, yellow, pink, brown, violet, and white on a black ground. The field was divided by rows of red and blue fleurettes forming rhombuses which contained various objects. Thirty-two rhombuses were cleared showing images of birds (all these were later obliterated by iconoclasts), flowers and fruits, baskets of bread, etc. In a rhombus in the center of the floor was a Greek dedicatory inscription of seven lines, which mentions a certain Georgios. Excavations thus far have revealed three phases of building and repair. The church appears to have been built in the fifth century and continued in use in the sixth and seventh centuries.

KURSI. HISTORY. This site comprises two separate areas: 1. Tell Kursi on the shore of the Sea of Galilee (map reference 21032480), with remains of an ancient fishermen's wharf. 2. The monastery of Kursi east of the mound (map reference 21112480) near the 'En Gev–Ramot road. Tell Kursi has not yet been excavated. The site of the monastery was first discovered in 1970 by M. Nun of Kibbutz 'En Gev during road construction. D. Urman identified it with Geresa or Gergesa where, according to Christian tradition, Jesus performed the miracle of "healing the man with an unclean spirit," also known as the "miracle of the Gergesene or Gadarene swine" (Matthew 8:28–34; Mark 5:1–17; Luke 8:26–37).

Kursi is mentioned several times in the Talmud. The tanna Rabbi Jacob son of Ḥanilay, who was the teacher of the young Patriarch Judah I, is also called by the name of his birthplace, Jacob of Kursi (Palestinian Talmud Shabbat 10:5). According to a tradition attributed to him, there was an idolatrous temple at Kursi called the House of Nebo (Babylonian Talmud 'Abodah Zarah 11b).

Kursi became famous as a result of Jesus' miracle. Origen (about A.D. 250) describes Gergesa (Γέργεσα) as "an ancient city near the lake, close to the hillside which the herd of swine descended." Cyril of Scythopolis (about A.D. 550) states that in 491 Saint Saba and his pupil Agapetus traveled along the Jordan and the Sea of Galilee to pray at Chorsia (Χορσία). Pilgrims frequently mention Kursi-Chorsia = Geresa-Gergesa — sometimes confusing it with Kerazeh-Chorazain.

EXCAVATIONS. The area of the monastery was excavated in three seasons. The first two (June–August, 1970; April, 1971) were directed by D. Urman on behalf of the Department of Antiquities, the third (November, 1971–January, 1972) by D. Urman and V. Tsaferis. The monastery was found to date to the Byzantine period. It was surrounded by a wall 90 centimeters thick, which was cleared to almost its entire length. The wall enclosed a rectangular area of about 18 dunams, all of which

was occupied by buildings with the remains of a large church in the center. The main entrance was in the western wall. It was protected by a high tower, of which only the foundations and a well-built staircase survived. From the entrance, a road, 5 meters wide and 50 meters long and paved with basalt slabs, led to the church. The latter measured 23 by 45 meters and consisted of an atrium, a narthex, and a main hall with auxiliary rooms attached on the north and south sides. Two main phases of building were uncovered in the atrium. In the first phase, it was surrounded by four porticoes with the eastern porch serving as an open narthex. In the second phase, partition walls were added and the porticoes were turned into rooms, thus reducing the area of the open atrium and enclosing it by rooms on the north, south, and west. In the east a closed narthex was formed which spanned the front of the hall. Beneath the atrium, which was paved with finely dressed ashlar slabs, was a pool with a vaulted roof. The pool had a capacity of about 500 cubic meters of water. The narthex had benches built along the façade of the hall. A few fragments of a mosaic pavement with geometric and cross designs were preserved. Three doors led from the narthex into the hall of the church.

The hall was of a basilical plan, with nave, two aisles, and two rows of columns, each with six columns that stood on square plinths and Attic bases. Letters, i.e., Greek numerals, were carved on some of the columns and bases. Most of the capitals and columns were decorated with reliefs of crosses, some of which were mutilated in later times. The apse seems to have been paved with marble slabs. Along the rear wall of the apse were remains of the synthronos (bishop's seat) and the presbytery. In the chord of the apse was a reliquary that once contained the bones of a saint. It marks the place of the altar, which was not preserved. The schola cantorum, of which only the foundations have remained, was raised two steps above the floor of the hall. It had been severely damaged by walls built over it in the early Arab period. The apse was flanked by rectangular chambers (4.5 by 6 meters), both of which were ornamented with mosaic pavements in geometric designs. The northern room served as the prothesis, and the southern room was the baptistery. A small, oval-shaped baptismal font was found in the latter. At the entrance to the baptistery was a mosaic inscription of nine lines in Greek, which dates the laying of the pavement to the year 585/86.

The nave, 7.65 meters wide, was paved with very delicate mosaics, most of which were damaged by iconoclasts. In the intercolumnar spaces, the mosaic has a running pattern of two animals flanking a Jussiaea plant, which was common in the region of Kursi. The images of the animals were completely obliterated. The intercolumnar spaces near the schola cantorum are ornamented with various geometric designs.

The mosaic floors of the two aisles, both of which are 3.15 meters wide, have identical designs but contain different images in the medallions. The fields are surrounded by a band of stylized flowers turning alternately inward and outward. The floor of the northern aisle is divided into 160 rhombus-shaped medallions, arranged in forty horizontal rows of four medallions each. The mosaic of the southern aisle is similarly arranged but with only thirty-nine rows. The medallions are very variegated. Most of the rows contain figures of various birds, from domestic fowl to running and water-fowl. All of them suffered severe damage, but many can be identified from the surviving fragments. A peacock appearing in one of the medallions entirely escaped destruction. Other medallions not destroyed by the iconoclasts contain various fruits: grapes, figs, pomegranates, oranges, citrons, and gourds,

From Qisrin, below: Aramaic inscription: "[U]zi made this square (?)." Opposite page, top: Northwestern corner of the beth-midrash, during excavation. Constructed entirely of smooth basalt stone, the building at this spot is preserved to a height of about 3 meters. Bottom: Facade of the beth-midrash.

stylized flowers, goblets, baskets, etc. Several representations of fish were also effaced.

Along both of the long sides of the hall were service rooms. One room on the north served as a wine press. A mosaic with a vivid depiction of two doves flanking a wicker basket was found at the entrance to one of the rooms on the north side. The entrance was probably blocked in the early Arab period, thus allowing the mosaic to escape destruction. One of the rooms on the south was a chapel, which was preserved almost intact. In a crypt beneath it were found the skeletons of more than thirty males, probably monks. Four small crosses were incised above one of the arcosolia.

Judging from the finds, the monastery and the church were erected in the fifth century, renovated at least once in the Byzantine period, and destroyed at the beginning of the seventh century, apparently during the Persian invasion. The site was resettled shortly afterward, and from the ninth century up to the Middle Ages, the buildings were used as private dwellings.

In the first season of excavations, the Underwater Archaeological Society and the writer discovered a fishermen's wharf north of the mound. It covers an area of more than 1.5 dunams. Its entrance was toward the north–northwest, and its two bases are structurally connected with the buildings on the shore. It apparently dates to the Roman period and was in use until the early Arab period. Near the wharf were various building remains and a reservoir for fish.

QISRIN. A deserted village about 8 kilometers (5 miles) east of the Jisr Banat Ya'qub (map reference 21612661). In 1967, the Israel Archaeological Survey Society, directed by S. Gutman, found Qisrin to be a large site from the talmudic period. In April–May, 1971, and March, 1972, D. Urman, on behalf of the Department of Antiquities, carried out a salvage excavation in a large building, presumably a synagogue. The walls of a hall, 18 by 15.4 meters, were found oriented in a north–south direction. The walls were 90 centimeters thick and were built of well-dressed basalt ashlars. The hall had two entrances: one, 85 centimeters wide, in the southern part of the eastern wall and the other, 1.9 meters wide, in the middle of the northern wall. The latter entrance was preserved intact and was probably the main entrance to the hall. It is ornamented with reliefs. A plaited wreath in the center

of the lintel is flanked by pomegranates and vases. Both the lintel and the doorposts, which stand on carved bases, are decorated with carved profiles and egg-and-dart designs. Two rows of benches, built of basalt ashlars, ran along the interior of the hall. The center of the hall has not yet been excavated, so that the number of columns supporting the roof is not known. The original floor of the hall also has not yet been uncovered. Only the floor of the last phase of the hall has been cleared. It dates to the thirteenth century. Contemporary with it is a wall which crossed the center of the hall and is built in part of stones re-used from the walls. A well-dressed basalt stone, 1 meter long and 32 centimeters high, with an Aramaic inscription was found in secondary use in the wall. It reads: "[U]zi made this square (?)."

The western wall, which was preserved to a height of 3 meters, does not follow the plan of the hall but turns in a southerly direction. This fact, together with the discovery of two large stone doorposts (one bearing the relief of a menorah) and a decorated lintel near the hall, led the excavator to assume that the hall was not an independent unit but part of a complex of rooms whose plan is not yet clear. The direction of the hall (north–south) does not correspond to that of a synagogue. It may have been a school with a synagogue attached to it.

Although the excavation of the school and/or synagogue has not yet been completed, it seems certain that it was built in the first half of the third century A.D. and continued in its original use at least until the middle of the fourth century.

ṢURMAN. A Circassian village built on an ancient

site, about 2.5 kilometers (1.5 miles) southeast of Quneitra (map reference 22862784). D. Urman, on behalf of the Department of Antiquities, conducted a survey and salvage excavations in 1968. The site was found to have been first settled in the beginning of the second century B.C. Some intact buildings from the Roman and Byzantine periods were found roofed with basalt slabs, many of them ornamented. Thirty tombstones were found, as well as two lintels with Greek inscriptions from the Byzantine period.

Several tombs were excavated on the northern slope of the hill on which the site is situated. Typologically and chronologically, the tombs can be divided into three groups: 1. Tombs dug into the ground, covered with heaps of oval-shaped stones. On the headpiece of each tomb was a basalt

From Dabbura, both pages, counterclockwise: Inscription 5. Inscription on basalt lintel mentioning "Eleazar ha-Qappar." Inscription 4. Inscription 3.

mortar filled with crushed leaves. Also found with them were loom spindles, weights, and a number of coins. This group belongs to the Mameluke period. Many finds from this period were discovered in another area. 2. Tombs with stone-built sides covered with long basalt slabs. These tombs are dated to the sixth and seventh centuries A.D. 3. A single basalt sarcophagus containing bones but no other objects. It was covered with a marble lid. Two figures adorn one of its sides. The sarcophagus may be dated to the end of the fourth century A.D.

ZAMAL, KHIRBET. A ruined site extending over an area of 2 dunams, southeast of Kafr Buq'ata (map reference 22412890). In September, 1971, a rescue excavation was conducted there by D. Urman on behalf of the Department of Antiquities. In one room, which was excavated down to floor level, were fragments of three store jars of the type which was named Golan Ware by the survey of 1968. Their date was problematic. The sherds bore fragmentary Greek inscriptions that were difficult to read. On the floor of the room, together with the sherds, lay a bronze spearhead and two coins of the Seleucid period. In the light of these finds, the excavator proposed that the Golan Ware — at least at Khirbet Zamal — should be attributed to the Hellenistic period and the beginning of the Roman period (third to first centuries B.C.). This ware was probably the work of Iturean tribes who lived at that time in the Golan. From the trial soundings, it seemed that this site, like many others in the northern Golan, was settled during a single period only, from the third century to the end of the first century B.C.

SYNAGOGUES AND SCHOOLS. Since the surveys of Oliphant and Schumacher, various explorers in the southern Golan have found remains of monumental buildings from the talmudic period which have been identified as synagogues or schools. Presented below is a brief description of the main finds not mentioned above (Qisrin) or in other articles (Ḥammat Gader, Synagogues [Umm el-Qanatir, el-Dikke]).

BATHYRA (map reference 21382568). A ruined site on a cliff first discovered in 1968 by the Archaeological Survey Society. In the southern part of the site was a synagogue oriented to the west and built of finely dressed and ornamented stones. Around the building were found a dressed architrave, a stone with the carving of a wreath, a "Hercules" knot and vine, Ionic (Eastern) capitals of pillars, and a torus decorated at both ends.

DABBIYE (map reference 21842684). The remains of a synagogue oriented in an east–west direction were discovered here in 1968 by D. Urman. Still standing in situ were the doorposts of the main entrance in the middle of the eastern wall, foundation courses of the walls, and sections of the floor paved with basalt slabs. Inside the building and nearby were column bases, capitals, lintels, and other carved stones.

DABBURA (map reference 21241725). An abandoned village in which some of the houses were built of stones taken from synagogues and a school of the second to fourth centuries A.D. S. Gutman, who headed the survey team, and D. Urman discovered tens of decorated stones, including six with Hebrew and Aramaic inscriptions. The most important inscription was engraved on a basalt lintel, 170 centimeters long and 42 centimeters high, with a relief of two harrier eagles with outspread wings, each holding a snake in its beak. The two snakes intertwine to form a plaited wreath which encloses a Hebrew inscription: "This is the beth-midrash [school] of the Rabbi." Continuing on both sides of the wreath are the words "Eleazar ha-Qappar." This lintel is of great importance, in that it attests to the existence here of a school of Rabbi Eleazar ha-Qappar, known in Aramaic as Bar-Qappara. The other inscriptions read: 1. "...[s]on of Yudah." 2. "...[Ḥ]inanah...May he be blessed." 3. "They made the house...May he be blessed." 4. "Made the gate." 5. "El'azar the son of...made the columns above the arches and beams...[In Greek] Rusticus built [it]."

DALIYA, KHIRBET (map reference 21902554). An ancient ruin first discovered in 1968 by D. Peri and Y. Gal. In the southeast part of the site were the remains of a monumental building with a number of courses still standing. The building was oriented to the west, which indicates that it was a synagogue. Lying on the eastern wall of the building was a basalt lintel, 170 by 50 centimeters, with the slightly blurred relief of three rosettes. Another lintel of the same size was found west of the building. This lintel was carved with reliefs of vine branches issuing from two vases and forming in the center a plaited wreath with a "Hercules" knot.

Jerusalem. Mosaic in the Dome of the Rock.

DARDARA (map reference 21142576). Here in 1968, a team headed by D. Urman first discovered the remains of a monumental rectangular structure oriented in an east–west direction. It was most likely a synagogue. Above surface level could be seen four to six courses of the northern and southern walls. Several carved stones were also found.

DEIR 'AZIZ (map reference 21702525). An abandoned village in which L. Oliphant discovered the ruins of a building which he called a synagogue. The building is rectangular in plan, measuring about 25 by 15 meters, and is oriented north–south. Above surface level were three courses of the western and southern walls, as well as parts of the northern and

Top: 'Edriya; fragmentary lintel with incised menorah. Bottom: Fiq; basalt lintel with incised menorah, shofar, and ethrog.

eastern walls. The entrance was in the middle of the eastern wall. In the southeastern part a rectangular room, 10 by 2.5 meters, with a roof of long basalt slabs, was preserved intact. Because of the direction of the building, it is difficult to consider it a synagogue. D. Urman, who examined the building in 1968, proposed identifying it as a school.

'EDRIYA (map reference 21552694). A survey headed by S. Gutman in 1967–68 found architectural remains which almost certainly belonged to a Jewish public building from the talmudic period. Part of a lintel was found with an incomplete Aramaic inscription in two lines which reads: "...Ḥalfu son of...be blessed." In 1971, D. Urman, on behalf of the Department of Antiquities, conducted a survey and soundings at the site, uncovering walls of a monumental building oriented in a north–south direction. Thus far, only the southern and western walls have been cleared. The southern wall is preserved to a length of 14 meters and the western to 19 meters. Also found were broken lintels on which seven-branched menorahs were engraved, parts of gables, cornices, architraves, and other carved stones.

ELI-'AL (map reference 22002457). The remains of a monumental building were discovered there in 1972 by D. Urman. Scores of architectural fragments from the talmudic period with motifs typical of synagogues were discovered in the area of the village by G. Schumacher and in later surveys.

'EN NATOSH (map reference 21512687). In 1971, during the excavations at 'Edriya (see below), D. Urman discovered a large ruined site from the talmudic period above the spring of 'En Natosh, about 1 kilometer south of 'Edriya. Situated on a hill with valleys on three sides, the site was well protected and was not disturbed by later settlements. Scores of buildings have been preserved there, some to a height of from three to five courses. On the west side are remains of a monumental building that was probably a synagogue. Among the ruins of the building were fragments of columns, bases, capitals, architraves, cornices, and other carved stones. Of particular interest are two stones with carved lions and part of a lintel with a fine relief of a seven-branched menorah standing on two feet.

FIQ (map reference 21642425). A large site from the talmudic period and later times (identified with

Apheca of Eusebius, *Onomasticon* 22:20). Many architectural fragments, which undoubtedly belonged to a synagogue, were found there. These included a basalt column with a seven-branched menorah and, beneath it, an Aramaic inscription: "I, Judah the ḥazan." Also found was a basalt lintel with the relief of a circle in the center enclosing reliefs of a menorah, a shofar, and an ethrog. The building itself has not been found, but it was probably situated on the edge of Wadi Fiq and faced west toward the Sea of Galilee.

MIZRA'AT QANEF (map reference 21452531). An abandoned village built partly on remains of a settlement from the talmudic period. In 1885 L.

From Mizra'at Qanef, top: Ornamented stone fragments, from the synagogue. Bottom: Corner of synagogue with modern Arab house built around it.

Oliphant discovered there the corner of a monumental building which he identified as a synagogue. Near an Arab house can be seen many ornamented architectural fragments, including parts of the frieze of the synagogue. An Aramaic inscription of one line was found engraved on a lintel. It reads: "...[Bless]ing. Remembered by for good Yose son of Ḥalfu son of Ḥan..."

ER-RAFID. A ruined site on the eastern shore of the Jordan River, about 5 kilometers (3 miles) north of its issue into the Sea of Galilee. In 1905 H. Kohl and C. Watzinger found there remains of a synagogue which they dated to the third century A.D. Little of the building survives today.

ZAMIMRA, KHIRBET (map reference 21392614). A village from the talmudic period whose ruins were first discovered by Claire Epstein in 1968. Remains of a synagogue were found oriented to the west. Two to three courses of the western wall of the building projected above surface level. A doorway, 1.65 meters wide, in the western wall was found with the lower parts of the doorposts with carved profiles still standing. Near the entrance was a very skillfully carved stone on which was depicted a column with capital and base and a crouching lion along its length. This stone, like many others found on the site, probably belonged to the façade of the building.

In addition to the above sites, explorers have noted architectural fragments of synagogues and schools in many other places, especially in the southern Golan, but the buildings to which they belonged have not yet been located. Of these, the following sites should be mentioned: Aḥmadiye; 'Ayyun, Khirbet; Butmiye; Ḥushniye; Kafr Ḥarib; Kafr el-Ma; Kafr Nafaḥ; Lawieh; Mizra'at Quneitra; Peḥura; Qusbiye; a-Ṣefira; Sekufiye; and Yahudiyya.

D. URMAN

BIBLIOGRAPHY

L. Oliphant, *PEF QSt* (1885), 167–71 • G. Schumacher, *The Jaulan*, London, 1888; *idem, Across the Jordan*, London 1889, 62–71, 149–52; *idem*, articles in *ZDPV*, passim, especially 40 (1917) • B. Mazar, *EI* 3 (1954), 21 and n. 26 (Hebrew) • Z. Ilan, *The Land of Golan*, Tel Aviv, 1969 (Hebrew) • S. Gutman and A. Druks, *Qadmoniot* 7 (1969), 91–92 (Hebrew) • C. Epstein, *Qadmoniot* 12 (1970), 134–35; *idem, IEJ* 22 (1972), 209–17; 23 (1973), 109–10, 238–41; *idem, RB* 79 (1972), 404–07; *idem, Hadashot Archeologiot* 44 (1972), 1–3 (Hebrew) • M. Kochavi (ed.), *Judea, Samaria and the Golan — Archaeological Survey 1967–1968*, Jerusalem, 1972, 244–98 (Hebrew) • D. Urman, *IEJ* 22 (1972), 16–23 • S. Gutman, *Mibifnim* 35 (1973), 143–51 (Hebrew).

ḤAMADIYA

IDENTIFICATION. The Neolithic site on the lands of Kibbutz Ḥamadiya is located in the Jordan Rift east of the Beth-Shean–Zemaḥ road. The site lies on an ancient terrace of the Jordan Valley, about 200 meters below sea level. The soil is a dark-brown alluvium, which covers an area extending from the foot of the hills on which the kibbutz is situated to about 150 meters west of 'Ein es-Suda. The ancient remains were discovered in a shallow depression in the brown soil which overlaid a bedrock of basalt. In the center of the depression was a vein of basalt tuff with a diagonal incline. Into this tuff the Neolithic settlers managed to cut pits and depressions.

Left: Yarmukian occupation floor. Right: Yarmukian fertility figurines.

EXCAVATIONS

In November, 1964, J. Kaplan carried out excavations on behalf of the Israel Exploration Society near Khirbet es-Suda (west of the spring 'Ein es-Suda). Immediately below the surface, a Neolithic settlement of the Yarmukian stage was unearthed, extending over an area of about 100 square meters. No remains of buildings were found. The inhabitants apparently found shelter in huts or tents. Ovens and fireplaces were uncovered in a few places in the floor, as were a number of depressions and pits which were probably dug for storage purposes.

Among the objects found were a large number of potsherds of cooking pots, cups, and bowls. Some were decorated with an incised herringbone pattern common in Yarmukian pottery. This pattern encircles the outside of the body and forms zigzag lines. It is sometimes marked at the ends by two bands in red paint. The flints found included a large number of deeply serrated sickle blades showing a gloss from use, axes, chisels, awls, arrowheads, spears, and many other implements, as well as the waste of the lithic industry typical of the Yarmukian culture. Also found were basalt grindstones and numerous animal bones. One should also mention the spindle weights and two fertility figurines incised on stone, one of them apparently depicting childbirth.

A workshop for the production of flint sickle blades was of special interest. In the workshop, located outside the excavated area, were more than three hundred sickle blades ready for use, together with the industrial waste of thousands of chips. Among the sickles were a great many that had apparently been brought to have their blunt or broken serration reworked.

CONCLUSION

Trial trenches dug around the excavated area produced only sterile earth. Hence, it seems that the small area excavated was inhabited by a single household or, at most, a camp. This household was probably one link in the chain of similar small settlements scattered nearby. The discovery of such a site is therefore very significant, as it provides a model of a settlement of a Yarmukian social unit.

J. KAPLAN

BIBLIOGRAPHY

N. Tzori, *PEQ* 90 (1958), 44–45 • J. Kaplan, *RB* 72 (1965), 543–44.

ḤAMMAT GADER

IDENTIFICATION AND HISTORY. Ḥammat Gader is generally identified with the springs of el-Ḥammeh in the Yarmuk Valley. It is first mentioned, but not by name, by Strabo, who described the hot springs near the city of Gadara. Origines (third century A.D.) also mentions the hot springs near Gadara. Eusebius was the first to explain the name "Hammata." In his book on the life of Jamblichus, Eunapius mentions two springs on the site, Eros and Anteros. Epiphanius (fourth century A.D.) describes the celebrations in honor of the pagan goddesses there, in which the rich and idle young men from near and far took part. His description is based on the stories of the *Comes* Joseph, a converted Jew.

From talmudic sources, we learn that many scholars visited Ḥammat Gader — from Rabbi Meir (mid-second century A.D.) onward. Among them were the Patriarch Judah I, Rabbis Ḥaninah, Yonathan, Hamm'a bar Ḥaninah, and Ami, the latter with the Patriarch Judah II. These scholars discussed there problems of the Sabbath boundaries between Gadara and Ḥammat, at the foot of Gadara. In the second century A.D., mention is already made of the many food merchants who flocked to the place to sell their goods to the crowds of visitors who came to the hot baths. The synagogue inscriptions also testify to the numbers of foreign visitors to the place.

The site lies north of the Yarmuk River in a valley (1,450 meters long, 500 meters wide, 725 dunams in area). There are four hot springs in the valley: two, 'Ein el-Jarab and 'Ein Bulos, in the northern part near the artificial mound called Tell Bani (a corruption of the Greek word βαλανεῖον meaning "bath"); and two in the southern part, 'Ein er-Rih and Ḥamammet Ḥammet Selim, near which were found remains of a Roman bath. On another hill 320 meters to the east of Tell Bani are the remains of a Roman theater. Roman and later remains are scattered over the whole western part of the valley. In 1816, J. S. Buckingham saw a Roman bath here with the upper story still standing. In 1866, G. Schumacher still found extensive remains of these structures.

EXCAVATIONS

In 1932, N. Glueck made soundings in Tell Bani

Top: General view of the synagogue, after excavation.
Bottom: Southern panel of mosaic floor in nave of synagogue.

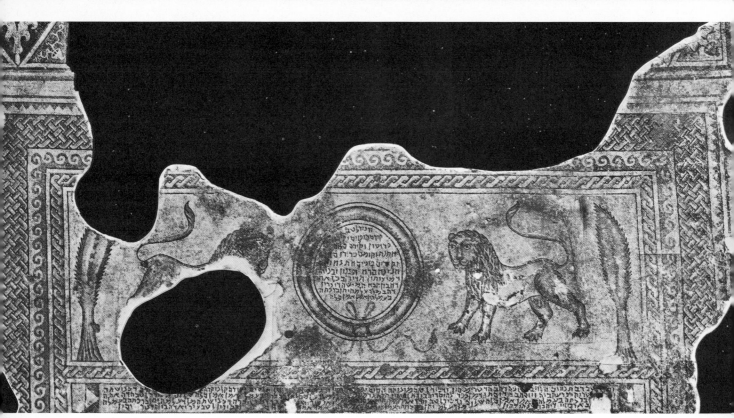

(Tell el-Ḥammeh) and found sherds of Early Bronze Age I–III. Sherds with band-slip decoration were particularly plentiful. Though Khirbet Kerak sherds were not found, in Glueck's opinion this was accidental. However, the absence of sherds from Early Bronze Age IV and Middle Bronze Age indicate that this settlement, like all those in Transjordan, was destroyed at the end of the Early Bronze Age. The site remained unoccupied till the Roman period.

In 1932, the Archaeology Department of the Hebrew University, under the direction of E. L. Sukenik, made a few soundings in the ruins of Ḥammat Gader. In the Roman bath near Ḥammat Selim, a hall was found (maximum width 12 meters, southern end rounded) with a niche east of the entrance to the hall. In front of it, at a depth of 5.2 meters, rose a hot spring. This hall was the caldarium (hot bath). West of it was a passage to another large hall (maximum width 18.4 meters). This was probably the entrance hall and apodyterium (dressing room) of the bath.

The University expedition also made soundings in the artificial mound (11 meters in height), built to support the theater. The *cavea* had fifteen rows of seats, each one 60–70 centimeters high, and a seating capacity of 1,500–2,000. The highest row was 6.6 meters above the orchestra (13 meters in diameter). The side entrances *(parodoi)* were about 3.6 meters wide. The stage was 1.5 meters higher than the orchestra and was 5.8 meters deep and 29.6 meters long.

THE REMAINS OF THE SYNAGOGUE

In the spring of 1932, the Department of Antiquities of the Mandatory Government discovered the remains of a synagogue on the summit of Tell Bani (unoccupied during Roman times). In the fall of the same year, the Department of Antiquities granted a license to the Hebrew University to complete the excavations. Some 700 square meters were excavated, and the synagogue hall and a few buildings in the vicinity were uncovered.

There were two entrances to the synagogue hall, both indirect. One entrance was through a narrow corridor (3.2 meters wide) on the western side, which led to an opening in the wall of the hall. At the end of the corridor was another opening which led to the western of the two rooms behind the apse (on the south side). The entire complex was surrounded by a wall 32.5 meters in length. The main entrance was from the east. Here, too, access was through a narrow passage (3.5 meters wide). It was divided into two rooms (5.45 and 6.9 meters long). In the second room, a mosaic floor with a geometric pattern was discovered. From the first room in this eastern passage there was an entrance to two side rooms (the first 4.9 by 4.7 meters, and the second 4.7 by 5.5 meters). Between them and the hall complex was a third corridor (2.6 meters wide). To the west of the latter were two rooms adjoining the synagogue hall. From the small room at the north (3.1 by 2.8 meters) one entered the second, larger room (6.65 by 3.65 meters) paved with stone. It could be entered either from the corridor or from the hall of the synagogue. Along the eastern wall of the larger room there was a bench. This room served for study or teaching, or as a place of prayer for women. Opinions are divided as to the existence of a women's gallery in this synagogue.

The hall was almost square (13 by 13.9 meters) and was divided by three rows of columns into a nave (7.8 meters wide) and two long aisles (the eastern one 3 meters wide and the western one 2.4 meters wide) and a transverse aisle opposite the apse (1.8 meters wide). The longitudinal rows had four columns each and the transverse row only two. At the corners of the rows were two angled, L-shaped, plastered columns. The columns stood on foundations under the mosaic floor. There were no bases. Along the walls were remains of benches.

In the center of the southern wall facing Jerusalem was a platform (bema), the same length as the apse (4.55 meters) and 1.2 meters wide, with two steps leading up to its center. There was a marble screen on either side of the steps. Remains of chancel posts and of one of its panels were also found. (After the excavation was completed, a fragment of a panel of the screen bearing a menorah within a wreath was found accidentally.) The apse itself was sunken 1.18 meters below the level of the bema. The thickness of its back wall was 1.45 meters.

The entire hall had been paved with mosaics. In the aisles, the mosaics were of simple geometric patterns (squares, flowers, circles, intersecting lines in guilloche, etc.). On both sides of the bema were lozenges, in the center a flame pattern, and in the corners jugs with plants winding out of them. The floor of the nave had a complex border in crowstep pattern, guilloche, and wave-crest pattern. The center of the mosaic was divided into three panels, each bordered by a guilloche. In the northern panel there was a pattern of intersecting lines, and between them large squares with guilloches inside and smaller ones with chess patterns inside. In this part of the mosaic was found the first inscription (I, below), a little west of the axis of the floor in a *tabula ansata*. There was most likely a matching inscription east of the axis, but that has not been preserved. The central panel of the mosaic in the nave was ornamented with patterns of *fleurons* in intersecting lines — with roses or pomegranates in the center of each lozenge. At the southern end of this panel, two inscriptions (II and III, below) were found side by side, both in a *tabula ansata*. Only in this section, closest to the bema, was the dominant abstract geometric pattern abandoned and a representational design adopted. Two cypresses stand at the edges of the panel. Between them, facing the viewer, are two lions with tongues protruding and tails rising above their backs. Inscrip-

tion IV was placed within a wreath with ribbons between the lions. Another inscription once existed in the western aisle, but nothing was left of it except the edge of the *tabula ansata*.

INSCRIPTIONS

I. "And remembered be (for) good Ada, the son of Tanḥum, the son of Moniqah, who has contributed one tremissis and Yoseh, the son of Qarosah(?) and Moniqah, who have contributed one-half denarius toward this mosaic. May theirs be the blessing. Amen. Selah. Peace."

II. (Right) "And remembered be for good Rab Tanḥum the Levite, the son of Ḥalif'a, who has donated one tremissis; and remembered be for good Moniqah of Susitha(?) the Sepphorite and Kyris Patriqios, of Kefar 'Aqabyah and Yoseh, the son of Dositheus, of Kefar Naḥum, who have, all three, donated three scruples. May the King of the Universe bestow the blessing upon their work. Amen. Amen. Selah. Peace. And remembered be for good Yudan...of...who has donated three [*i.e.*, 3

Plan of the synagogue.

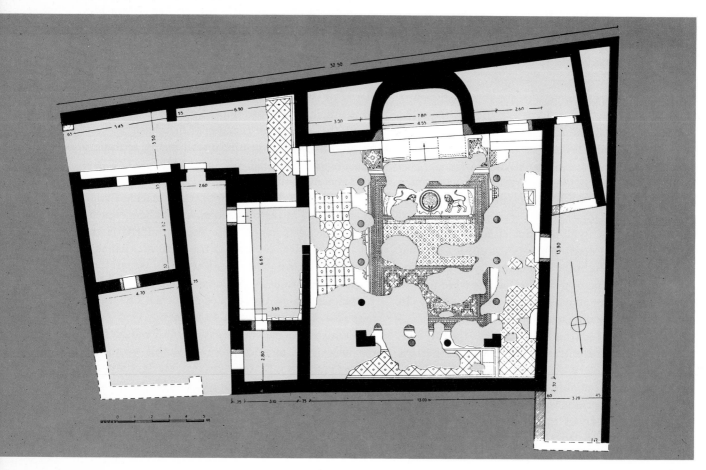

scruples?]. And remembered be for good the people of Arbela who have donated of their cloths(?). May the King of the Universe bestow blessing upon their work. Amen. Amen. Selah."

III. (Left) "And remembered be for good Kyris Leontios and Kyra Kalonike, who have donated... denarii in honor of the synagogue. May the King of the Universe bestow blessing upon his work. Amen. Amen. Selah. Peace. And remembered be for good one woman, Anatoliya, who has donated one denarius in honor of the synagogue. May the King of the Universe bestow blessing upon her work. Amen. Amen. Selah. Peace. (And remembered be for good the inhabitants of the town [or the wakeful] who have donated one tremissis)."

IV. "And remembered be for good Kyris Hoples, and Kyra Protone, and Kyris Sallustis his son-in-law, and *Comes* Phroros his son and Kyris Photios his son-in-law, and Kyris Ḥaninah his son — they and their children — whose acts of charity are constant everywhere and who have given here five denarii of gold. May the King of the Universe bestow the blessing upon their work. Amen. Amen. Selah."

DATE OF THE SYNAGOGUE

The excavator dated the synagogue to the first half of the fifth century A.D. on the basis of the names in the inscriptions, the like of which occur from the fourth century A.D. onward, and also on the basis of the title *"Comes,"* which Jews could not hold after A.D. 438. The plan of the synagogue is of a mixed type. The transverse row of columns and the square hall are characteristic of early synagogues. The apse and mosaic pavement are typical of the later types. Because of the absence of human images and the paucity of faunal and floral representations, this synagogue should be assigned either to the earliest period of the laying of mosaic pavements in synagogues, or to the time when resistance to images and figures was beginning and interest in geometrical patterns was again on the increase (from the middle of the sixth century A.D. onward). In comparison with the mosaics of the synagogue in Ḥammat Tiberias, a later date should perhaps be assigned.   M. AVI-YONAH

BIBLIOGRAPHY

Sukenik, *Ancient Synagogues*, 81 f.; idem, *JPOS* 15 (1935), 101–80 • S. Klein (ed.), *Sefer ha-Yishuv* 1, Jerusalem, 1939, 45–47 • M. Avi-Yonah, *BJPES* 12 (1946), 17–19 (both Hebrew).

From top to bottom: Panel from the chancel screen of the synagogue. Inscription (no. 1) in mosaic floor of synagogue mentioning the donors. Remains of Roman theater.

HAZOR

IDENTIFICATION. Hazor, a large Canaanite and Israelite city in Upper Galilee, was identified by J. L. Porter in 1875 with Tell el-Qedah (also called Tell Waqqas) some 14 kilometers (8.5 miles) north of the Sea of Galilee and 8 kilometers (5 miles) southwest of Lake Ḥuleh (map reference 20322691). This identification was proposed again in 1926 by J. Garstang who conducted trial soundings at the site in 1928.

HISTORY

Hazor is first mentioned in the Egyptian Execration Texts (published by G. Posener) from the nineteenth or eighteenth century B.C. It is the only Canaanite city mentioned (together with Laish-Dan) in the Mari documents of the eighteenth century B.C.,

Plan of the site, showing excavated areas.

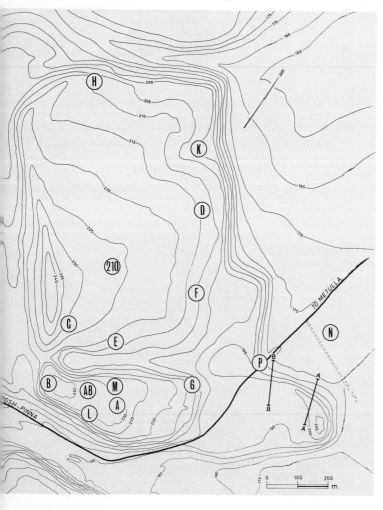

which points to Hazor having been one of the major commercial centers in the Fertile Crescent. The caravans plying between Babylon and Hazor passed through other large centers, such as Yamkhad and Qatna. Hazor is also mentioned frequently in Egyptian documents of the New Kingdom, such as the city lists of Thutmose III's conquests, the Papyrus Leningrad 1116-A, and the city lists of Amenhotep II and Seti I. The role of Hazor in the el-Amarna letters is of particular significance. The kings of Ashtaroth in the Bashan and of Tyre accuse 'Abdi-Tirshi, king of Hazor, of having taken several of their cities. The king of Tyre furthermore states that the king of Hazor had left his city to join the Ḥabiru. The king of Hazor, on the other hand, one of the few Canaanite rulers to call himself king (and to be called so by others), proclaims his loyalty to Egypt. In the Papyrus Anastasi I, probably dating from the time of Ramses II, the name of Hazor occurs together with that of a nearby river.

Hazor is first mentioned in the Bible in connection with the conquests of Joshua (Joshua 11:10–13). The Bible relates that Jabin, king of Hazor, was at the head of a confederation of several Canaanite cities in the battle against Joshua at the Waters of Merom. Especially noteworthy are the verses: ''And Joshua at that time turned back, and took Hazor, and smote the king thereof with the sword: *for Hazor beforetime was the head of all those kingdoms* ...and he burnt Hazor with fire....But as for the cities that stood still in their strength, Israel burned none of them, save Hazor only; that did Joshua burn.'' Here, then, is a direct reference to the role of Hazor at the time of the Conquest.

Hazor is also indirectly mentioned in the account of Deborah's wars in the prose version preserved in Judges 4 in contrast to the ''Song of Deborah,'' which describes a battle in the Valley of Jezreel without mentioning Hazor.

In I Kings 9:15, it is related that Hazor, together with Megiddo and Gezer, was rebuilt by Solomon. According to II Kings 15:29, Hazor, among other Galilean cities, was conquered in 732 by Tiglath-pileser III.

The city is again mentioned indirectly in I Maccabees 11:67 which relates that Jonathan and his army marched northward from the Valley of Ginnosar in his campaign against Demetrius. Jonathan camped on the plain of Hazor (πεδίον Ἀσωρ) near Cadasa. Josephus describes Hazor as situated above Lake Semachonitis (*Antiquities* V, 199).

TOPOGRAPHY

The site comprises two distinct areas: the mound proper, covering 120 dunams (at the base) and rising about 40 meters above the surrounding plain, and a large rectangular enclosure of about 700 dunams (1,000 by 700 meters) to the north of the high mound. On the west, this enclosure is protected by a huge rampart of beaten earth and a deep fosse, on the north by a rampart alone, and on the east by a steep slope reinforced by supporting walls and a glacis. On the south, a deep fosse separates the enclosure from the mound.

EXCAVATIONS

The results of Garstang's trial soundings (1928) in the mound and the enclosure were not published in detail. He concluded, *inter alia*, that the enclosure, which he called the camp area, was a camping ground for infantry and chariotry, rather than an actual dwelling area. As no Mycenaean pottery was found, Garstang dated the final destruction of the site to about 1400 B.C., the period to which he assigned Joshua's conquest. On the west side of the mound proper stood a structure which he dated to the Israelite and Hellenistic periods (see below, area B). In the center of the mound (see below, area A), he found a row of pillars and assumed them to be part of a stable from the time of Solomon.

In the years 1955–58, the James A. de Rothschild Expedition, under the direction of Y. Yadin, conducted excavations on the site on behalf of the Hebrew University in conjunction with PICA, the Anglo–Israel Exploration Society, and the Government of Israel. Among the members of the expedition were Y. Aharoni, Ruth Amiran, M. Dothan, Trude Dothan, the late I. Dunayevsky, Claire

Aerial view of the site, looking north.

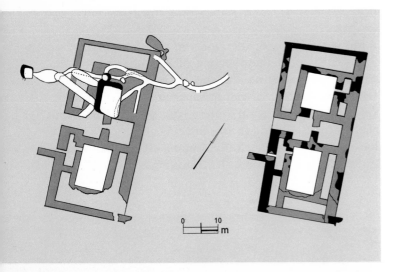

Both pages, counterclockwise: Area F, stratum 3; on the right, the palace; on the left, the underground tunnels shown beneath the palace. From area C, fourteenth–thirteenth centuries B.C.: Basalt statue of deity or king from the stelae temple; basalt stele from the stelae temple. Silver-plated cult standard of bronze; pottery cult mask.

Epstein, and J. Perrot. A further campaign was carried out in 1968 by Y. Yadin, assisted by A. Ben-Tor, Y. Shiloh, A. Mazar, A. Eytan, and Malkah Batyevsky. During the five seasons of work, several areas were excavated, both on the mound and in the enclosure (the latter proving to be the Lower City in the Bronze Age). The results of the excavations in each area are briefly presented below. Because of the great distances between the areas, separate strata numbers were assigned to each. These were later synchronized and arranged in an overall scheme.

THE LOWER CITY

Area C is located at the southwestern corner of the Lower City, adjoining the earth rampart. Five levels were distinguished (from top to bottom: 1-a, 1-b, 2, 3, 4). The buildings unearthed in this area provided the first evidence that the enclosure was in fact the Lower City.

STRATUM 4, the lowest level, is assigned to the beginning of Middle Bronze Age II-B, that is, the mid-eighteenth century B.C., when the first fortifications and the ramparts of the Lower City were constructed. A jar bearing an Akkadian inscription (the earliest found in Israel), incised before firing and bearing the name of the owner of the vessel, most probably belongs to this period.

STRATUM 3, which was destroyed by a conflagration, belongs to the end of Middle Bronze Age II. Many infant burials in jars were found beneath the floors of the houses of this level.

STRATUM 2, above a thick layer of ash, represents the city inhabited during the Late Bronze Age I. Various dwellings were excavated in this level. The results of the 1968 excavations indicated that the orthostats (see below, area H) most likely originated in this stratum, which probably represented the Hazor of Thutmose III.

STRATUM 1-b represents the peak of Hazor's prosperity in the Late Bronze Age II. A small, broadhouse temple was discovered on the inner slope of the rampart. In a niche in its western wall were a number of small stelae and statuettes that were re-used in the next stratum. Benches for offerings line the walls. Nearby are several large houses, including potters' workshops, complete with their installations. These evidently served the temple. The local and imported (Mycenaean III-A) pottery place the city in the el-Amarna period (fourteenth century B.C.). Noteworthy finds include a pottery cult mask, discovered in a potter's workshop and similar to another mask found in area D, and a bronze standard plated with silver. It bears a relief of a snake goddess and was apparently attached to a pole by means of a tang.

STRATUM 1-a. The city of this stratum is a reconstruction of stratum 1-b. The structures of stratum 1-a are essentially similar to those of 1-b. Since they are quite close to surface level, they have been poorly preserved. The temple was also reconstructed in this stratum, and all the accessories of the former stratum were found in situ — a row of small basalt stelae, one with two hands stretched toward a divine lunar symbol (crescent and circle), and a statuette of a seated male figure. Its head had been deliberately broken off and was found lying on the floor.

Mycenaean III-B sherds, together with the local pottery, indicate that this city came to an end before the close of the thirteenth century B.C., when occupation ceased in the Lower City. This destruction was most probably caused by the Israelites, as is recounted in the Book of Joshua.

Areas D, E, and 210, located at various points in the Lower City, corroborated the conclusion that the entire area of the enclosure was indeed a Lower City which met its destruction in the thirteenth century.

In area D, at the eastern edge of the Lower City, rich Middle Bronze Age II graves were uncovered, as well as Late Bronze Age I–II building remains containing many Mycenaean vessels. Among the finds was part of a sherd inscribed in paint in Proto-Canaanite script (thirteenth century B.C.):...*lt*.

Area E, at the southern edge of the Lower City, considerably enriched the knowledge of the pottery at Hazor in the Late Bronze Age I. A number of vessels were found which have no parallels in Canaan but resemble Late Bronze Age I ceramic types from Anatolia.

Area 210, a trial sounding in the center of the Lower City (measuring 5 by 5 meters), proved that the sequence of strata here is similar to that found in area C. As in area C, here, too, a large number of infant burials in jars were found beneath the floors of stratum 3.

Area F is located in the eastern section of the Lower City south of area D. Buildings and installations

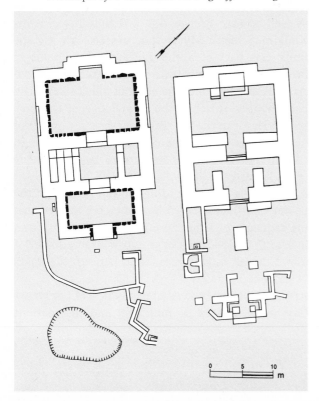

Area H, the temple: Top: Plan of stratum 1-b on the left, of stratum 2 on the right. Bottom: Aerial view of the temple after excavation showing different stages.

from all phases of occupation in the Lower City were uncovered in this area. A remarkable find, attributed to stratum 4, were rock-cut tombs with an elaborate network of tunnels connecting them. As a rule, these tombs consisted of a large, rectangular shaft, with caves hewn in varying shapes branching from its base. The eastern extension of the tunnel network, which was not cleared, may have also originally served for the drainage of water that had collected in the shafts. Except for a few pottery vessels, the tombs were found to be empty. They probably had been rifled already in antiquity.

In STRATUM 3 (Middle Bronze Age II-C), a large building with very thick walls was found, constructed on a rectangular plan. It was perhaps a double temple, dedicated to two deities.

In STRATUM 2 (Late Bronze Age I), part of the double temple was reconstructed, while other parts of the structure remained disused. The building is square in plan and divided into chambers around a central area. It, too, is perhaps a temple, similar in plan to the one discovered in 'Amman. A number of burials nearby contained a large assortment of Bichrome ware.

STRATUM 1-b (el-Amarna period) has a clear cultic nature. A stone altar — a huge ashlar stone taken from the Middle Bronze Age II temple — with de-

pressions for draining the sacrificial blood, stood in the southwestern part of the area. A drainage canal leading from the altar joined the earlier drainage and tunnel systems. Around the altar were a number of structures (evidently of a cultic nature), in which were found alabaster incense burners and other ritual vessels. A large tomb belonging to this stratum contained hundreds of vessels, including much Mycenaean III-A ware. The tomb served as a burial place during the entire period of stratum 1-b in the fourteenth century B.C.

In STRATUM 1-a most of the buildings surrounding the altar were renovated. Many incense burners and Mycenaean III-B vessels were found also in this stratum, which was completely destroyed in the thirteenth century B.C.

Area H lies at the northern tip of the Lower City. A series of four superimposed temples was unearthed here against the inner face of the earth rampart, similar to the location of the temple in area C.

In STRATUM 4, no remains of buildings were uncovered. This was the phase in which the rampart was erected, since in the course of constructing the earliest of the temples, that of stratum 3 (Middle Bronze Age II), the entire area had been leveled and filled up to the edge of the rampart. A number of stone structures found within the fill may have been part of the fill itself. It has been established, however, that the large rampart also found in this area was constructed during stratum 4, *i.e.,* in Middle Bronze Age II-B.

The temple of STRATUM 3 consisted of a broad hall, with a small rectangular niche, a sort of holy of holies, on the north side. The remains of two basalt capitals, or bases, indicate that two columns supporting the roof stood in the center of the room. This was necessary because of the dimensions of the hall. Two square areas on either side of the wide entrance on the south were evidently the foundations of two towers which flanked the entrance to the hall. South of the hall was a raised platform, which was reached by several steps made of finely dressed basalt. The entire area around the temple was paved with very small cobblestones. In several respects, this temple is similar in plan to those found at Shechem and Megiddo (stratum VIII), except that here the temple consists of a broadhouse rather than a long hall.

The temple plan of STRATUM 2 is identical with

From area H, top to bottom: On the left, bronze plaque in relief (stratum 2; sixteenth–fifteenth centuries B.C.) and on the right, basalt incense altar from the temple holy of holies (stratum 1-a; fourteenth–thirteenth centuries B.C.). Ritual vessels in situ in the temple holy of holies (stratum 1-a; thirteenth century B.C.). The lion orthostat in situ as found in pit; fourteenth–thirteenth centuries B.C.

that of the one above. The floor, however, had been raised and paved with large cobblestones. These stones were plastered with a white limey clay, typical of the Late Bronze Age I constructions at Hazor. The major modifications were made around the temple. South of it was a closed court paved with cobblestones, and farther to the south was a large open court, paved in a similar manner. The closed court was entered through a broad propylaeum, the threshold of which consisted of basalt slabs. A large, rectangular bamah ("high place") and several smaller altars were found in the court. Near the bamah, where the sacrificial animals were slaughtered, a single drainage channel was discovered, consisting in part of disused incense stands. On the other side of the court was a pottery kiln that still contained a large number of votive bowls. To the east of the main bamah was a heap of broken ritual vessels, including fragments of clay models of animals' livers for priestly divining. One of these bore an Akkadian inscription that mentioned various evil omens. Another noteworthy find in the court was a delicately hammered bronze plaque of a Canaanite dignitary enveloped in a long robe. It is possible that the orthostats mentioned below originated in this temple.

The plan of the temple in STRATUM 1-b is essentially different from that of the two earlier structures, although it was built partly on their foundations. Only on the northern side was the later

Area K, stratum 3. The gate; MBA II.

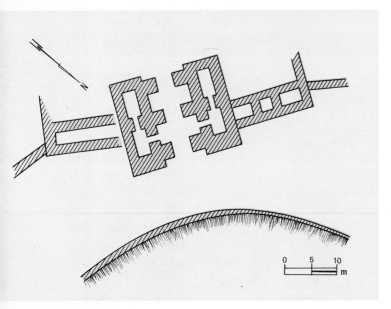

temple influenced by the plan of the earlier ones. The temple comprised three main elements built in succession from north to south, with the doorways on a single axis leading into each chamber.

1. THE PORCH. Situated on the southern side of the temple, this constituted the main innovation in the previous plan. It is somewhat narrower than the hall and served as a sort of entrance hall to the temple proper, but, unlike that of stratum 2, it was attached directly to the main structure.

2. THE HALL. This chamber was identical in its basic features with the porch of the previous temples.

3. THE HOLY OF HOLIES. This was a broad-room, similar to that of the previous temples, with a rectangular niche in its northern wall. In the center of the room were two bases of columns which supported the roof.

In its general plan, this temple resembles several of those found at Alalakh, as well as Solomon's Temple. From an architectural point of view, the most important feature in temple 1-b is the row of well-dressed basalt orthostats forming a dado around the lower part of the interior of the porch and the holy of holies. This feature clearly reflects northern influence and has close parallels at Alalakh and other sites. These orthostats most probably originated in the temple of stratum 2 and were re-used here. On either side of the entrance to the porch stood a basalt orthostat with a lion in relief. However, only one lion was found, buried in a pit deliberately dug for this purpose near the entrance. In style, the lion resembles the small orthostats found in the temple in area C and in the palace in area A. A basalt obelisk also stood near the entrance. No traces of fire were evident in this temple, and the finds were relatively scarce. It is very likely that most of the ritual vessels found in stratum 1-a originally belonged to this temple.

The temple of stratum 1-a is identical with the previous one, with only minor repairs and alterations. The floor of the holy of holies was raised and two new column bases were found resting on it, one of them still bearing the lower part of a stone column. The hall was widened at the expense of a side room on the east. The porch was reconstructed in such a manner that it is difficult to establish whether it was roofed or enclosed by walls. In front of the entrance leading from the porch into the hall, two round bases were found in situ. Their location indicates that they had a cultic significance similar to that of the pillars "Jachin and Boaz" in Solomon's Temple. A basalt table for offerings was found in situ in the hall near the entrance to the holy of holies.

Of particular interest in this temple are the cultic furnishings. These were found in a thick layer of ashes, especially in the holy of holies, showing that stratum 1-a was brought to an end by a conflagration. Among the ritual vessels that probably originated in the temple of stratum 1-b, the excavators discovered a basalt altar in the form of a square pillar having on one side the divine symbol of the storm god in low relief—a circle with a cross in its center. As indicated by the traces of fire on its upper part, this altar was used for burning incense. A large, round basin made of basalt, somewhat like the "Sea" of Solomon's Temple, was found next to the altar, as were several libation tables and a deep basalt bowl with a running-spiral design in relief on its exterior, a statuette of a seated figure, a large group of cylinder seals of the Late Mitannian type and a scarab with the name of Amenhotep III (similar to scarabs discovered in other temples of the thirteenth century B.C., such as those of Beth-Shean and Lachish).

Outside the area of the temple proper, fragments of a statue of a deity were found. This statue, which stood on a bull-shaped base, had a divine symbol on its chest, similar to the one on the incense altar described above.

Area K is situated on the northeastern edge of the Lower City not far from the northern corner. In this area, which is lower than its surroundings, the excavators uncovered a series of city gates, whose dates range from the founding of the Lower City down to its final destruction in the thirteenth century.

STRATUM 4. Very little was found of the gate of this stratum, which dated from the beginning of the Lower City and was built on virgin soil, although enough has survived to indicate its general plan. A simple gate passageway was flanked on either side by a solid brick tower on stone foundations and measuring about 8 square meters. This gate, which is similar to the southern gate at Gezer, apparently had a number of pilasters in the passageway. The city wall near the gate stood on lower ground and consisted of two parallel walls, each of which was about 1.5 meters thick and also built of brick on stone foundations. The space between the walls was filled with beaten earth, similar to the Middle Bronze Age II fortress found in area B. On both sides of the gate, the wall joined the rampart and the glacis at the point where it reached the natural, higher level of the Lower City. The gate was situated slightly to the rear of the natural slope and was approached by means of a gradual ascent constructed of beaten earth laid in alternate layers of basalt flakes and clay, crushed yellowish chalk rock, and brown brick clay.

STRATUM 3. This gate, built at the end of the Middle Bronze Age II, is completely different from the gate of stratum 4, both in plan and in position. It is patterned after the "classical" gate plan of this period. Three pairs of pilasters narrowed the width of its passageway to 3 meters. The entrance to the gate was flanked by two large towers. The southern tower (the only one excavated) is divided into two interconnected chambers. To this gate belongs the adjoining true casemate wall—the earliest of its type thus far found in Canaan (a similar one has now been uncovered at Taanach). The wall evidently continued for only a short distance before joining the main defenses of the city on a higher level of the Lower City. The great revetment wall built of large basalt boulders discovered on the slope east of the gate probably belongs to this phase. This wall supported the causeway leading up to the gate from the north along the slope. In front of the gate, the road made a right turn at an angle of 90 degrees on a large, artificial platform supported on the east by the revetment wall. This wall has been preserved to a height of more than 5 meters and is one of the finest examples of Middle Bronze Age II fortifications.

STRATUM 2. The gate of this phase, built during the Late Bronze Age I, is identical with that of stratum 3. Its huge, well-dressed, ashlar stones indicate, however, an altogether different construction technique. The casemate wall was strengthened in this period by the construction of additional upper courses.

STRATUM 1-b. The gate of this stratum, which dates from the Late Bronze Age II (fourteenth century B.C.), is that of stratum 2 with several modifications and the addition of a cobblestone floor of the type found in areas A and H in the parallel strata. South of the gate there are a number of workshops and a small cult installation containing several stelae similar to those discovered in area C. The section of the wall adjacent to the gate was rebuilt, and the casemate wall of the previous stratum was replaced by a brick wall 3 meters thick.

STRATUM 1-a. In this stratum, the gate is identical with that of stratum 1-b, except for minor repairs and additions. A thick layer of ash and rubble on the cobblestone floor of the passageway contained the fallen brickwork of the gate and towers. The excavators differ as to the date of this layer. In one opinion, the gate of stratum 1-b was no longer in use. It was not newly renovated in stratum 1-a and the conflagration is, therefore, to be assigned to stratum 1-b. This theory is based on the fact that a flimsy structure, apparently constructed on the city wall, was found south of the gate, thus proving that the fortifications had ceased being used. In the opinion of the director of the excavations, however, the destruction of the gate is to be attributed to stratum 1-a, paralleling the conflagration in the temple of stratum 1-a in area H. The nature of the small house mentioned above was not satisfactorily established during the excavations, nor did a trial sounding in 1961 succeed in proving that it was indeed built upon the wall.

Area P. This area is situated at the corner between the east and north sides of the eastern spur of the Lower City. Here, too, as in area K, a sequence of five city gates was found, ranging in date from the beginning of the Middle Bronze Age II-B to the end of the Late Bronze Age (strata 4, 3, 2, 1-b, 1-a). The discovery of a well-preserved gate of stratum 1-a further corroborates the conclusion that the latest gate in area K should be attributed to stratum 1-a. An important contribution of this area to the understanding of the Middle Bronze Age fortifications was made by the discovery near the gates of the joint between the gate and the eastern rampart. The excavation proved that the joint was achieved by means of a number of stone-built terraces, gradually rising from the gate to the top of the rampart. These terraces served as foundations for a thick, brick wall which joined the rampart farther to the east. In a short trial dig made in 1965, farther to the east, the method of the construction of the earthen rampart was ascertained. In some sections, it consisted of a brick-built core.

THE UPPER CITY

Three main areas were excavated in the Upper City in the 1955–58 seasons: area A in the center, area B on the western edge, and area G on the eastern edge. In 1967, two additional areas were opened— M in the north and L in the south—and area A was expanded. A small area, BA, was also excavated in both campaigns.

Area A, at the center of the mound, was the site of Garstang's trial excavation. He found there a row of pillars, which he identified as a stable from the time of Solomon (see below, stratum VIII). In one section of area A, the 1955–58 excavations reached bedrock and obtained a clear section of the levels of occupation in the Upper City from the first settlement onward.

STRATA XXI–XIX. Immediately above bedrock, building remains of three Early Bronze Age strata were found. Stratum XXI contained some pottery datable to the end of Early Bronze Age II. In stratum XX, a large number of sherds of Khirbet Kerak ware (Early Bronze Age III) was found.

STRATUM XVIII. No buildings were uncovered in the small sector cleared. The pottery found here is typical of the Middle Bronze Age I.

STRATA XVII–XVI. These two strata, which parallel strata 4–3 in the Lower City and represent the Middle Bronze Age II-B–C, are separated from one another by two floors of a large building originating in stratum XVII. Although only a small part of this structure was uncovered, it is clear from its size and location that it was either a palace or a citadel. Another building of the Middle Bronze Age II found in area A and most probably originating in stratum XVI was a rectangular temple. This temple —16.2 by 11.6 meters (exterior measurements)— was re-used and rebuilt in the following stratum XV (see below).

In a sectional trench dug east of the excavated area, a massive wall attributed to these two strata was discovered. This wall, which is 7.5 meters thick and built of plastered bricks on a stone foundation, probably protected the inner part of the Upper City. A good part of the wall still survived in the Late Bronze Age. It was again used, together with its moat, in Solomon's fortifications (see below), apparently as a sort of outer defense. The 1968 season indicated that prior to the fortification of the city of stratum XVII, there existed a small, unfortified settlement, of the very beginning of Middle Bronze Age II-B. In the chart below, this phase is called pre-XVII. In 1971, a chance find of

Jerusalem. Fresco fragments; Herodian period.
Upper rows: From excavations in the Jewish Quarter.
Bottom row: From excavations on Mount Zion.

Jerusalem. Top: Terra sigillata bowl from Citadel excavations; Herodian period. Bottom: Herodian bowls painted in "Pseudo-Nabataean" style from the excavations adjacent to the Temple Mount.

a rich tomb in area L (see below) confirmed by its position and contents the existence of this settlement. Furthermore, the latest excavations showed that after the destruction of stratum XVI, the site was used as a burial ground by squatters at the end of the Middle Bronze Age II. This phase is now called post-XVI.

STRATUM XV (which parallels stratum 2 in the Lower City) included among the typical Late Bronze Age I pottery uncovered here a number of sherds of Bichrome ware. The rectangular temple (mentioned above) was reconstructed in this stratum and an impressive orthostat entrance added to it.

STRATUM XIV parallels stratum 1-b in the Lower City. The remains of this stratum were extensively dismantled by the later settlers, but enough remained to indicate its date (fourteenth century) and magnitude. The orthostat temple was not rebuilt, although many shrines and cult installations were found in its vicinity.

STRATUM XIII, the last Late Bronze Age level on the mound, parallels stratum 1-a in the Lower City. With the destruction that occurred in this level, Canaanite Hazor was brought to an end in the thirteenth century B.C. As in the Lower City, few new houses were built, the ruins of the previous stratum being reconstructed and some structures erected here and there around the reservoir. A small cult installation, including stelae, found near the derelict temple, may be assigned to this stratum.

STRATUM XII. After a certain gap, a small settlement rose at the beginning of the Iron Age on the ruins of stratum XIII. This settlement, which can hardly be called a city, consisted mostly of deep silos, hearths, and foundations for tents and huts. The pottery is typical of the twelfth century B.C. and closely resembles that found in similar poor Israelite settlements in Upper Galilee. The settlement may be assigned to the first efforts of the Israelites to settle on the site.

STRATUM XI. No definite structures of this level were uncovered in this area.

STRATUM X. This stratum represents Hazor rebuilt as a fortified city. Its main features are a casemate wall and a large gate with six chambers, three on either side, and two towers flanking the passageway. On the basis of the stratigraphy, pottery, and biblical references, these fortifications are to be attributed to Solomon. The resemblance of the plan of the gate and the wall to similar Solomonic structures at Gezer and Megiddo (qq.v.) confirm this conclusively. This stratum has been subdivided by the excavators into two phases (X-a and X-b).

STRATUM IX, which is also divided into two phases (IX-a and IX-b), shows a certain decline in the quality of the buildings. This stratum is assigned to the period between Solomon and the rise of the Omrid dynasty. It was destroyed by fire.

STRATUM VIII. The main discovery in this stratum, in which extensive building activity is evident, is a large storehouse with two rows of pillars along its center and two halls attached to the north side. The rooms of the earlier casemate wall now served only as storerooms. The northern row of pillars was that uncovered by Garstang and mistakenly attributed by him to Solomon. In general plan these buildings differ completely from the structures of strata IX–X. The construction of this city by the Omrid dynasty represents a definite turning point in the history of Israelite Hazor. (See also, below, for the water system discovered in area L.)

STRATUM VII. The pillared storehouse continued in use in this level, although the floor was raised and laid over the debris of the fallen roof of stratum VIII. More basic changes occurred in the structures around the storehouse. This stratum was completely destroyed, and the pillared storehouse and other buildings were not reconstructed in the following strata.

STRATUM VI. The public buildings of the previous level were not re-used, and the entire area became a residential quarter with workshops and stores. There are clear signs that this city was destroyed by the earthquake in the days of Jeroboam II, which is mentioned by Amos. In one of the houses, a sherd was found bearing an incised inscription למקברם "belonging to Makbiram." An ivory cosmetic palette was also found here.

STRATUM V. In this level, most of the buildings of the previous stratum were reconstructed. The city was destroyed by a conflagration, traces of which were evident throughout the area. With this destruction, which is ascribed to the conquests of Tiglath-pileser III in 732 B.C. as recorded in II Kings 15:29, Hazor as a fortified Israelite city came to an end.

STRATA IV–I. With the exception of several

burials of stratum II (see below, area B), little was found in this area.

Area B is located at the western edge of the mound. Most of this area was occupied in the Israelite period by a large citadel, which was not removed in the recent excavations. Most of our knowledge of the older periods, therefore, derives from the excavation of a small sector east of the citadel. Only poorly preserved remains from the Bronze Age were revealed here.

STRATA XVII–XVI (Middle Bronze Age II). From this period were found the remains of a large citadel constructed of brick, with the spaces between the foundation walls filled with beaten earth as in stratum 4 in area K. It is attributed to the Middle Bronze Age II-B.

STRATA XV–XIII (Late Bronze Age). Remains were found indicating the existence of a settlement here during the Late Bronze Age, but there were not enough to ascertain their nature. The local pottery and imported wares point to Late Bronze Age I and II-A–B.

STRATUM XII (Iron Age). As in area A, here, too, remains were found of the first poor Israelite settlement built on the ruins of the last Canaanite occupation of the thirteenth century B.C. It resembles the settlement in area A and consists of silos, tent and hut foundations, and the like. The pottery is homogeneous and identical with that found in the small Israelite settlements of the twelfth century B.C. scattered through Upper Galilee.

STRATUM XI was uncovered mainly in area B. The remains indicate that another unfortified settlement existed in several parts of the mound after the first Israelite settlement but before Solomon established a city at Hazor (stratum X). Unlike stratum XII, which still had a semi-nomadic character, stratum XI shows definite traces of a permanent settlement. The most important find in this level is a sort of bamah, or "high place," in which were found incense vessels and a jar containing a cache of bronze objects as a foundation deposit. Among these were a number of weapons and a statuette of a deity. The stratigraphy and pottery date this stratum in the eleventh century B.C.

STRATUM X. The remains of the Solomonic city, in particular the casemate wall surrounding the mound, are also well preserved in this area. At the western edge, the fortifications were expanded to form a sort of citadel, but because of the later

Opposite page: Area A; Solomonic gate and casement wall in the foreground; ninth century B.C. Pillared building in the background. This page, top: Area A, stratum IV; sherd inscribed: lmkbrm; *eighth century* B.C. *Bottom: Plan of area A:* ▨▨ *Strata X-IX* ■ *Strata VIII-VII* ▭ *Stratum VI.*

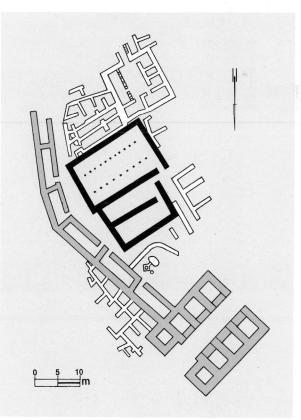

0 5 10
m

Aerial view of the ninth-century B.C. water system.

citadel of stratum VIII, built upon it, it was impossible to ascertain its exact plan.

STRATUM IX. Very few traces of this level were found here, and no plan could be established with certainty.

STRATUM VIII. The main feature of this stratum was a large citadel that covered practically the entire excavated area. The erection of this edifice in stratum VIII marks a turning point in the character of Israelite Hazor (see also area A, above, and areas G and L, below). It is of a rectangular plan and measures 21 by 25 meters, with walls about 2 meters thick. Two long halls, running from west to east, are surrounded by a series of rooms on three sides (north, south, and east). It is probable that these remains represent the cellars of the citadel and that the upper parts, reached by means of stairs (discovered intact), were built on brickwork that has not survived. Nearby were a number of buildings, which evidently were used in the administration of the citadel. Since this fortress occupied almost the entire mound here, its walls also formed, in effect, the city wall at this spot. The city wall, which extended from the east, was the earlier casemate wall, which was now filled with earth and stones to form a solid construction typical of all the Palestinian city walls from the end of the tenth or the beginning of the ninth century B.C. A similar change is evident in the fortifications at Megiddo (q.v.). The large citadel, built in the first half of the ninth century B.C., continued in use throughout the Israelite period until (in stratum V) it was destroyed to its very foundations. Of special interest is the entrance to the open area between the adjoining buildings and the citadel. This was a monumental entrance adorned with proto-Aeolic capitals and a monolithic lintel — all found near the citadel in secondary use in a later level (end of stratum VII).

STRATUM VII. In this stratum, several additions are plainly evident in the citadel, although the general plan was not altered.

STRATUM VI. The citadel continued in use for the duration of this level, with some changes and additions to the surrounding buildings as well.

STRATUM V. Drastic changes are evident in the first phase of this stratum. To meet the imminent Assyrian menace, the citadel was strengthened by an additional offset-and-inset wall on the west, north, and south. Some of the adjoining buildings had to be sacrificed in this process, the wall being constructed directly on their ruins and joined to the older wall. At the northwest corner, a single tower was erected which commanded the terrain to the north. In this phase, two buildings of the four-room type were constructed east of the citadel and evidently replaced the buildings destroyed.

The citadel met its final, complete destruction at the end of this level (the conquest of Tiglath-pileser III). The entire area was covered with a layer of ash and rubble about 1 meter thick. The most noteworthy finds in this citadel are an ivory pyxis and several Hebrew inscriptions, including one incised on the shoulder of a store jar, לפקח סמדר "belonging to Pekaḥ, *semadar*" (a type of wine), and another, לדליו "belonging to Delayo."

STRATUM IV. After the destruction of the citadel, a temporary, unfortified settlement arose. Its remains were found directly above the foundations of the fortress and the city wall. This occupation, stratum IV, from the end of the eighth century B.C., is probably to be ascribed to the Israelites who returned to the spot after the fall of the city.

STRATUM III also contains a large citadel, evidently constructed by the Assyrian conquerors. It consists of an inner courtyard surrounded by rooms on all four sides. On the east side there was another large courtyard enclosed by a wall.

STRATUM II is ascribed to the Persian period. The citadel of stratum III continued to be used, although it had undergone many alterations. The pottery — which includes Attic ware — indicates a span over the fourth century B.C.

STRATUM I contained the remains of another citadel attributed to the second century B.C., *i.e.*, to the Hellenistic period.

Area BA. East of area B, a small trial trench was excavated. It confirmed the stratigraphical sequence obtained in areas A and B from the Middle Bronze Age II on.

Area G, located on the northern edge of the eastern terrace of the mound, furnished important information regarding the extent of the Upper City in the various periods and the fortifications in this sector.

BRONZE AGE. An important find from the Middle Bronze Age II were the fortifications in the northeastern corner of the terrace, centered around a large, rounded stone bastion whose battered outer walls were protected by a deep, narrow fosse. The abundant pottery shows an occupation throughout

the Middle and Late Bronze Ages.

IRON AGE. There is not enough evidence to establish the character of the settlements before stratum VIII. But from this level onward, the remains clearly indicate that the city defenses were expanded to include area G as well, where they formed a sort of outer citadel to protect the terrace and the approach to the main gate (not yet excavated) on the south. The main city wall passed along the western edge of the terrace, which was, in turn, enclosed by another wall. All the phases of the Israelite occupation are represented here. Especially noteworthy is a four-room building originating in stratum VIII, found to the west of the terrace and a huge silo whose walls were lined with stone, dug into the center of the terrace. A postern gate in the northern part of the wall led from the outer citadel to the fields on the north. Sometime during stratum V, this gate was apparently blocked in the course of strengthening the fortifications against the Assyrians (see above, area B). Traces of the fire that destroyed the city in 732 B.C. are also clearly visible in this area. As in area B, remains of an unfortified Iron Age settlement (stratum VI), built over the ruined fortifications, were uncovered. Above these, the traces of buildings from the Persian period (stratum II) indicate that in this phase settlement was not limited to the citadel alone.

Area L. The most important discovery made in the 1968 season was the underground water system, constructed in stratum VIII. This system (area L) is located near the southern edge of the mound, where natural springs are still found 40 meters below. The water system comprises three elements: an entrance structure, a vertical shaft, and a sloping tunnel. The upper part of the shaft was cut through the strata of the mound, while its lower part was quarried out of the rock. The upper part measures about 19 meters from west to east and 15 meters from north to south, and was revetted by huge supporting walls. The total depth of the shaft is about 30 meters. The sloping tunnel (some 4.5 meters high), beginning at the bottom of the shaft, extends for about 25 meters and descends for a

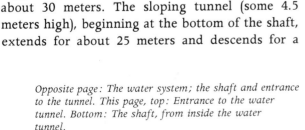

Opposite page: The water system; the shaft and entrance to the tunnel. This page, top: Entrance to the water tunnel. Bottom: The shaft, from inside the water tunnel.

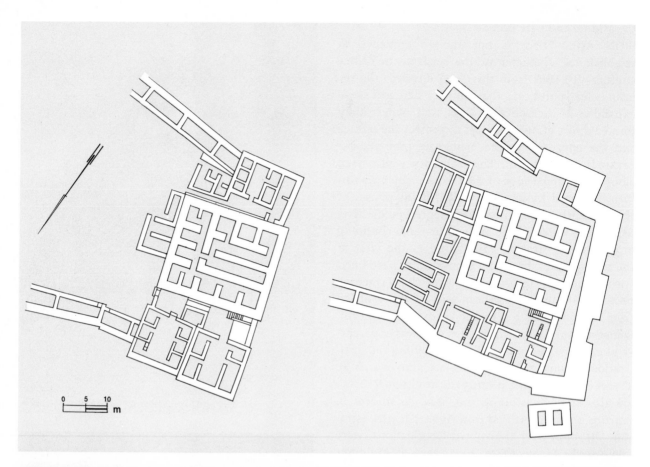

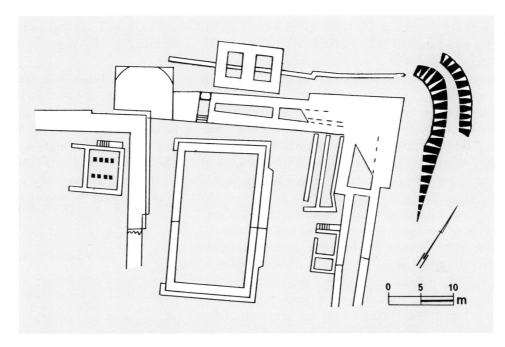

Both pages, counter-clockwise: Area B; IA citadel: On the left, stratum VIII; on the right, stratum V-a. Area B: view of the ninth-century B.C. Israelite citadel and eighth-century fortifications, looking south. Area G; stone glacis and fosse; MBA II. Area G; general plan.

further 10 meters. The tunnel ends in a sort of pool situated at the natural water level. This system, in many ways the largest of its kind, further testifies to Hazor's might in the ninth century B.C.

SUMMARY

The results of the excavations at Hazor enable us to reconstruct the history of the site and the nature of its settlement. In the third millennium B.C., the city was confined to the mound. At the end of this period there was a gap in occupation until the Middle Bronze Age I, when the mound proper was resettled.

The great turning point in the development of Hazor started in the Middle Bronze Age II-B (mid-eighteenth century B.C.), when the large Lower City was founded. Excavations in all the areas of the Lower City prove that it should not be termed an enclosure or a camp but that it was a built-up area with fortifications, constructed by a new wave of settlers too numerous to settle within the Upper City alone. Unlike the mound with its natural fortifications, here it was necessary to dig a large, deep fosse on the west, the excavated material being used to construct a rampart on the west and north. The slopes of the eastern side of the Lower City were strengthened by the addition of a glacis. Thus, a fortified area came into being, within which were built the various structures of the Lower City, the temples, public buildings, and private houses. Since the mention of Hazor in the Mari documents presumably refers to the city only after the large Lower City had been established, the results of the excavations lends support to the "lower chronology" for dating these documents, i.e., to the second half of the eighteenth century B.C. The Lower City flourished throughout the Late Bronze Age, being alternately destroyed and re-built. In these periods, Hazor was the largest city in area in the whole land of Canaan.

The final destruction of Canaanite Hazor, both of the Upper and the Lower Cities, probably occurred in the second third of the thirteenth century B.C., at which time a conflagration destroyed the city. This destruction is doubtless to be ascribed to the Israelite tribes, as related in the Book of Joshua.

Important evidence for understanding the process of Israelite settlement are the remains of stratum XII. These remains, which clearly belong to the twelfth century B.C. when Hazor ceased to be a real city, are essentially identical with the other remains of the earliest Israelite settlements in Galilee, indicating that the Israelite settlement, which was still of a semi-nomadic character, arose only after the fall of the cities and provinces of Canaan.

Only from the time of Solomon onward did Hazor return to some extent to its former splendor, although on a smaller scale than in Canaanite times. Occupation was henceforth limited to the Upper City.

In 732 B.C., Hazor was destroyed by the Assyrian invaders. It remained uninhabited thereafter, except for occasional temporary occupations or lonely forts overlooking the valley of the Ḥuleh and the important highways that passed it.

The dating of the strata at Hazor and the correlation between the Lower and Upper Cities are presented in the table on the following page.   Y. YADIN

BIBLIOGRAPHY

J.L. Porter, *Handbook for Travellers in Syria and Palestine,* London, 1875, 414–15 • J.J. Garstang, *Joshua-Judges,* London, 1931 • Y. Yadin, Y. Aharoni, R. Amiran, T. Dothan, I. Dunayevsky, J. Perrot, *Hazor 1–4,* Jerusalem, 1959–64 • Y. Yadin, *IEJ* 8 (1958), 1–14; 9 (1959), 74–88; 19 (1969), 1–19. **The temple in area C:** W.F. Albright, *Supplement to VT* 4 (1957), 242–58 • K. Galling, *ZDPV* 75 (1959), 1–13. **The conquest of Hazor by the Israelite tribes:** F. Maass in: *Von Ugarit nach Qumran,* Beihefte *ZAW* 77 (1958), 108 ff. • Y. Elitzur, *Bet Hamikra* 1 (1956), 2–8 (Hebrew) • Y. Aharoni, *The Settlement of the Israelite Tribes in the Upper Galilee,* Jerusalem, 1957, 2 ff. (Hebrew) • Y. Yadin, in *Deliberations on the Book of Joshua (Proceedings of the Bible Circle at the home of D. Ben-Gurion),* Jerusalem, 1961, 234 ff. (Hebrew). **On the status of Hazor:** A. Malamat, *JBL* 79 (1960), 12 ff. • Y. Yadin, *Hazor,* The Schweich Lectures, 1970, London, 1972.

Area B. Two proto-Aeolic capitals from the ninth-century B.C. citadel, in secondary use as a shelter for an oven.

Chronology of the strata of the Upper and Lower Cities at Hazor.

UPPER CITY	LOWER CITY	PERIOD	REMARKS
I		Hellenistic (3rd–2nd centuries B.C.)	Citadel
II		Persian (4th century B.C.)	Citadel, farmhouses, graves
III		Assyrian (7th century B.C.)	Citadel
IV		8th century B.C.	Unfortified settlement
V		8th century B.C.	Destruction by Tiglath-pileser III, 732 B.C.
VI		8th century B.C.	City of Jeroboam II, destruction by earthquake
VII		9th century B.C.	Reconstruction of parts of stratum VIII
VIII	No longer settled	9th century B.C.	Omrid dynasty
IX		End 10th–beginning 9th century B.C.	Conflagration (Ben-hadad I)
X		Mid-10th century B.C.	City of Solomon
XI		11th century B.C.	Limited Israelite settlement
XII		12th century B.C.	Temporary Israelite settlement, semi-nomadic
XIII	1-a	13th century B.C.	Destruction in second half of 13th century by Israelite tribes
XIV	1-b	14th century B.C.	Amarna period
XV	2	15th century B.C.	Thutmose III–Amenhotep II
Post-XVI		MBA II-C transitional	Graves in the ruined city
XVI	3	17th–16th centuries B.C.	Destruction by conflagration (Ahmose)
XVII	4	18th–17th centuries B.C.	Lower city founded in mid-18th century B.C. (the Mari documents)
Pre-XVII		Early MBA II-B	Unfortified. Mainly burials and some structures
XVIII	Not yet founded	21st–20th centuries B.C. (MBA I)	
XIX–XX		26th–24th centuries B.C. (EBA III)	Khirbet Kerak culture
XXI		27th century B.C. (EBA II)	

ḤEDERAH

EXPLORATION. In the summer of 1934, in the course of quarrying *kurkar* near the Naḥliel school in Ḥederah, fragments of pottery ossuaries and decayed human bones were brought to light at the foot of a hillock called Giv'at Bilu. Under the 1.5 meter thick *kurkar* layer, was a layer of sand from which fragments of ossuaries protruded. Some ossuaries were broken by the workers, but others had been damaged in antiquity. In December, 1934, E. L. Sukenik carried out excavations on the site on behalf of the Hebrew University.

EXCAVATIONS

With the removal of part of the *kurkar* layer, two complete ossuaries and many fragments were uncovered. Since the quarry workers had not dug at that spot, the discovery confirmed that some of the ossuaries had been broken in ancient times, either when they were deposited or while being moved aside to make room for more ossuaries. In the course of the excavations, many specimens were recovered. One contained human bones covered with sherds from a large vessel. Pottery vessels were found near the ossuaries: bowls, incense burners, and jugs. Of special interest was an ossuary with a pointed arched roof standing on four legs. A few chalices and bowls were found beneath it, apparently arranged in some definite order. Behind the ossuary were sherds of a large vessel covered with bones.

From the condition of the ossuaries and from the geological data, Sukenik inferred that the *kurkar* layer was formed after the chests had been deposited.

The bones found inside and around the ossuaries clearly show that these receptacles served for burial. Many ossuaries were decorated with red paint or in a pattern of parallel lines, visible on numerous sherds.

Sukenik distinguished three main types of ossuaries: (1) A rectangular type, open at the top like a box. (2) An oblong type, with a vaulted roof and a rectangular opening in one of the short sides. This was the commonest type. One specimen was found somewhat apart from the others. It had no opening and no bones inside. A fragment of the front elevation of another ossuary had the shape of a human face with a protruding nose and round eyes. (3) A rectangular type, with a pointed arched roof, standing on four legs. A square opening in one of the narrow sides was flanked at mid-height by lug handles. The other narrow side (at the rear) had three small openings at the top, arranged in the shape of a triangle with the point upward.

CONCLUSION

At the time of excavation, no comparable sites were known. Owing to the similarity of the pottery with Ghassulian ware, Sukenik dated the finds to the Ghassulian Chalcolithic, *i.e.*, to the fourth millennium B.C. The shapes of the ossuaries, reminiscent of house models, led Sukenik to conclude that they were meant to represent the houses of that period. He compared the ossuaries — the oblong type with an opening on the narrow side — with similar house plans discovered at Tuleilat Ghassul, Megiddo (stage V), Jericho, and other sites. He also found common features with the shape of Egyptian "soul houses" and especially European "house urns," where the ashes (not the bones) of the deceased were kept. From the study of the legs of one of the ossuaries, Sukenik suggested, although with reservations, that, at least in that area, the houses of that period had rested on stilts because of climatic conditions.

Since the discovery of the Ḥederah ossuaries, similar objects have been found at other Palestinian sites, confirming Sukenik's main conclusions as to the date of the finds and the architecture of that time. (See Azor, Bene-Berak, Tel Aviv, and additional bibliography there.)

Y. YADIN

BIBLIOGRAPHY

E. L. Sukenik, *JPOS* 17 (1937), 1 ff.

Fragment of pottery ossuary.

HEPTAPEGON
('En ha-Shiv'ah; eṭ-Ṭabgha)

IDENTIFICATION AND HISTORY. A Byzantine church on the northwestern shore of the Sea of Galilee. The Arabic name eṭ-Ṭabgha derives from the Greek ἐπτάπηγον (χωρίον), "(Land of) the Seven Springs." The area is probably first mentioned by the pilgrim Aetheria at the end of the fourth century A.D. The Multiplication of Loaves and Fishes (Matthew 14:13 ff.; Mark 6:34 ff.; Luke 9:11 ff.; John 6:1 ff.) was localized here. Further mention of the site was made in Byzantine times by Cyril of Scythopolis: *Life of St. Sabas* (d. 532) and in the itineraries of Theodosius (who visited Palestine about 530) and Antoninus Placentinus (about 570). Neither mentions a church. Later references to the site in sources of the seventh and eighth centuries seem to refer to another spot.

The discoveries and the Arabic name are reliable evidence for identification of the site. It appears

Ḥederah: Pottery ossuary.

that a chapel was erected on the spot in the fourth century and a church built toward the middle of the fifth. It was probably destroyed in 614, at the time of the Persian invasions, and soon forgotten.

EXCAVATIONS

The property, belonging to the Deutscher Verein vom heiligen Lande, was explored by Z. Biever at the end of the nineteenth century and by P. Karge in 1911. In 1932, A. E. Mader, assisted by A. M. Schneider, cleared the main remains. In 1936, the latter explored the earlier chapel.

FINDS

The length of the whole complex of church, court, and hospice was 56 meters from north to south, 33 meters on the western side and 24.3 meters on the eastern. The church was a basilica measuring 25 by 19 meters with transept. The level of the church was .3 meter above the narthex, .5 meter above the atrium. Walls were found standing up to 1.45 meters high. They were .6–.95 meter wide, on foundations .8–.95 meter wide. Except for the sills and stylobates (which were of white *mizzi* limestone), the whole was built of local, roughly dressed basalt, covered on the interior with mortar (a mixture of cement and lake sand) in which ribbed potsherds were set. The top layer was made of plaster mixed with straw and was painted red.

The church has a straight eastern wall. Between the eastern wall and the rear wall of the apse (1.2 meters wide with a radius of 3.3 meters) was a narrow corridor. The apse was flanked by two rooms (prothesis and diaconicon). In front of the apse extended the presbytery (6.9 by 6 meters), separated from the nave and transept by a chancel railing. The altar stands in front of the chord of the apsidal arch. It was shaped like a table, resting on four square legs. Below the table was a block of undressed limestone (1 by .6 by .14 meter). Traces of a metal cross and the chipped appearance mark it as the traditional "mensa (table) of the Lord." Behind the altar a semi-circular seat 1.1 meters wide served as a synthronos for the clergy. In front of the presbytery, a transept projected 1.75 meters on either side. A row of four pillars separated transept and nave. The central two pillars bore a triumphal arch that collapsed in an earthquake. The central pillars were reset, with two columns having a narrower range supporting it in the nave. This and the addition of an enlarged chancel screen, set parallel to the prothesis and diaconicon, were the main later

*Below: Plan of the church. 1. Court. 2. Cantharus.
3. Narthex. 4. Aisle. 5–6. Transepts. 7. Mensa Domini.
8. Schola cantorum. 9. Synthronos. 10. Prothesis.
11. Diaconicon. 12. Triumphal arch. Opposite page:
Mosaic near the altar, showing basket of loaves
flanked by fishes.*

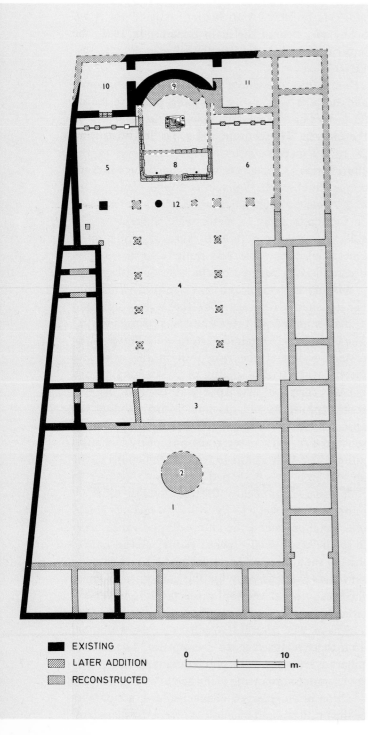

EXISTING

LATER ADDITION

RECONSTRUCTED

0   10
|_____| m·

additions. The rest of the church consisted of a nave (7.9 meters wide) and two aisles (each 3.58 meters wide). The aisles were separated from the nave by two rows of five columns each, set 3.3 meters apart. The main entrance was probably 3.2 meters wide, the aisle entrances 1.85 meters. A narthex, 3.3 meters wide, led to an atrium in the form of a rough trapezoid (23 by 13 meters) surrounded by the rooms of a hospice on the east, south, and west. A diagonal wall closed the complex on the north. It was slightly below the level of an ancient road. A cantharus, 5 meters in diameter, stood in the center of the atrium.

Below the basilical church, an earlier chapel was found, orientated 28 degrees more to the south. It measured 15.5 by 9.5 meters, with an apse 2.6 meters deep. The single room was roofed over by beams from attached pillars, 3 meters apart, 1 meter wide. Smaller finds included coins of Justin II (from the years 565 and 574), a fragment of a chancel screen, clay lamps of the sixth century, and a re-used Jewish epitaph of a certain Joseph.

THE MOSAICS

The principal interest of the Heptapegon church are its mosaic pavements. The atrium, narthex, aisles, the area between the transept pillars to the west, the presbytery, and the side rooms were all paved with ordinary geometric patterns. In the northern intercolumnary spaces (those on the south are lost) are represented two birds of the *Francolinus vulgaris* species holding garlands, two herons, two barnacle geese, and a bird fighting a badger. In the space between the pillars, in the northern transept, are two peacocks. In the presbytery, the altar is surrounded by a representation of a basket with loaves of bread (marked with crosses) and flanked by two fishes. An inscription nearby commemorates a "holy father" (whose name is missing). Another, east of the left transept, mentions a certain Saurus.

The two principal mosaics are in the left and right transepts. Each consists of a rectangular panel, bordered by lotus flowers turned alternately inside and out. Within each field (6.5 by 5.5 meters) are strewn — seemingly irregularly but actually arranged in long lines — representations of plants and animals, with a few buildings interspersed. The faunal and floral elements are depicted with much naturalism so that each species can be identified. The unrealistic element of Byzantine art appears in the lack of proportion between the various figures (houses, birds, and plants all being of equal size) and the lack of both shading and ground lines. The north panel shows, a red-crested duck poised on an Indian lotus flower, next a snipe, farther to the right two ducks, a red oleander bush, and a heron, then a barnacle goose. Below, we find, from left to right, a dove on an Indian water lily, bulrushes and a duck, another heron, a stone curlew and a *Spatula clypeata,* and, far to the right, a mountain duck. Returning to the left, a swan with two cormorants below, a flamingo killing a water snake, a bearded titmouse poised on a lotus bud. The pavement also includes bulrushes and thistles that could not be identified. The buildings include a city gate, a pavilion, and a (tomb?) tower. There are many restored places and traces of fire.

The parallel panel in the south transept is less well preserved. It shows a duck *(Anas boschas),* then an *Anthropoides virgo* attacking a young water snake springing out of a leaf. A crane stands to the left of a tower marked with stories numbered 6–10 in Greek (a type of Nilometer, which could also be used to measure the water level of the Sea of Galilee). A stork is perched on top of the tower. In the lower left are shown two ducks and a crane.

The colors include two hues of blue, light gray, three hues of red, and two of yellow. All the material is of local limestone. The number of tesserae in a square decimeter is 100–105 in the transept, 105–107 in the intercolumnia, seventy-six in the presbytery, 105 in the original part of the nave, fifty-three in the rest of the church, twenty-three in the narthex, and seventeen in the atrium.

DATE AND SIGNIFICANCE

The existence of the earlier chapel (which cannot

antedate the second quarter of the fourth century) is a *terminus a quo* for the later church. The excavators suggested a date in the late fourth or early fifth century, basing their estimates on stylistic grounds. In view of the stylistic similarity with the mosaics of the Great Palace in Constantinople, now dated to the middle of the fifth century, a similar date seems reasonable for the upper church of Heptapegon. The presbytery mosaics and inscription seem to belong to a repair of the sixth century.

Apart from their intrinsic artistic value (and they are the work of a great master), the mosaics are interesting from two aspects: They mark the introduction of the figurated pavement into the repertory of church pavements in Palestine, which until then, as far as can be seen, was exclusively geometric. This new freedom was of course limited by symbolic considerations. The other characteristic is the adaptation of a Nilotic landscape, popular in Hellenistic and Roman art, to the fauna and flora of the Sea of Galilee and its shores. These mosaics thus are a precious document for the natural history of Palestine.   M. AVI-YONAH

BIBLIOGRAPHY

A.M. Schneider, *Die Brotvermehrungskirche von et-tabga am Genesarethsee und ihre Mosaiken*, Paderborn, 1934 (English ed., London, 1937) • Unesco, *Israel Ancient Mosaics*, New York, 1960 (Introduction by M. Shapiro and M. Avi-Yonah), 9, 16–17, 20–22, pls. 1–3.

Opposite page: Mosaic in the northern (left) transept.
Below: Mosaic in the southern (right) transept.

HERODIUM

IDENTIFICATION. The fortress of Herodium is situated on a hill rising 758 meters above sea level. It is about 12 kilometers (7.5 miles) south of Jerusalem as the crow flies. Its position accords with the distance noted in several passages by Josephus, who locates it 60 stadia from Jerusalem (see *e.g., Antiquities* XV, 324). Josephus describes the hill, which is in the form of a truncated cone, as being shaped like a woman's breast. The Arabic name of the site, Jebel Fureidis, evidently preserves the name Herodis, as it was called in documents from the time of Bar Kokhba. Excavations at the site have definitely confirmed the identification of Jebel Fureidis with Herodium.

HISTORY

The main literary source for the history of Herodium are the writings of Josephus. The fortress is also mentioned by Pliny and in several documents from the time of the Bar Kokhba War. Herodium was built on the spot where Herod, when retreating from Jerusalem to Masada in flight from Matthias Antigonus and the Parthians, achieved one of his most important victories over the Hasmonaeans and their supporters in 40 B.C. (*Antiquities* XIV, 359–60; *War* I, 265).

Herodium appears to have been built after Herod's marriage to Mariamne, the daughter of Simeon the Priest of the House of Boethus. Its construction was probably not before 24 B.C. but prior to the visit of Marcus Agrippa to Judea, including Herodium, in 15 B.C. (*Antiquities* XV, 323; XVI, 12–13). According to Josephus, Herodium was built to serve as a fortress and the capital of a toparchy, as well as a memorial to Herod (*ibid.* XV, 324; *War* I, 419; III, 55). Josephus also gives a full description of Herod's funeral procession to his burial place at Herodium (*ibid.* I, 670–73; *Antiquities* XVII, 196–99). During the First Revolt, Herodium was the scene of some of the internal strife between the Zealots (*War* IV, 518–20). It is listed together with Masada and Machaerus as one of the last three strongholds, in addition to Jerusalem, remaining in the hands of the rebels on the eve of the siege of Jerusalem *(ibid.* 555). Herodium was the first of these strongholds to be captured by the Romans after the fall of Jerusalem (*ibid.* VII, 163). According to documents from the time of the Bar Kokhba War found at Wadi Murabba'at, Simeon, Prince of Israel (Bar Kokhba), had a command post at Herodis, where, among other things, land transactions were carried out and a treasury was kept — perhaps storehouses of grain.

EXPLORATION

In the fifteenth century, the Italian traveler, F. Fabri, gave "Mountain of the Franks" as the name of Herodium, the place where, as he assumed, the Crusaders made a stand after the Muslim conquest of Jerusalem. It retained this name until the nineteenth century. The first sketch plan of Herodium was made by E. Pococke during a visit in 1743. E. Robinson, in 1838, gave a detailed description of its buildings, dating them to the Roman period and noting their resemblance to Josephus' description. In 1863, the French explorer and traveler, F. de Saulcy, recorded important details and drew sketches and plans of the buildings at the foot of the hill, especially of the pool. In his opinion, the round structure in the pool was Herod's burial place. Several years later, V. Guérin accurately described the outer wall with the three semi-circular towers and eastern round tower. Until the recent excavations, the fullest account of the remains was made in 1879 by C. Schick, with plans and cross-sections. He noted that the lower part of Herodium was a natural hill and the upper part an artificial one. Schick traced the staircase leading to the structure on the summit of the hill, and he was later confirmed in his assumption that the steps led to the courtyard of the building through a tunnel-like passage dug in the artificial fill. His further assumption that cisterns had been dug in the lower part of the hill was also later verified. In addition Schick was correct in his belief that the upper structure had been designed as a grandiose mausoleum and not merely a stronghold.

In 1881, C. Conder and H. Kitchener prepared the first accurate plan of the site with the two circular walls, three semi-circular towers, and round eastern tower.

From 1962 to 1967, V. Corbo conducted four seasons of excavations at the site on behalf of the Studium Biblicum Franciscanum, uncovering most of the main building on the summit from the Herodian period, the period of the two wars with Rome, and

Aerial view of the site.

Below: Plan of the fortress. I. Round eastern tower with remains of later walls. II–IV. Semicircular towers. V. Corridor. VI. Foundations of the steps leading to the palace. VIII. Peristyle surrounding garden. XI, XXXIV. Exedrae. XII–XIII, XXXII. Entrances to the corridor. XVI–XVIII. Triclinium with four columns and adjoining rooms. XIX–XXII. Cross-shaped court. XXIII–XXXI. Bathhouse. XXXVIII–XL. Cellars.

Opposite page, counterclockwise: Bathhouse; caldarium. Exedra and stylobate. Remains of the peristyle, from the north. Area of the triclinium that apparently served as a synagogue in the period of the First Revolt, looking west.

the Byzantine period.

Preservation and restoration works were carried out in 1967 and 1970 by G. Foerster for the National Parks Authority. The entrance room to the palace was uncovered, as well as a complex network of cisterns and an elaborate system of tunnels dug in the hill and apparently dating to the time of the Second Revolt.

An impressive complex of buildings at the foot of the hill was examined in soundings made by E. Netzer in 1972 on behalf of the Hebrew University.

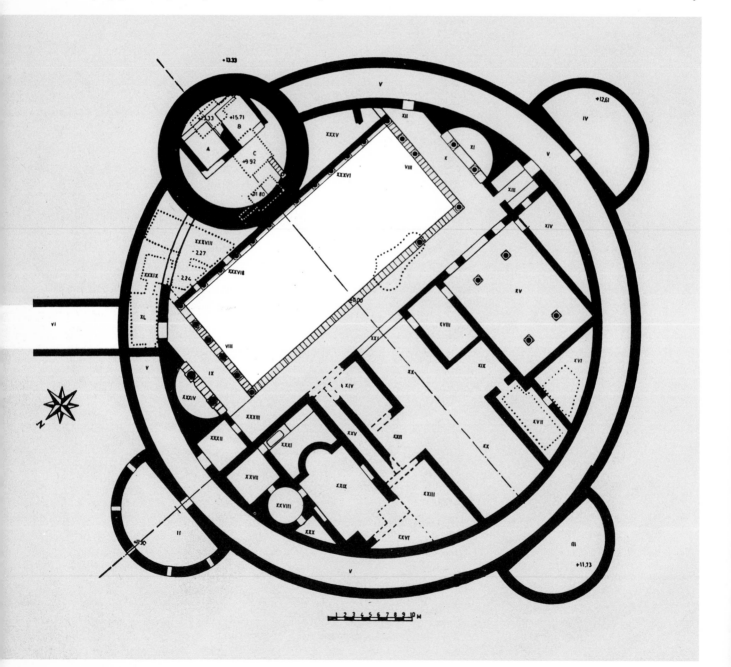

EXCAVATIONS

The investigations at Herodium have to a great extent confirmed Josephus' detailed description of the place in the Herodian period (*Antiquities* XV, 324–25):

This fortress, which is some sixty stades distant from Jerusalem, is naturally strong and very suitable for such a structure, for reasonably near by is a hill, raised to a (greater) height by the hand of man and rounded off in the shape of a breast. At intervals it has round towers, and it has a steep ascent formed of two hundred steps of hewn stone. Within it are costly royal apartments made for security and for ornament at the same time. At the base of the hill there are pleasure grounds built in such a way as to be worth seeing, among other things because of the way in which water, which is lacking in that place, is brought in from a distance and at great expense. The surrounding plain was built up as a city second to none, with the hill serving as an acropolis for the other dwellings.

Herodian Period. In its general plan Herodium

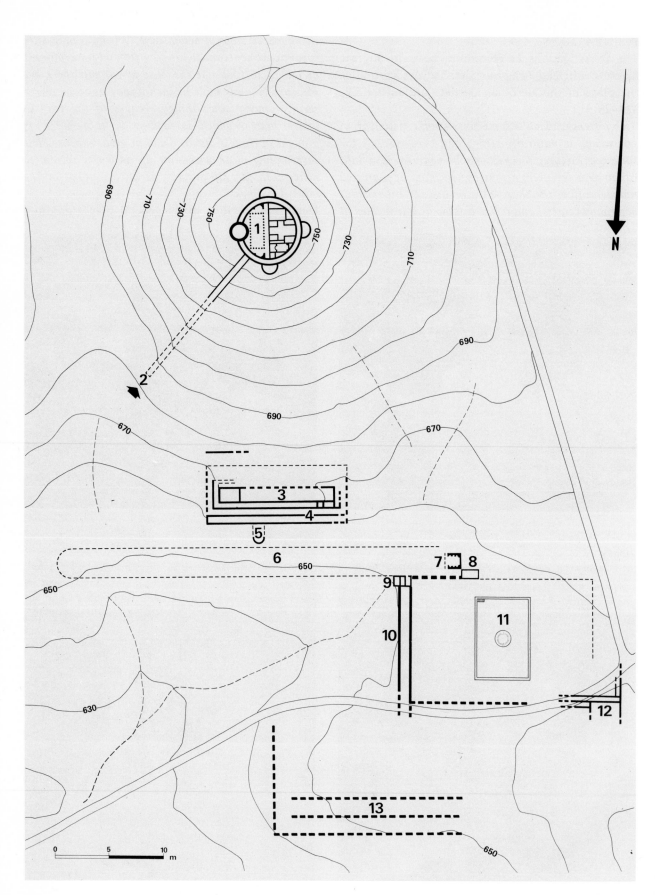

comprises two main areas: 1. a main building on the top of the hill; 2. a building complex at its base. This twofold plan, also mentioned by Josephus, has been decisively confirmed by the excavations.

On the summit of the hill, which rises 60 meters above its surroundings, a round building was erected, which is defined as a fortified palace or royal fortress. It consists of two parallel circular walls (diameter of the outer wall is 62 meters). The walls start on the east side at the monumental tower, which, according to its surviving remains, has an external diameter of 18 meters and is 16 meters high. A corridor, 3.5 meters wide, between the two walls, extended up to the eastern tower, which protruded from the outer wall. Three semi-circular towers also protruded from the wall due west, north, and south. The outer wall and the towers were built on a series of vaults (found in the excavations) designed to level the top of the natural hill. An earth and stone rampart was apparently poured over the towers and the outer wall (which rises at least 12 meters) immediately after their construction, leaving only their tops projecting from the fill. This is indicated by the great amount of building debris found in the fill of the rampart. Sections of a well-built, sloping retaining wall were discovered in the lower southeastern side of the rampart and probably served to support it. It is this rampart which gives the hill its distinctive conic shape and turns it into a giant tumulus—Herod's monument and grave.

Inside the artificial rampart was built an imposing entrance passage, which is still being excavated. The passage rises gradually from the base of the hill to a 5-meter-high vaulted entrance in the outer wall north of the eastern tower. The entrance leads into a gate chamber, which opens onto the palace garden. The entrance passage is 3.5 meters wide and apparently had two hundred marble steps

Plan of the site. 1. Mountain palace-fortress. 2. Steps leading up the mountain. 3. The lower palace (called a stable in the PEF survey). 4. Two halls with barrel vaulting. 5. Observation balcony. 6. Artificial terrace (hippodrome?). 7. Monumental building. 8. Building decorated with wall painting. 9. Rectangular towerlike structure. 10. Two retaining walls with elongated hall between them. 11. Pool with round structure in its center (pavilion?). 12. Service building with storerooms. 13. The northern complex of Herodian buildings. The Byzantine Church of St. Michael was situated here.

(mentioned by Josephus but not yet found). It was formed by two strong walls supported by a series of arches to counteract the pressure exerted by the artificial fill. Since the fill is of a homogeneous nature, it appears that the passage was deliberately sealed after Herod's burial.

The circular palace area is divided into two main sections. The EASTERN HALF of the area below the round tower was occupied by a garden, 33 by 12.5 meters, enclosed by columns on the north, south, and west. The east side of the garden was bounded by a pilastered wall. To the south and north of the peristyle garden were two symmetrical exedrae, both with two columns in their façades. Below the eastern tower on the south side was a third exedra. Its twin on the north side has not yet been uncovered because of the great amount of debris there. West of the south and north exedrae were two identical rooms, which led from the garden to the corridor between the double wall of the palace. Two entrances east of the exedrae also led to the corridor.

The WESTERN HALF of the area contains dwellings and service rooms and was divided into two parts by a cross-shaped(?) court (not yet excavated). In the middle of the southern part was a triclinium. A well-built bathhouse occupied the northern part. The triclinium was a rectangle, 10.6 by 15.15 meters, with four columns supporting the roof (only one column base was found in situ). Its entrance was in the center of the facade and was flanked by two windows. Doorways in its north and south walls led to additional rooms. The floor was laid in opus sectile, but only the base has survived. The triclinium is surrounded by four smaller rooms which also abut the inner circular wall on the south and west sides. Two well-plastered cisterns with barrel vaulting were found beneath the two western rooms. North of the triclinium was another room attached to it. Signs of at least one more story, used as living quarters, were found above these rooms and also above the bathhouse. Traces of upper stories (three?) were also noted in the corridor between the walls and in the northern tower where there were slits for inserting wooden ceilings.

The elaborately decorated bathhouse is situated northwest of the palace. The apodyterium (dressing room) had a mosaic pavement of which only fragments of two black borders on a white background

From lower Herodium: Top: Northwest corner of hall in monumental building. Bottom: Corner of Herodian tower southeast of pool complex.

have survived. The walls are ornamented with crustae in the Pompeian first style. The tepidarium (warm room) is circular, 4.15 meters in diameter, and is topped with a hemispherical dome 5 meters high. Three doors led from this room to the apodyterium, caldarium (hot room), and frigidarium (cold room). The tepidarium had a floor of white mosaic with a black band. The decoration in the center has not been preserved. The walls were decorated with frescoes in a geometric pattern in the Pompeian first style and were colored red, brown, blue, yellow, and black. Waterfowl were also depicted on the walls. The frigidarium, a small chamber abutting the inner wall of the palace, had a plastered pool in the center. The caldarium is rectangular in shape and terminates in an apse on the eastern side. It, too, is decorated with rectangular panels in the Pompeian first style in white, black, green, red, and yellow. Beneath its floor is the hypocaust. The hot air passing through its pipes was also conveyed to the north and south walls. East of the caldarium was a small chamber with a black and white mosaic pavement and a *fleuron* design within a black border.

In addition to the cistern found on the summit of the hill within the palace proper, a network of huge cisterns was also discovered dug into the interior of the hill. Thus far, four cisterns with hydraulic plaster have been excavated about 15 meters below the floor of the palace in the northeastern part of the hill. A number of staircases hewn in the rock led directly from the palace to the cisterns so that there was no need to leave the area of the palace. Since these cisterns were situated well above the aqueduct which brought water to Herodium from the springs of Urtas, they could not have received water directly from the aqueduct or from the pool at the foot of the palace. It can be assumed, therefore, that these cisterns were probably filled with water carried by pack animals from the lower pool. Herod's palace was built wholly of medium-sized ashlar stones, partly dressed with marginal drafting. All the walls, except perhaps the outer face of the exterior wall, were coated with plaster, and the lower part of the walls was painted in various colors and in various geometric panel designs in the Pompeian first style. The upper part of the walls was generally of white stucco molded to imitate architectural details. The column bases, Corinthian capitals, and the parts of the entablature found were also coated with a thin colored plaster. A number of Ionic capitals were also found. Some of the architectural fragments had stonemasons' marks in Greek or Hebrew and numerals. Several partly ruined mosaic pavements were uncovered with geometric ornaments in black and white alone. Some of the floors were laid in opus sectile.

The preliminary investigation at the foot of the hill has shown that there, too, Josephus' description agrees remarkably well with the finds. North of the hill is a huge building, 55 by 130 meters, constructed on two vaults. A level terrace, 25 by 300 meters, south of the building, is identified as a hippodrome. On the western edge of the terrace is a hall measuring 10 by 10 meters, with pilasters, niches, and a vaulted roof. A complex of buildings was examined on the northwest side. In its center was an open pool, 70 by 45 meters, in the middle of which was a structure which seems to be the foundation of a circular building in the form of a tholos. The area around the pool may have been a garden. There are traces of a portico east of the pool. Another building was found northwest of the pool with storerooms containing scores of store jars from the end of the Second Temple period. Pieces of colored and molded stucco were scattered throughout the area, as were various architectural fragments which closely resemble those found in the upper palace.

Remains from the Period of the Two Wars with Rome. Many traces were found of settlement from this time. The settlement is also known from literary sources. The new inhabitants occupied various parts of the palace, changing them to suit their needs. Signs of building were found in the area of the peristyle garden on the east and in the bathhouse and the triclinium on the west. The building activities of the new settlers were not extensive, being generally limited to the addition of walls in dry construction and the re-use of stones from the decaying palace. Many ovens for domestic use were found, some of which may have been used for smelting iron for making weapons. More basic changes of a religious and cultic nature were made in the triclinium, where rows of stone benches, constructed of building materials taken from the palace, were added along three of its walls. Apparently it now served as a synagogue for the rebels who had taken refuge at Herodium. A *miqve*, found in front of the hall, evidently was

added when the building became a synagogue.

In the opinion of V. Corbo, the intersecting walls in the three semi-circular towers on the north, south, and west were also built at this time. Building activities were also noted on the upper part of the eastern tower. One of the vaults beneath the corridor near the eastern tower was used as a cistern. Also built clearly for defensive purposes in this period was a network of subterranean passages dug into the northeast part of the hill. These passages, which are later than the cisterns from the Herodian

Lower Herodium; Greek inscription in mosaic floor of the Byzantine Church of St. Michael, situated north of the Bethlehem-Tekoah road.

period, contain traces of habitation, such as walls, pottery, and signs of fire, and may serve as confirmation of Dio Cassius' description of the defensive measures taken by the rebels during the Bar Kokhba War.

Corbo emphasizes the difficulty of differentiating between the two strata from the First and Second Revolts. The important finds from this time include large rolling stones, ballista stones, arrowheads, some scores of coins of the First Revolt, and an unusual hoard of about eight hundred bronze coins of Bar Kokhba from the three years of the war found near the southern exedra of the palace.

The small monastic settlement of the Byzantine period at Herodium is not mentioned in the ancient sources, but it has left its mark on several parts of the destroyed palace. The monks lived mainly in the parts of the bathhouse which were still roofed, and they built cells and ovens there. They also erected a small chapel in one of the rooms of the palace south of the bathhouse. They apparently abandoned the place in the seventh century.

Inscriptions. The written material found at Herodium comprises graffiti scratched on the stucco coating of the palace walls, ostraca, and inscriptions on jars. The inscriptions, which were written in Greek, Aramaic, and Hebrew, belong to the three main periods of settlement. Unlike the inscriptions from the Byzantine period, those from the time of Herod and from the two Revolts are difficult to differentiate. Graffiti from the various periods were found mainly on the walls of the bathhouse and in its vicinity. One, written in Greek, mentions Herodium(?) as a palace—Basileion—in the words of Josephus. In the bathhouse were several erotic inscriptions written by soldiers. The ostraca include one in Hebrew which mentions Herod. Others contain personal names, and several have the Hebrew alphabet.   G. FOERSTER

BIBLIOGRAPHY

Surveys and history: F. de Saulcy, *Voyage en Terre Sainte* 1, Paris, 1865, 171–76; 2, 332–35 • Guérin, *Description* 3 (Judée), 122–32 • C. Schick, *ZDPV* 3 (1880), 88–99 • Conder-Kitchener, *SWP* 3, 315, 330–32 • Benoit et alii, *Discoveries* 2, index (p. 296) s.v. • Y. Yadin, *IEJ* 11 (1961), 51–52 • A. Segal, *IEJ* 23 (1973), 27–29.
Excavations: V. Corbo, *Liber Annuus* 13 (1962/3), 219–77; 17 (1967), 65–121; idem, *Qadmoniot* 1 (1968), 132–36 • A. Spijkerman, *Herodion, Catalogo delle Monete* • E. Testa, *Herodion, I Graffitie gli Ostraca* • G. Foerster, *IEJ* 19 (1969), 123–24 • E. Netzer, *IEJ* 22 (1972), 247–49; idem, *Qadmoniot* 6 (1973), 107–110.

HESHBON

IDENTIFICATION. Eusebius' *Onomasticon* (84:5) locates "Εσσεβών, now called Εσβοῦς," 20 Roman miles east of the Jordan River opposite Jericho. Three Roman milestones on the road from Esbus to Livias and on to Jericho and Jerusalem record distances from Esbus (second to fourth centuries). Together with the general biblical references to the location of Heshbon in the "Plain of Moab" across from Jericho, the identification of Tell Ḥesban with Roman Esbus is certain, and the identification with the Heshbon of Isaiah's and Jeremiah's time is most likely correct. Since the excavations of Tell Ḥesban have so far produced no evidence for an occupation earlier than the seventh century B.C., the location of Sihon's Heshbon remains uncertain (see below). Tell Ḥesban lies 3 kilometers (2 miles) south-southwest of 'Ein Ḥesban and 9 kilometers (5.5 miles) north of Madeba on a modern asphalt road. Its size is approximately 50 acres. The summit is 895 meters above sea level. The village of Ḥesban covers the southeastern and southern slopes of the mound.

HISTORY

Heshbon first appears in the Bible as a Moabite city conquered by Sihon, king of the Amorites (Numbers 21:26). However, the city remained in Sihon's control only a short time, for the invading Israelites fought a successful battle against him under Moses and occupied it (*ibid.* 21:21–25). Heshbon was then allotted to the tribe of Reuben, which built, or rebuilt, it (*ibid.* 32:37). Later, the city changed hands and became a Gadite possession (Joshua 21:38–39). The Israelites probably lost Heshbon in the ninth century (together with other territories belonging to Gad) to King Mesha of the Moabites, whose rebellion against Israel is partly described in II Kings 3 and on the Moabite Stone. Hence, it is not strange to read that about a century and a half later Isaiah mentions Heshbon, together with Madeba, Eleale, and other former Israelite cities, as a Moabite possession (Isaiah 15:2, 4; 16:8–9). This situation still prevailed a hundred years later when Jeremiah in a prophecy denounced Heshbon with other Moabite cities (Jeremiah 48:2, 34, 45). In a later oracle of Jeremiah, however, Heshbon appeared to be in the hands of the

Below: Acropolis of Tell Ḥesban, showing
areas A–D of the 1968 and 1971

excavations. Bottom: Tell Ḥesban, seen
from the northeast.

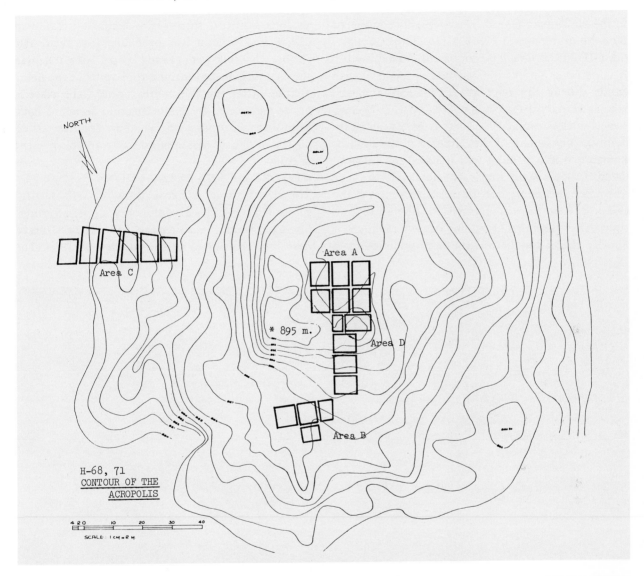

Ammonites (*ibid.* 49:2–3), who seem to have taken it during an invasion of Moabite territory referred to in Ezekiel (25:9–10).

In the Hellenistic period, Heshbon was conquered by John Hyrcanus in 129 B.C. (Josephus, *Antiquities* XIII, 255, although it is not mentioned directly). It is listed as one of the Moabite cities in Jewish hands during the reign of Alexander Jannaeus, who ruled from 103 to 76 B.C. (*ibid.* XIII, 397). King Herod settled a military colony at Esbus, as Heshbon was then called. At the outbreak of the Jewish-Roman war in A.D. 66, it was attacked by the Jews (*War* II, 458). Soon afterward, however, the city recovered its importance. In the third century, the emperor Heliogabalus granted Heshbon full city rights, including that of coining its own money. Shortly thereafter there is the first evidence for a

Christian community at Esbus. Its bishop, Gennadius, took part in the Council of Nicaea in 325. It remained the seat of a bishopric until at least the seventh century. During the Persian invasion in 614, Esbus' church was probably destroyed. The Arabs who followed twenty years later renamed the city Ḥesban and made it the capital of the Belqa district. After the thirteenth century, the place is never mentioned by historians and seems to have been deserted until some Bedouin families settled on the slopes of the mound early in the present century.

HISTORY OF THE EXCAVATIONS

The first season of excavations at Tell Ḥesban, sponsored by Andrews University, Berrien Springs, Michigan, and the American Schools of Oriental Research, took place in the summer of 1968. The

second was carried out in the summer of 1971. Both expeditions were directed by S. H. Horn of Andrews University, with R. S. Boraas of Upsala College, East Orange, New Jersey, as chief archaeologist.

During the first season (1968), excavations took place in four areas: area A, on the summit, where remains of a Roman or Byzantine public building protruded from the surface; area B, on the shelf separating the acropolis from the lower slopes of the mound, where a 7 by 7 meter square was excavated to ascertain the number of occupation layers in the mound; area C, on the western slope of the mound, in the hope of intercepting the city wall; and area D, on the southern ascent to the acropolis.

During the 1971 season, work in all four areas was continued and expanded. A fifth team worked in a Roman cemetery, recently discovered by the local villagers, in order to clear and study some unique but recently robbed graves.

RESULTS OF THE EXCAVATIONS

The earliest building remains so far discovered date from the Early Roman period, which in all four excavated areas rested on bedrock. However, evidence of an earlier occupation going back to the sixth and seventh centuries B.C. was found in the form of fills and pottery in areas B, C, and D. In area B, square 1, a 5-meter thick fill was encountered that contained large amounts of seventh-sixth century B.C. Ammonite pottery. This is the first time that such pottery has come to light in a stratigraphic excavation. Previously it has been found only in a number of tombs in and around 'Amman. An ostracon found in 1968 in the late Iron Age fill of area B and dated to about 500 B.C. contains a list of five names — of which one is Egyptian and one Babylonian — indicating that sixth-century Heshbon had a mixed population.

Another ostracon found in 1971 in the same fill can be dated to about 525 B.C. It contains the common Ammonite name *Tamak 'el* and also mentions the Edomite tribe of the Bene Gubla', referred to in Psalm 83:8.

The Roman period is represented by foundation

walls in all excavated areas, by a large subterranean cave in area A that seems to have served as an artisan's workshop, and by a number of tombs south of Ḥesban. Several of the excavated Roman walls belonged to domestic quarters, while some that were re-used in the later Christian church had been part of a public building, perhaps a temple. A fine flagstone pavement on the summit of the mound may also have been part of an important structure in Roman times.

One of the tombs, to be dated before A.D. 70, had a rolling stone in front of its entrance, the first such tomb found east of the Jordan. Inside were twelve loculi radiating from a central hall. Another Roman tomb, probably of the second century, had a swinging stone door and six arcosolia cut in the rock. Both tombs had already been rifled before the

Opposite page: Church, during excavation, looking east. The apse is seen in the right background; in the center are three column bases in situ; to the left is the northern side wall of the church. This page, top: Early Roman tomb with rolling stone in front of entrance. Bottom: Roman flagstone pavement with mouth of the huge underground cistern at lower left.

expedition began its work. Another Early Roman tomb with nine loculi, although entered and robbed of its jewelry in ancient times, still contained a large amount of pottery, glassware, and other objects when it was re-discovered.

The remains of the Christian church were the chief witnesses of the Byzantine period. It was a typical basilica-type structure, with rows of columns separating the central aisle from those in the north and south. Fragments of mosaics were found in three places. The mosaic found in the apse dates the last restoration or rebuilding of the church to the second half of the sixth century.

During the Arab period, the church ruins were covered up and the space was converted into an open plaza with vaulted buildings surrounding it on three sides — north, west, and east. Water channels drained rainwater into cisterns, some of which had already been in existence and were re-used, while others were new constructions. Altogether seven cisterns, large and small, have been discovered and excavated on the summit alone. One of them is a huge basin, over 10 meters deep, 8.5 meters long, and 4.5 meters wide, which, when full, could hold more than 300,000 liters of water.

The Mameluke period of the thirteenth–fifteenth centuries was the last era of occupation at Hesban until modern times. Whether a devastating earthquake destroyed the city and drove the population away or whether a plague made the people of Hesban vanish is not known, but the coins and pottery clearly show that the city ceased to exist in the early fifteenth century.

SUMMARY

Although the excavations at Tell Hesban have not yet been completed, it seems that the mound covers only the remains of the city from the seventh century B.C. to the fifteenth century A.D. In spite of some searching around 'Ein Hesban, no other candidate for the Heshbon of King Sihon has been found so far.   S. H. HORN

BIBLIOGRAPHY

Most of the pertinent information on Heshbon has been published in the *Andrews University Seminary Studies*.
On the history: W. Vyhmeister, *AUSS* 6 (1968), 158–77.
On the 1968 excavations: R.S. Boraas, S.H. Horn, et al., *AUSS* 7 (1969), 97–239 • A. Terian, *AUSS* 9 (1971), 147–60 • E.N. Lugenbeal and J.A. Sauer, *AUSS* 10 (1972), 21–68 • S.H. Horn, *BA* 32 (1969), 26–41.
On the 1971 excavations: Boraas, Horn, et al., *AUSS* 10 (1972).

HESI, TEL

IDENTIFICATION. Tel Hesi (Tell el-Hesi) stands on the west bank of Wadi Hesi (Shiqmah Brook), 25 kilometers (15.5 miles) northeast of Gaza and about 7 kilometers (4.5 miles) south of Qiryat Gat (map reference 124106). The area of the acropolis mound is about 11 acres, but W. M. F. Petrie discovered a large "enclosure"—a lower city, with an area of an additional 22 acres, surrounding the southern and western sides of the mound. The natural dune on which the earliest city was built is about 20 meters above the level of the valley, and the top of the mound is about 40 meters above it. The depth of the accumulated strata in the lower city varies from about 3 meters to none in the low-lying internal portions that were stripped by subsequent erosion and modern deep plowing.

Petrie believed that his excavations confirmed C. R. Conder's hypothesis that Tel Hesi was to be identified with Lachish. He based his conclusions in particular on the apparent similarity between the name "Lachish" and the Arabic name of the site "Khirbet Umm-Lakis," which is 4.5 kilometers (3 miles) northwest of Tel Hesi. Today, most scholars agree that Lachish is to be identified with Tell ed-Duweir (see Lachish), whereas Tel Hesi may be identified with Eglon, one of the important cities of the Shephelah, in the district of Lachish (Joshua 10:34, 15:39, etc.).

THE INVESTIGATION OF THE SITE

Tel Hesi was the first site in Palestine to have been excavated by scientific archaeological methods. In the spring of 1890, Petrie conducted the first excavation under the auspices of the British Palestine Exploration Fund. The excavations were carried out in a single six-week campaign. In 1891–93, F. J. Bliss continued Petrie's work and conducted excavations on the site for another four seasons. In 1970 a long-term American team project of excavation, survey, and a complement of scientific investigations was begun on the site under the direction of J. E. Worrell, assisted by L. E. Toombs, L. E. Stager, W. J. Bennett, Jr., and a team of specialists.

According to Bliss, in Petrie's six weeks of excavations he had succeeded in distinguishing all the main features of the site — the stratigraphy and the

Above: The mound during the 1973 excavations, looking northwest. Petrie's trenches are seen in the wadi face and on the southern slope. Bliss's cut makes the angular gap on the right. IA fortifications in Field III at base of mound with rounded tower just above the wadi. Below: General plan of the mound: 1. Acropolis. 2. Lower city.

periods of the cities built there. He excavated mainly the slopes of the mound, where he discovered sections of several city walls. Worrell's excavations have disclosed that much of this peripheral construction was designed for the primary purpose of consolidating the slopes against erosion, as well as for expanding the usable space on the upper portions of the acropolis. Petrie also carried out several small soundings in the lower city. Bliss, in his four long seasons, managed to excavate the northeast third of the acropolis area down to virgin soil and attempted to complete the details of the investigation begun by Petrie.

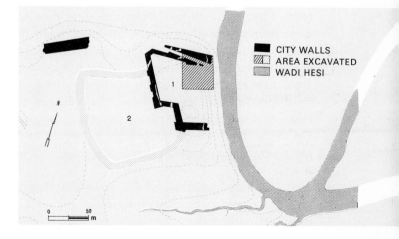

CITY WALLS
AREA EXCAVATED
WADI HESI

Worrell's excavations are located on the quadrant of the acropolis to the south of Bliss's cut, down the south slope, at its base, and in the lower city.

EXCAVATIONS

Bliss distinguished eight levels (I–VIII) and three sub-levels (I-b, II-b, and IV-b)—a total of eleven "cities." In spite of Bliss's systematic work, his division of the levels has recently been shown by the Worrell project to have discerned only a fraction of the actual strata on the acropolis. In the lower city, both Petrie and Bliss conducted only small trial soundings (Bliss made thirty), and both of them reported having discovered only "early" sherds in the area. Systematic survey and trial probes conducted during the first three seasons of the recent American project have demonstrated that the lower city had no significant occupation after the Early Bronze Age III. A section of a thick city wall, which was discovered in the lower city by the early excavators, must also be assigned to the large Bronze Age city enclosure.

Cities I-b and I. In the lowest strata excavated by Bliss, apparently only small traces of building were discovered, and these, he said, could not be described because of their miserable condition. According to the small amount of pottery published by the two investigators, the earliest settlement on the site has been dated to the Early Bronze Age. The recent American expedition, however, discovered some Chalcolithic habitations, and its survey has produced considerable Middle Paleolithic evidence. Bliss claimed that the group of bronze vessels, the crescent-shaped ax blade, the spearheads, and the few adzes discovered in a small sounding on the southeast part of the mound belonged to cities I-b and I. Kathleen Kenyon, who compared these implements with an ax found in tomb 114-A at Jericho, determined their date as Early Bronze Age III. However, the room in which these vessels were found is quite distant from the main excavation. This makes it difficult to ascertain their stratigraphic relationship to Bliss's divisions in his major cut. In any case, it is perilous to establish the chronology of the different strata on the basis of this single group of implements, and the Worrell excavations have not yet exposed those levels.

Bliss attributed to these levels the wall and rectangular tower, whose excavation he completed after Petrie's departure. The tower had two rooms, and traces of conflagration seem to prove that there were three or four phases in its history. The glacis described by Petrie may belong to this wall.

Cities II-b and II. It is not clear whether the two rows of adjoining rooms described by Bliss in his map of these "cities" belong to the new wall, or whether the wall, tower, and glacis described above belong to "cities" II-b and II. The pottery attributed to these cities is late Middle Bronze Age and Late Bronze Age I. The cemetery discovered by Petrie on the slope of the "enclosure" should be attributed to these two "cities" and to "city" III. Noteworthy in this context is a round "oven" discovered there, its function being unknown. Bliss described it in detail and emphasized that chemical examination showed that this kiln was not intended for iron smelting. The American team has found significant evidence of other such locations of intense industrial activity and confirmed Bliss on the absence of smelting residue. However, analysis of the slag has shown temperature action on materials far in excess of those used in pottery kilns of the period, so the enigma is as yet unresolved.

City III. A section of a wall with a row of rooms adjoining it belong to this "city." In one of the rooms, in a layer of debris and ashes, was discovered a tablet written in cuneiform script of the type used in the el-Amarna letters. City III has therefore been dated to the fourteenth century B.C. The letter was written by an Egyptian official named Papu, apparently residing in Lachish, and addressed to his superior, apparently in Tel Ḥesi. Papu complains that the Canaanite rulers of Yarmuth and Lachish lead bands of highwaymen and defy the Pharaoh. This document supplies important evidence of the anarchy that reigned in Palestine in the Amarna period, which was caused not only by the weakness of the central government but also by the cupidity of its officials in Canaan.

Both Petrie and Bliss emphasized that a thick layer of ash was discovered in every sounding made on the site and that it separated the five lower levels (I-b–III) from the six upper levels (IV-b–VIII). This ash layer is located at approximately mid-height of the mound and is 1–2.5 meters deep. Petrie thought it belonged to "alkali burners." Bliss, however, tried to find a connection between it and the kiln discovered in the previous level, which, he thought, would prove that there was extensive "industrial activity" in the city. While stratigraphy denies him that specific association, recent analysis by the American team of materials from the multiple bands of this "ash layer" suggests either extensive industry or considerable burned foundations distributed over the whole surface of the mound toward the end of the Late Bronze Age.

Cities IV-b and IV. City IV-b was built on the above-mentioned ash layer. A large, strong citadel was discovered in this stratum (about 18 by 18 meters; walls 1.6–3 meters thick). It was built of bricks and its interior was subdivided symmetrically. In the eastern part of the mound, Petrie uncovered a building (about 7 by 8 meters) in which he found carved stones which he considered to be jambs of openings. He called it, therefore, the Pilaster Building. Bliss assigned this building to "cities" IV-b and IV. However, the pilasters are of the Phoenician-Israelite type (called Proto-Ionic or Proto-Aeolic), which date from the time of Solomon or Ahab. It follows that Bliss's dating of the building to these cities is unacceptable. To complicate the issue further, Petrie was convinced that the sculpted stones were in architectural re-use in the structure. Stratigraphically, also, it must be later than Bliss's city IV.

The pottery, cylinder seals, and scarabs found in levels IV-b and IV indicate that these "cities" are to be dated close to the end of the Late Bronze Age. Among the finds is a sherd of a bowl belonging to the final phase of city IV on whose inner side was incised the Canaanite inscription bl' (בלע). This inscription can be attributed to the fourteenth century B.C.

There is an occupation gap between "cities" IV-b/IV and V–VIII. It should be mentioned that Petrie claimed the period of the Judges was not represented in the buildings on the site, without explaining, as usual, how he reached this conclusion. Among the pottery drawings appearing on plate VIII in his book, only two Philistine sherds are presented (Figures 180, 181). The survey and the recent excavations, while they have not yet reached that level, have found practically no early Philistine evidence.

City V. Of special interest in this level are six rows of stone bases with brick walls between them, covering an area of 15 by 37 meters. Some investigators have compared these "structures" to the Solomon/Ahab "stables" discovered at Megiddo. Today, however, it is thought more likely that this structure had served as a storehouse. The Pilaster Building, which Petrie discovered with its carved stones (which had apparently been originally used for other purposes), may be assigned to Bliss's city V and dated, as Petrie suggested, to 1000–900 B.C. — i.e., the time of Solomon, or more accurately, the time between Solomon and the Omrid Dynasty. Also, according to the two bowls Petrie found in the building, it should be dated to the tenth or the beginning of the ninth century B.C. This is the period of a massive fortification system discovered at the southern base of the acropolis by the recent American excavators — a wall and tower complex, built in the tenth/ninth centuries which remained in use through the Iron Age and underwent total restructuring early in the Persian period. Bliss admitted to great perplexity in determining function and phasing in cities VI–VIII. Worrell's excavations have revealed some of the complexity of causes for the confusion that makes Bliss's plans of those levels less useful than could be hoped. Petrie probed in separated trenches around the entire perimeter of the acropolis, leaving undisturbed remains between them which allow firm linkage with his elaborate plans. Bliss, on the other hand, in removing the entire northeast quadrant of the mound left nothing conclusive to key into, especially in the severely disturbed upper levels. The recent American excavations in the south sector of the mound have begun to connect up firmly with Petrie's plans, but those of Bliss remain conjectural in many points.

City VI. Both Petrie and Bliss described the course of a wall on the north slope which Bliss assigned to city VI. It is difficult to understand the nature of this wall as depicted on Bliss's plan, as well as the sections of buildings with thick walls set at acute angles one to the other. Is is quite possible that his plan contains elements belonging to at least two different strata. Petrie traced the wall around the perimeter to the point of its apparent loss by erosion at the eastern valley face. He assigned it to the period of King Manasseh and related it to two other fortifications, which were farther down the south slope and which he suggested belonged to Kings Uzziah and Rehoboam, respectively. The American excavations have revealed details of construction of Petrie's large "Manasseh" wall, a

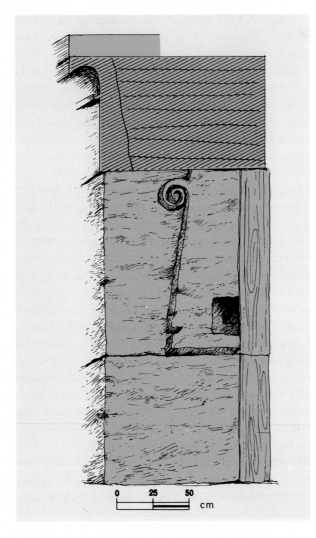

7.5 meter thick structure stepping up the slope upon, and at points cutting through, an earlier thick, plaster-over-stone glacis. Preliminary indications are that Petrie's dating for this wall is probably more accurate than Bliss's but that the other phases of fortification of the south slope are far more complex, both structurally and chronologically, than Petrie revealed.

Bliss attributed to city VI the sherd (defined by him as a fragment from the neck of a store jar) that Petrie discovered outside the wall assigned to the city. Bliss is of the opinion that the inscription on the sherd, which is generally read *Lsmkh* — לסמך — was incised after the vessel was fired. City VI apparently dates to the ninth/eighth centuries B.C., if the stratigraphy is properly recorded.

City VII. On the basis of the contents of two houses of this level described by Bliss, they are to be dated to the eighth or seventh century B.C. This settlement was completely destroyed by a conflagration. Because of the paucity of material available, it is difficult to assign this destruction to any specific event in these centuries. It has become clear from

Both pages, counterclockwise: Doorjamb of "pilaster building"; reconstructed. Citadel plan. "Pilaster building"; plan. Battered brick corner tower of IA fortification system.

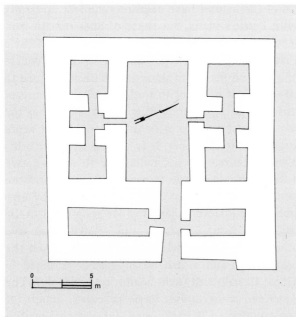

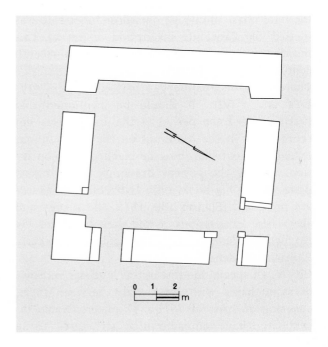

the American excavation, however, that the complicated stratigraphy perplexing Bliss in this level —with a massive fill unphased and never explained by Bliss—is due to the confusion of pre-destruction architecture with massive, post-destruction, terraced filling operations topped by sporadic industrial ash, perhaps a century and a half later. In the sector under excavation by the American team, preliminary indications are that, subsequent to the late Iron Age destruction described by Petrie and Bliss, the area was made into a platform more than 3.5 meters in height by a technique of building irregular walls as retainers for finely sorted, compacted fill material brought in from elsewhere than the primary living areas. This is evidenced in Petrie's plan by a "long range of chambers," which he was at an apparent loss to explain functionally. He assigned it tentatively to about 800 B.C. by its relative position alone. His date now appears to be about two centuries too early. In approximately the same period the base of the slope was built up in a similar fashion. The Iron Age lower fortification system was turned into a

massive consolidation by cutting into the slope inside the earlier wall and building irregular retaining piers abutting the rebuilt interior. These were then filled with mostly virgin soil. There is evidence that the whole construction may have been capped by a brick platform extending well up the south face of the mound. Signs of heavy loss by erosion preceding the operation suggest that in this later period the fortification was directed more against natural than political enemies.

City VIII. Little can be learned about the history of this level from the few items of pottery published by Petrie and Bliss. The American excavations indicate that Bliss's city VIII is at best a composite of two major strata, each with multiple sub-phases but both severely disturbed by late pitting and a recent Muslim cemetery.

Late Strata as Revealed by the American Excavations. During the first three seasons of excavation by Worrell, *et al.*, five major phases were disclosed in the southeast quadrant of the acropolis in the levels phasing with the complex designated city VII by Bliss. Phasing of structures on the south

slope, in correlation with Petrie's plans, and at the base of the south slope — examined by neither of the previous excavators — has been described above. (Soundings in the lower city have determined the extent of the surviving Early Bronze Age occupational material and some architecture of prominent proportions.)

PHASE 5 — PERSIAN PERIOD. Four significant sub-strata (5-D–5-A) characterize the period following the massive platform fill described above and preceding the Hellenistic period. The earliest of these (5-D), already post-Iron Age II, is characterized by a heavy occupational surface extending over the areas excavated to that level in the first three seasons, and by the lower courses of a large, finely plastered mud-brick structure at the south end of the mound. Replacing this, but with no evidence of a period of disuse, was a series of ash-covered surfaces, exterior retaining walls, and debris suggesting an area of livestock quartering and perhaps animal slaughter (5-C). Level 5-B showed slight architectural re-alignment, multiple intentional re-surfacings — one of heavy mottled limestone — and a square subterranean structure 1.5 meters on a side and 3.5 meters in depth from contemporary surfaces. No domestic architecture was found in the sectors excavated, and analysis of debris suggested primarily agricultural and storage usage. Level 5-A dates to the very end of the Persian period. It is characterized by re-use of the earlier architecture, heavy and consistent resurfacings, and especially the honeycombing of the acropolis with deep, cylindrical storage pits. The pits — perhaps better termed subterranean silos — have characteristically baked walls, sometimes mud plastered and frequently brick lined. They vary in diameter from 1 to 2.8 meters, and in depth from 2.5 to 5.5 meters. Used as grain storage silos in 5-A, they were subsequently filled with rubbish in the Hellenistic period. The scientific team has been given significant material for reconstructing the ecology of these agricultural phases.

PHASE 4 — HELLENISTIC PERIOD. City VIII of Bliss overlaps phase 4 and the upper materials of phase 5 of the American excavations. The "rude stone walls" mentioned by Bliss as characteristic of this level are found in the quadrant of the American excavation as well, but nearly all other occupational evidence was destroyed by the late cemetery and military intrusions. Where occupational surfaces remained, they were well prepared, showing considerable use, and rich in imported Aegean pottery. The site clearly shows domestic use with at least two clear phases in the Middle and Late Hellenistic periods.

PHASE 3 — EARLY ISLAMIC. This was not recorded by Petrie and Bliss, and scant evidence — a few well-prepared occupational surfaces, minor installations, and badly preserved mud-brick walls — has survived the later intrusions and agricultural activity.

PHASE 2 — MUSLIM CEMETERY. The American team analyzed more than six hundred individual burials from the cemetery. Careful excavation revealed three main phases of burial, all Islamic and at least two phases probably Bedouin. The earliest cemetery perhaps dates to phase 3. All information pertaining to crypt construction, corporal placement, and osteological data was computerized, allowing complementary stratigraphic, ethnographic, and pathological analysis.

PHASE 1 — MILITARY INSTALLATIONS. This phase consists of trench and bunker systems, ranging from Turkish and World War I to 1947–48.

SUMMARY

The dates which Petrie and Bliss assigned to the various cities from Late Bronze Age onward have been accepted as relatively accurate, although their dates for the earlier periods were too low. Despite the matters they left unsolved in their excavation reports, there is no doubt that here Petrie clearly established for the first time the connection between the stratigraphy of a mound and the pottery and other finds discovered on the site. The Worrell team of excavators and scientists have purposely fielded a project alongside those pioneering efforts in order to incorporate the full complement of ecological as well as cultural data and, in the process, to refine the history previously exposed.

RUTH AMIRAN AND J. E. WORRELL

BIBLIOGRAPHY

W. M. F. Petrie, *Tell el Hesy (Lachish),* London, 1891 • F. J. Bliss, *A Mound of Many Cities,* London, 1898 • W. F. Albright, *AJSLL* 55 (1938), 345 • G. E. Wright, *AJA* 43 (1939), 462 • W. F. Albright, *BASOR* 87 (1942), 32–38 • K. M. Kenyon, *Annual Report, Institute of Archaeology,* University of London, 11 (1955), 1 ff. • J. E. Worrell, *Newsletter of ASOR,* April 1970, December 1970 • J. E. Worrell and L. E. Toombs, *IEJ* 21 (1971), 177–78, 233–34; 24 (1974), 139–41 • L. E. Toombs et al., *PEQ* (1974), 19–31.

HIPPOS (Sussita)

IDENTIFICATION AND HISTORY. Hippos, a Greek city, known in Arabic as Qal'at el-Ḥuṣn, is situated some 2 kilometers (about 1 mile) east of the Sea of Galilee on a promontory rising 350 meters above the sea (map reference 212242). It was founded by the Seleucids in the Hellenistic period, possibly on the site of an earlier settlement. The town continued to exist until the Arab conquest, being known by its Greek name, "Antiochia Hippos" (*hippos* — "a horse"). In Aramaic it was known as Sussita. It was conquered in one of the campaigns of Alexander Jannaeus (*Antiquities* XIV, 75). Pompey took it from the Jews and included it in the Decapolis (League of Ten Cities) founded by him. Augustus gave the city to Herod, much to the dissatisfaction of the inhabitants. After Herod's death it became part of the Province of Syria (*Antiquities* XV, 217; XVII, 320; *War* I, 396; II, 97). During the First Revolt, the Jews attacked Hippos (*ibid.* II, 459, 478). Jews from the city were among the defenders of Migdal-Taricheae (Magdala) (*ibid.* III, 542). The territory of Hippos extended down to the Sea of Galilee (*Life* 153), and the city was the sworn enemy of Jewish Tiberias on the opposite

Coin of Hippos-Sussita; second century A.D.

shore of the lake (*Lamentations Rabba* 19), despite the trade connections between them (Palestinian Talmud, *Shevi'it* 8:38a). Jewish villages east of the lake were included in the territory of Hippos and were exempt from tithes in the time of the Patriarch Judah I, being considered beyond the frontiers of the Land of Israel proper (Tosefta, *Shevi'it* 4:10, Tosefta, *Oholot* 18:4). Remains of ancient synagogues have been found at Fiq (Aphek) and at Umm el-Qanatir, both of which lay within the territory of Hippos (see Synagogues). In the Byzantine period, Hippos was the seat of a bishop, being one of the sees of Palaestina Secunda. Like many other towns in the Byzantine period, it enjoyed great prosperity, and many churches and public buildings were built. The city was probably abandoned after the Arab conquest at the beginning of the seventh century. Isolated buildings were erected on its ruins in later times.

In the past, Hippos was identified with the neighboring village of Sussiyeh, which preserves the city's ancient name (Sussita), while Qal'at el-Ḥuṣn, whose natural shape resembles a camel's hump, was considered to be the site of ancient Gamala. However, since recent surveys of the ruins at Qal'at el-Ḥuṣn, its identification with Hippos has been generally accepted.

With the settlement of 'En Gev in 1937, surface surveys were again carried out at Hippos by members of the kibbutz. These owed much to the earlier, thorough researches made by G. Schumacher during the latter part of the nineteenth century. However, the new information from observation on the spot, as well as from aerial photographs, made possible a reliable reconstruction of the city plan, on which the positions of its chief public buildings were correctly plotted.

Although Hippos is known to have been founded in the Hellenistic period, few remains from that time have been found, probably because of the comparatively small size of the Hellenistic town. The inhabitants were entirely dependent on a natural water supply, which was inadequate for the requirements of a large population. After its conquest by Pompey in 63 B.C., Hippos, as one of the cities of the Decapolis, was rebuilt in accordance with standard contemporary town planning. The town plan, which has been preserved, is essentially that of the Roman period, although many buildings were erected later. The streets of the city ran at right angles to one another over the length and breadth of the town, forming the characteristic insulae. The public buildings stood at the intersections of the important streets. Of these, the cardo (main street) is easily distinguishable. It is paved with large basalt flagstones and runs from east to west through the center of the town. It is still in use today as a path. Halfway along the cardo was the nymphaeum. Close to it was a large subterranean cistern with vaulted roof and plastered walls and a flight of steps leading down to water level. After the water had been brought to the numphaeum and used in its ornamental fountains, it was collected in the cistern for further use. In Hippos, water was a valuable commodity, the main water supply coming from some distance by a specially constructed aqueduct (see below). Not far from the cistern are Byzantine baths that also required a considerable amount of water.

Evidence that this town of the Decapolis had imposing buildings in Roman times can be seen in the many architectural remains which lie strewn over the surface: massive red granite column shafts, numerous capitals (Corinthian and Ionic), decorated pilasters, molded lintels, carved cornices, and the like, many of which were re-used in the Byzantine period. Most of these lie along the cardo or in the center of the city.

The town wall has also been well preserved. It is provided with a number of towers at strategic points. The wall follows the contours of the hill and makes use of the natural cliff wherever possible. On the south side, sectors of the wall still stand to a considerable height, providing an excellent view of the Roman road which ascends from the lakeside through Wadi Jamusiyeh. It is very likely that there was a harbor of some kind at the point where this valley opens upon the lake and where the Roman road coming from the city turned south to continue along the eastern shore of the Sea of Galilee. Evidence of such a harbor may be seen in the heaps of stones extending for some distance into the water at this spot.

At the eastern end of Wadi Jamusiyeh is a small promontory or bluff in which there are caves containing niches, stone sarcophagi, ornamented tomb doors, and other evidence of burials. This was doubtless one of the places the people of Hippos used as a cemetery, other graves having been found in the west, also outside the city walls.

THE EXCAVATIONS

In 1951, a small excavation was made in an area north of the cardo, where buildings dating to the Byzantine period were found, including houses and a small church with apse and mosaic floor. This is one of four churches discovered so far at Hippos, the largest and most impressive of them (20 by 40 meters) having been excavated during the years 1952–55. The latter was probably the cathedral. It is situated to the south of the cardo, not far from the nymphaeum at the center of the city. Like many churches of the period, it was built as a triapsidal basilica (with inscribed apse). Two rows of nine columns (average height: 5 meters) of differently colored marble and granite separated the nave from the aisles. The columns were found lying on the floor of the building, having been thrown down in a single direction by an earthquake. Close by were the Corinthian capitals of pink and white marble which the columns had originally supported. The floor was laid in opus sectile of colored marble (parts being executed in a lozenge-shaped flower pattern). It is almost certain that the walls, as well as the apse itself, were lined with marble, since many slabs of various colors were found lying on the floor, and a number of copper clamps to hold them in position were still in situ in the apse wall. Around the main apse, where the altar had stood, the sockets for the chancel screen and for the posts which supported its panels were found set into the floor. One of these panels (of white marble) was found broken. It was decorated with a relief showing the entrance to an ornate public building. From its architrave hangs a large circular object, perhaps a basket commemorating the Miracle of the Loaves and Fishes. Above the molding of the surrounding frame is an inscription in Greek: "In the time of Procopius, Presbyter." The back of the panel was decorated with a large dolphin in relief, apparently dating from the time of its original use, since attempts to efface the outlines of the dolphin are clearly visible.

Entrance to the cathedral was through three doorways in the west wall. They were approached through a corridor which gave on to a colonnaded atrium beyond. The southern aisle was not completely excavated. It appears to have matched the northern one in all respects, except that in the latter the external wall served as a party wall for the adjacent baptistery building.

The baptistery was also triapsidal. Its nave was separated from the aisles by two rows of four white marble columns (two of them unusually fluted). In the central apse was a cruciform font with rounded ends set into the floor, and with the mosaic around it. The floor of the baptistery was completely covered with colored mosaics laid in a variety of geometrical designs. It included three inscriptions in Greek and the Monogram of Christ (north apse). In the southern aisle there was an intact dedicatory inscription to Saints Damian and Cosmas in a *tabula ansata*. These were two Syrian brothers who, as physicians, gave free service to the poor and were martyred in the early fourth century. The remains of another inscription framed in a medallion, of which only a few words remain, was found in a central position in the nave. This fragment, however, does contain the date of the building of the baptistery — January, 654, according to the Pompeian era of Hippos, which is the equivalent of A.D. 591. In the northern aisle, a third inscription was found, also framed in a circular border. Here, the end of most of the lines is missing. The name "Procopius," mentioned also on the cathedral chancel screen, is still legible. He was apparently responsible for the building of the baptistery and the laying of its mosaic floor. Here, too, the date, which is the same as that in the nave inscription, can be made out.

The Hippos baptistery is unusual, in that it is built in a triapsidal plan and divided into nave and aisles and also that it is dedicated to special patron saints. All these characteristics are more often associated with the mother churches, to which baptisteries served as annexes.

In the east, a rocky saddle links the hill on which the city was built to the north–south range beyond it. The road to the city passed over this natural ridge, branching off from the main highway, which ascended from the lakeside through Wadi Jamusiyeh and continued eastward into the Golan hills. The approach to ancient Hippos was by way of this saddle. Over it ran also a massive, basalt aqueduct that conveyed water into the city by gravitation from the 3.5 kilometer distant spring at Fiq. Sections of this aqueduct can still be seen at various points within the city itself, as well as on the saddle ridge. During the excavations of 1952, twenty-four sections were found in situ below the *cardo* pavement near the East Gate. Each section is square without but circular and hollow within (average internal diameter: 30 centimeters). The sections are joined by spigots and sockets reinforced with plaster. Some had a venthole in the upper wall to enable the air bubbles caused by the uprush of the water to escape. The aqueduct entered the city by the East Gate and continued beneath the *cardo* to the nymphaeum.

The East Gate, which was the main gate into the city, had a paved area within. Its southern pier was built as an integral part of the city wall (it is well preserved at this point). The wall was strengthened here by a well-built circular tower (external diameter, 9 meters), which commanded the road leading into the city from the east. Built into the rocky slope of the hillside, the lower part of the tower contained a stone fill coated with a thin layer of plaster — probably the floor. In the round tower and the gateway, two phases of building could be distinguished from the Roman and Byzantine periods (but no trace of Hellenistic). On the north side, only the foundations of the gate pier have survived (giving a probable internal width of 3.1 meters). From here, the wall, which follows the contours of the hill, turns abruptly west at a point not far from the gate. At this corner position was erected a two-storied square tower that commanded the northeastern approaches to the city. Its lower section appears to have been used as a plastered cistern, probably by the garrison manning it.

In the west, the *cardo* terminated at a much smaller city gate, whose chief purpose was to provide easy access into and out of the town for those of its inhabitants who cultivated the terraces on the western slopes of the hill. In the west were also found remains of a well-preserved city wall. Below it, the hillside falls away steeply, making a hostile approach from this direction extremely hazardous. A little below the West Gate there is a group of big rocks which in times of emergency could undoubtedly be used for defense purposes (as is borne out by the signs of building found between them). Not far from these were found graves cut into the rock face, which can be dated by their contents to the Byzantine period.　　　CLAIRE EPSTEIN

BIBLIOGRAPHY

G. Schumacher, *ZDPV* 9 (1886), 327 ff.; *idem, The Jaulan,* London, 1888, 194 ff. • Schurer, *GJV* II, 155 ff. • E. Anati and A. Schulman, *'Alon* 5–6 (1957), 30–33 • M. Avi-Yonah, *ibid.,* 33 (Hebrew).

ḤUSIFAH

IDENTIFICATION. Ḥusifah is identified with the site of the modern village of 'Isfiye on Mount Carmel, about 12 kilometers (7.5 miles) southeast of Haifa. In the Roman-Byzantine period, a Jewish settlement existed on the site, of which the remains of a synagogue were discovered. The existence of this early settlement is also attested by ancient graves found within the boundaries of the village and by coin finds. The latter include a hoard of 4,560 silver coins, the latest among them dating to A.D. 52/53. In a Hebrew elegy discovered in the Cairo Genizah, the destruction of the Jewish settlement of Ḥusifah is mentioned. Most scholars accept the suggestion of S. Assaf that this Ḥusifah be identified with 'Isfiye.

EXCAVATION OF THE SYNAGOGUE AND THE FINDS

In 1930, a mosaic floor with the representation of a seven-branched candlestick was discovered in one

Plan of the synagogue and mosaic pavement.
■ *Excavated* ▨ *Conjectured.*

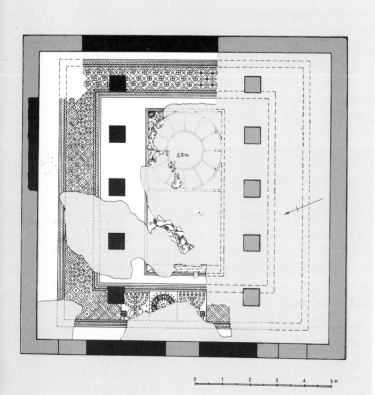

of the village streets. In 1933, excavations were conducted at this spot under the direction of N. Makhouly and M. Avi-Yonah, on behalf of the Department of Antiquities of the Mandatory Government. Because part of the remains lay beneath one of the village houses, little more than half of the synagogue could be uncovered. A floor and the foundations of a hall (probably square) were discovered. The northern wall was cleared for its full length of 10.1 meters, whereas the eastern wall and the foundations of the western wall could only be partially uncovered (6.2 and 5.5 meters of them respectively). In the mosaic floor in the hall there were square gaps, the traces of a row of five pillars or columns, set at unequal distances. The second row of columns apparently stood in the unexcavated part. In the western wall, remains of a threshold were noted, and west of it, the bed of a mosaic pavement. These finds point to the existence of a narthex.

THE MOSAIC PAVEMENT

Along the walls of the hall there was a broad band of mosaics (about 1 meter wide) containing geometric motifs: steps, double diagonal lines, stylized guilloche, rhombuses, and meanders. This border terminated on the western side (in front of the threshold but not on the axis of the building) in three square panels, each 1 square meter. In the middle panel was depicted a wreath composed of three rows of elongated flowers with leaves and intertwined branches. The wreath surrounds an inscription, partially preserved: שלום על ישראל "Peace upon Israel."

The lateral panels were occupied by two seven-branched candlesticks. The menorah on the left had a trunk consisting of squares and circles, and branches of circles (knops) and heart-shaped "flowers" alternately. The lamps at the top of the branches have a triangular base and a handle. The lamps themselves are depicted in profile, and at the top of each, a flame is shown burning (on the left side, the three flames are represented as inclined to the right, and on the right side, the single surviving flame points to the left). The central lamp, above the trunk, shows two flames. The menorah is made of red, orange, and golden (yellow) tesserae. In the center of each link is a cube of green glass (to represent a precious stone?). Beneath the branches of the menorah are depicted, from right to left, a lulab (only its tip survived), an ethrog (with a green glass mosaic cube in its center), a shofar, and an incense shovel. The trunk and branches of the menorah on the right are made of alternate square and round links, with a green stone in the center of each. At the top of each branch there is a square from which a flame rises. Near the menorah can be seen an incense shovel and the end of a shofar.

A band of geometric designs, similar to that along the walls, surrounds the main field of the mosaic floor in the center of the hall. This field is divided into three parts (from west to east):

1. An inscription in three lines, 2.8 meters long (of which 1.3 meters is preserved) and .27 meter wide, which reads: "...and blessed be...Halifu, the wife of the Rabbi... Honored be the memory of every one who promised and gave his donation, be he blessed... Honored be the memory. Honored be the memory of Josiah who gave..."

2. A vine trellis (of which only a narrow diagonal band is preserved) presented in a naturalistic manner, with bunches of grapes, leaves, and tendrils. At the western end there are two heads of peacocks. Among the branches of the vine, a bird is standing, facing the direction opposite to that of the peacocks.

3. A zodiac. The inner circle of the zodiac is .6 meter in diameter, the outer is 1.38 meters. The center of the circle was almost completely destroyed. Of the twelve signs of the zodiac, fragments of only the five from the sign of Sagittarius to the sign of Aries have remained. Sagittarius is pictured as a nude figure with a yellow mantle thrown over one shoulder, similar to Hercules' lion skin. Of the Capricorn, only the ends of the horns have survived. The sign of Aquarius is depicted as an amphora with water flowing out of it. Pisces was apparently represented by two fish swimming in opposite directions. Of Aries, only the hind legs have remained. In the corner of the square field still preserved is pictured the head of a woman (one of the Seasons), with a necklace of green tesserae and the head covered with a yellow and white scarf. Near the head were drawn pomegranates and other symbols (possibly a cluster of dates, or a sickle). The head apparently symbolized autumn (*Tequfat Tishri*), although the zodiac signs near it are those of spring. A similar discrepancy appears in the Na'aran mosaic.

The mosaic is of fine quality — sixty-five tesserae to 10 square centimeters. Most of the material is local

Below: The inscription "Peace upon Israel." Part of the menorah and ethrog can be seen to the left.
Bottom: Figure of one of the four seasons in the zodiac.

red, yellow, white, pink, brown, and orange lime-stone. Bluish marble and an abundance of green glass are also employed. Its artistic level is reasonably good. In one place, the mosaic was repaired with coarse red tesserae.

DATE AND EVALUATION

The synagogue in Ḥusifah represents a mixture of early and late features (see Synagogues, Vol. IV). Like the early synagogues, it did not seem to have had an apse, but like some of the late synagogues, it is built in the form of a basilica. Its entrances are in the west, on the side opposite Jerusalem (like the other synagogue remains on Mount Carmel, which were all assumed to be situated on the sea, i.e., due west), and it is paved with mosaics. Judging by the quality of the mosaic, the synagogue at Ḥusifah was later than that of Ḥammat-Tiberias, which also has no apse, but earlier than the synagogue at Ma'on, where representations of vines and animals were found but no human images. The synagogue may be dated, therefore, to the beginning of the sixth century A.D. The structure bears obvious signs of conflagration. Parts of the mosaic had faded because of heat, and a layer of ashes had accumulated in its southeastern corner. It seems that the building was destroyed during the riots against the Jews in the reign of Justinian, and perhaps the lament found in the Genizah elegy should be attributed to that event. The style of the pavement is popular and vigorous.

The synagogue was built according to Halakhic rules, that is, on the highest spot in the village. This modest building can be associated, on the one hand, with a group of synagogues in which the zodiac is depicted, such as Beth Alpha, Na'aran, Ḥammat-Tiberias, Japhia (in the opinion of some scholars, however, it is the symbols of the tribes that are depicted in Japhia; see article). On the other hand, it can be linked with such later synagogues as Ḥammat Gader and Ma'on. The mosaic bears no traces of iconoclasm, which seems to indicate that it was destroyed before the appearance of iconoclastic tendencies among the Jews of Palestine.   M. AVI-YONAH

BIBLIOGRAPHY

N. Makhouly–M. Avi-Yonah, QDAP 3 (1934), 118–31 • Goodenough, Jewish Symbols 1, 257–59 • S. Assaf, BJPES 7 (1943), 62, 66 • L. Kadman, Yediot Numismatiot 1 (1962), 9–12 • M. Avi-Yonah, Essays and Studies in Palestinology, Tel Aviv-Jerusalem, 1962, 11–22 (the last three in Hebrew).

EL-ḤUṢN

IDENTIFICATION AND EXCAVATION. This dwelling and burial cave lies near the town of el-Ḥuṣn in Gilead, about 1 kilometer (.5 mile) south of Tell el-Ḥuṣn and 22 kilometers (13.5 miles) north of Gerasa. It was discovered during construction work and excavated by L. Harding. Due to collapses inside the cave, its original form was not preserved. In the course of the excavations, a shapeless cavity was discovered in the soft limestone, containing a confused mixture of implements and skeletons.

The examination of the finds showed that they represented two different periods, about one thousand years apart. To the first period of occupation belong sherds and fragments of big, coarse store jars with flaring rims, simple ledge handles, and band-slip decoration. Pottery without a slip was also discovered, made of a very gritty material, similar to cooking pots. Most were hole-mouth jars, or store jars with slightly flaring rims. In Harding's opinion, these finds are to be dated to the Early Bronze Age II. J. Isserlin, on the other hand, assigned them to the Early Bronze Age I.

During the second period, the cave was probably used for burials. Most of the pottery vessels were preserved in good condition. They were probably placed in the cave, together with copper pins, as burial offerings. More than fifty pottery vessels were discovered, including store jars with flared

Selection of pottery from the later period.

rims and folded ledge handles, store jars with globular bodies, some of them with incised decoration on the shoulders, amphoriskoi (comprising more than half of the objects found), some decorated like the store jars, others with red-painted decoration, as well as jugs with handles joining the rim to the shoulder, some of them painted in the style of the amphoriskoi, and some red slipped. Other finds included a "teapot" with a loop handle, two copper pins with convoluted heads, and a lamp of the four-pinch type. In the opinion of Harding, these finds belong to the period from Early Bronze Age IV to Middle Bronze Age I. Isserlin ascribes them to the beginning of Middle Bronze Age I, as represented in stratum I at Tell Beit Mirsim.

The objects from the earlier period are similar to Early Bronze Age I finds from the north of the country, especially from the Jordan and Jezreel Valleys. Cave dwellings were not unusual in the Proto-Urban period (as defined by Kathleen Kenyon). People then lived in the open country, in caves and casual structures. The pottery repertoire from the later period is also characteristic of the culture of that time in the north of the country, having analogies in Megiddo and Ma'ayan Barukh. The pottery belongs to Families B and C, according to the classification of Ruth Amiran.

M. KOCHAVI

BIBLIOGRAPHY

G. L. Harding–J. B. S. Isserlin, *PEFA* (1953), 1–13 • R. Amiran, *IEJ* 10 (1960), 209–13.

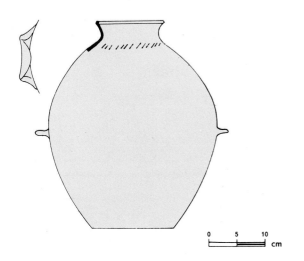

'IRAQ EL-EMIR

IDENTIFICATION AND HISTORY. 'Iraq el-Emir lies on a nearly direct line between Jericho and 'Amman, 29 kilometers (18 miles) east of Jericho and 17 kilometers (10.5 miles) west of 'Amman. The site includes a mound partly occupied by modern habitation, which has re-used some of the architectural fragments of the ancient site. Situated on the heights above the west bank of Wadi es-Şir, it commands a view of the spectacular plunge of that valley southward into the Wadi Kefrain. Two hundred meters northwest of the mound are cliffs with natural and man-made caves. Down a fairly steep slope, some 500 meters southwest of the mound, is the megalithic Qaşr el-'Abd with retaining walls and gates. Between the Qaşr and the cliffs lies the Square Building, near which is an area irrigated in antiquity by a canal. The canal can be traced northward to the base of the cliffs and toward a source beyond. The source ensures a year-long flow of water through the site.

'Iraq el-Emir is probably to be identified with the Ramath-Mizpeh of the Bible and Birtha ("stronghold") of the Ammonites in the Land of Tobiah mentioned in the Zenon papyri. It is certainly the fortress Tyros built by the Tobiad Hyrcanus in the early second century B.C. Of the sites proposed for Ramath-Mizpeh (Khirbet Jel'ad, Khirbet eş-Şar, Khirbet eş-Şireh), only 'Iraq el-Emir has both a geographically satisfactory position and evidence of Iron Age I occupation. The two "Tobiah" inscriptions on the facades of the two largest halls carved in the cliffs, and the name "Qaşr el-'Abd" ("Fortress of the Servant," in obvious reference to "Tobiah, the Ammonite servant" mentioned in Nehemiah 2:10) stamp the site as a Tobiad center. The family and land of Tobiah have been traced in biblical and other sources to the eighth century B.C., but the archaeological evidence available so far indicates that there was no substantial occupation of the site from the eleventh century until about 200 B.C. This situation is probably best explained by considering the site as the country estate from which the Land of Tobiah was administered. Birtha perhaps consisted of a manor at or near the mound, with the nearby caves offering a defensive stronghold. A few coins and sherds of

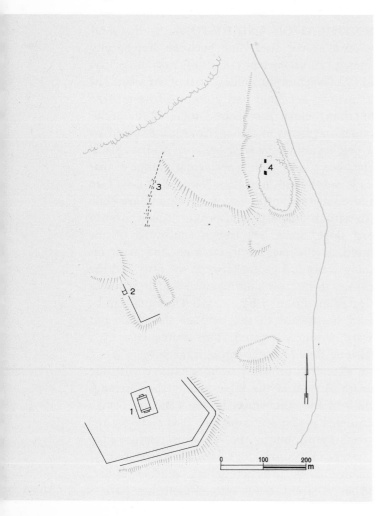

the early third century B.C. may be associated with the estate. It seems dubious, however, that 'Iraq el-Emir had been the center of the Tobiad dominions since the eighth century B.C. Josephus' description of the building of Tyros could be interpreted as construction on a previously unimportant site.

There are so many links between the description of Hyrcanus' Tyros by Josephus and 'Iraq el-Emir that this identification has never been seriously contested. The name "Tyros" itself is still preserved in the name Wadi eş-Şir. The Qaşr el-'Abd can hardly be dissociated from the "strong fortress" which Hyrcanus "constructed entirely of white marble up to the very roof, and had beasts of gigantic size carved on it, and he enclosed it with a wide and deep moat." (*Antiquities* XII, 230). The two large halls with the two "Tobiah" inscriptions correspond to the chambers carved in the rock with narrow entrances "so that only one person and no more could enter at one time." The Plaster Building, excavated in 1962, is almost certainly one of Hyrcanus' "large enclosures." Excavation has undermined the attempts of many scholars to attribute to the Qaşr a date before the operations of Hyrcanus in the first quarter of the second century B.C. The Qaşr is now clearly dated by archaeological evidence to Hyr-

Both pages, counterclockwise: Map of the site.
1. Qaşr el-'Abd. 2. The "square building." 3. Canal.
4. Mound. Qaşr el-'Abd: Relief on lowest course of
east wall. Northeast corner. Reconstruction. The
"plaster building"; ca. 175 B.C.

canus' time, and the Plaster Building is contemporary with it. The dating of the cave inscriptions has been much disputed, a fifth century B.C. date having been accepted by a majority of scholars of paleography for many years. Recently F. M. Cross, Jr., has proposed a date about 300 B.C. on epigraphic grounds. The epigraphic evidence is not clearly decisive, however, and the excavator has proposed that the reliability of Josephus' account be accepted in this matter, too. He has even suggested the revival of an early view that the "Tobiah" of the inscriptions is the Jewish name of Hyrcanus.

EXPLORATION

The environs of the Qaṣr have been described by early travelers and scholars beginning with C. L. Irby and J. Mangles in 1817. The visits of E. M. de Vogüé in 1864, F. de Saulcy in 1868, and C. R. Conder in 1881 resulted in publications that were superseded only by those of H. C. Butler, whose Princeton Expedition survey team spent six days at the site in October, 1904. Little attention was paid to the mound by these explorers, and Conder was the only one who provided detailed plans of the caves. Little was added to Butler's amazingly complete descriptions of the Qaṣr before the recent excavations, except that a number of his conclusions were refuted in a dissertation by M. Etchemendy in 1960.

EXCAVATIONS AND STRATIGRAPHY

Three campaigns were undertaken at 'Iraq el-Emir in 1961 and 1962 under the direction of P. W. Lapp, with most of the budget supplied by the American Schools of Oriental Research. Most of the staff members were appointees and residents of its Jerusalem School.

The stratigraphic history of the mound indicates six main strata of occupation. A few Chalcolithic sherds have been found but always in later contexts. Small patches of undisturbed Early Bronze Age occupation have been discovered on the site (stratum VI) and a contemporary stratum has been excavated in the Square Building. A second series of layers (stratum V) produced pottery from an occupation of the mound from the beginning of the eleventh century B.C. until close to its end. Its major feature was a 17-meter segment of a 1.5-meter wide defensive wall. This could have been part of a Gadite fort at Ramath-Mizpeh abandoned at the end of the eleventh century B.C., when Ammon is presumed to have eliminated the Gadites from the area.

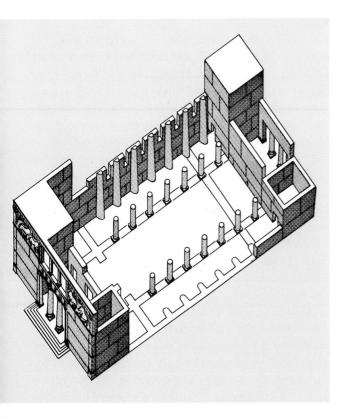

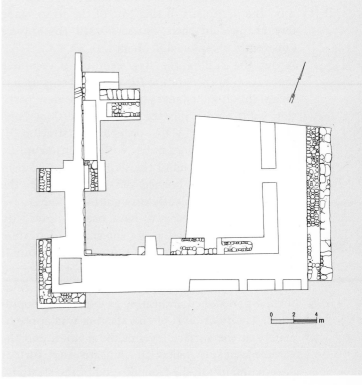

Stratum IV follows a long gap and belongs to an occupation in the early second century B.C., the period when Hyrcanus was building Tyros. There is scattered evidence of occupation in the third century B.C., and it is hoped that a future campaign will uncover the stratigraphy of this time, but as yet it cannot be isolated as a separate stratum. Hyrcanus began building Tyros about 182 B.C. and perhaps as early as 210 B.C. Pottery in the fill under the floors of stratum IV belongs to the beginning of the second century B.C., and pottery in the ash layer on the floor, marking the destruction of the Plaster Building, belongs to a ceramic horizon of about 175 B.C. Unfortunately, except for the Plaster Building, the major construction of Hyrcanus on the mound was cleared to floor level by the next major rebuilding of the site. It seems likely that there was a break in occupation from the time of Hyrcanus' death in about 175 B.C. until near the end of the century.

In about 100 B.C., at least in the northwest quarter of the mound where excavation has taken place, there was a major rebuilding of the site (stratum III-B), which established the defensive limits of the town by a kind of casemate construction and a large plastered court inside the casemate. Except for importing a .5 meter of fill for the floors of the casemate rooms in the first half of the first century A.D., the occupants of this part of the town made few changes in their quarters until these were apparently abandoned in about A.D. 50.

About the end of the first century, a complete renovation of the stratum III structures was undertaken, involving changes in entryways, new partition walls, and a fill which raised the floor level another .5 meter. This occupation (stratum II) seems to have continued without interruption until close to the end of the second century when, judging from the burned destruction layer, the occupation was violently brought to an end.

This destruction seems to have been followed by immediate re-occupation, for the sherds of stratum I are only slightly later than those of the stratum II destruction. In stratum I, the floor level was raised .8 meter with an imported fill, and rooms were further partitioned, indicating an expanding population. The floor level of this stratum was approximately at the surface level of the mound, and the surface remains failed to indicate any further occupation of the site from the end of the stratum I

occupation just after A.D. 200 to the present.

The Qaṣr environs were inhabited in the Early Bronze Age (stratum IV), the early second century B.C. (stratum III), and in the Byzantine period (strata II and I). Stratum IV consisted merely of debris into which foundations for Hyrcanus' building were cut. No Hellenistic layers related to the Qaṣr were found, for the Byzantine occupants cleared the environs of the Qaṣr to below Hellenistic floor level, and the earlier stratum II floors rested directly on stratum IV debris. Some sherds of the early second century B.C. were mixed with the Byzantine debris. The Byzantine occupation could be quite closely dated by coins and pottery. The occupation of stratum II, which ended in a violent destruction of much of the Qaṣr, belongs to the middle half of the fourth century and probably ended with the major earthquake that rocked Transjordan in A.D. 365. In the final occupation of the site, a 2-meter fill was required to level the quake debris. This level lasted through the fifth century A.D.

The stratigraphy of the Square Building is identical with that of the Qaṣr, with the addition of two pits containing pottery of about A.D. 200. It was built with re-used architectural fragments of Hellenistic buildings. None of the latter have been examined so far.

The results of the excavation included the elucidation of the plan and dimensions of the Plaster Building. The walls surrounding the large inner court were covered by thick plaster with a fine, dark red surface, beveled edges, and white borders. The plaster and carefully dressed rectangular blocks at the doorways contrast strikingly with the bricky dirt core of the wall, the thinner plaster layers in the corridor around the court, and the small stone outer walls. The structure belongs stratigraphically to the early second century B.C. and can be identified as one of the large enclosed courts that Josephus attributes to Hyrcanus.

THE QAṢR EL-'ABD

Excavations at the Qaṣr involved a trench through the main hall, trenches against the east, west, and north walls, and scattered probings. The results have shed light on the date, function, unfinished state, and a number of architectural details of the megalithic building. The only precise evidence for the date of the Qaṣr's construction comes from a group of early second century B.C. sherds found in the Byzantine fill. Since this was the only occupation in the vicinity of the Qaṣr between the Early Bronze Age and Byzantine period, it provides clear support for Josephus' attribution of the Qaṣr to Hyrcanus.

Until the recent excavations, scholars had interpreted the Qaṣr as a fortress, a temple, a palace, or a mausoleum. The architectural details of the stairwell located in the northeast tower were studied by the architect M. Brett during the third campaign. The five flights of the gradually rising staircase gave access to a gallery at the north end of the main hall, and led to a tower above the frieze course and presumably also to a terrace roof which (as the large interior half-columns indicate) covered all or part of the main hall. These elements — stairway, terrace, and tower — have been convincingly associated with temple-cult function by R. Amy. The opisthodomos and megalithic voussoir blocks found in the adytum area also support the temple interpretation. The Qaṣr emerges as a unique, indigenous example of the old Syrian temple type in the Hellenistic period, providing a link between the stair temples of Ugarit and Jerusalem and those characteristic of the Roman East. It has a striking contemporary parallel in the temple of Onias IV Leontopolis, mentioned by Josephus but not located with certainty.

A number of architectural fragments point to the incomplete state of the building. The frieze blocks of the eastern towers still in situ bear weathered reliefs of what are usually considered lions. One of the frieze megaliths unearthed near the southwest tower, which had probably fallen during the fourth-century A.D. earthquake, displayed only the roughed-out head, back, hind leg, and tail of the beast that was to have been sculptured in situ. A fragment of the string course (lower cornice) with dentils still uncut and the only partial removal of the bosses of the lowest course of the east wall further indicate that, while the main walls of the building had been erected, the finishing of architectural details was never completed. There is no evidence that the terrace roof over the main hall had ever been constructed, but it could have been entirely obliterated by Byzantine operations.

The most interesting discovery of the recent excavations was a fountain head, with the representation of a feline sculptured in high relief on a large block of mottled red-and-white dolomite. It was located in the lowest course of the east wall of the Qaṣr on a line with the spur by which one crossed the moat to the Qaṣr from a gate to the east. A study by Dorothy Hill concludes that this is a unique example of provincial Greek sculpture of the early second century B.C. The stone used in the relief is available locally, and, it may be added parenthetically, the quarry for the Qaṣr megaliths has been discovered at the very top of the hills directly west of it.

The Byzantine re-use of the Qaṣr involved a major building operation, and the series of piers unearthed in some of the large rooms, together with related artifacts, suggests that it may have been used by a monastic group.   P. W. LAPP

BIBLIOGRAPHY

H. C. Butler, *Syria*, Div. II, Sec. A, Leyden, 1919, 1–22 •
P. W. Lapp, *BASOR* 165 (1962), 16–34; 171 (1963), 9–39 •
M. J. B. Brett, *ibid.*, 39–45 • Dorothy K. Hill, *ibid.*, 45–55 •
M. Etchemendy, *Le site d'Araq el-Emir* (Unpublished dissertation; Jerusalem, 1960).

ISKANDER, KHIRBET

IDENTIFICATION. Khirbet Iskander, a site which was occupied from the end of the Chalcolithic period until the beginning of Middle Bronze Age, lies on the northern bank of Wadi el-Wala, a tributary of the Arnon River, on the top of a hill commanding the "King's Highway" which crosses the valley there (map reference 22331072). The site, discovered in 1879 by C. Schick and also mentioned by A. Musil, was first described by N. Glueck.

EXCAVATIONS

Trial excavations were conducted at the site in 1955 under the direction of P. Parr, with the assistance of the Ashmolean Museum in Oxford. Up to now, only a preliminary report has been published. The excavation was limited to two trial trenches, one on the eastern slope of the mound and the other at its northern extremity. From the first occupation period — which was encountered in the eastern trench only — six courses of the foundations of a well-constructed wall (2.3 meters thick) were discovered. This wall rests on a foundation trench cut into the rock of the hill and was, in the excavator's opinion, part of the city wall. A small number of potsherds from the Late Chalcolithic period or beginning of the Early Bronze Age were found. From the second occupation period, deposits of debris covering the earlier wall were found in the eastern trench, while in the northern one a stone wall was discovered. Pottery finds are similar to those of the preceding period, but some Early Bronze Age II ware also uncovered.

Between the second and the third periods there was a considerable gap which was marked by erosion of the soil. Period 3(i) could be distinguished in the eastern trench only, where the foundation trench of a wall (2 meters deep, 3 meters wide) was cleared. Remains of the wall itself were found inside the trench. From period 3(ii), which was found in the eastern trench, a courtyard (2.5 by 4 meters) was uncovered, paved with cobblestones and divided by low walls into working areas. In the center of the courtyard was a perforated stone, presumably a base for a wooden ceiling support. In one of the walls surrounding the courtyard were incorporated the remains of a wall dating from the preceding stage (.75 meter thick and preserved to a height of 1.5 meters). In the northern trial trench, a rectangular chamber (9.5 by 7.5 meters, thickness of the walls .75 meter) was discovered, practically at surface level. Pottery from both stages of this period is attributed by the excavator to the Middle Bronze Age I, although it clearly preserves traditions from the Early Bronze Age.

The excavator is not certain of the date of the early period, and the later period was not sufficiently elucidated by the excavation. The description of the site by N. Glueck, who surveyed the area, presents the image of a stronghold, surrounded by a strong, tower-flanked wall, outside of which were circular structures and numerous menhirs, reaching a height of 4 meters. The pottery, the architectural finds, and the menhirs are all characteristic of settlements such as Bab edh-Dhra' (q.v.), Ader (q.v.), and other sites in Transjordan.

M. KOCHAVI

BIBLIOGRAPHY

N. Glueck, *Explorations in Eastern Palestine* 3 (*AASOR* 18/19 [1939]), 127–28 • P. J. Parr, *ADAJ* 4–5 (1960), 128–33 • K. H. Bernhardt, *ZDPV* 76 (1960), 154–58 • A. Kuschke, *ZDPV* 77 (1961), 30.

JAFFA

IDENTIFICATION AND HISTORY. Ancient Jaffa was built on a high promontory jutting into the sea and in Arabic was called *Yāfa el 'Atiqa* ("ancient Jaffa") or *el Qal'a* ("the fortress"). The name "Jaffa" is derived from the word "beautiful."

Jaffa is first mentioned in Egyptian sources as one of the cities conquered by Thutmose III in the fifteenth century B.C. The Harris Papyrus describes the capture of the city by a stratagem in a folk tale reminiscent of "Ali Baba and the Forty Thieves." The city is mentioned in the el-Amarna letters as an Egyptian stronghold sheltering royal granaries. The Papyrus Anastasi I, a satirical letter, provides additional interesting information about the city in the thirteenth century B.C. Jaffa and the surrounding towns, Azor, Bene-Berak, and Beth-Dagon, are mentioned later in the "prism stele" of Sennacherib, the king of Assyria, who conquered them in his campaign of 701 B.C.

Jaffa is mentioned in the Bible in the description of the boundaries of the tribe of Dan (Joshua 19:46). Cedars from the Lebanon were brought by sea to the port of Jaffa for the building of the First and Second Temples (II Chronicles 2:15; Ezra 3:7). The prophet Jonah sought to flee from the Lord via Jaffa (Jonah 1:3). The Greek legend of Perseus and Andromeda was located in the sea of Jaffa, on

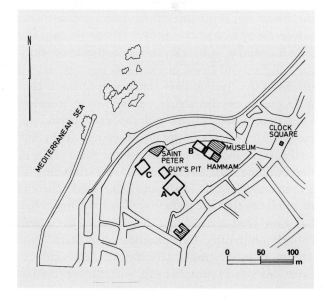

Map showing areas of excavation.

*Jerusalem. Herodian mosaic pavement
found in excavations in the Jewish Quarter.*

rocks to which the heroine was chained to be devoured by a monster from the sea. According to the inscription of Eshmunazar of Sidon (probably fifth century B.C.), the "Lord of Kings" (king of Persia) presented him with Dor and Jaffa. The Sidonian occupation of Jaffa in the Persian period is also known from the description of the coastal towns of Syria and Palestine attributed to Scylax.

In the Hellenistic period, Jaffa was colonized by Greeks. The Papyri of Zenon, an Egyptian treasury official who visited the country in 259/258 B.C. during the reign of Ptolemy II, throw some light on the history of the city in his time.

In the Hasmonaean period the city was captured

Area A. Plaque of nude woman with Hathor hairdress.

from the Seleucids and became the port of Judea. During the war with the Romans, it was destroyed first by Cestius Gallus and then by Vespasian but was quickly rebuilt. Tombstones from the Jewish cemetery of Jaffa (at Abu Kabir) dating from the first to the fifth centuries A.D. provide information about the inhabitants of the city and their occupations.

The ancient harbor, protected by a chain of large rocks which formed a kind of breakwater, was situated at the foot of the promontory. In the years 1937–38 and 1950–54 a number of crumbling buildings were cleared in old Jaffa, making possible the beginning of archaeological exploration in some areas of the mound.

EXCAVATIONS

In 1948–50 P.L.O. Guy carried out the first exploratory excavations in Jaffa on behalf of the Israel Department of Antiquities. In 1952, Guy's excavations were continued down to virgin soil by J. Bowman and B.S.J. Isserlin, on behalf of the University of Leeds. The excavators established that the earliest remains at that spot were sherds dating from the fifth century B.C. and that the site was uninhabited prior to that date. They also discovered a structure from the fourth or third century B.C. of which only the floor of one of the rooms was preserved. The walls of the building were repaired in the second century B.C., and in the following century the level of the floor was raised. During the Byzantine period the area was settled anew.

In 1955, J. Kaplan undertook a systematic excavation of ancient Jaffa on behalf of the Museum of Antiquities of Tel Aviv–Jaffa. By 1964, three areas (A, B, C) in different sections of the mound had been excavated during six seasons of excavations. Limited soundings were also carried out in the Clock Square of Jaffa where part of the cemetery of the gentile population of Jaffa, dated to the Late Hellenistic and Roman periods, was uncovered.

Area A. Seven occupation levels, the latest dating from the first century B.C., were excavated here, and the stratification was established as follows:

LEVEL I. — HELLENISTIC. This level is divided into two sub-levels, I-A and I-B. Level I-A contained a section of a wall of dressed stone, 2.2 meters wide, with a casemate construction adjoining it. They date from the first century B.C., i.e., from the Hasmonaean period. In Level I-B the corner of a square fortress, also built of dressed stone, was uncovered, with a wall 2.5 meters wide. The fortress is dated to the third century B.C. To this level are also assigned a group of five round stone floors, .8–1.2 meters in diameter, each with a small, stone basin. These floors were found in the southern section of the excavation and had no connection with the walls.

LEVEL II. — PERSIAN II-A. A section of a dressed stone wall, 2.5 meters wide, and some adjacent structures were cleared. The wall dates from the second half of the fifth century B.C. and was apparently built by the Sidonians.

LEVEL III. — IRON AGE. This level is also divided into two sub-levels. Remains of sub-level III-A were preserved at the eastern edge of the excavation, and remains of III-B were found at the western edge. In sub-level III-A a rough stone wall, approximately .8 meter thick, was found adjoining a stone floor sloping eastwards. These constructions were assigned to the eighth century B.C. Level III-B contained a section of a courtyard with a floor of beaten earth and an ash pit nearby. The floor and pit contained Philistine sherds of the eleventh century B.C.

LEVEL IV. — LATE BRONZE AGE II-A. This also consists of two sub-levels. Sub-level IV-A contained the threshold of the citadel gate and two entrance walls, 18 meters long and 4 meters apart, built of gray mud bricks. The walls run in an east–west direction from the gate into the citadel. The passageway between the walls was paved with stone and pebbles. The walls and gate were destroyed by fire, apparently late in the thirteenth century B.C. The bronze hinge of the gate was discovered in situ near the bottom of the left jamb.

Beneath the structures of sub-level IV-A were revealed the remains of sub-level IV-B. These included the lower part of an earlier gate, fallen stone doorjambs, and two entrance walls, all of which followed the same line as the structures of sub-level IV-A. It is thus clear that sub-level IV-A had been built on the ruins of a previous occupation level IV-B, which had also been burned, apparently in the third quarter of the thirteenth century (in the published interim reports, sublevel IV-B appears as level V). The entrance walls are built of yellow and red-brown mud bricks, while the doorjambs of the gate were of hard

From area A: Below: Fragmentary doorjamb of city gate inscribed with the name of Ramses II; LBA. Bottom: Bronze hinge of citadel gate; stratum IV.

Both pages, counterclockwise: Brick wall of fort at right; "Lion Temple" in foreground. Area G; ashlar wall built in headers and stretchers; third century B.C. Wall of Sidonian masonry; ashlar piers with rubble interstices. East mud-brick wall of fort. The "Lion Temple."

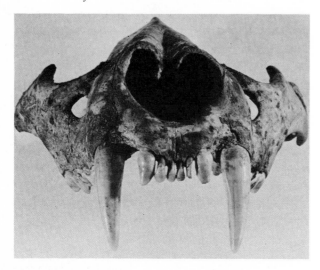

Skull of lion.

dressed sandstone. Inscribed upon four of the stone jambs were the five titles of Ramses II and part of his name. It seems that the inscriptions were originally set symmetrically on both sides of the gateway.

The gate and the entrance walls dating from the time of Ramses had been dug deep into the eastern part of the ruined citadel of Jaffa. As a result, remains from the eighteenth–fourteenth centuries B.C. situated to the north and south of the entrance walls lay at a higher level than the threshold of Ramses' gate. These strata were only partially cleared.

LEVEL V — LATE BRONZE AGE II-B. Some building remains were found, as well as a small silo built of rough stones set between the southern entrance wall of Ramses' gate and parts of the structures of level VI south of it. Quantities of potsherds of the fourteenth century B.C. were found in the silo and its vicinity.

LEVEL VI — LATE BRONZE AGE I. This level contained some remains of mud-brick buildings on stone foundations. North of the northern entrance wall, a locus of pottery vessels was uncovered, including Bichrome and gray-burnished ware. South of the entrance wall was a heap of sherds probably thrown there when the inhabitants had cleared an adjacent area. These broken vessels are of Cypriot origin and include base ring and Monochrome type wares. Level VI is dated from the second half

of the sixteenth century to the second half of the fifteenth century B.C.

LEVEL VII — MIDDLE BRONZE AGE II-C. Sections of two brick walls were found at the northern and southern edges of the excavated area. It seems that subsequently occupation levels VI–IV were concentrated in the space between these two walls. The outer face of the northern wall did not adjoin any visible glacis, while the southern wall was set on a rampart of beaten earth and *kurkar*. This rampart belongs to an earlier, unexcavated layer, probably level VIII. Level VII is tentatively dated to the period between the second half of the seventeenth century and the first half of the sixteenth century B.C.

The excavations in area A were resumed in 1970, and the area was extended on the south and west sides. Here, too, as in the excavations in the 1950's, settlement strata of the Early Arabic, Byzantine, and Roman periods are absent. Some scattered remains attest the destruction and damage caused to these strata in the last century. The same is true for the remains from the late Second Temple and Hasmonaean periods found in Jaffa.

LEVEL I — HELLENISTIC. Reasonably well-preserved strata begin in the early part of the Hellenistic period. The remains consist mainly of sections of walls built of brick-shaped, ashlar blocks set on their narrow end. In most cases, these walls were constructed on top of walls from the Persian period. Of special interest is an altar (2.4 by 2.4 meters) built of field stones uncovered in square L–4. It stood in a room whose measurements were only 3.9 by 5.3 meters. This type of cult hall is also known from the same period in Cyprus.

LEVEL II — PERSIAN. Remains from the Persian period cover almost the entire excavated area. They date from the second half of the fifth century to the Macedonian conquest, *i.e.*, to the period in which, in the excavator's opinion, the Sidonians held Jaffa. The Sidonian settlement in Jaffa is mentioned in a number of sources, such as Eshmunazar's inscription and a fourth-century B.C. document attributed to the navigator Scylax (who lived in the fifth century B.C.). Several building stages of that period were uncovered, notably sections of walls of a large structure extending from east to west across the entire area. It apparently served as a temple. In its western part were found fragments of dividing walls and a mud-brick floor, probably belonging to a holy of holies. The method of construction of these walls and of other structures in Jaffa from this period is unusual. They are built of regularly spaced ashlar pilasters with a fill of field stones between them.

Also discovered in this level were the remains of an ironworks. In the excavations in the 1950's, great heaps of blacksmith's waste were discovered in various places in the Persian stratum. This waste was also found in the later excavations, along with part of a forge. Near wall W.800 was cleared the floor of the forge, black from the soot mixed into it. A stone container was set against the wall, an iron sickle lay on its bottom, and a knife lay nearby. A pile of stones near this container probably belongs to the same period. It was apparently the remains of a furnace for heating the metal to be worked. In another corner lay a heap of charcoal. When the floor (about 7 centimeters thick) was excavated, it yielded a large quantity of iron filings and many complete weapons — arrowheads and spearheads. All the evidence suggests that this iron smithy continued in use in the beginning of the Hellenistic period. In square K-3, an early Persian stratum with the foundations of a pre-fifth century building was discovered for the first time in Jaffa. The structure was found under the ashlar walls. This stratum was designated stratum II-B and that of the ashlar structures stratum II-A.

LEVEL III — IRON AGE. The Israelite period (Iron Age II) is represented by layers of earth mixed with ashes but no building remains. At the bottom of this stratum were found two cattle burials dug into the Iron Age I stratum with stone markers standing by them. The burial of the cattle whole clearly points to some religious ritual. And indeed, this was a sacred site hundreds of years earlier (see below). A different picture emerged under the ashlar blocks of the Persian stratum in squares I_2–I_3. Here an Iron Age II stratum was found and underneath that a stratum from Iron Age I. In depressions and pits belonging to this last level was found Philistine pottery of the eleventh century B.C. The pits and depressions were partly dug into a layer of rubble and clay bricks fallen from a nearby structure. Under these strata were cleared the foundations of a long hall. A citadel with mud-brick walls was attached to it on the south side.

Below: Coin of Jaffa, from the time of Heliogabalus (A.D. 218–22). Bottom: Fragmentary stone door from a burial cave; second half of second/first half of third century A.D.

PRE-PHILISTINE TEMPLE. The hall measured 4.4 by 5.8 meters and was entered from the north. The floor was covered with a coat of white plaster. On the floor were two round stone bases of wooden columns which had supported the beams of the roof. The pottery finds were meager — only two bowls and some fragments of other vessels. On the floor, however, was found the skull of a lion with half of a scarab seal near its teeth. This find suggests that the building was a temple where a lion cult was practiced. Evidence for such a cult is found in the city names Layish (Dan), Hakefirah, and Beth Levaot. Despite the paucity of the pottery finds, the building could be dated to the end of the thirteenth century–beginning of the twelfth century B.C. The northern temple at Beth-Shean from the time of Ramses III which is identical in plan with the temple at Jaffa also supports this date. It should be added that the reconstruction of the inscription on the half-scarab found near the lion's teeth produced the name of Queen Tiy, wife of Amenhotep III, but at the same time it should be remembered that scarabs of kings of the Eighteenth and Nineteenth Dynasties continued in use as talismans or jewelry for generations afterward, and therefore they cannot serve as evidence.

Area B. Excavations in this area were concentrated in the premises of the Ḥammam building adjoining the Jaffa Museum and on the slope to the west of it. In the Ḥammam a sandwich-built glacis was uncovered sloping from west to east. The external revetment was made of thin stone slabs which rested on layers of sandy soil. Beneath them were courses of mud bricks laid in a layer of gray soil. The potsherds unearthed in this layer indicated that the glacis is not later than the eighth century B.C. This would make it contemporary with level III-A in area A.

Beneath the brick and gray layer, the excavation revealed a thick layer of *kurkar* indicating that there must have been an earlier glacis here. And indeed layers of beaten earth and *kurkar* were found also on the slope of the mound west of the Ḥammam. These are situated at a lower level than the glacis of the eighth century B.C. and rest on the eastern slope of a rampart of beaten earth, trapezoid in section, running south to north. This rampart dates to the eighteenth century B.C., *i.e.*, to the beginning of the Hyksos period. It probably enclosed Jaffa in a square area.

Area C. The excavation of this area revealed six occupation levels and a catacomb built of dressed stone. The levels of this area are later than those excavated in area A and in effect continue them.

The first (upper) level contained a rough mosaic floor from the sixth-seventh centuries A.D. The second level had structures from the fifth century A.D., situated immediately beneath the mosaic floor. In the third level was found a section of a fourth century A.D. building of large proportions built on thick rubble foundations and containing a floor made of large stone slabs. The fourth level, dating from the third century A.D., contained a section of foundations lying under the stone floor slabs of the large building of the previous occupation level. The fifth level dates from the beginning of the second century. It contained a two-room structure, whose foundations were sunk deep into the earlier levels. In this level were found pottery, a stone bowl, a bronze jug, and a hoard of bronze and silver coins, all not later than the reign of Trajan. The sixth level contained a section of a private dwelling from the first century A.D. with a courtyard and cistern. A doorway, approximately 2 meters high, of which two jambs had survived, was situated in the wall facing the courtyard. Numerous pottery vessels and lamps were found on the floor of the courtyard. Behind the eastern wall of the fifth occupation level was uncovered part of the courtyard of a burial cave of extremely fine construction — ashlar blocks laid as headers and stretchers. The catacomb consisted of three chambers. The first to be found was damaged by the collapse of the ceiling and its entrance blocked with ashlar stones. The ceiling of the second chamber was also destroyed, while the third, the front chamber, had been reconstructed after the collapse of its ceiling. It was fitted with a new roof supported by arches of ashlar stone. These supported stone slabs that formed the floor of a private dwelling erected above the chamber.

Among the finds excavated in area C, two Greek inscriptions deserve special mention. One of them, engraved on limestone, mentions in three identical versions that during the reign of Trajan, Judah the son of . . . was the *agoranomos* of Jaffa. The second is a fragment of a votive inscription from the third century B.C. which mentions Ptolemy IV Philopator. Many jar handles with Greek and Latin stamps were also found, as well as a tile fragment with the stamp of the Tenth Legion and a pyramidal seal engraved with the name "Ariston."

Area Y. Area Y is located near St. Peter's Church, at the intersection of Mifratz Shlomo Street and the ring road. Some remains were found beneath the square in front of the church. The site was first excavated in August, 1964, and again in May, 1968. It is located west of the edge of the western glacis of the Jaffa citadel. The area was not inhabited prior to the Persian period. The finds consisted mainly of tombs and various installations (see above, the results of the excavation carried out nearby by the Leeds Expedition). Two strata of settlement were uncovered in area Y: Hellenistic I-B and Persian II-A. Beneath the latter was virgin clay soil containing tombs and other installations from the Middle Bronze Age II.

The Hellenistic remains were found immediately below the ruins of modern buildings. In the southern part of the area, a section of an ashlar structure was uncovered with walls preserved to a height of 1 meter. The northern part of the area contained the corner of a large building, also built of ashlar in which were several square rooms side by side. This building may have been part of the agora of Jaffa. The Persian period is represented only by layers of ashes. There were no building remains. Many fragments of Attic pottery were found. An infant burial in a jar, dating from the seventeenth century B.C., was discovered in the virgin soil. In addition to the remains of the body, it contained a red-burnished juglet, and outside near the burial was a scarab seal. In the northern part of the site two furnaces were discovered dug into the loam. One furnace was almost intact, except for its vaulted roof. It was constructed over a Middle Bronze Age II tomb. The tomb contained funerary offerings and a scarab seal. A bed of ashes and pits dug into the loam in the eastern part of the area were found filled with ashes and animal bones. These remains date from Late Bronze Age I. In one of the pits were found full length leg bones of domestic beasts preserved from the upper end to the hoof. These finds suggest that a cult place was located close by.   ḤAYA AND J. KAPLAN

BIBLIOGRAPHY

J. Bowman–B. S. J. Isserlin–K. Rowe, *Proceedings of the Leeds Philosophical Society* 7 (1955), 231–50 • J. Kaplan, *Archaeology* 17 (1964), 270–76; idem, *BA* 35 (1972), 66–95; idem, *IEJ* 20 (1970), 225–26; 24 (1974), 135–37.

JAPHIA

IDENTIFICATION. Japhia, an Arab village in Lower Galilee, called Yafa, is situated about 2 kilometers (1 mile) southwest of Nazareth. In the Bible, Japhia is mentioned as one of the cities of Zebulun (Joshua 19:12). The place is apparently mentioned in the el-Amarna letters (fourteenth century B.C.), where it is called Iapu. During the Jewish War, Josephus Flavius strengthened the defenses of the city, whose inhabitants took an active part in the revolt. Titus captured the city in the summer of 67 and killed most of its inhabitants (*War* II, 573; III, 289; *Life* 45, 230; 52, 270). According to a late Christian tradition, the apostle James, son of Zebedee, was born here. The location of the Roman-Byzantine city is certain, but the site of the ancient settlement of the Bronze and Iron Ages is not known.

EXCAVATIONS

In 1921, L. H. Vincent published two lintels which had been re-used in the village. On one is carved a menorah with a rosette on either side, and on the second is carved a wreath flanked by eagles with outspread wings holding small wreaths in their beaks. These finds proved that the remains of a synagogue of the early type (third–fourth centuries A.D.) should be sought here. In the summer of 1950, E. L. Sukenik and N. Avigad excavated the remains of the synagogue on behalf of the Hebrew University.

The excavations established that the synagogue had stood on a peak to the north of the village and that only few remains had survived. Of the south wall, a segment 2.7 meters long and .65 meter thick was discovered. At a distance of 2.9 meters north of the wall, a row of four column pedestals, with Attic bases attached, and the foundation stones of a fifth pedestal were found. Seven meters north of them were found several foundation stones, which apparently belonged to a second row of columns. It became evident, therefore, that the synagogue was built as a basilica, slightly more than 15 meters wide. The eastern and western ends of the building were found destroyed, and it proved impossible to establish the original length of the building. However, it is clear that it was at least 19 meters long. Only a few fragments of the mosaic pavement of

the synagogue were preserved. It was multi-colored (black, brown, red, gray, and white—altogether thirteen different hues). In the southern aisle, the pavement is decorated with squares, rectangles, and simple geometric patterns, surrounded by bands of guilloche. The few remains of faunal and floral decorations found in the nave indicate that the floor there was richly decorated. In it was depicted a circle 3.8 meters in diameter with twelve circles within it, all enclosed in an interlocking guilloche, which presented a pattern similar to the zodiacs discovered in the synagogues at Naʿaran, Beth Alpha, Ḥusifah, and Ḥammat-Tiberias. The excavators believed, however, that it was not the signs of the zodiac that were portrayed here but the symbols of the Twelve Tribes. Of these symbols, only two are extant: a buffalo, and beside it the fragmentary legend רים.([Eph]raim?), and an ox, the symbol of Menasseh. This description is not in keeping with that in the Midrash (Rabba, 82), where the ox is the symbol of Ephraim, and the buffalo the symbol of Menasseh. We find it difficult, nevertheless, to accept the opinion of E.R. Goodenough that the zodiac is represented here, too. In the southwest end of the nave, one panel of the pavement was preserved in its entirety. On it is a depiction of an eagle with outspread wings, standing on two pairs of volutes and between the volutes is the head of Helios (in the opinion of Goodenough, the head of Medusa). On the basis of style, the pavement may belong to the late third or fourth century A.D., but it is not known if it was part of the original building.

The orientation of the synagogue is from west to east, and its facade apparently faces east. This differs from the other early Galilean synagogues, whose facades are oriented south, toward Jerusalem. Sukenik claimed that this change of orientation could be explained by the fact that Japhia was in Zebulun, presumed (according to Genesis 49:13) to be located on the sea, i.e., west of the Holy City.

In this synagogue there is a mixture of features of the early type of synagogue (pedestals of columns, and perhaps the lintels published by Vincent) and of the late type (the mosaic floor). M. Avi-Yonah was therefore of the opinion that it should be attributed to the transitional type (see Synagogues).

D. BARAG

BIBLIOGRAPHY

S.L. Loewenstamm, Enc. Miqr. 3, 744 (Hebrew) • L.H. Vincent, RB 30 (1921), 433 f. • E.L. Sukenik, Bulletin of the L.M. Rabinowitz Fund 2 (1951), 6–24 • Goodenough, Jewish Symbols 1, 216–18, s.v. index • G. Foerster, Yediot 31 (1967), 218–24 (Hebrew).

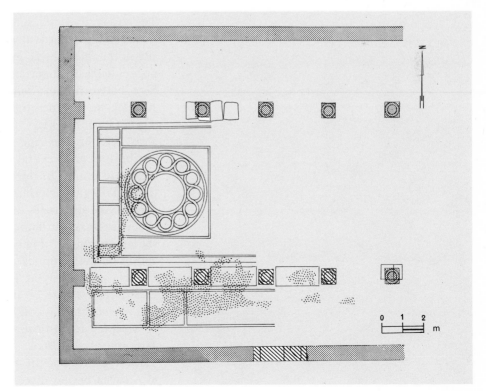

Right: Synagogue; plan. Opposite page: Remains of synagogue and details of mosaic pavement.

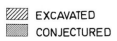

EXCAVATED
CONJECTURED

JARMUTH, TEL

IDENTIFICATION. Tel Jarmuth (Hebrew, Yarmut; Arabic, Khirbet Yarmouk) is located at map reference 14751240, about 5 kilometers (3 miles) southwest of modern Beth Shemesh. The site consists of an acropolis, about 15 dunams in area, and a lower city of about 140 dunams.

F. M. Abel, W. F. Albright, J. Garstang, and others identified this site with Jarmuth, listed in Joshua 12:11 among the conquered cities of the Shephelah. Most scholars were unaware of the fact that the site consisted of both an acropolis and a lower city. In their descriptions of the site they referred to the acropolis only.

EXCAVATION

Up to now, only a brief trial excavation has been carried out at the site (in 1970) by the Institute of Archaeology, Hebrew University, and directed by A. Ben-Tor. Two areas (A and B) were excavated in the northwestern corner of the lower city.

Area A, close to the edge of the site, is occupied by two rectangular stone-built platforms, the larger of the two measuring 12.5 by 31 meters. The platforms consist of retaining walls, built of large stones. The area between them is filled with small rubble. The surface of the platforms is quite level. No answer can yet be offered as to the function of these structures. One possibility is that they served as platforms for structures which later disappeared completely. The meager amount of potsherds found within the rubble fill of the platforms is exclusively of the Early Bronze Age.

In the main area of the excavation — **area B** — the following strata were noted:

STRATUM I. A large building, about 5 dunams in area, is attributed to this level. The building, undoubtedly of public character, was mostly destroyed to below its floor level. It dated to the beginning of the Byzantine period.

STRATUM II. Several building remains, mainly of three houses situated on both sides of a stone-paved alley, belong to this stratum. A large number of pottery vessels, dating to Early Bronze Age III, were found in the houses.

STRATUM III. Several fragmentary walls, also of private dwellings, were found below the structures of stratum II. These walls, too, are associated with Early Bronze Age III pottery, which included some sherds of Khirbet Kerak ware.

The pottery assemblage is rich and varied. A considerable number of outsize vessels were found, which differ from the usual size of similar known vessels.

The excavation and survey conducted at the site uncovered potsherds attesting to a settlement at the site in the Chalcolithic period. At this stage there is no evidence to determine whether a gap existed here between the Chalcolithic and Early Bronze Age III, or whether there are any earlier Bronze Age strata at the site.

Two Late Bronze Age sherds (both of doubtful attribution) and several sherds from the Iron Age were also found. In the excavated area the Byzantine building is superimposed directly on the Early Bronze Age structures. If Late Bronze and Iron Age occupations did in fact exist at Tel Jarmuth, they should be sought in another part of the lower city and/or on the acropolis.

Unless future study at Tel Jarmuth establishes the existence of a Late Bronze Age settlement, the inevitable conclusion will have to be that the generally accepted identification of the mound with the Jarmuth of the Book of Joshua — and with the Yarmut mentioned in an Akkadian letter of the el-Amarna period discovered by F. J. Bliss at Tell

Map of mound.

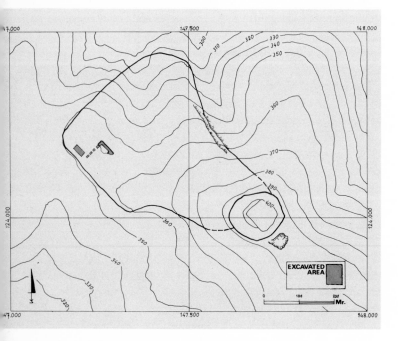

el-Ḥesi — is untenable.

The date and nature of the finds discovered in stratum I seem to justify the identification of the site with the Iermous of Eusebius (*Onomasticon* 106:9). A. BEN-TOR

BIBLIOGRAPHY

Guérin, *Judée* 2, 371 ff. • W.F. Albright, *JPOS* 8 (1928), 243 • J. Garstang, *Joshua-Judges*, London, 1931, 171–72 • Abel, *GP* 2, 356 • W.F. Albright, *BASOR* 77 (1940), 31; 87 (1942), 32–38 • A. Druks, *Hadashot Archeologiot* 5 (1963), 20–21 (Hebrew) • P. Thompson, *Loca Sancta*, Hildesheim, 1966, 71–72 • H.N. Richardson, *BASOR* 192 (1968), 12–16 • A. Ben-Tor, *Qedem* 1 (1975), 55–87.

From top to bottom: Stratum II; EBA: Two views of large platter. Large basin.

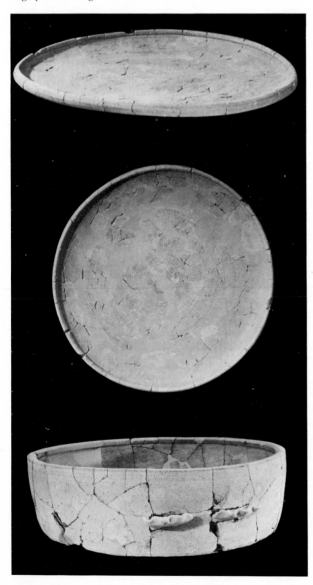

JEMMEH, TELL

IDENTIFICATION. Tell Jemmeh is located about 10 kilometers (6 miles) south of Gaza, on the southern bank of the Besor River (Wadi Ghazzeh, map reference 097088). It was the site of a flourishing city during the Middle Bronze Age II, Late Bronze and Iron Ages, and the Persian and Hellenistic periods. There is also evidence of a Chalcolithic occupation at the site and a large Byzantine city in the fields directly south of the mound. F. Petrie considered Jemmeh to be the site of ancient Gerar (Genesis 20:1; 26:1–12, etc.), but the majority of scholars disagree with that identification. B. Mazar's suggestion that the site is ancient Yurza seems more acceptable. Yurza was a Canaanite city-state mentioned in the Egyptian topographical lists of the New Kingdom and in the el-Amarna letters. Thutmose III describes Yurza as the southernmost city to have revolted against Egypt, which corresponds well with the location of Tell Jemmeh. Jemmeh is almost certainly the "Arṣa near the Brook of Egypt" mentioned in the lists of Esarhaddon, since excavations have shown that the site was extremely important in the time of Assyrian domination.

EXPLORATION

In 1922, W.J. Phythian-Adams dug a trial step trench. During 1926–27, Petrie spent six months excavating a large area along the western sector of the site. This was the first of three mounds in the northwestern Negev excavated by Petrie in the 1920's and 1930's (see articles Tel Sharuhen, Tell el-'Ajjul). In 1970, a Smithsonian Institution expedition, directed by G. Van Beek, resumed the excavation of the site which is still continuing.

EXCAVATIONS

The northern side of the mound has been partially cut away by the Besor River, and about 15 meters have been destroyed in this manner. The southern area has also been deeply eroded. The present surface of the mound has the shape of the Roman numeral "I." All investigators have chosen the western side of the mound for excavation. It is about one meter higher than the eastern end, and Petrie correctly suggested that the most important buildings on the site were to be found in this area which faces the sea breezes. In the 15-meter

View of the mound.

accumulation on the mound, Petrie excavated to a depth of about 11 meters, reaching virgin soil in only two places. He distinguished five strata, in addition to the granaries which were sunk into the top stratum and which represent a separate occupation. Focusing on the area immediately north of Petrie's excavations, Van Beek discovered remains of a substantial Hellenistic settlement of the third-second centuries B.C. Petrie had found no evidence of a city wall. However, some remains of walling have been found at the extreme northwestern slope of the mound (near the escarpment), indicating fortifications.

Petrie's finds were published in his customary corpus system, which is not convenient for study. In addition, there is a serious technical flaw in his method of excavation and of assigning material to strata. Petrie attributed the objects found at the top of a stratum to the stratum immediately above. Thus, the finds must be reassigned, and careful attention must be paid to the altitude recorded for the finds. In the table at the bottom of the page, revisions are suggested for Petrie's dates. These revisions are based on the studies of W. F. Albright and G. E. Wright, and on Van Beek's excavations.

In his soundings to virgin soil, Petrie found traces of a settlement of the Late Bronze Age, and this has been confirmed by the Smithsonian excavations, which have also yielded a few Middle Bronze Age sherds. The only architectural feature of significance, apart from badly eroded mud-brick walls, is a large section of a courtyard paved with large rounded stones from the valley. In addition, in one area on the lower eastern slope of the mound, Chalcolithic sherds were found, indicating a limited occupation in that period.

Stratum JK. This is the lowest continuous stratum exposed in Petrie's excavations. Parts of three buildings were discovered, but it is difficult to ascertain their plan except for one that seems to consist of a series of rooms arranged around a court (JF). The stratum should be dated by the Philistine pottery, and not — as did Petrie — by the scarab inscribed with the name of Thutmose III.

Stratum GH. In this stratum was exposed a larger area than in the previous stratum. Several buildings were discovered, all fragmentary. Two of the buildings (HA and GC) are probably four-room structures. The largest of the four ovens found on the mound belongs to this stratum. Petrie thought that the ovens were used for smelting iron, but preliminary analyses of the slags which abound in

NAME OF STRATUM	HEIGHT IN FEET	DATE ASSIGNED BY PETRIE	SUGGESTED REVISION
	158–166		MBA II-B
	166–174		LBA
JK	174–183	Thutmose III — 1489 B.C.	IA I
GH	183–189	Ramses III — 1194 B.C.	IA II-A
EF	189–192	Shishak — 932 B.C.	IA II-B–C
CD	192–197	Amaziah — 810 B.C.	IA III-C
AB	197–206	Psamtek — 660 B.C.	
		Persian — 457 B.C.	Persian and Hellenistic

the site have failed to yield any traces of iron. Yet all were produced at temperatures above 1100 degrees centigrade, suggesting that iron smelting may have been involved. Many iron utensils were found by Petrie, but this fact alone does not constitute proof that the ovens were intended for iron production.

Judging from the pottery, it is certain that the stratum is to be dated to the tenth century B.C., e.g., bowls with horizontal loop handles, which had degenerated from Philistine bowls. It should be noted that the pottery also indicates that the stratigraphy of Petrie's excavation is irreparably disturbed. Several of the numerous human and animal figurines found in the excavation belong to this stratum, as for example, that of a man sitting in a chariot (the wheels are missing).

Stratum EF. The area uncovered from this stratum is larger than that in the other strata. The main architectural features include blocks of buildings with long parallel rooms, a possible street, and three ovens. One wall (EC–ED) is of Assyrian type with header and stretcher bricks, mud plaster on the wall surface, and remains of vault bricks at the top. This wall is certainly contemporary with the Assyrian structures which were found in the recent excavations. Moreover, the plans of some of the buildings of this stratum bear a striking resemblance to that of the Assyrian building which will be described below.

In the table above, this stratum is attributed to the Iron Age II-B–C, but the pottery also includes seventh-century B.C. types, indicating a probable stratigraphic mix-up in the excavations. Provisionally, however, this stratum should be attributed to the end of the eighth–seventh centuries B.C., rather than up to the reign of Amaziah, as Petrie had thought originally.

Stratum CD. The latest excavations by Van Beek have shown that this stratum belongs to the seventh century B.C., the time of the Assyrian occupation of Philistia. The most outstanding find is a building of at least six rooms with mud-brick barrel vaults, parts of which are still standing in four of the rooms. The walls are constructed of brick with a row of headers backed by a row of stretchers, rectangular in shape and alternating in successive courses. The vault bricks are differently shaped and have four deep grooves on the lower surface to key the mud mortar. They are laid in the pitch-brick technique,

which developed in Mesopotamia in the third millennium B.C., continued in use in the second millennium B.C., and appeared again in Nubia, Constantinople, and Mesopotamia in the first millennium A.D. The Tell Jemmeh example is the only one known from anywhere in the Near East in the first millennium B.C. and the only example of mud-brick vaulting as yet found in Israel. Both walls and vaulting were coated on the inside with mud plaster. An intact doorway in the wall of the center room gave access to the room, probably from a corridor. A large quantity of Assyrian Palace Ware was found on the fallen vaulting in one of the rooms. It probably came from a pantry on an upper floor. A portion of this may also have been preserved. Petrie also found a considerable amount of Palace Ware, but all of it came from a rubbish pit in the southeast corner of his excavation. The bricks of the walls of this structure are of the same size as those of Petrie's CD buildings, and the plan of the latter bears a resemblance to Assyrian constructions at Nimrud. In addition to the stratified Palace Ware, noteworthy finds include an ostracon, probably a receipt, written in a Phoenician script of about 650 B.C. and an ivory inlay engraved with the voluted palmette design so common in the Nimrud ivories.

This structure seems to have been the residence of the Assyrian military governor of the district, following Esarhaddon's conquest of Arṣa in 679 B.C., and the entire site probably served as a forward Assyrian military base in anticipation of Esarhaddon's campaigns against Egypt in 674, 671, and 669 B.C., and possibly of Ashurbanipal's campaigns of 667 and 663 B.C.

Stratum AB. To this stratum belong the best preserved structures found by Petrie. These include two very large buildings each consisting of at least one central court surrounded by smaller rooms, a plan known in Assyrian and Persian architecture. It seems likely that they belong to the end of the seventh or the sixth century B.C. and were constructed either by Necho or Nebuchadnezzar. In the recent excavations, only one short section of a wall could be assigned to this period. The finds include a jug with a schematic relief of a man's head, a type common in Egypt during this period. Also belonging to this and the succeeding period is a Fikellura bowl and Ionian cup fragments of the sixth century B.C., and a number of black- and

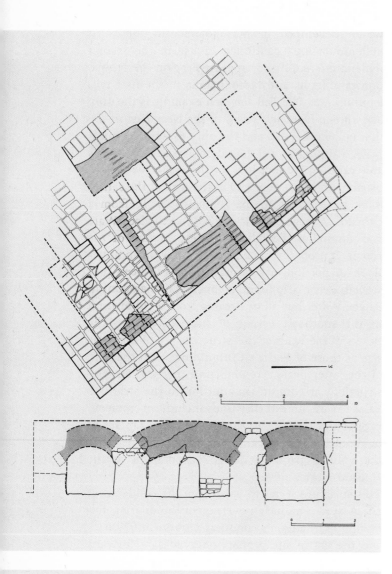

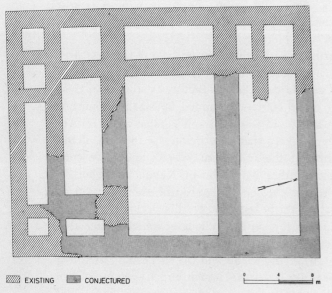

EXISTING   CONJECTURED

red-figured Attic imports of the late sixth and fifth centuries B.C., the finest of which is the large red-figured lekythos kept at the Rockefeller Museum in Jerusalem.

Persian and Hellenistic. The AB buildings were succeeded by a series of seven large mud-brick granaries. Three others were found by Petrie along the southern edge of the mound, and another by the current Smithsonian excavations to the north of Petrie's excavation. The latter measures 6.2 meters in diameter and is preserved to a height of 2.2 meters. The granary was entered through two doorways on the southeast and northwest sides. From these, steps led down to a high platform projecting on each side inside the structure. A portion of a high conical dome may be preserved near the doorway. The structure has two successive mud-brick floors. Whether these granaries were constructed in the Persian period, as Petrie thought, remains to be confirmed. It is certain, however, that they continued in use until about 150 B.C., as is shown by the vast quantity of local Hellenistic store jars and other pottery, as well as early second century B.C. imported black-slip Hellenistic vessels. An important find from the granary fill is a sherd of a locally made store jar with a painted South Arabic monogram, reading 'bm ('abum), a name known in both Sabaean and Minaean inscriptions. This indicates the presence of South Arabs at the site, no doubt in connection with caravan traffic in frankincense and myrrh destined for Gaza, the chief incense port on the Mediterranean in Hellenistic and Roman times, and perhaps earlier as well. To the Hellenistic period belong several walls which do not form a coherent plan because of later intrusive Arab pits. One of these walls, however, has associated with it two successive floors near the granary. The latter was probably filled with the bricks and walls from the collapse of this building.

RUTH AMIRAN–G. W. VAN BEEK

BIBLIOGRAPHY

On the identification of the site: K. Galling, *ZDPV* 52 (1929), 242–50 • B. Mazar, *BIES* 16 (1951), 38–41 (Hebrew); *idem, PEQ* (1952), 48–51 • Y. Aharoni, *Enc. Miqr.* 2, 561–64 (Hebrew); *idem, IEJ* 6 (1956), 26–31.
On the excavations: W. J. Phythian-Adams, *PEF QSt* (1923), 140–46 • W. M. F. Petrie, *Gerar*, London, 1928 • G. E. Wright, *AJA* 43 (1939), 458–63 • W. F. Albright, *AASOR* 21–22 (1943), 23 f., 144 • G. W. van Beek, *IEJ* 20 (1970), 230; 22 (1972), 245–46; 24 (1974), 138–39, 274–75.

Both pages counterclockwise: Plan of the Assyrian vaulted building (above); sections of the east wall with vaults restored (below); seventh century B.C. *Fort; sixth century* B.C. *"Assyrian" bowl; seventh century* B.C. *Red-figured lekythos; ca. 450* B.C. *Iron tools; tenth century* B.C.

JERICHO

IDENTIFICATION. The town of Jericho is situated in the wide plain of the Jordan Valley, about 10 kilometers (6 miles) north of the Dead Sea and close to the steep cliffs that fringe the valley to the west. At a depth of 250 meters below sea level, it is the lowest town on the surface of the earth. This very low site, shut in by mountain walls to the east and west, has a climate that is tropical in summer and usually mild in winter. The amount of rainfall is small, about 140 millimeters a year, most of which falls in a few violent downpours, whereas in some years there is virtually none. The flourishing agriculture of which the area is capable is dependent on the spring known today as Elisha's well, or 'Ein es-Sultan, a perennial spring flowing at the rate of 1,000 gallons per minute. With irrigation based on the spring, the alluvial soil of the valley can produce crops of almost every kind, tropical and temperate in habitat — dates, green vegetables, or wheat. In times of expansion, the waters of 'Ein es-Sultan can be supplemented by those of 'Ein Duq, some 3 kilometers (2 miles) to the northwest, which, as in the Early Arabic period and today, can be brought to Jericho by aqueduct. With irrigation an extensive oasis can be created, but when it is neglected the area reverts to the parched scrub of the adjacent valley, as is seen in nineteenth-century photographs taken in the immediate neighborhood of 'Ein es-Sultan. Destruction of the irrigation system by enemies, or the interruption of the water supply as a result of earth movements to which the Jordan Valley is liable, may account for the periodic abandonments of the ancient site that excavation has revealed.

HISTORY

Jericho enters written history as the first town west of the Jordan to be captured by the Israelites approaching from the east. Joshua's instruction to his spies to "go view the land even Jericho" (Joshua 2:1) is an illustration of the position of Jericho in the age-long process of penetration by nomads and semi-nomads from the desert area in the east into the fertile coastal lands. It stood near the Jordan fords between a good valley route down the eastern side of the Jordan Valley and another going up the western mountains. As it dominated one of the few routes leading directly from east to west, it was liable to attack by successive invaders.

The identification of the main mound of the oasis, Tell es-Sultan, with the oldest city is generally accepted. The mound rises to a height of 21.5 meters and covers an area of about 4 hectares. It stands quite near 'Ein es-Sultan (Elisha's well). As regards the Jericho of the Book of Joshua, there are some chronological difficulties, as will be seen below. Following its destruction by Joshua, the Bible states, Jericho was abandoned for centuries until a new settlement was established by Hiel the Bethelite in the time of Ahab, in the ninth century B.C. (I Kings 16:34). Other biblical references do not suggest that Jericho ever recovered its im-

portance. The archaeological evidence shows that occupation on the ancient site came to an end at the time of the Babylonian Exile. The centers of the later Jerichos were elsewhere in the oasis.

EXCAVATIONS

Soundings at Tell es-Sultan were first made by C. Warren as part of the early campaigns of the Palestine Exploration Society. Warren sank a number of shafts into the mound and concluded that there was nothing to be found. Two of his shafts were identified in the 1957–58 excavations, one of them penetrating through the Early Bronze Age town wall and the other missing the great pre-pottery Neolithic stone tower by only one meter.

The first large-scale excavations were those of an Austro-German expedition, from 1907–09, under the direction of E. Sellin and C. Watzinger. The expedition cleared the face of a considerable part of the Early Bronze Age town wall and traced the line of about half of the revetment at the base of the Middle Bronze Age defenses. Within the town, a large area of houses was cleared at the north end and a great trench was cut across the center. Re-excavation in 1953 showed that it had penetrated well into the pre-pottery Neolithic levels. The excavations were conducted and published by the best standards of the time. Unfortunately, at that time, there was no accepted chronology, so that the results of this early work can be used only to a limited extent.

By the time new excavations were undertaken by the Neilson Expeditions, directed by J. Garstang, from 1930 to 1936, the knowledge of pottery chronology had greatly increased. Excavation technique lagged, however, and the absence of detailed stratigraphy still often made the dating of the structures mere guesswork. The dating of the successive Bronze Age defensive systems by Garstang has, in fact, proved to be wrong. No Late Bronze Age wall survives. Also, as our knowledge of pottery chronology increased, the dating given to the scanty Late Bronze Age levels from the mound and the tombs was shown to be incorrect. The most important discovery of Garstang was that beneath the Bronze Age levels there was a deep Neolithic accumulation, usually of the pre-pottery stage. It was believed that there was a transition to the use of pottery at the site, but this was a mistake, and the detailed stratification of all levels is unreliable.

A third major series of excavations was carried out

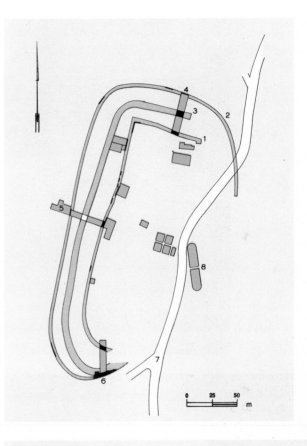

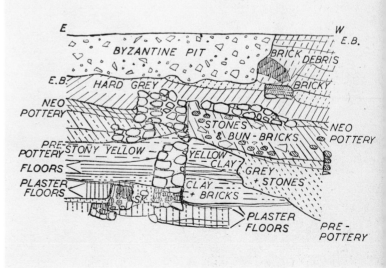

between 1952 and 1958, directed by Kathleen M. Kenyon on behalf of the British School of Archaeology in Jerusalem. The results are described in the following.

ARCHAEOLOGICAL RESULTS

Although extensive excavations have been carried out at Tell es-Sultan, the great depth of deposit in the lowest levels has allowed their examination only in limited areas. The mound survives to a maximum height of 21.5 meters above the surrounding plain, and to an average height of 17 meters. Bedrock has been reached in a sufficient number of places to show clearly that all of this height was built up by human occupation. The original settlement was on a surface sloping gently down to the east. Its position was doubtless dictated by the position of the spring, the actual source of which is now buried beneath the accumulation of the mound.

The earliest remains, found in an area near the north end of the mound, are Mesolithic. Carbon-14 dates for the deposit range from 9687 B.C. $\pm$ 107 to 7770 B.C. $\pm$ 210. The nature of the remains is not clear, but an oblong structure enclosing a clay platform, with a group of sockets for uprights set in a wall, too close together to be structural, may represent a sanctuary. The associated flint and bone industries, including a harpoon head and a lunate, are clearly related to the Lower Natufian of Mount Carmel. It is possible that this was a sanctuary set up by Mesolithic hunters by the spring of Jericho, for water sources are often treated as sacred in the Orient.

In the limited area excavated to bedrock, only at this one spot were definite Mesolithic levels found. But in a number of other places, levels were found which link these first Natufians of Jericho with the subsequent Neolithic stage. The most important of these sites was Square M. At this site the very lowest deposit consisted of a depth of 4 meters composed of a close succession of surfaces bounded by slight humps. The humps clearly represent the bases of flimsy walls, perhaps little more than the weighting down of tents of skins, although rudimentary mud bricks were present in the form of balls of clay. The area excavated was too limited and the traces so slight that no plan could be estab-

Fragments of wall paintings. Above, from the Hasmonaean palace. Below, from the Herodian palace.

lished, but the humps were visible in section. The surfaces that made up this 4 meters of deposit represent the remains of a succession of slight structures, huts, or tents suitable to the needs of a nomadic or semi-nomadic group. But the creation of this great depth of deposit indicates that these people were no longer nomadic, or at least that they returned to Jericho at regular and frequent intervals, perhaps in the practice of some form of transhumance. It is a truly transitional stage of culture, and the flint and bone industries are clearly derived from the Mesolithic Natufian. Though in square M-I there is no preceding Mesolithic stage, it is reasonable to presume that the stage represented is that of Mesolithic hunters, of whom evidence was found in site E, settling down to a sedentary way of life.

From such slight shelters the first solid structures are clearly derived. The actual transitional stages were not found. In square M-I they may even have been destroyed, for a thickish deposit containing fragments of clay-ball bricks intervened between the earlier succession of surfaces and the first solid structures, probably representing the leveling over of a nucleus mound that had become too small and steep. Above this deposit, the solid structures appear already fully developed, but their circular plan, usually single roomed, is clearly derived from that of a primitive hut.

These circular structures are built with solid walls of plano-convex mud bricks, often with a hog-backed outline. The walls are inclined somewhat inward and the amount of brick in the debris of collapse suggests that the roofs were domed. The interiors of the houses were sunk below the level of the courtyard outside, and there were porches with a downward slope, or steps of stone or wood, projecting into the room.

Rich industries of flint and bone were found in the houses: many axes and adzes, with polished or partially polished cutting edges, pestles, mortars, hammerstones, and other stone implements, which are clearly derived from the Lower Natufian. Dishes and cups of limestone represented the only surviving utensils.

The construction of these solid houses marked the establishment of a fully sedentary occupation, and the expansion of the community was rapid. Over all the area occupied by the subsequent Bronze Age town, and projecting appreciably beyond it to the north and south, houses of this type have been identified. The total area covered was almost 40 dunams.

The expansion of the settlement was soon followed by a step of major importance, the construction of a town wall. This was best preserved in trench I on the western side, where the first of a succession of defensive walls was still standing to a height of 5.75 meters. At the south end, a structure that was probably the same wall survived to a height of 2.1 meters, but at the north end, though the line could be identified, only one course survived. In each case, the foundations of the wall cut through the remains of pre-existing houses, but not of a long succession, so the enclosing of the site by a defensive wall followed soon after the growth of the settlement.

On the west side, the first town wall was associated with a remarkable structure, a great stone tower built against the inner side of the wall, 8.5 meters in diameter at the base and still surviving to a height of 7.75 meters. The tower was constructed solidly of stone, except in the center where a staircase provided access to the top of the tower from the interior of the town.

The tower is not only a monument to remarkable architectural and constructional achievement, but tower and wall together furnish evidence of a degree of communal organization and a flourishing town life wholly unexpected at a date which, as will be seen, must be in the eighth millennium B.C.

In all the areas excavated to this level there was a long succession of structures belonging to this first Neolithic stage. In the house areas, the ruins of successive houses were built up on a deposit of up to 6.5 meters. In trench I there was a sequence of four stages of the town wall, all incorporating the tower. The second stage was associated with a rock-cut ditch 9.5 meters wide and 2.25 meters deep. At the north and south ends of the town, in trenches II and III, these later walls lie farther out, obscured by the Middle Bronze Age revetment.

A number of Carbon-14 datings have been obtained for different stages in the deposits of this period. They range from 8340 B.C. $\pm$ 200 to 6935 $\pm$ 155, but the majority suggest a date for the beginning of the period in the late ninth millennium.

In all the areas excavated, the town of the period seems to have been fairly closely built up. In its area of about 40 dunams there may have been 2,000 or so occupants. A sedentary population of this size must have been largely dependent on agriculture. The favorable conditions provided by the perennial stream must have led to the very early development in food production, a development beginning in the Proto-Neolithic stage and increasing with the growth of the town. It is also possible to assume that the developing agriculture was accompanied by developing irrigation, for the spring in its natural state could not have watered an area large enough for the fully grown town. The organization required to create a system of irrigation could produce the community organization of which the imposing defenses provide evidence.

This pre-pottery Neolithic A culture of Jericho came to an abrupt end and was succeeded by a second, pre-pottery Neolithic B, which arrived at Jericho fully developed. Between the two there was a period of erosion, although it is uncertain whether it was caused by a destruction wrought by the newcomers, or whether natural causes such as disease or an interference in the water supply caused an abandonment of the site by the inhabitants. It is also uncertain whether there was an interval in time between the two occupations.

Pre-pottery Neolithic B differed from its predecessor in almost every respect. The most immediately obvious contrast was the architecture. The houses were far more elaborate and sophisticated. The rooms were comparatively large, rectangular in plan, and grouped around courtyards. The plan seems to have been stereotyped, with central suites divided by cross walls in which there were entrances at either end and in the center, with smaller rooms adjoining. No complete house plan was recovered, as the size of the houses was such that in no case was an entire building within an excavated area. The walls were of handmade mud bricks of an elongated shape with a herringbone pattern of thumb impressions on the top. Floors and walls were covered with a continuous coat of highly burnished, hard lime mortar. It is presumed from the rectangular plan that the roofs were flat. There was no evidence as to whether there were upper stories. In the courtyards, whose floors were usually of mud mortar, were fireplaces, and there was often an innumerable succession of charcoal spreads.

The material equipment was also almost completely different from that of pre-pottery Neolithic A. The flint industry was distinct and is not derived from the Natufian. The bone industry was very poor, being confined to simple implements such as pins and borers. Polished axes and adzes were rare, and in fact there were very few heavy stone implements. A very characteristic object was a trough-shaped quern with the grinding hollow running out to one edge and a flat border round the other three sides. This type was never found in pre-pottery Neolithic A, and the types of grinding stone were also distinct. Bowls and dishes of white limestone, some of them very well made, become very common.

Two structures were found which probably served religious purposes. In one, a room had been cut off from part of the usual suite of rooms. In its end wall was a small niche with a rough stone pedestal at its base, and in the debris nearby was a carefully trimmed stone pillar, which must be interpreted as a representation of the deity. The plan of the other structure was unique. It consisted of a large central room with a burnished plaster floor, at each end of which were annexes with curvilinear walls. At the center of the large room was a rectangular basin, also plastered. It is likely that this structure had a ceremonial use.

The most remarkable evidence bearing on religious practices was the discovery of ten human skulls with features restored in plaster, sometimes with a high degree of skill and artistic power. Eyes inlaid with shells, delicately modeled ears, nose, and eyebrows, flesh-colored tinting, combined to make the heads extraordinarily life-like. These plastered skulls were most likely associated with a cult of ancestor worship. The normal practice was to bury the dead beneath the floors of the houses, and many of the bodies had the cranium removed, presumably to ensure that the wisdom of the individual was preserved for the benefit of the descendants. The skulls were found in three groups, two close together, but the tenth skull came from a house some distance away, so the practice must have been followed by a number of separate families.

The pre-pottery Neolithic B settlement seems originally to have been undefended, for the earliest town wall found was later than a long series of house levels. Like that of pre-pottery Neolithic A, it was built of rough stones, some of them of very great size. It was traced only on the west side of the site, where in trench I it overlay the earlier wall,

though separated from it by a considerable depth of fill. Its probable continuation was found in site M. At the north and south ends, in trenches II and III, the houses of the period were truncated by the Middle Bronze Age revetment, and the contemporary town wall must have lain farther out.

The town of this period had a long existence, for the houses were rebuilt time and time again. Usually the houses were rebuilt in approximately the same position and on the same plan, but there was nearly always evidence that the preceding destruction was very severe, and the walls had to be rebuilt almost from floor level. The Carbon-14 datings have a range from 7379 B.C. $\pm$ 102 to 5845 B.C. $\pm$ 160.

Whereas pre-pottery Neolithic A had every appearance of being an indigenous development, this was not the case with pre-pottery Neolithic B. The latter arrived at Jericho with a fully developed architecture and an industry that owed nothing to its predecessor on the site. Other related sites have now been found. Some 180 kilometers to the south Diana Kirkbride has excavated the site of Beidha (Seyl Aqlat) near Petra. The plastered floors, flint industry, and typical querns indicate clearly that the culture of the two sites is related, though differing in some details. There are indications of similar sites elsewhere in Palestine. At Catal Hüyük in Anatolia, J. Mellaart in 1961 began the excavation of a site that must also be related. The plans of the houses have the same rectangular layout, the same abundant use is made of burnished plaster, the dead are buried beneath the floors of the houses, and there are other similarities. The relationship, however, is probably collateral. The material equipment of the Anatolian site, with molded plaster decoration and elaborate wall paintings, is much more sophisticated than that at Jericho, and pottery is found, although in the lower levels it is not common. The earliest period is dated by Carbon-14 to about 6700 B.C. It is very probable that the cultures of the Anatolian and Palestinian sites are derived from a common ancestor, which, geographically, might be sought in northern Syria, although so far no evidence has been found.

Thus, there were two successive and quite separate pre-pottery Neolithic cultures at Jericho, and in each case the settlement assumed the character of a walled town. Of the first indigenous culture, all the stages of development can be traced on the spot.

JERICHO

Right: Round tower, pre-pottery Neolithic A. Below: Defences of the Neolithic city showing ditch, wall, and tower. Bottom, left to right: Plastered human skull; pre-pottery Neolithic A. Plastered human skull; pre-pottery Neolithic B. Head molded of unbaked clay with hair marked by lines and eyes by shells (pre-pottery Neolithic B?), from Garstang's excavations.

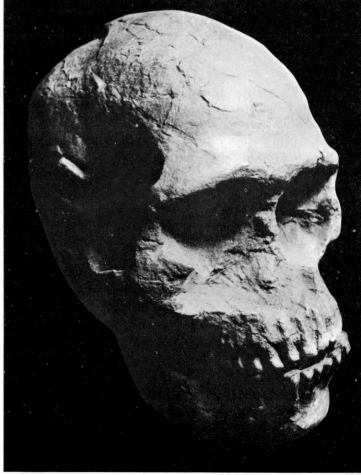

The second had evolved elsewhere. These two early Neolithic cultures are probably examples of a considerable number of trial evolutions from a hunting economy to a village or town economy based on developing agriculture.

Like pre-pottery Neolithic A, its successor pre-pottery Neolithic B also came to an abrupt end. In all the areas excavated, the buildings and surfaces of the period are eroded on an angle sloping down to the exterior of the town, often very steeply. The terrace walls which were an essential part of the layout on the slopes of the mound had collapsed in whole or in part, and the fill and floors behind them had been washed out, often to the depth of several layers. It is impossible to estimate the length of the period of abandonment that produced this erosion. Once an earthquake or violent rains had made breaches in the terrace walls, the washout process could have proceeded rapidly if there were a series of heavy rains, but less violent conditions might have slowed down the erosion over a long period.

The evidence of the next period of occupation appears in the form of pits cut into this erosion surface. These pits, which often were as deep as 2 meters and about 3 meters across, and in at least one instance as deep as 4 meters, were at first interpreted as quarry pits sunk to obtain material for brickmaking. It was suggested that the characteristic fill of angular stones represented material sieved out in the brickmaking process. Subsequently, however, it became clear that the pits contained a series of floors and occupation levels, including in one case a well-constructed oven, and it was also observed that the stones originated from walls revetting the edges of the pits. It is therefore clear that these were occupation pits, or the emplacements of semi-subterranean huts. Closely similar phenomena, including the angular stones, were observed at Tell el-Far'a (q.v.) in the levels which

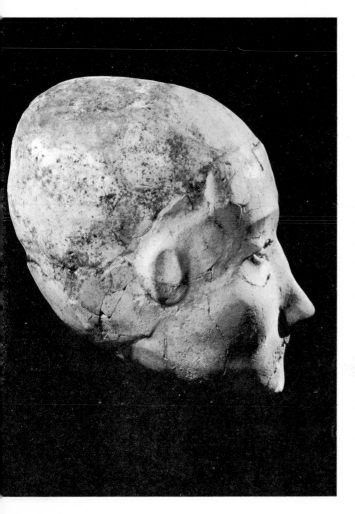

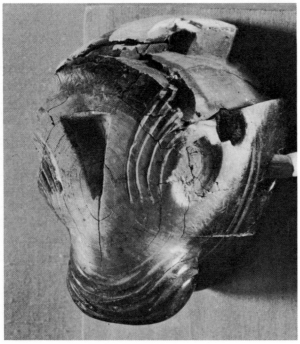

preceded the Early Bronze Age structures. The use of subterranean dwellings may also be compared with those of the Chalcolithic period, with a culture allied to the Ghassulian, at Tell Beer Matar and Tell Beer Safad near Beersheba (q.v.).

In these pits at Jericho appears the first pottery. The analysis of the earliest pottery of Jericho suggests that two different and successive groups are represented, which are called pottery Neolithic A and pottery Neolithic B. The A pottery, consisting of vessels decorated with burnished chevron patterns in red, and also of extremely coarse, straw-tempered vessels, corresponds with that ascribed to stratum IX by J. Garstang, while the B pottery, consisting of jars with bow rims, jars and bowls with herringbone decoration, and vessels with a mat red slip, corresponds with that ascribed to stratum VIII. The former was believed to appear as an indigenous development out of the pre-pottery Neolithic. A re-examination of Garstang's trench and fresh evidence from other parts of the mound, however, make it quite clear that this is not so, that it was a conclusion arrived at only because the pits containing the pottery were not observed, and it was believed that the pottery belonged to the latest plastered-floor houses instead of being intrusive. With the appearance of pottery there was a change in the flint industry, most noticeably the use of coarse instead of fine denticulation for the sickle blades.

By far, the greatest amount of the finds of the period came from the pits. Above the pits, however, there were some scanty remains of buildings. Too little was found to establish any house plans, but their characteristic feature was the round and plano-convex (bun-shaped) bricks, not found at any other period. The relation of the two types of pottery to the successive stages is not yet clear.

Scattered examples of the characteristic pottery Neolithic A pottery have been found on a number of Palestinian sites, i.e., Tell Duweir, Megiddo, and Tell Batashi, but usually only in mixed groups (or collections published as such) found at the lowest levels, with a range from the Neolithic to the Early Bronze Age. Such finds indicate that the people who used this pottery were fairly widespread in Palestine at this time, but tell us little about them.

Top: EBA II jug from Tomb II, from Garstang's excavation. Bottom: Ivory head of bull, 4.75 cm. high; EBA.

Objects comparable with the finds of pottery Neolithic B are found over a wide area. Pottery and flints, particularly the former, can be closely paralleled at Sha'ar ha-Golan on the Yarmuk. Similar pottery is also found in the Enéolithique A of Byblos, with the additional link of incised pebbles, so common at Sha'ar ha-Golan, and also found at Byblos. It would appear, therefore, that this element in the pottery Neolithic of Jericho had Syrian or at least northeastern connections. But it must be admitted that this period in the life of the site is at present rather obscure.

Between the pottery Neolithic and the next stage at Jericho there is another gap, perhaps covering the period of the Ghassulian culture. The gap is evidenced by the usual erosion stage and by a complete break in the artifacts, particularly the pottery.

Toward the end of the fourth millennium, a completely new people arrived in Palestine. It is probable that some of the earliest evidence of their arrival is to be found at Jericho. Both groups of pre-pottery Neolithic people buried beneath the floors of the houses. There is no evidence as to how the pottery Neolithic people buried. The newcomers for the first time buried in rock-cut tombs, a practice which was to become standard at least down to the Roman period. They brought with them pottery of simple forms, bag-shaped juglets and round-based bowls, not previously found in Palestine. In earlier excavations, at Ai, Tell el-Far'a, and Megiddo, these vessels had been found, together with vessels more elaborate in form or decoration. The Jericho tombs showed that such combinations represented a later stage, since at Jericho the components could be shown as separate entities. The Jericho evidence suggested that the newcomers could be divided into A, B, and C groups. The A group, with the bag-shaped juglets and the round-based bowls, were the first to arrive at Jericho. Upon this group supervened the B group, who decorated their vessels in elaborate patterns of grouped lines. Elsewhere, at Tell el-Far'a and Megiddo, for instance, the A group was mingled with a C group not found at Jericho, with vessels characteristically gray-burnished and known as the Esdraelon ware.

These combinations and permutations suggest immigrant groups arriving successively and mixing differently in the various areas. Nowhere is there evidence that they were responsible for true urban development, for almost all the evidence concerning them comes from tombs. But at sites where there is evidence of them, urban development subsequently took place, unlike the sites at which the people of the Ghassulian culture are found, and it is for this reason that the classification Proto-Urban is suggested.

The stage of Jericho in which this Proto-Urban phase, with the combination of the A and B elements, developed into the urban civilization of the Early Bronze Age has not yet been fully investigated. The process was clearly a gradual one, and other immigrant groups may have provided the impetus toward urbanization. From the amalgamation of influences emerged a culture responsible for the walled towns which at Jericho, as elsewhere, are the characteristic feature of Palestine for the greater part of the third millennium B.C.

Jericho at this stage had grown into a steep-sided mound beside the spring which was the reason for its continued existence. Round its summit can be traced the line of mud-brick walls by which the Early Bronze Age town was defended. The line is uncertain only on the east side, due to the intrusion of the modern road. This line was traced by the earlier excavations. Sections cut across and into it during the 1952–58 excavations showed that the history of the walls was complex. The section cut completely through the walls on the west provided evidence of seventeen stages. There were buildings completely destroyed, sometimes probably by earthquakes, sometimes by enemies, and sometimes apparently through neglect. It is impossible to estimate a time scale for the successive events, and it is impossible to correlate the succession observed in one area with that in another, for one length of wall might have collapsed or have been destroyed while other sections remained intact.

It was also impossible, because of the much cut-into and eroded state of the site, to relate the detailed history of the defenses with the successive building stages within the town. In the areas in which the interior of the town has been investigated, there was a sequence of building periods, though not the same number of destructions found in the defenses. The remains, however, showed a succession of solidly built and spacious structures that confirm the impression that this was a period of full urban development.

A number of tombs were found covering the same period. All were large rock-cut tombs, and contained a large number of burials. The interpretation of the evidence was complicated by the fact that in every case erosion had removed the roof of the chamber and the greater part of the shaft by which the chambers presumably were approached. It is clear, however, that there were multiple successive burials, numbering up to a hundred (based on the number of recognizable skulls). At intervals the tombs were cleared, and in many cases the greater part of the bones were discarded, leaving mainly the skulls and the pottery vessels and other objects that had accompanied them. Many successive burials were therefore made in the tombs, but on the present evidence it is not known whether they represent family vaults covering a long period, or whether they were simply the current burial site for all the members of the community.

The end of Early Bronze Age Jericho was sudden. A final stage of the town wall, which in at least one place shows signs of having been hurriedly rebuilt, was destroyed by fire. The next building stage consisted of houses quite different from those of the Early Bronze Age, more slightly built, of irregular plan and distinctive greenish bricks. These houses, however, did not immediately succeed those of the Early Bronze Age, for between the layers associated with the two types of houses was an accumulation of pottery of a new type,

Left: MBA I tomb; plan and section. Right: MBA II-B tomb. On the right, skeleton lying on burial bed; on the left, offering table with wooden bowl, basket, and pottery.

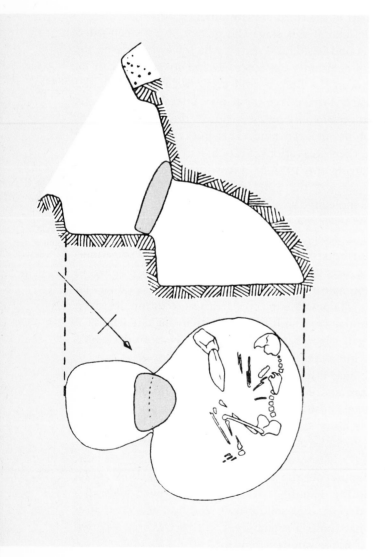

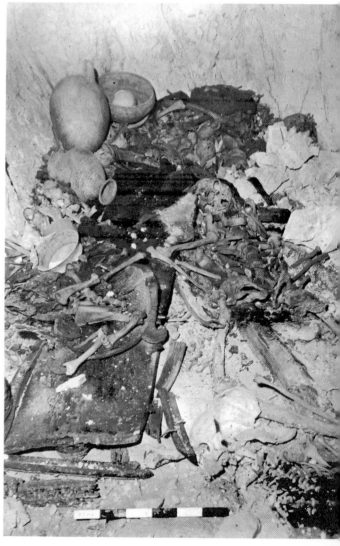

associated with newcomers who apparently were not yet building houses but must still have been living in tents.

The stage (elsewhere called Middle Bronze Age I) is best called the Intermediate Early Bronze–Middle Bronze period, for it represents an intrusion between the Early Bronze and Middle Bronze Ages, differing from both in every important respect. The newcomers were nomads and pastoralists. Even when they started to build houses, they did not develop a true urban center. The houses straggle down the slopes of the mound and over the surrounding country, and there is no evidence of a town wall. The tribal and nomadic character of the population is shown by their burial customs. The dead were buried individually in separate tombs, a feature that sharply distinguishes this period from the preceding and succeeding ones. But within this general practice there are distinctive variations, grouping the tombs into seven categories. The variations cover disposition and state of the body, form and size of the tomb and shaft, and type of offerings. These differences may represent the practices of separate tribal groups. One feature occurring in several of the groups is the very careful burial, in large deep tombs, of skeletons that are largely disintegrated and often incomplete. This must be taken as evidence of a nomadic way of life, in which those who died during seasonal migrations were brought back for burial when the tribe returned to some focal spot.

The Early Bronze–Middle Bronze period people are found all over Palestine, although the differences in equipment and customs from site to site further emphasize the tribal nature of their organization. They can also be traced in Syria, where it can be shown that their appearance is part of the great expansion of the Amorites, to which reference is made in Sumerian records as early as the time of Sargon of Akkad (2371–2316 B.C.) and the Third Dynasty of Ur (2113–2004 B.C.), and who were responsible for the destruction of Byblos at about the end of the Sixth Egyptian Dynasty. It thus seems clear that it was at this stage that the Amorites, who formed an important element of the population both in Palestine and Transjordan at the time of the entry of the Israelites, arrived on the scene.

An equally abrupt break marks the beginning of the Middle Bronze Age. The evidence at Jericho is very clear. The break is again in type of settlement, burial customs, tools and weapons, and pottery. Unfortunately, very little survives of the town of the period. The greater part of the summit of the mound has suffered very severe erosion during periods in which the site was unoccupied. As a result, with one exception, the latest houses to survive in all the areas excavated within the line of the Bronze Age defenses belong to the Early Bronze Age. Those of the Early Bronze–Middle Bronze period that survived did so because they were protected by the Middle Bronze Age rampart. The exception to this considerable erosion was in the center of the east side of the town, immediately

Below: Drawing and reconstruction of a chair, from a MBA II-B tomb. Bottom: MBA II rhyton, from Tomb 9 of Garstang's excavations.

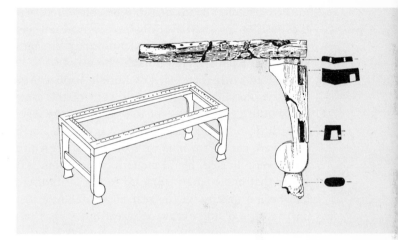

adjacent to the spring. Here, presumably for reasons of access to the spring, the accumulation of earlier levels had not raised the mound to such a height, so there was a crescent-shaped hollow in this area. In the hollow, the Middle Bronze Age levels have survived. Only a limited area of the lower levels has been excavated, but the evidence is sufficient to show that from the earliest stages the buildings were substantial, and in this respect and in the regularity of their plans, they resemble those of the Early Bronze Age and not those of the Early Bronze–Middle Bronze period. Like the Early Bronze Age houses beneath them, they were built in terraces ascending the side of the mound. An interesting feature was that in one of the earliest stages occurs a brick-built tomb containing multiple burials. Other burials were found in graves nearby. These burials appear to be earlier than any found in the cemetery. It can possibly be concluded that the position of the new inhabitants was not yet very strong, and fear of desecration by enemies kept them from burying outside the walls.

Associated with these earliest Middle Bronze Age levels was a succession of town walls of the same brick-built type as those of the Early Bronze Age. Very little of them was exposed, as to the north they were cut by the modern road and to the south they were buried by a modern water point. It seems that immediately adjacent to the south there had been a gate, with the rear of a gatehouse just on the edge of the excavated area, but it was impossible to explore this further. It is probable that elsewhere the line of these early Middle Bronze Age walls followed approximately that of the Early Bronze Age walls that had created a crest around the edge of the mound. But for the greater part of the circuit the earlier walls alone survived, and the destruction of the summit of the later Middle Bronze Age rampart (see below) showed that there had been much erosion on the line of the walls.

It appears that the first Middle Bronze Age occupation at Jericho does not belong to the beginning of the period. No evidence was found of anything comparable with the Middle Bronze Age I remains at Ras el-'Ain, in the Tell el-'Ajjul Courtyard Cemetery, or at Megiddo. Only one tomb in the cemetery area is likely to belong to Middle Bronze Age I, and although the pottery on the mound has not yet been fully studied, very little of it appears to belong to Middle Bronze Age I. It is probable,

therefore, that the site was first occupied at the end of Middle Bronze Age I, perhaps toward the end of the nineteenth century B.C.

For the final stage of the Middle Bronze Age, something more of the plan of the town can be established. The houses excavated in the 1930–36 and 1952–58 expeditions were small dwellings, with small and rather irregular rooms, lining two roads that in parts had shallow cobbled steps going up the slopes. In the 1930–36 expedition, these houses were called the Palace storerooms, for at the time of their final destruction many of them contained a large number of jars filled with grain. This interpretation is improbable, both because the roads show that it was an ordinary quarter of the town, and because the building called the Palace is quite obviously later in date. The houses were, in fact, of the type common then and down to the present time, in which the living rooms were on the first floor, and storerooms and shops on the ground floor. In fact, there were clear examples of the little one-room shops found in modern suqs, which have a door onto the street and no connection with the rest of the house. This quarter of the town may have been one in which corn millers lived, for in one house, having a store of grain on the ground floor, no fewer than twenty-three grinding querns were found in the debris fallen from the upper story.

This final Middle Bronze Age building phase, and several of the preceding ones, is later than the town wall described above, and extends over its top to the east, where it is truncated by the modern road and the water installations beyond. It is reasonably certain, however, that these building phases belonged to the new type of defenses that appear at Jericho, as at many other Palestinian sites, the type in which the wall stands on top of a high glacis. The surviving portion at Jericho consists of a revetment wall at the base (without the external ditch found at some sites), an artificial glacis overlying the original slope of the mound and steepening the slope to an angle of 35 degrees, with the face of the glacis surfaced with hard lime plaster. On the summit of this glacis was the curtain wall, at a height of 17 meters, above the exterior ground level and set back 26 meters from it. Inside the wall was a lesser slope down to the interior of the town. Only in one place, at the northwest corner of the town, did the glacis survive to its full height, with above it the foundations of the wall. Elsewhere, erosion had removed some 6 meters of it and, with it, all traces of the previous Middle Bronze Age walls that may be presumed to have existed beneath the glacis and can probably be identified beneath its surviving high point.

Three stages of this glacis can be traced. The final one had a very massive revetment wall placed in front of earlier and less massive walls. This wall can be traced around nearly two thirds of the circuit of the mound and swinging out at the north end well to the east of the present road. Here, the glacis had left the crest of the sloping edge of the mound and must have formed a freestanding rampart on level ground, as it does in some other sites with this type of defenses, for example at Qatna and Tell el-Yahudiyeh.

The evidence of the Middle Bronze Age at Jericho from the town was considerably supplemented by that from the tombs. Once more there was the practice of multiple burials, additional evidence of a break with the preceding period. From the evidence of a succession of forms of pottery and other objects, it is possible to establish a series covering the whole period of Middle Bronze Age II. The normal practice was to provide each burial with a provision of food, furniture, and personal toilet equipment. As new burials were made, the skeletal remains and associated offerings of previous ones were pushed to one side, thus creating a heap of bones and objects around the rear of the chamber. Some property in the Jericho tombs, not as yet fully understood, arrested the total decay of the organic material, and objects of wood and basketry, therefore, often survived in recognizable form. In the pushing-aside process, many of the larger objects were broken. But a number of tombs were found in which groups of simultaneous final burials remained undisturbed. Most of these belonged to the latest stage of Middle Bronze Age Jericho and are probably evidence of a period of high mortality so soon before the final destruction of the town that the tombs were never re-used.

From these tombs, therefore, it was possible to obtain evidence of the full normal equipment of the tombs of the period. Almost without exception there was a long narrow table, usually found laden with food. The structure of the table, with two legs at one end and one at the other, presumably was designed to enable it to stand on an uneven floor.

Stools and beds were also found, but these were rare and only occurred in tombs of apparently important persons. In other tombs, the dead person lay on rush mats, and it can be concluded that beds and stools were luxury articles. Most adults were provided with baskets containing toilet equipment, alabaster vessels, wooden combs and boxes with applied bone decoration. Wooden vessels, from huge platters to small bowls, cups, and bottles, clearly supplemented the pottery vessels. In most cases, the dead were buried clothed. The garments were not well preserved, but fragments of textile, usually of a rather coarse texture, were found extending at least to the knees and held in place by toggle pins on the shoulder, chest, or at the waist. Personal ornaments were not numerous. From the position of a number of wooden combs, it appears that they were worn in the hair. There were a few beads that in some cases may have belonged to necklaces. A considerable number of scarabs were found, sometimes worn on finger rings but more often apparently as pendants.

It is reasonable to assume that the equipment provided for a dead person in a tomb was the same equipment to which he was accustomed during life. The objects found in the Jericho tombs in conjunction with the pottery and metal objects from tombs elsewhere are thus a very important addition to the knowledge of the period.

The final Middle Bronze Age buildings at Jericho were violently destroyed by fire. Thereafter, the site was abandoned, and the ruins of two buildings on the lower part of the slope gradually became covered with rain-washed debris. The date of the burned buildings would seem to be the very end of the Middle Bronze Age, and the destruction may be ascribed to the disturbances that followed the expansion of the Hyksos from Egypt about 1560 B.C. During the rest of the sixteenth century and probably most of the fifteenth, the site was abandoned. The conclusion formed during the 1930–36 excavations that there was continuous occupation in this period was due to a lack of knowledge of the pottery of the beginning of the Late Bronze Age, so that the significance of its complete absence was not appreciated.

Only very scanty remains survive of the town that overlies the layers of rain-washed debris. These include the building described by Garstang as the Middle Building, the building he calls the Palace (although there is no published dating evidence and it could be Iron Age), and a fragment of a floor and wall in the area excavated in 1952–58. Everything else has disappeared in subsequent denudation. The small amount of pottery recovered suggests a fourteenth-century date. This date is supported by the evidence from five tombs of the period excavated by Garstang that were re-used at this period. It is probable that the site was re-occupied soon after 1400 B.C. and abandoned in the second half of the fourteenth century. The pottery on the mound and in the tombs is certainly later than 1400–1380 B.C., the date that a calculation based on biblical evidence led Garstang to suggest for the destruction of the site, and is probably not as late as the thirteenth century, which is the date supported by other scholars for the entry of the Israelites into Palestine after the Exodus.

Of the defenses of the period, nothing at all survives. The double wall ascribed to the Late Bronze Age in the 1930–36 excavations is composed in part of two successive walls of the Early Bronze Age. For most of the circuit, only stumps survive. Even of these walls and of the Middle Bronze Age glacis that buried them, only the part on the slopes of the mound is intact. At the highest preserved point of the mound, the northwest corner, the glacis is intact, but of the wall that crowned it, only the bare foundations are still in position. There is not the slightest trace of any later wall, and it is unlikely that even the most thorough search will produce any remnants.

Jericho, therefore, was destroyed - in the Late Bronze Age II. It is very possible that this destruction is truly remembered in the Book of Joshua, although archaeology cannot provide the proof. The subsequent break in occupation that is proved by archaeology is, however, in accord with the biblical story. There was a period of abandonment, during which erosion removed most of the remains of the Late Bronze Age town and much of the earlier ones, and rainwater gulleys cutting deeply into the underlying levels have been found. According to the biblical account, Hiel the Bethelite was responsible for the first re-occupation, occurring in the time of Ahab (early ninth century B.C.). No trace of an Iron Age occupation as early as this has so far been observed, but it may have been a small-scale affair. In the seventh century B.C., however, there was an extensive occupation of the

ancient site. Evidence of this does not survive on the summit of the mound but is found as a thick deposit, with several successive building levels, on its flanks. On the western slope, a massive building of this period was found, with a tripartite plan common in the Iron Age II. The pottery suggests that this stage in the history of the site goes down to the period of the Babylonian Exile. Thereafter, the site by 'Ein es-Sultan was abandoned, and later periods are represented only by some Roman graves and a hut of the early Arab period.

KATHLEEN M. KENYON

JERICHO FROM THE PERSIAN TO THE BYZANTINE PERIODS

Identification. Although the evidence available at present is not sufficient to establish the size of the town of Jericho in the Second Temple period, it can be assumed that at the beginning of the period it lay within the confines of the modern town. At that time the town received its water supply mainly from the spring of 'Ein es-Sultan. Like the modern town, Jericho then was also most probably spread out among gardens and plantations.

In the Hasmonaean period and in the time of Herod, the area of cultivated lands was greatly enlarged around Wadi Qelt following the construction of a network of aqueducts which carried the waters of the springs of 'Ein Duq, 'Ein Nureimah (Na'aran), and Wadi Qelt.

Because of the rich agricultural land, the mild winter climate, and the relatively short distance to Jerusalem, a number of winter palaces were erected at the site called today Tulul Abu el-'Alaiq. The rich and upper classes of Judah also built winter homes there. The entire valley of Jericho was protected by a chain of fortresses built by the Hasmonaeans on the hills around the valley. Herod continued this practice and, like them, combined the fortresses with palaces.

In the Late Roman and Byzantine periods, the town was again reduced to the area of modern Jericho. A number of synagogues and churches from the Byzantine period have been found in the vicinity (see below).

E. NETZER

History. Historians of the Hellenistic-Roman period (*e.g.*, Strabo, Pliny, Josephus) stress Jericho's economic and military importance. In the tropical climate prevailing in the Vale, the groves of Jericho

(Tosefta *Arakhin* 2:8) produced high quality dates and various medicinal plants and spices, particularly balsam which thrives on intensive irrigation. Because of these products, famed throughout antiquity, Josephus considers the Vale a veritable paradise (*War* IV, 469).

Since it was situated on the eastern approaches of Judea, the Jericho district was also of great strategic importance. This was the main reason for the establishment there of fortresses at various times. These served also to defend the rich plantations that constituted an important source of revenue for all rulers of the area.

Jericho served as district headquarters during the Persian period. Later rulers retained this administrative pattern. It seems that the Jericho district already constituted a portion of the private domain of the ruler at the time of Alexander's conquest. It became the property of the conqueror and his heirs, being "spear-won" land, according to Hellenistic custom. Consequently, the Jericho area was not urbanized and thus did not prejudice either the king's revenue or his estates. In any event, the flourishing of the oasis on a large scale can be connected with Hellenistic irrigation works.

According to I Maccabees (9:50) and Josephus (*Antiquities* XIII, 15), the Syrian general Bacchides fortified Jericho. These fortifications were probably built on the hills around Jericho. Among them is the fort of Doq (Dagon), which is mentioned in I Maccabees 16:11–16; Josephus, *War* I, 56; *Antiquities* XIII, 230. According to these sources, Simon the Hasmonaean was murdered at Doq by the commander of his army, Ptolemy, son of Habubu. The forts of Thrax and Taurus were apparently also part of these fortifications. They were destroyed by Pompey during his Jerusalem campaign (Strabo XVI, 2, 40). The two mounds of Tulul el-'Alaiq were mistakenly considered by scholars to be the remains of these forts. Under Gabinius (58 B.C.), Jericho had the administrative status of a sanhedrin (*Antiquities* XIV, 91; *War* I, 170). According to talmudic sources a large number of priests resided there. In the struggle between Herod and the last Hasmonaeans, the Vale of Jericho played a prominent role. It was here that Antigonus concentrated the bulk of his military force and waged a bitter campaign against Herod and his allies. Herod was extremely active in the building of Jericho and the development of its environs.

It was only natural that Antony should consider Jericho a present fit for Cleopatra, who thereafter leased it to Herod. Octavian (Augustus Caesar), however, restored Jericho to Judean rule in 30 B.C. Herod built his winter residence there (*War* I, 407; II, 59), as well as an amphitheater (*Antiquities* XVII, 161), a hippodrome (*War* I, 659), and a theater (*Antiquities* XVII, 194). He also erected the fortress Cypros, named for his mother, on the spot called Tell 'Aqaba today (map reference 190139). One of the forts built by the Hasmonaeans was probably situated on Tell 'Aqaba. In the area between the fortress and the palace, Herod had residences built for his courtiers. Both he and Archelaus, his successor, developed the irrigation installations until, according to Josephus, the Vale was replete with ponds and gardens. Surveys and explorations have brought to light five aqueducts that distributed water throughout the city and the Vale.

Upon Herod's death, his slave Simeon declared himself king and set fire to his master's palace and other edifices (*War* II, 57). Archelaus, however, after succeeding to power, reconstructed the palace in a magnificent fashion (*Antiquities* XVII, 340).

Apparently, no alteration occurred in the status of Jericho when, on the extinction of the Herodian dynasty, it became an estate of the Roman emperor. Throughout the Second Temple period, Jericho was occupied by a Jewish community, which, as may be concluded from talmudic sources continued to exist there in the post-destruction period. During the third century A.D., Jericho contained a Christian community. Christian literature mentions by name five local bishops in accounts down to the seventh century. The city remained in a state of perpetual quarrel with its Jewish rival at Na'aran.

G. FOERSTER–GABRIELLA BACCHI

Tulul Abu el-'Alaiq. Exploration. In 1838, the site was first discovered by E. Robinson. Thirty years later, C. Warren conducted excavations at the two mounds of 'Alaiq as part of his examination of nine mounds in the Jericho area. He cut trenches in an east–west direction and ascribed his finds to the Roman period. On the northern mound he exposed walls of stone and of sun-dried brick, some of the latter decorated with colored plaster.

An expedition headed by A. Nöldeke, C. Watzinger, and E. Sellin conducted excavations in the two mounds (this time in a north–south direction) in

1909 and 1911. They also dug trenches near the southern mound.

The most extensive excavations were carried out in 1950 by a joint expedition of the American Schools of Oriental Research and the Pittsburgh-Xenia Theological Seminary. The work was directed by J. L. Kelso and D. C. Baramki. They cleared most of the remains on the southern mound (which they called mound 1) and identified them as the remains of a Hellenistic tower with two superimposed Herodian levels. To the west of the mound they uncovered a monumental facade, with a sunken garden in front of it, and buildings flanking it. The excavators called this Jericho's civic center and attributed its construction to Herod. On the other side of Wadi Qelt they uncovered a number of walls built of Roman concrete (the sunken garden and the remains on the southern mound were similarly constructed). On the northern mound (called mound 2) they made several cross-sections and distinguished the remains of "towers," whose dates they could not establish, with remnants of a Hellenistic "fort" beneath them.

In 1951, the American Schools conducted another campaign of excavations which were directed by J. Pritchard. They uncovered buildings southwest of the southern mound and also cleared a large structure which was identified by Pritchard as a gymnasium.

Further excavations were carried out in 1973–74 by a Hebrew University expedition headed by E. Netzer. The excavations concentrated mainly on the northern mound and its surroundings and in the area north of Wadi Qelt opposite the southern mound. Soundings were also made in the southern mound. The results of these excavations are given below.

HASMONAEAN PERIOD. A palace from this period was uncovered north of Wadi Qelt. Built by one of the Hasmonaean kings, it consisted of a main building (about 50 by 70 meters) and a swimming pool surrounded by a spacious court.

The main building was constructed mainly of sun-dried bricks on a rubble foundation. It had survived almost two stories high in some places because of an artificial mound which was built above it in the Herodian period. To create this artificial mound, massive stone foundations were built in the palace, and an earth fill, six to seven meters high, was then poured into the foundations.

The palace seems to have been made up of a large central court surrounded by rooms. Some of its walls were decorated with colored plaster. Kelso and Baramki, who also found some of these

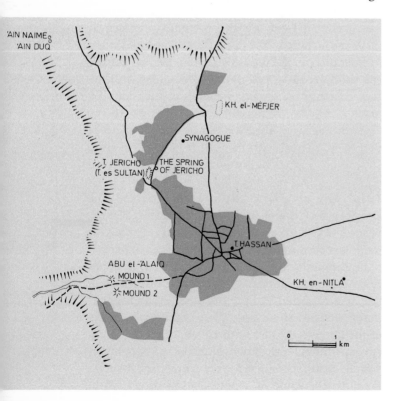

Left: Jericho and neighboring sites in Roman and Byzantine periods.

Opposite page, top: General plan:
A. Hasmonaean winter palace complex. 1. Main palace. 2. Pavilion (?) 3. Pool surrounded by large court. B. Herod's winter palace (early). 4. Palace (gymnasium), excavated in 1951 and today covered over. C. Herod's enlarged winter palace (later). 5. Southern mound. 6. Sunken garden, with the "Grand Facade" south of it. 7. Northern wing. 8. Pool. 9. Villa (?) built over main building of Hasmonaean palace.

Opposite page, bottom: Plan of northern wing of Herod's palace. 1. Portico in the facade, on the banks of Wadi Qelt. 2. Great reception hall. 3. West court (Ionic style). 4. East court (Corinthian style). 5. Entrance halls and passageway. 6. Rooms oriented toward central court. 7. Apodyterium. 8. Tepidaria. 9. Caldarium. 10. Frigidarium. 11. Service court. 12. Earlier structures.

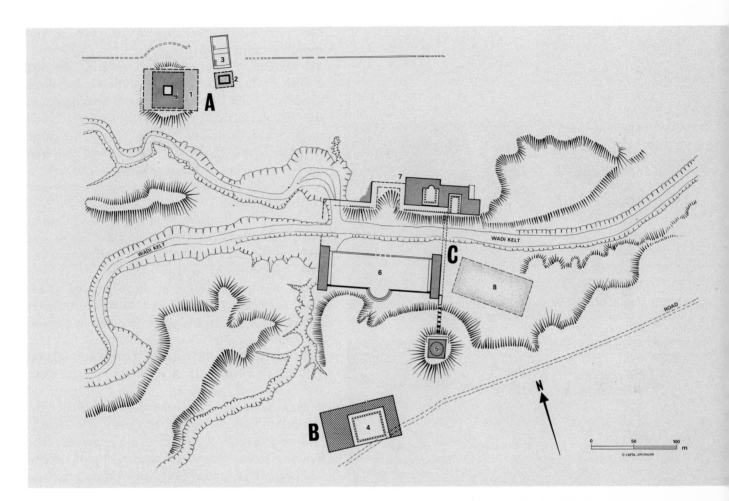

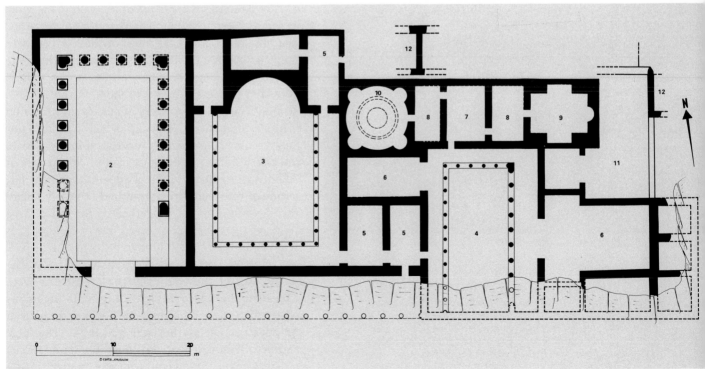

decorated walls, mistakenly dated them to the second or third century A.D.

The swimming pool, 35 by 20 meters, was fed directly by the aqueduct built by the Hasmonaeans to convey water from the springs of Nureimah and Duq. It was divided into two halves by a broad ramp that rose halfway up the pool. The large court surrounding the pool had a fine plastered floor. The foundations of what was probably a pavilion, about 20 by 17 meters, were uncovered south of the pool.

A hoard of twenty coins from the time of Matthias Antigonus, the last of the Hasmonaean kings, was found in the court near the pool. As can be learned from Josephus, Antigonus used the palace and Herod was a guest there at the beginning of his reign. Josephus also relates that Aristobulus III was put to death by drowning in the pool at Jericho (*Antiquities* XV, 50–55).

HERODIAN PERIOD. THE EARLY PALACE. Herod built his first palace at 'Alaiq south of Wadi Qelt, after having developed the area by building aqueducts to bring water from the springs of Wadi Qelt. His palace was discovered in Pritchard's excavations and identified by him as a gymnasium. The building was rectangular in plan, 46 by 87 meters, and had a large central court enclosed by rooms on three sides. West of the court was a large hall with rows of columns along three of its walls. This room served as the triclinium. The palace also contained a bathhouse of six rooms, most of them paved with mosaics. Although Pritchard thought that the building was constructed of ashlar stones, which were later carried away by robbers, in the writer's opinion it was built entirely of sun-dried bricks on a rubble foundation. A group of 122 pyriform unguentaria for oils or spices was found in the palace.

THE LATER PALACE. The most magnificent palace at 'Alaiq was erected by Herod apparently in the last decade of his reign. It incorporated the early palace (the "gymnasium"). Altogether, it formed a large royal estate which comprised the southern artificial mound, an exotic sunken garden, a large pool east of the garden, and an extensive wing on the north bank of the wadi. All these elements were conceived and executed according to an ingenious master plan. Two building techniques were used in the construction of the later palace: 1. The local method of sun-dried bricks on rubble foundations. 2. The Roman method of concrete poured into a

Both pages, counterclockwise: Tulul Abu el-'Alaiq, mound 1; Herodian ashlar blocks on top of Hellenistic partition walls. Niches built in opus reticulatum, from the area of the sunken garden. Herod's palace; western part of reception hall; note marks left by column bases and floor tiles. Herod's palace; frigidarium of bathhouse. Flower pots, from Herod's enlarged palace.

stone facing—opus reticulatum in which the concrete is poured into an outer facing of small square
stones set at an angle of 45 degrees. It gives the
impression that the wall is covered with netting.
Opus quadratum was used in constructing the
corners, which were reinforced with square brick-
shaped stones laid in horizontal courses. This
Roman method was characteristic of the Augustan
period in Italy and was probably executed at 'Alaiq
by a team of Roman builders.

A square building, apparently containing a round
hall of Roman concrete, was situated on the highest
point of the southern mound. Ashlar walls were
found which were probably part of its substructure. The remains of a bathhouse belonging to the
building were also found. The stone foundations,
20 by 20 meters, were mistakenly interpreted by

Kelso and Baramki as a Hellenistic tower. Around the foundations a fill was poured which created slopes encircling the mound. On the northern slope facing the wadi, an imposing stepped bridge built of Roman concrete was exposed.

In the sunken garden stood a monumental façade which had porches with double rows of columns on its sides. A stepped hemispheric structure was found in the center of the façade. It was flanked by twenty-four decorative niches on each side. A narrow water channel ran along the façade. Flower pots were found in situ on the steps of the hemisphere as well as in the area of the garden.

In the 1974 excavations, a pool, about 40 by 90 meters, which belonged to the palace complex, was uncovered east of the garden.

The largest wing of the palace was located north of Wadi Qelt. It contained a huge triclinium, two courts, a bathhouse, and groups of rooms with another, smaller, T-shaped triclinium. The large triclinium, 19 by 29 meters, is identical in plan with the triclinium in Herod's early palace (the "gymnasium"), but two and a half times larger. It was paved entirely with colored stone and marble in opus sectile. The stones were all removed by robbers but their impressions still remain. Since the columns were set at a distance of 13 meters from one another, the wooden ceiling beams must have been of giant proportions, Beams of such great size, as well as the colored stone floors, closely recall Josephus' description of the tricliniums in Herod's palace in Jerusalem (*War* V, 178–79).

The bathhouse contained five rooms. The most magnificent room was the frigidarium which was round (8 meters in diameter), with four circular niches equally spaced on the periphery. The bathhouse was built wholly of Roman concrete; the other parts of the wing were mostly constructed of mud brick. All the walls were plastered and decorated for the most part with wall paintings and stucco ornamentations.

The north wing had two courts: one on the east containing Corinthian columns and one on the west with Ionic columns. A large semi-circular niche was set in the north wall of the west court.

A row of columns along the greater part of the north wing furnished a link between the north bank of Wadi Qelt and the sunken garden on the opposite bank, combining them into a single unit enclosing the wadi.

A few building remains and some decorative stucco are the only remnants of a building, perhaps a royal villa, which stood above the Hasmonaean palace on the artificial mound. Ornamental gardens were laid out around the pool in the earth fill and bathing facilities were also added.

LATER FINDS. No traces were found of the burning of the palace by the rebel Simeon nor of its rebuilding by Archelaus. Subsequent to the abandonment and partial destruction of the palace there are some signs of occupation in several parts of the palace at the end of the Second Temple period.

The area thereafter suffered a decline as a result of the destruction of the aqueducts and only in a few spots are remains found from after 70 A.D. or from the Byzantine period. A Roman villa of the second century was built above the ruins of the north wing of the palace.

A small building, probably a fort, from the Early Arab period, was found on the southern mound. It contained a number of rooms around a central elliptically shaped court.

E. NETZER

Tell Ḥassan. Plan of the church. ▓▓ *Existing* ▢ *Conjectured.*

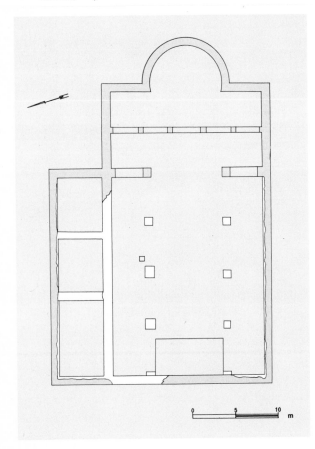

THE CHALCOLITHIC SETTLEMENT AT TULUL ABU EL-'ALAIQ. The various excavations found Chalcolithic objects; undisturbed Chalcolithic layers with pottery implements were first uncovered in 1951.

Under the supervision of W.H. Morton, an exploratory pit was dug south of the large Herodian facade (see above) in an area 3 by 5 meters and to a depth of 3.75 meters down to virgin soil. Thirteen layers were encountered. The excavators found no evidence of a typological development of the pottery in the different strata. Since there were no structural remains and the strata consisted of rather thin layers, the excavators suggested that this was not stratification in the ordinary sense, but rather superimposed alluvial deposits from the Chalcolithic settlement apparently located at the top of the cross-section. It is possible, however, that these strata are linked to a yet undisclosed structure, since the area of the cross-section was a limited one. Note should be taken of the gray-burnished ware uncovered here, which is usually attributed solely

From the synagogue: Detail of mosaic pavement and inscription in mosaic pavement.

Plan of the synagogue.

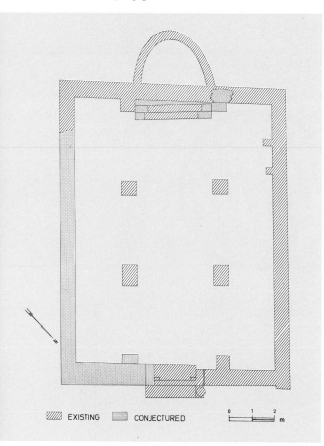

EXISTING   CONJECTURED   0 1 2 m

Nestorian monastery. Mosaic pavement.

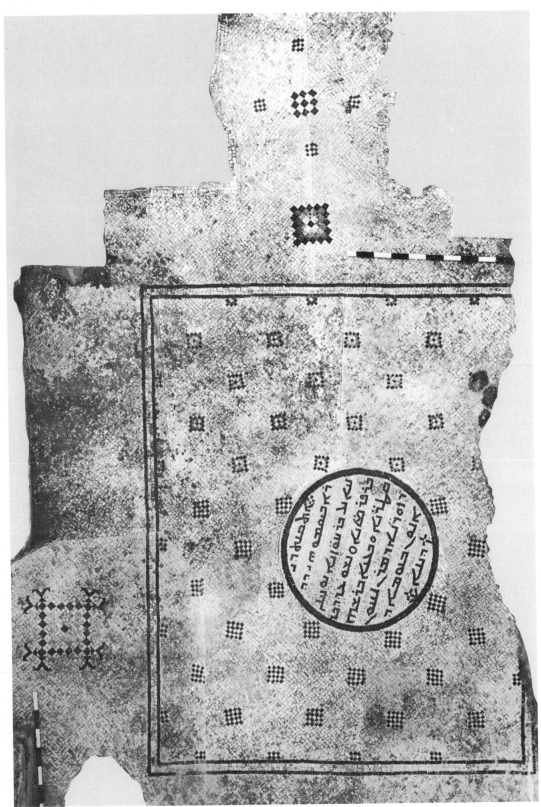

to the northern parts of the country. This ware seems to date from the Late Chalcolithic, a period paralleling part of the chronological gap between strata VIII and VII at early Jericho.

The Synagogue. At Tell es-Sultan Byzantine remains were found and, nearby, a synagogue. Obviously, a settlement which included a Jewish community existed here in the Byzantine period. It is not altogether clear, however, whether this settlement is identical with Byzantine Jericho. Today the latter is identified with the site occupied by modern Jericho, some 2 kilometers southeast of the mound.

In 1936, D. C. Baramki excavated the synagogue on behalf of the Mandatory Department of Antiquities. The rectangular building (10 by 13 meters) is divided into a nave and two aisles by two rows of square pillars. The apse, facing southwest in the direction of Jerusalem, is semi-circular in shape. Two steps lead to it from the nave. On the northeastern side of the structure can still be identified a doorway, in front of which two columns had once stood. The synagogue pavement consisted of a mosaic with stylized geometric and floral patterns. The nave mosaic is surrounded by a guilloche border and divided into two sections. The southern one was laid in lozenges, containing a pattern of heart plants (ivy), alternating with rhomb-shaped plain lozenges. On the northern side, the mosaic is laid in alternating interwoven squares and circles. Along the aisles and in the spaces between the pillars are simple geometric motifs. In the southern portion of the nave, the mosaic is decorated with the image of the Ark of the Law standing on four legs with a stylized conch above it. This is one of the few instances of a mosaic in which the Ark is represented with a shell ornament, rather than a gable motif above it (cf. Ḥammat-Tiberias, Beth-Shean, Beth-She'arim, Beth Alpha). The front of the Ark shows two locked doors decorated with panels, the latter crossed by diagonals to give an impression of lighter and darker triangles. Beneath the Ark of the Law is a medallion containing a seven-branched menorah with a lulab on its left side and a shofar on its right side. Beneath it is the inscription: "Peace upon Israel." In this mosaic pavement, decorated mainly with geometric patterns, one may notice the strong tendency then prevalent throughout Palestine to exclude human and animal figures from synagogue mosaics.

Near the entrance is a six-line Aramaic inscription which reads: "Remembered for good be the memory of the entire holy community, the old and the young, whom the Lord of the Universe aided and were of strength and made the mosaic. He who knows their names and those of their children and of their families may He inscribe them in the Book of Life [together] with all the pious, friends to all Israel. Peace. Amen."

Noteworthy among the finds are three glass vessels, fragments of menorahs, and other objects made of bronze apparently dating to the fifth–seventh centuries A.D. Three early Arabic coins found among the rubble show that the synagogue was in use as late as the eighth century. Baramki suggested that the synagogue was constructed at that time. It is more likely, however, that it was erected during the seventh century or at the end of the sixth century A.D.

Tell Ḥassan. After the accidental discovery here of a section of a mosaic floor belonging to a basilica, Baramki excavated at the site in 1934, on behalf of the Mandatory Department of Antiquities. Two strata of settlement were encountered, one from the early Byzantine and the second from the Arab period.

The Byzantine stratum revealed a basilica with a nave and two aisles, and two additional chambers and a portico attached to the north side. Two rows of arches separated the nave from the aisles. The floor is paved with mosaics. All the walls had been completely destroyed and the plan of the basilica was reconstructed solely on the basis of gaps in the flooring left by the original walls. The plan of the apse was similarly reconstructed. It apparently contained two altars separated by a row of pillars supported by a stylobate built of black stone. Save for a small section, the mosaic floors of the aisles decorated with geometric patterns were well preserved. Adjoining the wall of the northern aisle was a portico (A) flanked by two chambers (B, C). All have mosaic floors. The area south of the basilica has not been excavated.

ARAB PERIOD. Stones taken from the walls of the Byzantine basilica were used in the construction of the building dated to the Arab period. During its construction, the mosaic pavement of the basilica suffered some damage. The plan of the chambers and the position of the walls being almost identical, the pavement remained throughout on the same level, and the mosaic floor, where undamaged, continued in use.

IDENTIFICATION OF THE SITE. Procopius related that the emperor Justinian (A.D. 527–65) restored the Church of the Holy Virgin in Jericho. One can infer, therefore, that a church dedicated to the Virgin Mary had existed previously at Jericho. No details are forthcoming from Procopius as to the repairs ordered by Justinian. However, on the basis of the other buildings the emperor construct-ed throughout the country, it is reasonable to assume that this church, too, was built in grandiose style. There is no information available in literature on the early church. Mosaic portions found be-tween the pillars of the southern aisle of the basilica resemble the mosaic in the Church of the Nativity at Bethlehem, which has been assigned to the fourth–fifth centuries A.D. (q.v.). The fragments described above may possibly belong to the early church alluded to by Procopius and the entire basilica may conceivably be attributed to the days of Justinian, *i.e.*, to the sixth century A.D.

Khirbet en-Niṭla. The excavation undertaken in February, 1954, was restricted to five small ex-ploratory pits. In four of these were revealed Byzantine or early Arabic walls. It could not be determined to what kind of buildings the walls belonged. In the fifth pit, a church was unearthed which apparently had existed from the fourth or fifth century until the ninth century A.D. During this period the structure underwent many archi-tectural modifications.

THE FIRST CHURCH. This was a basilical church built of ashlar. Sections of the south wall, parts of a rectangular apse, fragments of a mosaic pavement, part of the foundations of the atrium, as well as parts of the monastery and diaconicon were ex-cavated. Most of the foundations of the nave and of the northern aisle were destroyed. The width of the rectangular apse indicates that the nave was wider than the aisles. The mosaic floor of the apse, which was severely damaged, was decorated with a hexagon and square pattern, and with a six-line Greek inscription in the center. At the facade of the church were discovered foundations of pillars and of a stylobate. This church was erected in the fourth or fifth century and destroyed at the time of the Samaritan revolt in the sixth century.

THE SECOND CHURCH. This building contained a single hall that covered approximately the area of the southern aisle of the first church. The diaconi-con of the first church became the apse of the second. This church may have been smaller than its predecessor because of insufficient financial support from the west resulting from the dispute between the eastern and western authorities at the time of Pope Gregory I. It appears that the church was destroyed during the invasion of the Persian king Khosrau II in A.D. 614.

THE THIRD CHURCH. This church was constructed between 614 and 636, immediately after the de-struction of the previous church. Nothing remains of its walls, and the reconstruction of its plan was based on foundation trenches and the still extant fragments of a mosaic floor. The third church was smaller than its predecessor. In fact, it was but a small chapel with a narthex, apparently built of dried, plaster-coated brick. The narthex was paved with white mosaic containing an inscription at the entrance. The church apparently was destroyed by the earthquake of 747.

THE FOURTH CHURCH. Erected a short time after the destruction of the previous church, this was also only a chapel. It was built of dried brick overlaid with a thin coating of plaster. Its area was enlarged somewhat to the north and south (roughly 30 centi-meters in either direction), although the overall plan was similar to that of the previous church, and the earlier mosaic pavement was also re-used. The small chambers adjacent to the southern side of the church testify to the existence of a small monastery. This church was not destroyed but was converted into a storage room for the fifth church, which was built on top of it.

THE FIFTH CHURCH. This was a small chapel built as a second story over the previous church. This ad-ditional story was supported by a row of six square-shaped pillars set in the mosaic floor and running from east to west along the central axis of the build-ing. The chapel was entered by means of an exterior stairway built against the northern wall of the fourth church. The walls of the chapel were also built of dried brick, and its area was equivalent to that of the fourth church. Above the ground-floor level were found architectural fragments and debris of a mosaic floor that had fallen from the upper story. The fifth and fourth churches were erected at the end of the eighth or beginning of the ninth century — the period of Charlemagne. At that time, the country was already under Islamic rule, a fact that may explain the poverty of its construction. The church seems to have collapsed of its own accord in the ninth century. Ceramic finds confirm the building's existence until that time.

Aside from the architectural remains, a small altar pillar of bituminous limestone came to light, as well as glass fragments from windowpanes, door nails, pieces of a bronze shovel, and a small pottery incense burner.

In the vicinity of the church were found the ruins of modest dwellings contemporaneous with the various churches. Ceramic finds in the area prove the existence of settlement in this area at a time when Tulul Abu el-'Alaiq was deserted. The finds at both sites testify to a continuity of settlement from the end of the Hellenistic until the Arab period.   G. FOERSTER — GABRIELLA BACCHI

BIBLIOGRAPHY

Early excavation reports: C. Warren, in Conder-Kitchener, *SWP* 3, 224 ff. • E. Sellin and C. Watzinger, *Jericho*, Leipzig, 1913 • J. Garstang, *AAA* 19 (1932), 3–22, 35–54; 20 (1933), 3–42; 21 (1934), 99–136; 22 (1935), 143–68; 23 (1936), 67–76 • I. Ben-Dor, *ibid.*, 77–90 • G.M. Fitzgerald, *ibid.*, 91–1000 • J. Garstang, *The Story of Jericho*, rev. ed., London, 1948.
Kenyon excavation reports: K.M. Kenyon, *PEQ* (1951), 101–38; (1952), 62–82; (1953), 81–96; (1954), 45–63; (1955), 108–17; (1956), 67–82; (1960), 88–113; *idem, Excavations at Jericho I, The Tombs Excavated in 1952–1954*, London, 1960; 2, ... 1955–1958, London, 1965.
Other studies: N. Avigad, *Enc. Miqr.* 839–58 (Hebrew) • F.E. Zeuner, *PEQ* (1954), 64–68; (1955), 70–86, 119–28 • I.W. Cornwall, *PEQ* (1956), 67–82 • K.M. Kenyon, *Digging up Jericho*, London, 1957 • F.E. Zeuner, *PEQ* (1958), 52–55 • D. Kirkbride, *PEQ* (1960), 114–19.
From the Persian to the Byzantine periods, history of the site: M. Avi-Yonah, *The Jews of Palestine*, Oxford, 1973, *passim; idem, The Holy Land*, Grand Rapids, Michigan, 1962, *passim* • G. Alon, *A History of the Jews in the Land of Israel* 2, Tel Aviv, 1955/56, 261 ff. (Hebrew) • A. Schalit, *Koenig Herodes*, Berlin, 1969 (includes bibliography) • Schuerer, *GJV* 2, 3–4, 380 n. 67, 382 • L. Mowry, *BA* 15 (1952), 33 ff.
Surveys of the site: Conder-Kitchener, *SWP* 2, 224–25 • C. Watzinger–E. Sellin–A. Nöldeke, *MDOG* 41 (1909), 30 ff. • E. Sellin–C. Watzinger, *Jericho*, Leipzig, 1913, 12, n. 1, 88–92 • J.L. Kelso–D.C. Baramki, *Excavations at New Testament Jericho and Khirbet en-Nitla* (=*AASOR* 29/30 [1955]) • J.B. Pritchard, *The Excavations at Herodian Jericho, 1951* (=*AASOR* 32/33 [1958]) • R. de Vaux, *RB* 66 (1959), 155–58 • K.M. Kenyon, *Antiquity* 33 (1959), 231–34 • C.H. Kraeling, *AJA* 64 (1960), 302–03.
The synagogue: D.C. Baramki, *QDAP* 6 (1938), 73–77 • M. Avi-Yonah, *Rabinowitz Bulletin* 3 (1960), 35.
The churches: D.C. Baramki, *QDAP* 5 (1936), 82–86 • J.L. Kelso–D.C. Baramki, *AASOR* 29/30 (1955), *passim* • Y. Tsafrir, *Qadmoniot* 7 (1974), 24–26 (Hebrew) • E. Netzer, *ibid.*, 27–36; *idem, IEJ* 23 (1973), 260 (both Hebrew).

JERISHE, TELL

IDENTIFICATION. Tell Jerishe (in Arabic) or Tel Gerisa (in Hebrew) lies within the boundaries of Ramat Gan, near the southern bank of the Yarkon River, about 4 kilometers (2.5 miles) east of its estuary and near its confluence with Naḥal Ayalon (Wadi Muṣrara). It is the largest of the ancient sites in the region of the Yarkon River valley that once accommodated a chain of prosperous settlements, since the river provided a natural communication line between the sea and the interior of the country.

The mound is named after the nearby Arab village of Jerishe, which formerly stood near the Seven Mills — and is popularly known as "Napoleon's Hill." Its historic name is not known with certainty. B. Mazar has suggested identifying it with biblical Gath-Rimmon (Joshua 19:45, 21:24) and with the Gath (Knt) mentioned in the list of towns of Thutmose III (Number 63) between Jaffa and Lod, Ono and Aphek.

The mound consists of two hillocks: a higher one on the southern side, rising to 33 meters above sea level and about 20 meters above its surroundings, and a lower, northern one. The area of the mound (at its base) covers about 60 dunams. Its steep slopes show that it was once a fortified settlement.

EXCAVATIONS

Excavations were conducted on behalf of the Department of Archaeology of the Hebrew University under the direction of E.L. Sukenik, with the assistance of S. Yeivin, J. Pinkerfeld, and N. Avigad, during five seasons (between 1927 and 1950). Several areas on the mound were excavated, but only a small portion of the site was uncovered. Nevertheless, valuable information was obtained regarding the history of the site and details of the form and manner of construction of a Hyksos stronghold in Palestine. The settlement at this site dates from the second half of the third millennium B.C., as can be deduced from the remains of the buildings and pottery found in the lowest level dating to the latest phases of Early Bronze Age. The early settlement spread over a considerable area of the site, and the excavators reached this level in the center of the western part of the mound and in its southern part.

Upper part of "Hyksos" glacis.

In the Middle Bronze Age I, the area of the settlement was reduced, and it seems to have declined considerably. Judging by the isolated pottery objects from this period found in various places, only a temporary settlement seems to have existed on the site. Archaeological finds from this period are generally scarce in most of the excavated sites in the country.

Only in the Middle Bronze Age II did a prosperous and fortified city arise at Tell Jerishe. The finds attest to the high level of its material culture. From the very beginning of the period, the pottery is outstanding for its fine forms, especially the vessels covered with red slip and burnished to a metal luster. A pottery kiln with unusual curved walls was also discovered on the site. Other finds include bronze weapons, scarabs, jewelry, etc., providing much information about the daily life of the inhabitants. Building remains are scanty and yield no information about the layout of the city or the plan

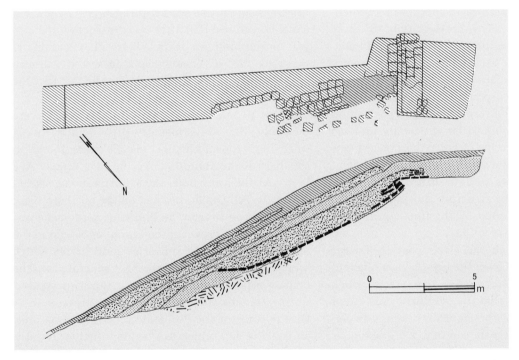

"Hyksos" glacis; plan and cross-section. On top of page: Giant scarab (6.5 cm. high) containing text of the "Book of the Dead"; LBA.

of the dwelling houses. In several places infant burials in jars, which were then customary, were discovered under the floors of the rooms.

The most interesting feature of the Middle Bronze Age II city is its defense system, which is based on a glacis — a form of fortification that came into use at that time in Western Asia and in Egypt. Judging by the nature and strength of the glacis, Tell Jerishe was probably an important link in the chain of fortifications of the Hyksos. The complex and

excellent structure of this glacis has no parallel in the country. Basically, it is formed by layers of earth and sand spread on the slopes and surrounding the whole of the mound. Only in the south and southeast were large parts of this outstanding construction cleared. At other places the construction is simpler.

At the upper edge of the mound, along its slopes, a wall of large, sun-dried mud bricks was built (about 3 meters wide up to a height of nearly 3 meters, according to topographical requirements). As could be seen after clearing, the wall was not visible from the outside, since its face was covered by the layers of the glacis sloping down from the wall to the foot of the mound. Of the upper part of the wall surrounding the city — which was exposed — no remains have survived.

The glacis proper was built as follows. The natural surface of the slope, consisting of friable *kurkar*, was covered with a layer of dark, beaten earth. On this layer sun-dried quadrangular mud bricks (40–50 centimeters a side) were set in one or two courses. Near the wall five to six courses were used. This layer of bricks was thickly covered with *kurkar* sand upon which were poured several alternate layers of beaten earth and sand to a thickness of 2–3 meters. The cross-section of these layers somewhat resembles a kind of "sandwich" with alternating dark and light stripes. The sandy layers were probably laid for the purpose of draining off the rainwater penetrating the uppermost layers. The steep slope was intended to prevent an enemy from undermining the city walls or from breaching them by means of battering rams. It was therefore of the utmost importance to prevent erosion of the slopes and to maintain them in perfect condition. The structure did indeed fulfill its purpose, as is attested by the fine condition of the glacis until the present day.

The layers of earth in the glacis contained large quantities of pottery from the pre-Hyksos phase of the period (Middle Bronze Age II-A), from which it can be deduced that the Hyksos built their fortress at the end of the eighteenth or the beginning of the seventeenth century B.C., using as filling debris taken from inside the town they had conquered. When the Hyksos were expelled by the Egyptians in the middle of the sixteenth century B.C., this fortress, too, fell and was destroyed.

The city itself was rapidly renewed, and it was rebuilt in its early form. The stratum of Late Bronze Age extends over the whole area of the mound and is rich in buildings and objects attesting to the economic prosperity of the Canaanite cities under Egyptian rule. At that time, nearby Jaffa was an important Egyptian base. In Tell Jerishe were found sherds with Bichrome decoration, the local luxury ware popular at the beginning of the period. An abundance of imported ware from Cyprus and Mycenae shows that the city maintained commercial relations with the Aegean region. Alabaster vessels, faience objects, scarabs, weapons, and jewelry attest to the existence in the city of a highly developed craftsmanship in which Egyptian influence is clearly discernible. Pottery figurines of nude goddesses of the Astarte type, connected with the Canaanite cult, were also found. Small finds include a very large scarab of green stone of the Egyptian "heart scarab" type in which passages of the 30th chapter of the *Book of the Dead* (from the Nineteenth Dynasty) were carved in hieroglyphics.

In about 1200 B.C., the flourishing Canaanite town was completely destroyed and the site was abandoned. It is difficult to establish at this time whether the destruction was brought about by the Israelites or by the Sea Peoples. In any event, excavation showed that after this destruction the city was not rebuilt on its previous plan and in its previous size. It remained limited to the southern part of the mound, which explains the fact that the mound is higher there.

The first people to re-occupy the ruined city were probably the Philistines (twelfth century B.C.), since numerous Philistine vessels were found in this part of the mound above the Late Bronze Age layer. At the same time, the Philistines also settled at nearby Tell Qasile, situated on the northern bank of the Yarkon River. The Philistine settlement was destroyed by a great conflagration, as is seen in the stratum of ashes and sun-dried mud bricks which were baked brick red by the heat generated by the conflagration. It seems that the city was destroyed during David's war against the Philistines.

On the ruins of the Philistine settlement was built an Israelite city which can be identified with Gath-Rimmon, one of the Levitical cities. It has not yet been ascertained clearly whether the city was walled. In the Israelite layer remains of buildings and numerous finds were discovered, including pottery of workmanship that is fine but inferior to the preceding Canaanite pottery. The Israelite city did not last long. It was destroyed after the division of the United Monarchy, perhaps during the expedition of Pharaoh Shishak at the end of the tenth century B.C., when the site was finally abandoned.

N. AVIGAD

BIBLIOGRAPHY

E.L. Sukenik, *QDAP* 4 (1935), 208–09; 6 (1938), 225; 10 (1944), 198–99 • J. Ory, *ibid.*, 55–57.

JERUSALEM

PREHISTORY

THE SITE IN THE VALLEY OF REPHAIM

A prehistoric site is situated in the Greek Quarter of Jerusalem in the upper part of the Valley of Rephaim, several hundred meters from the line of the watershed. The ridge is about 780 meters above sea level; the bottom of the valley is from 720 to 740 meters above sea level. The slopes of the ridge show a moderate declivity.

Prehistoric implements have been collected during the digging of the foundations of the numerous buildings that today cover nearly the entire valley and during the construction of the railway tracks. Although the exact extent of the site is not known, the finds indicate that the area must have been quite extensive.

Excavations. The site was discovered by J. Germer-Durand. The first excavations were conducted in 1933 by M. Stekelis, with the participation of R. Neuville, on behalf of the Institute of Paleontology of Man in Paris. Additional excavations were carried out in 1962 on behalf of the Israel Department of Antiquities, under the direction of B. Arensburg and O. Bar-Yosef.

Since the 1933 excavations were restricted to a pit of 8 by 5 meters, the stratigraphical and geological results arrived at by P. Solomonica are valid only for this one spot and not for the entire site.

The 1962 excavations were carried out about 100 meters southeast of the 1933 excavations in an area 4 by 4 meters. In addition, about 150 meters of cross sections of building foundations were also examined. On the basis of these investigations, the following stratigraphy was established:

STRATUM 1. Alluvial layer up to 2 meters thick, containing lentil-shaped inclusions of angular or semi-angular pebbles. Within these inclusions were found some hand axes, flakes, and sherds of various periods.

STRATUM 2. Gravel layer gradually increasing in thickness along the bed of the valley and reaching 1.8 meters at the site of excavation. At a distance of about 100 meters northeast of the site this layer gradually disappears within the alluvial layer.

The gravel, composed of flint or limestone, is angular and slightly rounded. It varies in size from a few millimeters to blocks of 40 centimeters. It probably originated from the Campagnian beds exposed over a distance of several hundred meters toward the southeast. Part of the gravel is covered with incrustations. Within the stratum, the gravel is only very loosely compacted by brown-yellowish clay. In some spots, there are local concentrations of mostly smaller gravel, resulting from the fact that irregularities on the slope surface caused variations in the speed of the water carrying the gravel. This stratum contains a rich assemblage of hand axes, cores, and flakes.

STRATUM 3. Between the layer of gravel and the underlying rock are found scattered lentil-shaped inclusions of brown clay, devoid of stones.

STRATUM 4. At the base of the alluvial cut is found decomposed limestone *(Nari)* of reddish to white color and hard limestone, probably of Turonian Age. No bones were found in any of the strata.

Stekelis divided the industry found in these layers into nine groups according to typological criteria, degree of abrasion, and patina. He stressed the fact that early techniques were employed in numerous implements. Comparing the first three groups with finds from his excavations at Jisr Banat Ya'qub, he concluded that technologically they belong to the Abbevillian or early Acheulean.

Using the same criteria, the lithic finds made in 1962 were divided into four (instead of nine) groups. This reduction facilitated the classification of the essential characteristics of the lithic groups. The same general conclusions as Stekelis' were reached. The groups were labeled A_1 and A_2 (later); B and C (earlier).

The raw material used in making the implements is brecciated flint from the Campagnian formation. Since this material is not easily fissile, the results of its flaking are irregular, and proper shaping presented great difficulties to the toolmakers. No two pieces of this flint are equal in quality, and many implements had to be discarded during their fashioning; these remained at a stage of processing which recalls much earlier types. Completed implements were also found, and these determine the special character of each industry. The flint used in the A industries is for the most part of a homogeneous structure, and very little brecciated flint is found. This obviously influences the quality and appearance of the implements.

Characteristic of the early B and C industries are the hand axes, mostly cordiform, oval, and discoidal, and some retouched flakes. There is an abundance of unretouched flakes, cores, and debitage. The whole assemblage is heavily or moderately abraded and covered with yellow or gray patina. About 700 items were discovered, almost equally divided between the two industries. The A_1 and A_2 industries are characterized by an increase of retouched and utilized flakes, and a striking scarcity of hand axes. Abrasion is slight in A_2, and the patina is light yellow; in A_1 the implements are unpatinated. From the earlier industry about 200 items were found and from the later one, about 350.

Conclusions. The B and C industries belong to the Acheulean. Between these and the A_1-A_2 industries is a gap whose length is difficult to establish. The flakes in all the complexes show a clear connection with the Acheulean-Yabrudian industries. Stekelis thought that part of the industries in the Valley of Rephaim was even older than the earliest finds in caves in Israel. Although typologically the B and C industries have a close affinity with stratum F in the Cave of the Oven (Mugharet et-Tabun), they are earlier. Compared related to a group of sites located in mountainous areas mainly, such as Yiron, Sahel el-Koussin, etc. The A industries resemble the lowest level of stratum E of Tabun, but due to the absence of clear Levallois-Mousterian elements the upper chronological limit of these industries is circumscribed.

On the basis of the above data, it is possible to reconstruct an approximate history of the site as follows: The B and C assemblages were formed and their implements carried off and covered with patina a considerable time before the accumulation of the gravel layer. Only in a later period, contemporary with the A industries, were all the lithic materials, including the younger industries, deposited in the layer of gravels that covered the surface of the old slopes of the Valley of Rephaim.

O. BAR-YOSEF

BIBLIOGRAPHY

M. Stekelis, *JPOS* 21 (1948), 80–97 • B. Arensburg and O. Bar-Yosef, *Metequfat ha-Even* 4–5 (1963), 1–16 (Hebrew); *idem, Ampurias* 29 (1967), 117–33 • D. Gilead, *World Archaeology* 2:1–11 (1970).

JERUSALEM IN THE BIBLICAL PERIOD

Name. The name of the city, Jerusalem, occurs in the earliest history of the city. It is already mentioned in the Egyptian Execration Texts of the nineteenth–eighteenth centuries B.C., in a form probably to be read *Rushalimum.* In the el-Amarna letters, of the fourteenth century B.C., it appears as *Urusalim* and in the Sennacherib inscriptions (seventh century B.C.), as *Uruslimmu.* The early Hebrew pronunciation was undoubtedly *Yerushalem,* as is evidenced by the spelling in various inscriptions and by its form in the Septuagint. As for the meaning of the name, we can assume that it is a compound of the West Semitic elements *yrw* and *šlm,* probably to be interpreted as "Foundation of (the god) Shalem" (cf. Jeruel, II Chronicles 20:16 and Job 38:6). Shalem is known from a Ugaritic mythological text as one of the two "beautiful and gracious gods," Shahar and Shalim ("Dawn" and "Twilight," respectively). Salem, the shortened form of the name occurring in Genesis 14:18 and Psalms 76:2, as well as in later sources, also seems to be quite early.

The city was known also as Jebus, an ethnic name denoting the population of the city and its land in the period of the Israelite Settlement down to its conquest by David. Araunah *('wrnh, 'rwnh),* apparently the last pre-Israelite ruler of the city, is thus called Araunah the Jebusite. In the narrative of David's conquest, it is related that "the king and his men went to Jerusalem unto the Jebusites, the inhabitants of the land... David took the stronghold of Zion: the same is the City of David" (II Samuel 5:6–7). The name "City of David" was given to the citadel of Zion by the king himself: "And David dwelt in the fort and called it the City of David" (II Samuel 5:9; I Chronicles 11:7).

The early name "Zion" specified the eastern hill of the city, with its northern summit (Mount Zion), known also as the Temple Mount, the "mountain of the Lord," "mountain of the House of the Lord," where Solomon built the Temple and the royal palace. Over the generations, the name Zion took on poetic connotations as an appellation for the entire city. The Temple Mount is also identified as Mount Moriah (II Chronicles 3:1), the holy mountain in the "land of Moriah" (Genesis 22:2), vestiges of some early, obscure tradition.

There are still other early names for Jerusalem, such as the "city of Judah" (II Chronicles 25:28, as

Above: Silver shekel from the revolt against Rome, with Hebrew inscription. Left: "Shekel of Israel sh[nat] g[imel]"
("year three," i.e., A.D. 68). Right: "Jerusalem the Holy." Below: Aerial view of the city from the south, with the
Kidron Valley between the Siloam village (extreme right) and the Ophel and the Valley of Hinnom in the foreground.

Above: The inscription from the Siloam (Hezekiah's) tunnel; ca. 701 B.C. To the left, facsimile. Bottom left: The "Ophel ostracon," from the end of the Monarchy period. Below: The Siloam (Hezekiah's) tunnel.

well as in the *Babylonian Chronicle*), denoting its status as the capital of the kingdom of Judah, and "The City" (in the Lachish letters).

History.

THE PRE-DAVIDIC CITY. The archaeological finds and epigraphic and biblical evidence do not provide a well-founded basis for reconstructing the development and history of Jerusalem from its founding until its establishment as the royal city of the Israelite kingdom. Even so, archaeological research has been able to determine precisely where the city was located in earliest times — on the southeastern spur below the Temple Mount. This small hill is protected by steep slopes on three sides: by the Kidron Brook on the east, the Hinnom Valley on the south, and the Tyropoeon Valley on the west. This last valley separates it from the western hill. Besides its conveniently defended location, the site possessed other advantages, which made it suitable for a focal settlement: It had an abundant spring, the Gihon, and it lay near the watershed and the principal highways — from Shechem to Hebron, and from the Coastal Plain to Jericho and the Jordan Valley — which crossed close by.

The many changes in the city's history and the never-ceasing construction and destruction have largely obliterated the remains of the early settlement. Even so, various data point to the continuity of settlement on this historical site from the Early Bronze Age. Painted ware of the Early Bronze Age I (early third millennium B.C.) was discovered here (published by L. H. Vincent), as early as the Parker Expedition (around 1910). An imported Cypriot bowl of the Middle Bronze Age I has also been found. Pottery of the Early and Middle Bronze Ages, as well as of the Late Bronze Age, has been found in the debris overlying bedrock in the various excavations carried out on the southeastern spur and its slopes. Of greater importance is the discovery of the remains of a solid wall some 2.5 meters thick and of an adjacent tower built of rough boulders on the eastern slope in the excavations undertaken by Kathleen Kenyon. This fortification, it seems, was erected in the Middle Bronze Age II-A (twentieth–nineteenth centuries B.C.) and continued in use for a long time thereafter.

Also indicative of the early settlement are the cemeteries of the Middle and Late Bronze Ages on the western slopes of the Mount of Olives and in the Kidron Valley, opposite the eastern hill. In one

Plan and cut of 'En Gihon, Siloam channel, and Hezekiah's tunnel.

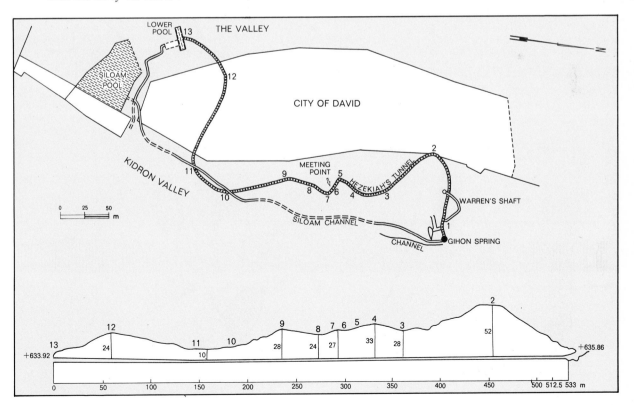

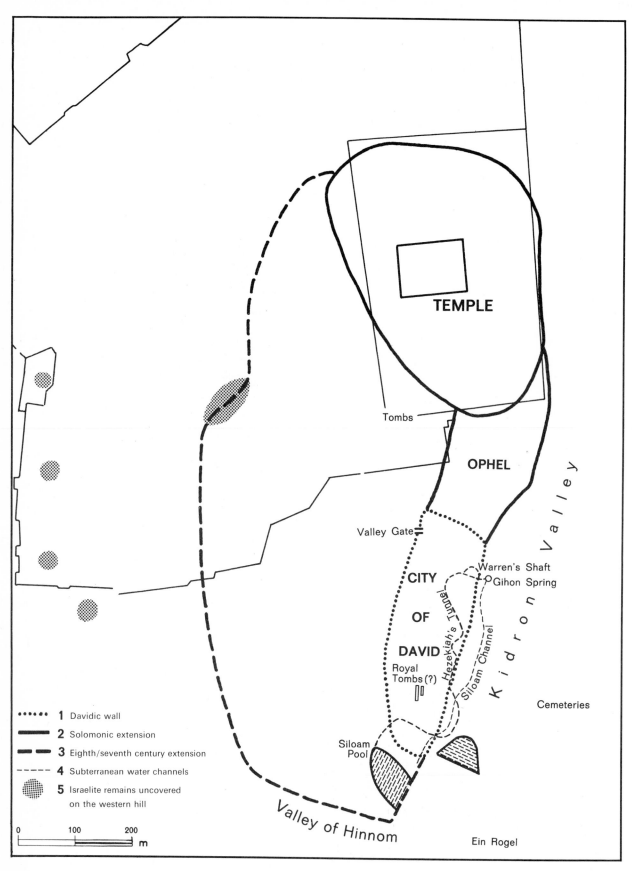

TEMPLE

Tombs

OPHEL

Kidron Valley

Valley Gate

Warren's Shaft
Gihon Spring

CITY

OF

DAVID

Hezekiah's Tunnel

Siloam Channel

Royal
Tombs (?)

Cemeteries

Siloam
Pool

Ein Rogel

Valley of Hinnom

	1	Davidic wall
	2	Solomonic extension
	3	Eighth/seventh century extension
	4	Subterranean water channels
	5	Israelite remains uncovered on the western hill

0   100   200
m

group, excavated by the Franciscan Fathers on the site known as Dominus Flevit, a very rich assemblage of pottery was discovered, along with a number of alabaster and faience vessels and Egyptian scarabs, mostly of the Middle Bronze Age II-C (sixteenth century B.C.) and the Late Bronze Age I–II-A (fifteenth–fourteenth centuries B.C.) Especially instructive are the numerous vessels from the fourteenth century B.C., mostly from the first half of that century (the el-Amarna period), generally of the same types as found in a tomb with a rich pottery collection in Naḥlat Aḥim, near Reḥavia, and in a pit on the grounds of the former Government House, south of the city. These discoveries apparently indicate sporadic settlement outside the fortified city. There is a surprisingly large number of imported pottery and other objects, especially from Cyprus, the Aegean, and Egypt.

Information on Jerusalem in the days of Egyptian rule in Canaan, in the first half of the fourteenth century B.C., is found in the el-Amarna letters — diplomatic correspondence between the kings of various Canaanite cities and their overlords, Amenhotep III and Amenhotep IV (Ikhnaton). They include six letters sent by the ruler of Jerusalem to the Egyptian king, confirming the allegiance of the "Land of Jerusalem *(mât Urusalim).*" This ruler, ARAD-ḤI-pa "Servant of Ḥipa" (a Hurrian goddess), wrote in the lingua franca of that period, Akkadian, but the peculiarities of usage indicate that the language spoken in Jerusalem at this time was a West Semitic dialect (Canaanite), closely related to the Hebrew of the Bible. He describes the situation in Canaan, requesting assistance in repelling Egypt's enemies — disloyal Canaanite rulers and their allies, the Ḥabiru — and of the rebelliousness of the locally stationed Nubian troops, part of the Egyptian garrison in Canaan. Another interesting letter, sent by Shuwardata, the ruler of a city in the Shephelah, informs the Egyptian overlord of the great danger posed by the Ḥabiru, especially after all his colleagues had abandoned him, only he and ARAD-ḤI-pa remaining to fight them. These ties between local kings, as mentioned here and in other letters, fully reveal the importance of Jerusalem in the fourteenth century B.C. It seems that the land of Jerusalem extended in this period over a large area of the southern hill country.

This picture may be of assistance in understanding

Above: Scaraboid seal bearing incision of griffin; from the Judean Monarchy period (eighth century B.C.). Opposite page: Jerusalem in the First Temple period. 1. Davidic wall. 2. Solomonic extension. 3. Eighth/ seventh century extension. 4. Subterranean water channels. 5. Israelite remains uncovered on the western hill.

the background of chapter 10 in the Book of Joshua, on the penetration of the Joseph tribes (Ephraim and Manasseh) to the west of the Jordan River and their fanning out over the mountains of Benjamin and Ephraim. Jerusalem was still the most important kingdom in the southern part of the country. The Israelites came into contact with the Hivite cities to the northwest and west of Jerusalem, the foremost of which was Gibeon, which apparently before the penetration of the Joseph tribes was subject to Adoni-zedek, the Amorite king of Jerusalem. The latter subsequently led an alliance of Amorite kings of the southern part of the country against Gibeon, and Joshua rushed to the aid of the city, defeating Adoni-zedek. Though this reduced Jerusalem's power, the city remained unconquered. In contrast to the Book of Joshua, Judges 1:8 tells of the sacking of Jerusalem by the tribe of Judah. If we assume that there were two waves of Israelite tribes in the thirteenth century

B.C. (the "Rachel" or Joseph tribes and the "Leah" tribes), we can draw the following picture: While in the first wave the king of Jerusalem was defeated but his city was not taken, in the second wave the tribe of Judah succeeded in destroying the city. Unfortunately, the archaeological evidence is too meager to substantiate or disprove this. We may note here that the Late Bronze Age vessels found in Jerusalem and its immediate vicinity are mostly of the fourteenth century B.C.

It should be noted that the biblical sources treating the early population of Jerusalem and its neighbors to the south (for example, Joshua 10) use the term "Amorite," while toward the end of the period of Israelite settlement and at the beginning of the period of the Monarchy the term "Jebusite" appears in this context. It seems that Jerusalem was not Jebusite until the time of the Israelite conquest, more specifically until the sacking of the city by the tribe of Judah. Some clue of the ethnic affiliation of the Jebusites may be hinted at in Ezekiel 16:3: "Thus saith the Lord God unto Jerusalem: Thy birth and thy nativity is of the land of Canaan; thy father was an Amorite, and thy mother an Hittite." And we may note that a well-known inhabitant of the city was Uriah the Hittite, who possessed a house in the City of David. Equally of interest is the name of the owner of the site of the Temple Mount, who was probably the ruler of the city when conquered by David — Araunah (or *the* Araunah, as the Hebrew has it in one passage, cf. II Samuel 24:16) seems not to have been a personal name but rather the Hurrian word *ewrine* ("lord"), which is found in Hittite (and as a personal name in Ugaritic) and refers to a ruler. Thus, the Jebusites are related to the Hittites, and they came to control the "Land of Jerusalem," remaining a foreign enclave surrounded by the Israelites during the twelfth–eleventh centuries B.C. (cf. Judges 19:10).

THE CITY OF DAVID AND THE TEMPLE MOUNT. The conquest of the stronghold of Zion and its becoming the City of David is described in II Samuel 5:6–9 as a daring deed on the part of the king, but in I Chronicles 11:4–7 it is ascribed to

Opposite page: Segment of Israelite city wall discovered in the Jewish quarter, looking north; late eighth or seventh century B.C. This page: The eastern slope of the Ophel. Kenyon's excavations between the city walls and the spring (top); section of wall and tower from the MBA II (bottom).

Joab, who thus gained his lofty position under David. It can be assumed that David took Jerusalem early in his reign, prior to the events around the pool at Gibeon (II Samuel 2:12–32) and the death of Abner (ibid. 3:20–27), at which time Joab was already the commander of the Judean army, and the foreign enclave between Judah and Benjamin had already been eliminated. The Jebusites were not wiped out but rather continued to live ''with the people of Benjamin in Jerusalem unto this day'' (Judges 1:21).

David seems to have transferred his seat from Hebron to the new capital at Jerusalem some seven years after he had conquered the stronghold of Zion. During this period several events occurred which led to the strengthening of David's kingdom, and the new capital became the royal estate, thus forging a bond between the City of David and the Davidic dynasty. This bond was a decisive factor in the history of the kingdom for many generations. There are few references in the Bible to David's building activities. His principal efforts — ''And he built the city round about even from the Millo round about'' (I Chronicles 11:8; II Samuel 5:9) — should be ascribed to his earlier years in the city. The construction of the House of Cedars (apparently on the Millo) by craftsmen sent by Hiram, king of Tyre, apparently took place later (II Samuel 5:11). We may assume that David extended the fortified city on the north, toward the Temple Mount. This seems to have led to the breaching of the older city wall on the north of the stronghold

of Zion, until Solomon "repaired the breaches of the city of David his father," strengthened the Millo (I Kings 11:27), and began to erect his new acropolis, including the magnificent structures on the Temple Mount itself.

On the west of the spur apparently stood the Valley Gate, in the vicinity of the later gate in the western wall of the City of David which was discovered in J. W. Crowfoot's excavations. The "Millo" may have been the terraces on the eastern slope of the southeastern spur, which formed supporting walls for the structures above. It seems to have been here that the more splendid of the buildings of the City of David were built, such as the "house of the mighty" (Nehemiah 3:16), the "house of cedar" (II Samuel 7:2), and "tower of David" (Song of Songs 4:4). Both man and nature had worked toward the obliteration of these structures, and even during the period of the Monarchy, it was necessary to repair the Millo from time to time. Indeed, only retaining walls and a massive substructure at the middle of the slope, fragments of two Proto-Aeolian capitals, ashlars, and other meager finds from the zenith of the Monarchy were discovered in the very limited excavations carried out there (by K. Kenyon).

When Jerusalem became the royal city of Israel, and high officials and a permanent garrison were stationed there, David brought there the Ark of the Covenant, symbol of the unity of the tribes and of the covenant between the people and God. Thus, he established Jerusalem as the metropolis

Both pages, counterclockwise. From the Ophel: Selection of EBA I pottery from tomb 3. City walls; right, from the eighteenth century B.C.; left, from the seventh century B.C. Remains of seventh century B.C. houses, beneath the so-called Jebusite rampart. Cultic building, ca. 800 B.C. Deep fill from the second century A.D. in a seventh-century B.C. quarry. Proto-Aeolic capital.

of the entire people and the cultic center of the God of Israel. In the latter years of his reign, David built an altar on Mount Zion, the Temple Mount; according to the tradition recorded in the Bible, David purchased the threshing floor of Araunah the Jebusite, upon God's command, for this purpose. It is clear that this site was held sacred even prior to David, for an elevated, exposed spot used as a threshing floor at the approaches to a city often served as the local cultic spot. The sanctity of Jerusalem, atop the Temple Mount, is inferred already in the Book of Genesis (Mount Moriah), though this is anachronistic. The tale of the connection between Abraham and Melchizedek, king of Salem and "priest of the most high God" — who blessed the Patriarch and assured him of victory over his adversaries, receiving "tithes of all" (Genesis 14:18–20) — is the outstanding example. Psalm 110 indicates the importance placed by tradition upon Melchizedek as an early ideal ruler, using his prestige to strengthen the claim on the city and the legitimacy of his successors there, the Davidic line. The story of the Sacrifice of Isaac (Genesis 22) is also revealing: The spot on one of the mountains in the land of Moriah, where Abraham built his altar, was the place called "the Lord provides," the site on which David built his altar much later. Thus, David is regarded as having rebuilt the altar of Abraham on this sacred spot.

THE ROYAL TEMPLE AND THE ROYAL PALACE. The acropolis of Jerusalem, which included the Temple and the royal palace, had apparently been already planned during the coregency of David and Solomon, under the inspired guidance of Nathan the Prophet (II Samuel 7). The actual construction, however, began only after the death of David, in the fourth year of Solomon's reign. The craftsmen, recruited from Tyre, labored for some twenty years, and the buildings were built according to the typical plan of Neo-Hittite and Aramaean royal cities in this period. This plan kept the acropolis — the royal precinct, with the military command and the civilian government, along with the priesthood — separate from the city proper. Solomon built the Temple first, for it was not his intention merely to build a house for God and for the Ark of the Law, but to establish the central Temple of Israel under the patronage of the Davidic dynasty, to forge a perpetual bond between the royal line and the Temple, a bond which lasted throughout the period of the First Temple.

Construction of the Temple lasted for seven years, and the palace complex — the palace proper, the House of Pharaoh's Daughter, the throne room, the Hall of Columns, and the House of the Forest of Lebanon — was built immediately to the south over a thirteen-year period. In both projects Phoenician craftsmen were employed, who left their imprint on the architecture, on the actual construction work, and on the decoration and furnishings within. Solomon was also active in the City of David and its fortifications, and it has been suggested that the small segment of a casemate wall located near the top of the eastern slope of the northern part of the spur — discovered by Kenyon — should be ascribed to his reign. At this time the city included within its walls not only the acropolis, but also markets which were of considerable importance in international trade. It may even well have been at this time that the city began its spread westward and northward outside the walls.

THE CITY OF JUDAH. From the time of the splitting of the Monarchy, following Solomon's death (about 930 B.C.), Jerusalem remained the capital of the kingdom of Judah alone. At the end of Solomon's reign there arose factional differences between the royal family and the priesthood over the division of authority between the secular and the religious powers. These differences recurred throughout the period of the Monarchy, with the varying foreign influences, at first Phoenician, later Aramaean, and finally Assyrian. Generally, this led to the strengthening of the purist faction and to religious reforms. Throughout, the Temple continued to serve as the focal point of the national-religious feelings which first arose during the days of David and Solomon.

The historiographical sources in the Bible provide much information on the persistent efforts of the kings of Judah to fortify and glorify Jerusalem. Special importance seems to have been attached to the establishment of the High Court in Jerusalem by Jehoshaphat (II Chronicles 19). Of interest also are the descriptions of the repairs carried out in the Temple, such as those of Joash, as well as of the fortification work carried out in the city's defenses. Uzziah and his son and coregent Joram seem to have done much to reinforce the fortifications of the city in the difficult days of Assyria's rise in the mid-eighth century B.C. (II Chronicles 26:9). Great attention was now given to the new citadel which was built to the south of the Temple Mount, between the royal palace and the City of David.

A new phase in the history of Jerusalem began under Hezekiah, when the destruction of the kingdom of Israel and its capital Samaria (722 B.C.) led to renewed ties between Judah and the remnant of the population of the northern kingdom. The new political and economic conditions which came about in the days of Sargon II of Assyria (722–705 B.C.) again raised Jerusalem to the status of the national-religious and economic center for the entire nation. This enabled Hezekiah to achieve a strong position for his country between Assyria and Egypt, to extend the political borders of Judah in the Negev and in Philistia "till Gaza," to take an important role in the trade with Egypt and Arabia, and to carry out religious reforms. However, the struggle of the Assyrian Empire for hegemony over the lands of the West and its conflict with Egypt brought Judah, too, into the maelstrom of war. Among the projects of Hezekiah in Jerusalem, on the eve of Sennacherib's campaign (701 B.C.), was the strengthening of the Millo and of the city wall with its towers and the construction of a new wall (II Chronicles 32:5), as well as the blocking of all sources of water outside the city. This also involved the diversion of the waters of the Gihon Spring through the famous Siloam Tunnel.

Another phase in the city's history began toward the end of the reign of Manasseh (698–642 B.C.) when that king was allowed to restore the autonomy of Judah, under Assyrian tutelage. Manasseh saw to the refortification of Jerusalem, the strengthening of its citadel, and the building of a new outer wall (II Chronicles 33:14). The city reached new heights, hower, during the reign of Josiah (639–609 B.C.) when Judah threw off the Assyrian yoke, expanding its borders and influence and undergoing an economic revival. During the reign of this king, the walled city of Jerusalem already included much of the area of the present-day Old City, including the Makhtesh (apparently in the Tyropoeon Valley) and the Mishneh (the western hill), undoubtedly the new residential and commercial center of the city. The city's expansion to the west is clearly indicated by the various recent excavations on the western hill, and especially the discovery of a section of a solid city

wall. The height of Josiah's efforts was reached in his concentration of the cult in the Temple in Jerusalem, basing it on the Scroll of the Law—apparently the nucleus of the Book of Deuteronomy—discovered during repairs in the Temple (622 B.C.). With the restoration of the glory of the Davidic line, the status of the Zadokite family of High Priests, which had served in the Temple in the days of Solomon, was restored. This dynasty of priests played an important role in Second Temple times also, in the religious and political spheres.

After the destruction of Jerusalem and the Temple by the Babylonians (586 B.C.), the city continued to be the focal point of the national aspirations of the exiles and those who had remained in Eretz-Israel. Pilgrimages to the Temple Mount continued, not only from Judah, but also from Samaria (Jeremiah 41:5). The decree of Cyrus, king of Persia (538 B.C.), gave expression to the reawakening of the Babylonian exiles, and with the movement of the Return, the establishment of an altar, and the beginning of work on a new Temple, Jewish settlement was renewed in Jerusalem.   B. MAZAR

BIBLIOGRAPHY

B. Maisler (Mazar), *AJSL* 49 (1932–33), 248–53 • J. Simons, *Jerusalem in the Old Testament*, Leiden, 1952 • Vincent-Stève, *Jérusalem* • Ruth Amiran, *EI* 6 (1960), 25–37 (Hebrew) • S. J. Saller, *The Excavations at Dominus Flevit 2: The Jebusite Burial Place*, Jerusalem, 1964 • K. M. Kenyon, *Jerusalem*, London, 1967; *idem, Digging up Jerusalem*, London, 1974 • B. Mazar, in: *Jerusalem Revealed*, Y. Yadin (ed.), Jerusalem, 1975, 7–14.

History of the Excavations. The first systematic excavations in Jerusalem were carried out by the Palestine Exploration Fund between 1864 and 1867 under the direction of C. Warren. By means of shafts and tunnels, Warren explored the walls of the ancient city and of the Temple Mount. In 1894–97, the excavations were continued under the same auspices and directed by F. J. Bliss and A. C. Dickie. In these excavations, which were also executed mainly by tunnels, the excavators attempted to trace the line of the walls south of the present Old City, that is, of the walls which encircled the southern spur of the ridges on the northern part of which is situated the Old City. Another British mission, the M. Parker Expedition, conducted excavations in Jerusalem in 1909 and 1911. Although its aims were of a spectacular rather than scientific nature, this expedition succeeded in tracing the tunnels and the shafts in the Kidron Valley connected with the Gihon Spring. The archaeological results of that expedition were published by L. H. Vincent. In 1913–14, R. Weill, with the support of Baron Edmond de Rothschild, carried out extensive excavations on the southern tip of the Ophel. More excavations were conducted in Jerusalem in 1923–25 on behalf of the Palestine Exploration Fund, under the direction first of R. A. S. Macalister and J. G. Duncan, and later of J. W. Crowfoot. Macalister excavated an area on the summit of the hill of Ophel and cleared a section of the strong defenses on its eastern crest.

Crowfoot excavated an area on the western slope of the same hill and discovered a gateway of strong fortifications which were in use in the Hasmonaean period.

In 1961 excavations were renewed under the joint sponsorship of the British School of Archaeology in Jerusalem, the Palestine Exploration Fund, and the British Academy, and with the participation of the Dominican Biblical School and the Royal Ontario Museum, under the direction of Kathleen M. Kenyon and R. de Vaux. In these excavations, which continued until 1967, the theories based on the results of the previous excavations were tested by modern methods of investigation.

The Site. The present Old City of Jerusalem is bounded on the east by the Kidron Valley, and on the south and west by the Valley of Hinnom. To the north the city rises and merges into the central mass of the Judean mountains. Through the center of the Old City runs a hollow in which the northern extremity of the valley that formerly divided the city into two ridges is now hidden under buildings and accumulations of occupational debris. The southern wall of the city runs across the two ridges from the Valley of Hinnom in the west to the Kidron Valley in the east.

The boundaries of the ancient city on the south were more sharply defined. They included the area of the eastern ridge, referred to by Josephus as the Ophel. The steepest slope of the Ophel is to the east, toward the Kidron Valley. The valley called by Josephus the Tyropoeon separated the Ophel from the higher and larger, western ridge. The Valley of Hinnom curves round the western ridge and enters the Kidron Valley at a point south of the confluence of the Kidron and Tyropoeon Valleys. The earliest settlement in Jerusalem was situated on the eastern ridge because of its proximity to the Gihon Spring in the Kidron Valley. A second source, 'En Rogel (Bir 'Ayub, the "Well of Job") lies farther south in the Kidron Valley. The Gihon Spring was however the only permanent spring used by the inhabitants of the earliest town.

Archaeology of Biblical Jerusalem. Excavations have shown that the original settlement in Jerusalem was situated on the hill of Ophel, the eastern ridge. During the last hundred years it was generally accepted that the wall of ancient Jerusalem lay south of the wall of the present Old City,

Opposite page: Kenyon's excavated areas in the city of David. 1. The Temple platform in its Herodian period form.
Above: The Ophel; Hasmonaean tower built on remains of houses from the seventh century B.C.

and that it was the wall discovered by Warren south of the southeastern corner of the Temple Mount running along the crest of the eastern ridge to its southern end where the Kidron and Tyropoeon Valleys converge. The only indication of an early western wall was the gate discovered by Crowfoot, which was in use in the Hasmonaean period but was believed to have been built earlier. From the excavations of Bliss and Dickie, it became clear that the eastern wall, which ran along the crest of the ridge, joined the wall at the southern extremity of the ridge, which crossed the issue of the Tyropoeon Valley and continued to the extremity of the western ridge and from there along the curve of the Hinnom Valley to the southwestern corner of the wall of the present Old City. This wall clearly marks the boundaries of the expansion of ancient Jerusalem, which initially had been built on the eastern ridge only. There was a difference of opinion, however, as to whether the town expanded after the time of Solomon. The excavation methods used at that time to trace the line of the walls could not resolve this question.

This was the state of archaeological research when Kathleen Kenyon began activity on the site in 1961. It seemed that the accepted theory regarding the eastern boundary of the early city was not satisfactory for two reasons. The earliest town would then have been very small, its length not exceeding 100 meters in some places. The water source, vital for the existence of the city, was situated, according to the above theory, well outside the city wall, lying within the valley at its foot. There was an extensive and ramified system of conduits to carry the waters of the Gihon Spring, the most famous of which is the Siloam Tunnel, cut under Hezekiah at the end of the eighth century B.C. to carry the water through the eastern ridge to the Central Valley (Tyropoeon). The earliest water supply system (as identified by Vincent in 1909–11, at the time of the Parker Expedition) consisted of a tunnel penetrating the ridge down to the foot of a vertical shaft. Steps descended from inside the city to this shaft, thus protecting the approach to the spring. The entrance to this shaft was, however, *outside* the wall built on the crest of the ridge. It was therefore impossible that it should have served the city, which was surrounded by this wall.

In order to elucidate this problem, the excavators dug a trench from the shaft on the ridge down the slope to the spring. Already at an early stage of the excavations, it became clear that the wall assumed to have belonged to the early city could not, in fact, be so. One reason was that the tower (cleared in 1923–26), which was considered to have been built by David to strengthen the Jebusite defenses, was found to have been erected over debris of buildings of the seventh century B.C. The tower itself, in fact, is to be dated to the Hasmonaean period. The finds in the trench dug in the slope showed that the uppermost layers consisted of debris and rubble from the third–first centuries B.C. Underneath them were remains of houses from the seventh century B.C.; such remains were discovered on the slope of the ridge to a distance of 50 meters outside the wall built on its crest. There the buildings disappeared. Beyond them were the remains of the defenses of Jerusalem, which had protected the city during a very long period.

The earliest wall was built on the edge of a scarp in the natural rock at the beginning of the Middle Bronze Age II–A (about 1800 B.C.). It is 2.5 meters wide and built of very large boulders. On the strength of the finds discovered in the foundation trench of the wall, it is definitely dated to Middle Bronze Age II. However, the layers on the slope beyond the line of the wall are not earlier than the seventh century B.C., and the excavators indeed found signs of several phases of rebuilding on the outer face of the wall. It is also evident that, on such a steep slope, the outer face of the wall and its lower parts are exposed to erosion, collapse, etc. This was the wall which protected the city until the period of the Israelite monarchy, and it was this wall which David conquered and afterward restored, although within the excavated area no signs of such repairs could be discovered. The wall continued in use in the times of the kingdom of Judah, and only in the seventh century B.C. was a new wall built to replace the old one.

From the topographical standpoint, it is quite clear why the wall had been built on this line. It was erected on the slope so that the entrance to the early shaft leading to the spring would be brought within the walled area. A wall which would have also included the spring would have had to be built nearly at the foot of the slope and would therefore not have granted any real protection to the city. Thus far the line of the wall has been identified only in one place. Because of the seventh-century wall built above the earlier wall, it proved impossible to trace its course on the north, and houses and gardens on the south make exploration on this side difficult.

It is impossible to obtain topographical evidence for the northern border of the earliest settlement of Jerusalem. Today the ridge rises with a gradual ascent to the north. Although there are some signs that several lateral valleys may have cut off the ridge to the north, such evidence is very scanty. It seems that the northern boundary of the Jebusite city, whose defenses were reinforced by David, passed south of the area of the Temple of Solomon, since the threshing floor of Araunah the Jebusite was probably situated outside the walled area of the town. During the following generations, there was extensive building on the summit of the ridge, while the foundations of the walls of the Roman and Byzantine periods reached bedrock itself. It is also possible that the walls that Macalister suggested identifying as the northern walls of the earliest settlement, in fact, belong to the Roman or Byzantine period. The recent excavations showed that the line of the early northern wall passed not far to the north of those walls. South of the northern area (field 3 in Macalister's plan) a broad wall was discovered, showing several phases of construction. Due to the difficulties of excavating within an area of gardens cut by property boundaries, paths, and water pipes, the excavators were unable to properly explore the stratigraphic evidence of the various stages of construction of this wall. But the limited excavations carried out in the north and south, for example, in the area of the north tower discovered by Macalister, enabled the excavators to reach several conclusions. In the north, traces were discovered of the earliest occupation in the area. This was an Iron Age settlement, probably dating from the tenth-ninth centuries B.C. In the south a deposit, .5 meter thick, was found containing pottery from the end of the Bronze Age to the Iron Age I. The earliest sections of the wall probably belong to the early northern wall, but this has not yet been sufficiently examined.

The excavators were also unable to trace the line of the wall on the western side. There is no doubt that the earliest sections of the city wall were built along the western side of the eastern ridge, which today is hidden in the Tyropoeon Valley under a thick accumulation of debris. Up to now, only remains of defenses from the post-exilic period have been discovered. Exploration in this area is still continuing. It has been definitely established, however, that in the period of the Monarchy, the area of the city south of the present Old City was restricted to the eastern ridge. The wall discovered by Bliss and Dickie on the western ridge, reaching the tip of the eastern ridge, is now ascribed to the time of Herod Agrippa I (A.D. 40–44), but excavations in several sites on the eastern side of the western ridge have uncovered no evidence of settlement there prior to the first century A.D.

There are few remains of the settlement situated within the area of the earliest wall. The wall itself is dated to the Middle Bronze Age II. Pottery from the Early Bronze Age, discovered outside the wall, attests to the existence there of an earlier settlement. Such pottery was found also by Macalister in his excavations on the summit of the ridge but unfortunately not in a stratigraphic context. Considering the strategic importance of the site, it may be assumed that a city had existed there in the Early Bronze Age, but no building remains from this period have been found as yet.

In addition to the city wall from the Middle Bronze Age, fragmentary evidence of building from this period was found along the slope of the ridge up to its peak. These few remains were of buildings which had been damaged by erosion and by the rebuilding of the city in the thirteenth century B.C. The small flat area on the summit of the ridge was expanded during the rebuilding by the construction of retaining walls on the upper part of the eastern slope. These retaining walls belonged to the Jebusite city. Houses were probably built on the terraces supported by these walls. The existence of the houses depended upon the durability of the retaining walls, which were, however, exposed to damage by man and nature. And indeed successive natural disasters destroyed these early structures. In the Iron Age, probably in the tenth century B.C., new retaining walls were erected in front of the earlier ones. (It will be possible to establish their exact dates only after further examination of the finds.) In the opinion of the excavators, these retaining walls may be identified as the Millo which David and his successors repaired. The literal meaning of Millo, "filling," seems to correspond to these terraces supported by retaining walls. The filling consisted of a large quantity of stones and earth supported by transversal walls. The fate of a considerable part of the city depended on the stability of this filling, and the archaeological evidence shows that the retaining walls were indeed frequently repaired. Due to the many collapses of the retaining walls on the eastern slope and the subsequent building activity on the peak of the ridge, all building remains prior to the seventh century B.C. have vanished. Fragments of two Proto-Aeolian capitals are the only evidence for the existence of a public building. Another building, whose remains were discovered outside the wall, can perhaps be interpreted as one of the non-official cult buildings, referred to in the Bible. Two upright stones may have been *massebahs*. On the same site a cave was discovered containing a large hoard of pottery vessels dating from about 800 B.C. It may have been a depository for discarded offerings. A square structure, perhaps an altar, was also found here.

The early eastern town wall continued in use until the seventh century B.C., when new strong defenses were erected slightly to its west. It will be possible to date this wall after the full assessment of the pottery has been completed. It is, however, clear that it is not to be ascribed to a later date.

To these later phases of the city wall belong the few houses which still survive, as well as several terraces on the top of the slope. These structures are not very impressive. The rooms are small and the walls built of rough stones, slightly dressed and coated with mud. One large room was built on the pattern of the three-room house, the usual plan in the Iron Age II. It was divided by two rows of monolithic piers standing on bases. Only one row has survived. The other side of the room with the second row of piers disappeared after the destruction of the house.

The destruction of these houses is attributed to the siege of Jerusalem by the Babylonians in 586 B.C. The floors of the rooms on the top of the slope are covered by a thick accumulation of stones from the collapsed walls. Rainwater cut these deposits of debris and the floors underneath and swept away most of the building remains on the slope and the entire city wall.

The first exiles returned from Babylonia to Jerusalem at the end of the sixth century B.C. and began rebuilding the Temple. When Nehemiah initiated the repair of the defenses of the city, probably in about 440 B.C., it was beyond his power to clear away the tumble of debris and the ruined terraces on the eastern slope and restore them to their original state. But since the population of Jerusalem was much reduced now, a smaller city was quite adequate for them. It therefore seems that the wall on the crest of the eastern slope, which had formerly been considered the early city wall, should be ascribed to Nehemiah. The trench, which was dug in 1962 perpendicular to this wall, showed that the earliest debris accumulated near it was not earlier than the fifth and fourth centuries B.C., thus providing evidence for the date of the construction of the wall.

The towers were incorporated in the wall during the following centuries. The strong tower, which was previously attributed to the time of Solomon, is now ascribed to the Hasmonaean period, on the strength of coins and pottery found in its foundation. The gateway excavated by Crowfoot in 1928 is dated to the same period, but the line of the western wall was not explored.

As stated above, the city did not expand beyond the southern end of the western ridge until the first century A.D. The northern end of the western ridge was, however, brought within the city walls in Herod's time during the last third of the first century B.C. The large tower, which forms the main part of the present Citadel, shows masonry typical of that period. We do not know, however, when the expansion of the city began and what extent it reached. No remains of the Hasmonaean and Herodian periods have been discovered in excavations in the southwestern corner of the present Old City.

It seems, however, that in Herod's time the city was bounded to the north by a wall leading from the Temple Mount to the Citadel on the western ridge. It was generally accepted that this wall followed a line approximately corresponding to David Street in the Old City and that it is to be identified with the First Wall or the old northern wall, referred to by Josephus. The Third Wall which existed when Titus besieged Jerusalem in A.D. 70 was the wall erected by Herod Agrippa I in approximately A.D. 40–44. Between these two walls ran the second northern wall which was the city wall at the time of the crucifixion of Jesus.

The sites of Golgotha and the Church of the Holy Sepulcher therefore lay outside this wall. According to Josephus' account, the wall ran from the Antonia Fortress at the northwest corner of the Temple platform wall, to the Gennath (Garden) Gate in the old (or First) north wall. Although there are numerous theories regarding this gate, there is no archaeological evidence to confirm its location.

It is very difficult to uncover archaeological evidence in such a densely built-up area as the Old City of Jerusalem. Nevertheless, the excavators succeeded in digging a small area south of the Church of the Holy Sepulcher. It was found that in the seventh century B.C. there was a quarry on the site but no building traces were discovered up to the deep fill made in the time of Aelia Capitolina in the second century A.D. There is no doubt that, until the second century A.D., this site was outside the city wall, as was therefore the site of the Church of the Holy Sepulcher. It is thus possible that this was the site of Golgotha, but there is no direct evidence for it. KATHLEEN KENYON

BIBLIOGRAPHY

Wilson–Warren, *The Recovery of Jerusalem,* London, 1871 • Bliss–Dickie, *Excavations at Jerusalem 1894–97,* London, 1898 • L. H. Vincent, *Jérusalem sous terre,* Paris 1911 • R. Weill, *La cité de David* 1–2, Paris, 1920–47 • Macalister–Duncan, *APEF* 4 (1926) • Crowfoot–Fitzgerald, *APEF* 5 (1929) • J. Simons, *Jerusalem in the Old Testament,* Leiden, 1952 • Vincent–Stève, *Jérusalem* • M. Avi-Yonah (ed.), *Sefer Yerushalayim,* Jerusalem, 1956 (Hebrew) • K. M. Kenyon, *PEQ* 1962, 72–89; 1963, 7–21; 1964, 7–18; 1965, 9–20; 1966, 73–88; 1968, 97–109 • A. D. Tushingham, *ibid.* 1968, 109–11 • K. M. Kenyon, *Jerusalem,* London, 1967; *idem, Digging up Jerusalem,* London, 1974.

The reuniting of Jerusalem in 1967 made possible widespread excavation activity, and the latest excavations have provided more positive data than all the previous fifty years combined. The innovations and changes stemming from the excavations and publications of the past decade have thrown much light on the problems of Jerusalem in the period of the First Temple and earlier: By ascertaining that the Jebusite city wall (and the wall of the subsequent City of David) ran along the middle of the eastern slope of the eastern hill, Kathleen Kenyon has solved one of the most difficult problems in the topography of ancient Jerusalem. The earlier belief that the eastern wall of the City of David ran at the top of the slope left the upper outlet of Warren's shaft outside the supposed line of the wall. According to Kenyon's proposal, both the entrance to the shaft and the tunnel were within the walled city. This in turn indicates that the Jebusite city and the City of David spread over a much larger area than previously considered. She was not able, however, to connect in a reasonable manner the line of the city walls with the Siloam Pool of Hezekiah.

The problem of the northern end of the City of David and of the expansion to the western hill (Josephus' Upper City; today's Jewish and Armenian Quarters, together with Mount Zion outside the modern walls) has not entirely been solved. The excavations of B. Mazar, N. Avigad, R. Amiran and A. Eitan, and M. Broshi have fixed two basic facts: There *was* an Israelite settlement on the western hill — at first unwalled and later fortified at least in part by a stout wall — from the eighth century B.C. on. The early existence of the Mishneh Quarter has been proved by pottery and building remains which have been discovered directly on bedrock, within a layer of reddish earth. It was also ascertained that the central valley between the eastern and western hills was outside the city until the eighth century B.C. This is evidenced by tombs hewn within the valley in the ninth–eighth centuries B.C. The continuation of the wall discovered by Avigad is still unclear, both on the north and on the south. We may assume, however, that on the south this wall joined up with the wall of the City of David, encompassing the Siloam Pool. This can solve the problem of why Hezekiah brought the waters of the Gihon Spring "within the city," to a reservoir once thought not to have had a defensive wall.

In the days of Nehemiah, the city seems to have shrunk again, being limited to the eastern hill. The wall and towers at the top of the slope, previously ascribed to First Temple times, are now to be considered Hasmonaean for they overlie ruins of houses from the period of the kingdom of Judah. M. AVI-YONAH

BIBLIOGRAPHY

Ruth Amiran and A. Eitan, *IEJ* 20 (1970), 9–17; *idem,* in: *Jerusalem Revealed,* 53 • N. Avigad, *IEJ* 20 (1970), 1–8, 129–40; 22 (1972), 193–200; *idem,* in: *Jerusalem Revealed,* 41–44 • M. Broshi, in: *Jerusalem Revealed,* 57; *idem, IEJ* 24 (1974), 21–26 • B. Mazar, *EI* 10 (1971), 22–23; *idem,* in: *Jerusalem Revealed,* 38–40.

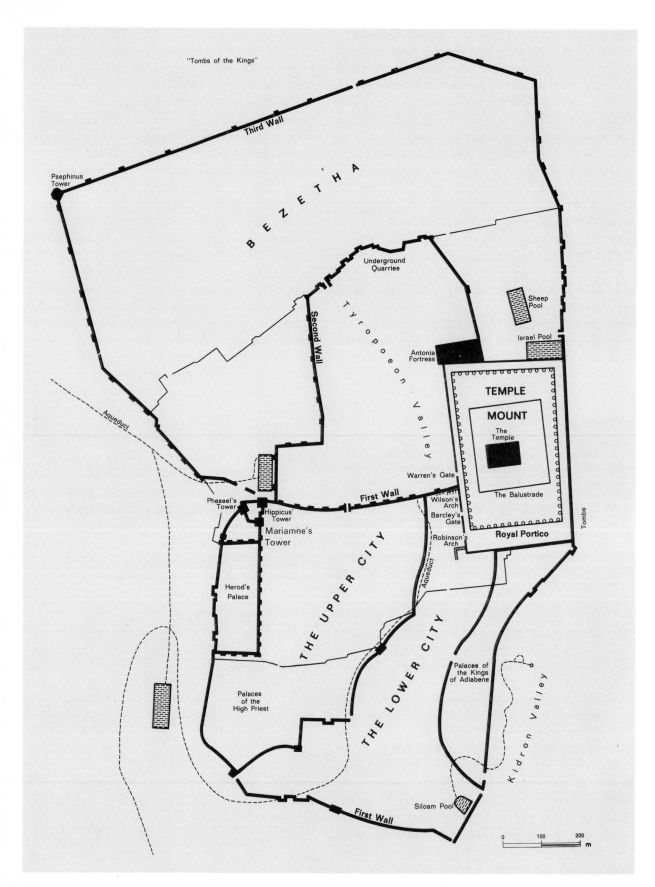

"Tombs of the Kings"

Third Wall

B E Z E T H A

Psephinus
Tower

Underground
Quarries

Sheep
Pool

Israel Pool

Antonia
Fortress

Second Wall

Tyropoeon Valley

TEMPLE

MOUNT

The
Temple

Aqueduct

Warren's Gate

The Balustrade

Wilson's
Arch

Barcley's
Gate

Robinson's
Arch

Royal Portico

Tombs

First Wall

Phasael's
Tower

Hippicus'
Tower

Mariamne's
Tower

T H E   U P P E R   C I T Y

Herod's
Palace

Aqueduct

Palaces of
the Kings of
Adiabene

Palaces
of the
High Priest

T H E   L O W E R   C I T Y

Kidron Valley

Siloam Pool

First Wall

0   100   200

m

JERUSALEM IN THE SECOND TEMPLE PERIOD

The Hasmonaean Wall. The remains of this wall were discovered by C. N. Johns during excavations carried out (1934–48) in the area of the Citadel. These excavations showed that the "Tower of David" (Phasael Tower, see below) was a later addition to an earlier wall and therefore the wall itself is pre-Herodian. The wall ran obliquely along the 765 meter altitude line and formed a rounded corner between the Phasael Tower and the southern continuation of the wall. The section uncovered consists of two segments of the wall and two towers. Johns distinguished four periods of construction in the wall:

1. The earliest phase is made up of coarsely hewn stones, which are noted mainly on the inner face of the central tower where the wall is built of courses of headers. In a trial section, Hellenistic pottery and arrowheads appeared in the stratum which is later than the wall, and it was preceded by potsherds from the period of the Monarchy. Signs of a breach and of its subsequent blocking are also discernible. The excavator dated this wall to the time of Jonathan the Hasmonaean and the breach to that of Antiochus VII (133 B.C.).

2. The southern half of the wall, between the Phasael Tower and the central tower, as well as the facade of the latter, is built of ashlars with margins and protruding bosses, laid in alternating courses of headers and stretchers. This masonry is similar to that of the fortress of Sartaba attributed to Alexander Jannaeus; coins of Jannaeus were found in strata connected with this construction of the wall. Further finds are fragments of thick

Opposite page: Jerusalem in the Second Temple period. Below: Fragment of Greek inscription from the Temple prohibiting entry to foreigners, found near the Lions' Gate. Right: Corner of the Herodian Phasael Tower ("David's Tower") in Citadel.

yellowish glass, grooved near the rims, as well as fragments of blown glass.

3. In the section between the Phasael Tower and the Second Wall, the masonry consists of alternating courses of headers and stretchers. The stones have margins, but the boss is flat and not protruding as in the previous section. Similar masonry also appears at the southern extremity of the wall, south of the central tower, where it served as an additional revetment for the section which had been breached. The excavator ascribed this type of masonry to the beginning of Herod's reign, before the erection of the Phasael Tower. It seems that it was used for blocking the breaches made during the siege of 37 B.C.

4. For the construction of this part of the wall ashlars from periods 2 and 3 were re-used. The excavator dated it to the First Revolt against the Romans but was undecided whether to attribute its construction to the Jews or to the Romans after the destruction of the city. It seems, however, more probable to ascribe it to the Jews. In the recent excavation in the Citadel by R. Amiran and A. Eitan, a massive tower preserved to a height of some 3 meters was uncovered along the interior of the Hasmonaean wall. This wall was also traced in new excavations in the Armenian Garden by M. Broshi.

The continuation of the Hasmonaean wall lies outside the Citadel and surrounds the western hill (the present Mount Zion). Bliss discovered it in 1894–97, while continuing H. Maudslay's work from 1874. Maudslay had discovered the rock-cut foundations of a section of the wall of the Upper City. The wall, cleared for a length of 177 meters, included two towers (length of the facade 14 meters projecting from the wall 15.24 meters) and between them a third, less protruding tower. In the fosse were found ashlars with margins and protruding bosses which correspond to period 2 of the Citadel. In 1894 Bliss continued clearing the wall around Mount Zion and found, near the last tower discovered by Maudslay, a fosse continuing within the city toward the northeast. Beyond the fosse the outer wall continues to the southeast to a gate and tower, and from there it runs eastward up to

Top: Column found in situ in quarry at Mahaneh Yehudah. Bottom: "Wilson's Arch."

Jewish cemetery on the Mount of Olives with   "Absalom's Tomb," Bene Hezir Tomb, and   "Zechariah's Tomb" in the foreground.

the Jewish cemetery on the slopes of the mount. Two periods of construction are distinguished in this wall: a later superstructure (see below) of smooth stones, and an earlier substructure of smooth stones on foundations. These are topped by courses of ashlars with margins and protruding bosses (similar to period 2 in the Citadel). Here, too, there are alternating courses of headers and stretchers, although some sections are built of headers only. In this section of the First Wall, a corner tower belonging to the earlier wall was discovered, as well as another tower and six casemate chambers projecting from the wall. Three other towers (each 10 meters wide) and various sections of the wall were found there (one 100 meters long, another 40 meters long, and two 10 meters long). Beyond the Jewish cemetery, Bliss discovered a further section of the earlier wall and a gate at the corner of the wall west of the Siloam Pool. In 1962–63, this gate and the adjoining section of the wall were re-examined by Kathleen Kenyon who ascribed them to the time of Herod Agrippa I. It seems, however, that this section of wall belongs mainly to the Hasmonaean period, especially to the end of the reign of John Hyrcanus I and the beginning of the reign of Alexander Jannaeus. The many repairs it underwent belong to later times. Kenyon also dated the remains of the upper wall, on the east side of the hill of Ophel, to the Hasmonaean period. Part of these remains were unearthed by her, and part were known from the excavations of Macalister in 1923–25. The gate discovered by Crowfoot in 1927 in the wall of the Ophel

is dated by Kenyon to the Hasmonaean period.

In recent excavations by N. Avigad in the area of the Upper City, considerable new data has been obtained, greatly clarifying the picture. Work in the Armenian Garden has confirmed that the First Wall on the western flank indeed lay beneath the present city wall there. The excavations in the northeastern part of the Jewish Quarter enable us to locate the Hasmonaean palace and possibly also the site of the Seleucid Akra. It would seem that Antiochus IV prepared huge columns for a temple (of the Olympian Zeus?) in the Hellenistic city he intended to found.

Opposite page: The Western Wall of the Temple Mount. This page, clockwise: Hebrew inscription from southwest corner of Temple Mount: "To the place of trumpeting..." Greek inscription from the synagogue of Theodotus, son of Vettanius; end of Second Temple period, from the Ophel. Fragment of monumental inscription in paleo-Hebrew script, discovered south of the Southern Wall.

Construction in the Time of Herod. Besides the repair of the breaches in the Hasmonaean wall in the Citadel, the building of the Phasael Tower, popularly known as David's Tower, should also be ascribed to Herod. Of the original tower, the main part (21.4 by 17 meters) is still preserved to a height of 20 meters. It is built of ashlars dressed in the monumental style of Herodian masonry, *i.e.,* with margins around the central boss which displays narrow borders of its own. Excavations in the courtyard of the Citadel revealed that eight courses were built on bedrock, and then the wall was withdrawn a little, and on the resulting platform eight more courses were erected, the upper ones sloping. Investigation showed that this tower had been incorporated in the wall running through the courtyard of the Citadel. The stone courses of the wall were broken up, and at the ends a filling of stones was inserted in order to adjust the line of the wall to the courses in the tower. In the recent excavations in the courtyard of the Citadel and in the Armenian Garden, identical remains were found of the foundation platform on which Herod's palace had been built. Of the palace itself nothing remains, but we can certainly determine that this building stretched from the Citadel to around the southwestern corner of the Old City. In Tushingham's excavations (within the framework of Kenyon's expedition), further remains of this platform were encountered, though the excavators did not appreciate the significance of their find.

THE TEMPLE MOUNT AND SURROUNDINGS. Besides the Phasael Tower, most of Herod's building activity was concentrated around the Temple Mount. While restoring the Temple, Herod doubled the area of the Temple platform and surrounded it with a retaining wall, the remains of

Restoration of Western and Southern Walls of the Temple Mount; Herodian period.

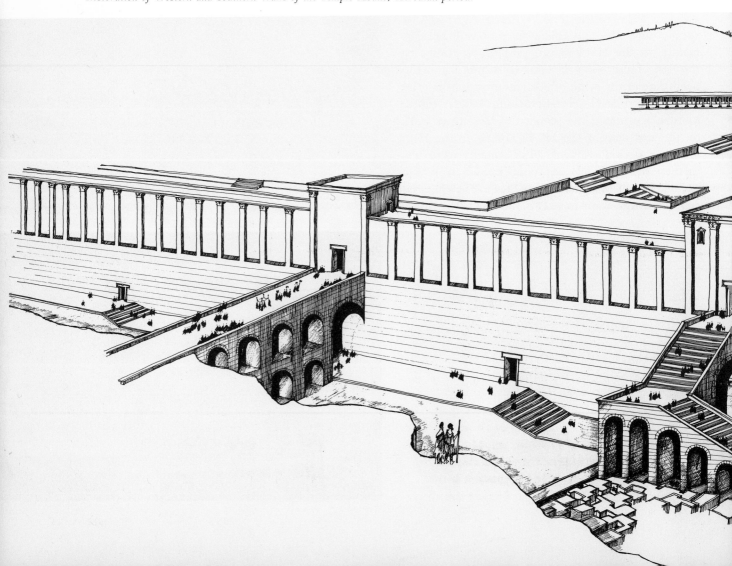

which are still visible (the Western Wall and parts of the Southern and Eastern Walls of the Temple Mount). The remains of this wall were explored by Wilson and Warren (1867–69). The fanaticism of the Muslims prevented them from excavating openly near the Temple Mount, and the explorers were compelled to sink shafts and then dig tunnels up to the wall and alongside it. Thus they could examine the bedrock, the foundations of the wall up to the level in Herod's time, and the accumulation of the later debris which covered the face of the wall. Herod altered the ground level while enlarging the area of the Temple platform, and the foundations of his wall followed the dips and rises of the bedrock. Thus the southern wall of the Temple Mount descends at its western corner 50 meters below the level of the platform and 4 meters more toward the east. From there the bedrock rises up to the threshold of the Triple Gate, and at the southeastern corner (known in the Talmud as Keren Ophel), it again dips down to 60 meters below the platform. In this corner there are fourteen courses above ground and twenty-one below the surface. The foundations of the wall are sunk into a rock-cut trench, and it is still possible to see that the two lowest courses were originally laid below surface level. Warren established that the Herodian wall was built of unequal courses varying in height from .75 to 1.2 meters; their average height is from 1 to 1.2 meters. The twenty-eighth course consists of unusually large ashlars (1.85 meters high). The corner stone is 7 meters long, and its weight certainly exceeds 100 tons.

The tooling of the stones is not uniform. The most outstanding ones are dressed in the Herodian masonry style, a flat boss surrounded by a smooth margin and around it another, deeper margin. In

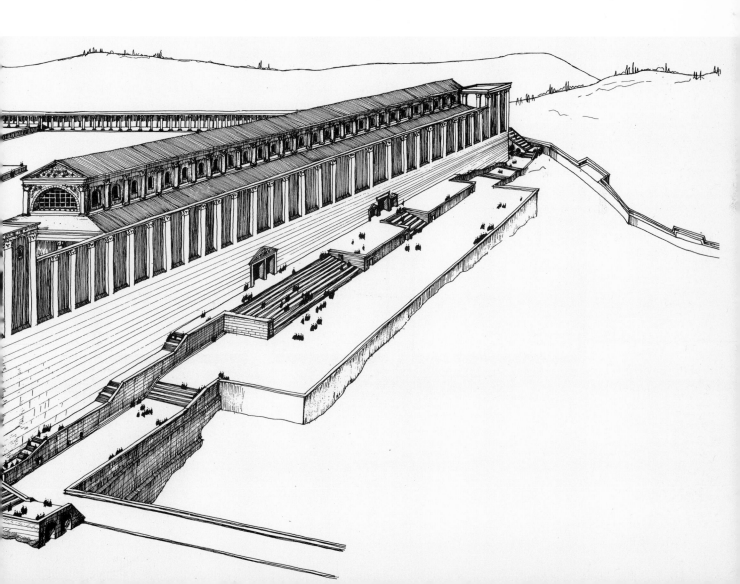

the Western Wall of the Temple Mount, sixteen to twenty-two Herodian courses have survived, including five visible courses, known today as the Western (Wailing) Wall.

At the southwestern corner of the Temple platform, emerges the so-called "Robinson's Arch," named for its discoverer. Warren excavated along its line and discovered the foundations of a pillar of the arch, at a distance of 10 meters from the wall. North of the Western Wall, Wilson and Warren discovered the remains of another arch ("Wilson's Arch") (13.4 meters wide; the height of the arches is 23 meters above bedrock). In 1931 R. W. Hamilton discovered a further section of the foundations of the arch. North of the arch, about 5 meters south of Bab e-Sarai, 52 meters from the northwestern corner of the Temple platform, a section of a wall was found built at a high level with the remains of the pillars which decorated the front of the upper part of the wall. Recently, one very important point has been settled in the excavations near the Western Wall of the Temple Mount: In contrast to previous theories, it was ascertained that "Robinson's Arch" was not a bridge between the Temple Mount and the Upper City, but merely a span supporting stairs leading

down from the Mount. The situation south of the Temple Mount is also clearer, revealing a quite detailed picture of the approaches to the Huldah Gates, the main entrance to the Temple precincts for the pilgrims.

It is now clear that there was only one bridge leading across the Tyropoeon Valley — that of "Wilson's Arch," north of the Western Wall plaza.

The houses of the Herodian and subsequent periods in the area of the Upper City bring the late Second Temple city to life — from the upper-class house covered over already in Herod's day by a street ascending opposite "Robinson's Arch," to the burned Kathros family house. To these, we may add the contemporaneous house uncovered by M. Broshi in the area of the Armenian cemetery on Mount Zion, notable for its frescoes. These latter include depictions of birds in the style of Pompeii —a so-far unique find in this country. Evidence of adherence to the injunction against depicting animal forms is found in the mosaic pavements found in other houses, which have purely geometric patterns.

Of the northern wall of the Temple platform, the eastern corner near the Israin Pool, and remains of

Plan of Southern Wall area, showing Herodian paved street and monumental stairway. Opposite page: Herodian paved street with flight of steps along the Southern Wall of the Temple Mount.

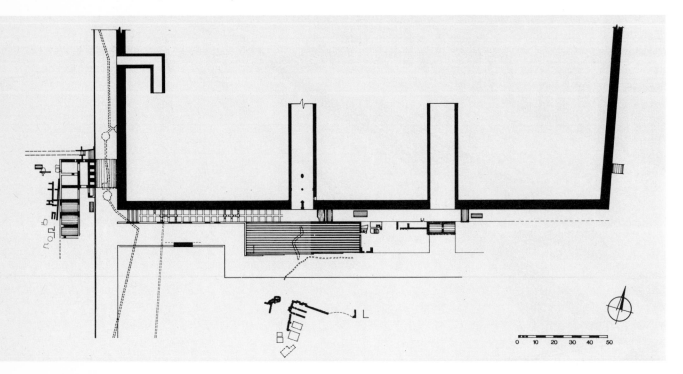

the Antonia Fortress (see below) are still extant.

At the Eastern Wall, Warren dug tunnels, mainly in its northern section. There, too, the wall crossed a small valley, and its foundations dip down 45 meters below the level of the Temple platform. At the northeastern corner, eleven courses are still extant above ground level, rising like a corner tower, 25 meters wide and projecting 2.1 meters from the front of the wall.

At the northwest end of the Temple Mount were discovered the remains of the Antonia Fortress, built by Herod on top of the old Baris — the Baris citadel of the Hasmonaeans. These remains were cleared during many years of work by the nuns of the order of Notre Dame de Sion, in whose convent the western part of this site lies. A double gate oriented to the west was found there and north of it, parts of a pillar-decorated facade and an oblong hall against the northern wall of the fortress, of which 3 meters was excavated. On the strength of these discoveries and of the rock diggings, part of which were excavated and part of which are visible in the area of the Temple Mount, L.H. Vincent reconstructed the plan of the Antonia Fortress with its four towers. In the center of the fortress was found an early stone pavement (area about 50 square meters) which is identified with the *Lithostrotos* mentioned in the Gospel of St. John, 19:13.

But recently the picture north of the Temple Mount has been clarified by the excavations in the Convent of the Soeurs de Sion and in the area of the Bethesda Pools. In the former, it was ascertained that the pavement was in fact contemporaneous with the Ecce Homo Arch, erected in the second century A.D., as part of Aelia Capitolina. In the opinion of P. Benoît, there is no archaeological basis for the accepted reconstructions of the Antonia Fortress as a very extensive structure with four massive corner towers. The fortress was limited, apparently, to the area between the Temple Mount and the Via Dolorosa, or even less than this.

The second discovery concerns the Bethesda Pool, also mentioned in John (5:2–4). In the excavations since 1956, it was found that the two pools there were Hasmonaean, and that they went out of use with the building of Birket Israin along the Northern Wall of the Temple Mount. The miracles performed at this spot by Jesus, according to

Christian tradition, are now ascribed to a cave east of the above pools. The waters of a nearby brook were gathered in this cave and, because of their reddish color, were held to have healing properties.

Since the course of the walls in the period from the reign of Herod until the siege of Titus is still controversial, we shall mention here only several discoveries connected with the problem. In 1937 a course of six ashlars dressed in Herodian style (1.03 to 1.1 meters high, one of them 3.8 meters long) was discovered in a pit west of the Damascus Gate. The course faces northwest and runs westward. It formed the foundation of a gate from the Second Temple period. Whether this was a gate of the Second or the Third Wall is still debated. West of the Damascus Gate, on the foundations of the Dominican Biblical School in the northwest corner of the Old City wall (on the site called Qaṣr Jalud), six engaged pillars built on two parallel

lines were discovered in 1912 and 1927. Southwest of the pillars was the corner of a tower built of smooth ashlars with margins. Vincent attributed these remains to the Psephinus Tower, an opinion not shared by others.

In 1962, Kathleen Kenyon excavated in the Old City a fill found at great depth, which may mark the line of the fosse in front of the Second Wall (and see above). But she also made a trial sounding in an open space near the Lutheran Church of the Redeemer, where she found layers of rubble down to bedrock. The results have been confirmed by excavations of the German Archaeological Institute in Jerusalem, directed by Ute Lux, beneath the foundations of the very church. It was ascertained that the wall beneath the church, ascribed since its discovery in the 1800's to the Second Wall, is actually from the days of Herod Agrippa I, at the earliest. Since the Second Wall was located in its entirety within the present-day Old City walls

General plan of the excavation of the "third wall," with two towers running from left to right and pierced by Roman burials. A large Byzantine complex overlies part of the wall.

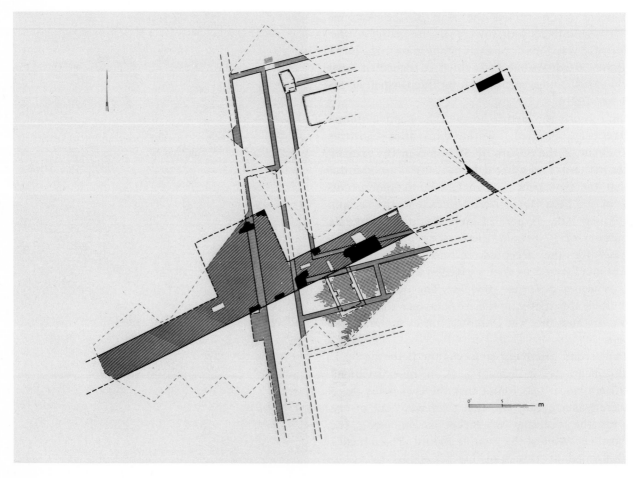

(reaching at most to the Damascus Gate), it is impossible to establish its course at present.

THE THIRD WALL. In 1925–27, E. L. Sukenik and L. A. Mayer conducted excavations north of the Damascus Gate along the line of walls running from west to east. In their opinion, these are the remains of the Third Wall, the foundations of which were built by Herod Agrippa I and which was hastily finished during the First Revolt. Vincent and others do not share this opinion.

In the excavations six stretches of wall were discovered: 1. a section 32 meters long, near the Swedish School; 2. a section 56 meters long, with a tower 12 meters wide; 3. a section 60 meters east of the preceding one. Its foundations reach a length of 81.7 meters, and above them is the line of a wall 46 meters long. To this section belongs the isolated stone block on Damascus Gate Road whose position indicates that it belonged to a tower 12.4 meters wide; 4. a small section, 8.8 meters long, visible in front of an open pool; 5. 70 meters east of the preceding was a section 10.4 meters long with a 16.1 meters wide tower; 6. a segment 15 meters long with a tower projecting 7.5 meters behind it, opposite the American School of Oriental Research; nearby stood the remains of a gate. In the opinion of those who consider this to be the Third Wall, this is the gate near the "Women's towers" mentioned by Josephus. In 1940, another two segments of the Third Wall were discovered: one, 23 meters long with a 12 meter-wide tower, lies about 150 meters east of the last-mentioned section. At a distance of 140 meters to the east were found the foundations of a large tower (20 by 7.5 meters), which marks a change in the direction of the wall. In 1965, E. W. Hamrick, on behalf of the Kenyon expedition, made a trial sounding in this wall and identified it with the Third Wall. The building technique of this wall is not uniform. The foundations were built of small stones, stone fragments, and cement. The stones in the courses are of various sizes with a fill of smaller stones between them. The large stones are dressed with bosses and margins, their length varying in different sections of the wall from 1.7 to 5.05 meters and their height from 1.1 to 1.75 meters. The width of the wall varies from 4 to 4.5 meters. The towers project about 9 meters beyond its face, the average width of their facade being 12 meters. Recently J. B. Hennessy, who excavated in front of

Damascus Gate, ascribed the triple gate there, with its flanking towers, to the Third Wall. His conclusions are based on an examination in a very limited area at the eastern gate and tower and disregard Hamilton's results from 1937, near the western gate there. Neither Hennessy nor Kenyon could explain satisfactorily the massive foundations of a wall discovered by Mayer and Sukenik far to the north. In the last few years, another attempt was made by D. Bahat to settle this controversy, just outside the northwestern corner of the Old City walls, but only a wall and fosse of the Crusader period were found, the medieval builders having thoroughly destroyed all earlier structures there.

In 1972, the Mayer-Sukenik wall was re-examined

Section of the "third wall."

in excavations by Sara Ben-Arieh. Another long stretch of wall with two towers projecting to the north was uncovered. The stratigraphy indicated that the wall dated to the first century A.D., and it is therefore identified as the Third Wall.

OTHER REMAINS. The other remains from the period of the Second Temple consist mainly of tombs. During excavations on the grounds of the Monastery of St. Peter in Gallicantu, the foundations of a house were discovered. The excavators ascribed it to the Second Temple period, but it seems more probable that it dates to the period of Aelia Capitolina and so will be dealt with in the following section. In 1914, R. Weill found on the southern Ophel the remains of foundations and water installations on which a synagogue and an asylum were built by Theodotus, son of Vettanius. The meager remains, however, do not allow a reconstruction of the building which was dated to the Second Temple only on the strength of the inscription found there. In 1963, Kathleen Kenyon found Herodian remains, probably of a street, in site N in the Central Valley.

AELIA CAPITOLINA

The Roman city, founded by the emperor Hadrian as a Roman colony, was built on a square plan crossed by two main streets, following the pattern of a Roman military camp. In 1937, Hamilton discovered sections of its walls, mainly near the present-day Damascus Gate and to the east of it. Other sections were published in 1878 and 1889 by C. Schick, but their description is not entirely accurate. Hamilton's excavations showed that Aelia Capitolina had not been originally built as a walled city but was an open one, like most cities in the Roman Empire. Fragments of an inscription have been found, in which the city is dedicated to the Antonine emperors in the name of the town fathers. Since these fragments were re-used in the city wall of Aelia Capitolina, the wall could not have been erected prior to the third century A.D., a fact confirmed by ceramic finds. The section of the wall discovered by Schick has an average width of 4 meters and is built of ashlars with margins. The height of the ashlars reaches 1.2 meters; they probably are re-used Herodian stones. Both faces are built of hewn stones, 1.2–1.5 meters wide. Between them there is a fill of rough stones. The wall supports a Byzantine wall, which is further evidence that it dates from the

Roman period. In the area of the Citadel in the Old City, Johns found that the Romans used part of the Herodian wall for the camp of the Tenth Legion (*Fretensis*).

For the study of the wall of Aelia Capitolina, Hamilton's excavations are of great importance. The excavations can be divided into several sections as follows: 1. The section at the corner between the present city wall and the western tower of the Damascus Gate, where up to twelve courses of the wall have been discovered, decorated on the sixth to eighth courses of the tower with high and sunken reliefs. On the front of the tower, up to the eighth to twelfth courses of the wall face, the ashlars have bosses and margins. Above these courses, the stones of the face of the wall are smooth without margins and are fitted to the other ashlars. 2. Along the front of the towers two sounding were made. A pit near the western tower revealed Herodian foundations (see above). The fill in front of the wall contains remains from the Late Roman and Byzantine periods, with the exception of some earlier potsherds. In the foundations of the front of the eastern tower was a carved arch, and above it was a re-used stone with an inscription ending with the following words: "according to the decision of the decurions of Aelia Capitolina." The style of the script can be dated to the time of Hadrian. The fact that this stone was put to secondary use proves that the wall was not built in the reign of Hadrian. 3. In the section of excavations between the Damascus Gate and Herod's Gate, cuttings in the rock were found in front of the line of the present construction. Here (like the walls described by Schick), the course of the wall of Aelia Capitolina passed at some distance from the present wall. In this section was found an aqueduct passing under the city wall. It was covered with the tombstone of a Roman officer who probably died a short time after the fall of Jerusalem (about A.D. 74). 4. East of Herod's Gate, ten courses were discovered below surface level. They are laid in alternating courses of headers and stretchers as was usual in the time of the Syrian dynasty and later. Here, too, ceramic finds confirm that the wall was built in the third–fourth centuries, although one coin was found from the time of Herod Agrippa I and another from that of the Roman procurators.

The excavations adjacent to the Temple Mount and in the Jewish Quarter have greatly supplemented our knowledge of the development of the city following the destruction of A.D. 70. Thus, the camp of the Tenth Roman Legion, stationed here from A.D. 70 to the third century, is now considered to have been much larger than was previously thought. Near the Temple Mount was found a monumental inscription dedicated to Septimius Severus and Caracalla.

Various Roman Buildings. At a distance of 350 meters north of the northern gate of the Roman city (which, as stated above, was identical with the Damascus Gate of today), and outside of it, were found in 1964 the remains of an arch with a triple entrance to which belong also fragments of a Roman inscription dedicated to Emperor Hadrian.

Opposite page: Interior of aqueduct beneath western street, looking south; Herodian period. Below: West wall of the west tower of Damascus gate, apparently part of the city wall of Aelia Capitolina.

The remains of Aelia Capitolina within the city itself include the Roman arch known as Ecce Homo, explored by E. Pierotti in 1860, Wilson in 1864, and Warren in 1872. Still extant from this arch are the large central entrance (5.2 meters wide, 6.25 meters high) and the smaller northern entrance (2.36 meters wide and 5.22 meters high). In the pillar between the entrances were niches.

The remains of the forum of Aelia Capitolina were discovered in the excavations of E. M. de Vogüé (1855, 1862), Pierotti (1857–60), Wilson (1864), Clermont-Ganneau (1873–74), and of the Russian authorities (in 1883, 1887–88) who owned the site (called the Russian Hospice or Alexander's Hospice). A monumental wall (1.5 meters wide) running from north to south, with a large gateway and a threshold (4.3 meters) and a southern, smaller gate (2.5 meters), was discovered. The wall is built of smooth, dressed ashlars, .76–1.84 meters long .96 meter high. Perpendicular to this wall, which was probably the entrance to the forum, stood another, narrower wall (1.1 meters wide) with two narrow entrances. On the southern side of this wall are recesses with pillars between them. East of the corner formed by these two walls one entrance of an arched gateway is visible. It stood perhaps at the entrance to the forum. Nearby stands a pillar of the middle entrance topped by a Corinthian capital.

From 1889 to 1912, the Assumptionist Fathers excavated on their land on the eastern flank of Mount Zion. They uncovered the remains of a large house (21 by 31 meters), consisting of a courtyard surrounded by rooms. On the northern front side of the house is a porch with pillars with a cantharus (large stone bowl) in its middle. In the center of the courtyard was a rock-cut pit, perhaps a natural cave. Here and there in the rooms were remains of mosaic floors. J. Germer-Durand, who published these excavations, had ascribed these remains to a Jewish house from the Second Temple period; however, careful comparison with Roman-Byzantine houses on the Ophel as well as other sites shows that it should probably be dated to the time of Aelia Capitolina.

In the years 1863–76, 1888–1900, and again in 1956 and 1962, the White Fathers excavated on their property in the Muslim Quarter of the Old City near St. Anne's Church. In addition to various medieval finds, they discovered remnants of two pools, partly cut into the rock and partly built on the surface. Between the pools, which are coated with watertight plaster, stands a dam 6 meters wide. The northern pool is larger (the length of one of its sides exceeds 45 meters), but the pools were not excavated in their entirety. At the southeastern corner of the northern pool is a structure which is perhaps a water-settling tank (16 by 16 meters). Between the pools there is also a subterranean passage decorated with frescoes. It is assumed that this was an underground sanctuary for the worship of one of the Oriental deities whose cult was widespread throughout the Empire at the end of the Roman period. This assumption is supported also by various objects with dedicatory inscriptions, as for example, a marble foot dedicated to "Pompilia Lucilia," and several reliefs depicting religious subjects inspired by related sources. Vincent assumed that the two pools were surrounded by colonnades. The base and pedestal of one of the columns (1.36 meters high) were discovered in situ.

In the Roman period, a colonnade was erected around the Siloam Pool, where Bliss excavated in 1896. Near the pool, a stepped street descended from the town (the southern wall of which was identical with the present city wall) to the well. The site was surrounded by a square wall enclosure (25 by 25 meters, 1.2 meters wide) in which there was a colonnade with pilasters or columns set at 3.5-meter intervals. The entrance was from the south and was reached by ten steps. Between the columns, there were probably steps leading down to the pool itself. The pool was filled with water conveyed through Hezekiah's tunnel, but its source was already forgotten in the time of Josephus, and the water flowing into the Siloam Pool was thought to come directly from a natural source. Vincent identified this building with the Tetranymphon mentioned among the buildings of Aelia Capitolina. The pool itself and the colonnade around it are mentioned by several pilgrims prior to the period of the empress Eudocia (see below).

Outside the walls of Aelia Capitolina were discovered several tombs of the late shaft-type grave ascribed to the Roman city. A shaft — at the bottom of which was a stone which sealed the burial chamber — led down to a vaulted room with a narrow passage in the center, on both sides of which were burial places enclosed by stone parapets. A tomb of this type was found from the third century. In the fourth century, the form of the tomb underwent a change. The shaft was replaced by an entrance with steps built on one of the narrow sides of the burial chamber. Such tombs were found near Birket es-Sultan ("Pool of the Snakes") in the Valley of Hinnom, on the slopes of the Mount of Olives and especially on the road leading to the village of e-Tur north of the wall of the Old City, between the Damascus Gate and the Tombs of the Kings and near the Church of Saint Stephen's outside Damascus Gate, along Jaffa Road and Mount Zion, and on the summit of the Mount of Olives. Since the transition from the Roman to the Byzantine period is not marked by any destruction, the tombs of the fourth century are distinguished only by the finds. Those of a clear pagan nature attest to non-Christian tombs. In 1934, graves of this type were discovered by Hamilton and Husseini near the intersection of Saladin and Damascus Gate streets, south of the Tombs of the Kings. Four types of tombs were discovered there: 1. Shaft tombs with a shelf in the lower part supporting stone slabs which covered the burial; 2. a similar type, but with two superimposed burials, in which the cover of one burial forms the bottom of the other; 3. tombs in which the shaft widens into a bell-shaped room, at the bottom of which the tombs are cut into the rock. The burial chamber is closed from above by a stone slab on which more stones are heaped; 4. tombs with an open shaft, with individual graves covered with stone slabs; each grave compartment contained either one or two super-imposed burials. Finds included lamps — by which the burials were dated — various kinds of jewelry, amulets, ivory pins, etc. Another type of tomb from the third century was excavated in 1932, west of the YMCA building in Jerusalem. Built of ashlars, the tomb consists of a narrow passage, near which are burials dug into the rock. The first tombs on this site date from the second and third centuries A.D., the tomb built of ashlars being from the third century A.D. Finds included three lead coffins; on one of them are represented bulls and two cupids with bunches of grapes. A similar coffin, showing a Nike and cupids, was found in a tomb excavated in 1879 near the Schneller area. In a shaft tomb excavated by Bliss in 1894–97 were found the remains of colored frescoes of masks,

wreaths, and depictions of Nikes with wreaths.
In 1935–36, a Roman tomb was discovered during the widening of the street in front of the Lions' Gate. It consists of two parts: the burial cave with a remnant of a vault above it and a structure with several rooms, the largest of which was also vaulted and perhaps formed the foundation of the structure prior to its destruction. During excavations at Givat Ram in 1949 (see below), the remains of the Tenth Legion's workshop for the production of bricks and tiles were discovered.

THE BYZANTINE PERIOD.

Emperor Constantine, who defeated his rival Licinius in A.D. 324, was the first Christian emperor to rule Palestine, and he undertook to make Jerusalem the Holy City of Christendom. At the Council of Nicaea (325), Macarius, bishop of Aelia, persuaded the emperor and his mother Helene to clean up the area considered to be the site of Jesus' sepulcher and to erect there a church. Byzantine building activity in Jerusalem began in the second quarter of the fourth century and continued until the seventh century, transforming Jerusalem into a city of churches and monasteries, of hospices and asylums for pilgrims, as it is depicted on the map of Madeba (q.v.). In the footsteps of the emperor came donors, mainly after the conquest of Rome by the Goths, when many Roman patricians took refuge in Palestine.

Tombstone of Tiberius Claudius Fatalis, Roman officer of the Tenth Legion; end of first century A.D. Discovered between Damascus and Herod's Gates.

Public and private money started flowing into the Holy Land, and Jerusalem had its full share. The numerous remains from that period are witness to the high standard of life in those days.

Byzantine building activity in Jerusalem is divided into three main stages: the time of Constantine and of his sons; the time of the empress Eudocia (middle of the fifth century), and the reign of the emperor Justinian.

Churches from the Time of Constantine. 1. The Church of the Resurrection *(Anastasis)* also called the Church of the Holy Sepulcher. This church, the largest and most important of all churches in Jerusalem, still stands on its original site, but most of its surviving structure stems from Crusader times. Understandably, no systematic excavations have been carried out in this church, but it has been explored several times during restoration work, the last time in 1962. Scholars have thus been able to study the plan of the Constantinian church, relying also on the representation on the Madeba map and on its description in the writings of Eusebius and of various pilgrims. The Byzantine architects used part of the gate of the Roman forum against which they erected a basilica, the rear wall of which (1.3 meters wide) was discovered on the line which crosses the Crusader apse from south to north. This wall terminates in a rocky knoll 5.4 meters high, considered to have been the site of the Crucifixion and known as Golgotha. On the top of this rock was set a gilded cross. Near the rock was an open court, and west of the court and the basilica was the rock-cut sepulcher surrounded by twelve columns (the present-day columns are from the Crusader period). A rotunda, about 35 meters in diameter, stood over the tomb. In the circular wall were three rounded niches, on the north, south, and west. Contrary to previous suppositions, it now appears that these niches were an integral part of the original wall. The presence of a straight wall that runs eastward near the southern niche makes it doubtful whether the rotunda indeed enclosed the tomb roundabout, or whether it had, perhaps, the shape of a giant semicircular apse.

2. The Church of the Eleona (Church on the Mount of Olives). No remains of this building are visible on surface level, but it was discovered by the White Fathers in 1910, and the Dominicans continued clearing it in 1918. Of the original church, mainly rock-cuttings and remains of the foundations have survived. The church, 72 by 12 meters, consisted of a court surrounded by colonnades and a basilica (about 30 meters long). In front of its apse, there is a crypt, perhaps an ancient tomb cave. The basilica terminates in an interior apse. Whether the apse was polygonal or rectangular is the subject of a controversy between Vincent and T. Wiegand. South of the church, there was a pit. On the site were found several fragments of mosaic (mainly with geometric patterns), a Corinthian, basketlike capital and parts of the chancel screen.

Other Churches from the Fourth Century. In A.D. 340, Maximus, bishop of Jerusalem, built a church on the traditional site of the Last Supper. This is the Church of the Apostles, also called the Church of Mount Zion. According to the same tradition, it was on this site that the Apostles gathered for the first time, and the church was therefore considered as the Mother of All Churches. Its meager remains were discovered in 1898–99 during excavations carried out by a German mission, at the time the Dormition Church and the Benedictine Monastery were built. H. Renard and Vincent are of opinion that these remains belong to the western end of the church. A wall, 2 meters wide, running for a length of 6 meters from north to south, is part of the outer wall of the church. The foundations of a stylobate 9.5 meters long extend from this wall eastward. At a right angle to the stylobate, at a distance of 4.5 meters from the outer wall and parallel to it, are foundations of a wall continuing for a length of 11 meters. The two excavators ascribed these foundations to the partition wall between the narthex and the nave of the church. However, the question of the location of the church and the identity of the other wall fragments discovered north of the exterior wall was disputed by them. Renard considered these walls part of the original church, bounding the northern aisle on the west, analogous to the southern remains which belong to the southern aisle. Vincent, on the other hand, did not attribute the remains on the north to the Byzantine church, but he ascribed to this church the foundations of the southeastern corner of "David's Tomb". Both scholars agreed that the church had four rows of columns, which divided it into a nave and four aisles, two on each side.

Vincent thought that there was one apse at the end of the nave, near the eastern wall. Renard, however, reconstructed the church with a triple apse. Meanwhile behind "David's Tomb", the remains of a wall were found with niches built of ashlars similar to those of the foundations on which Vincent based his theory, but these remains belong to a non-Christian building oriented toward the north (see below). This discovery obviously invalidates Vincent's main assumption, and Renard may be right in his suggestion for the location of the church.

In A.D. 378, the matron Poemenia founded on the summit of the Mount of Olives the Church of the Ascension (*Ascensio*, named for the ascension of Jesus to heaven after his resurrection). Excavations carried out in 1960 by the Franciscan Fathers under the direction of V. Corbo revealed evidence of a circular church (rotunda). Along its round wall stood a row of columns, and another circle of columns in front of this wall supported the dome. Arkoplas, a pilgrim from the end of the seventh century, describes the plan of the church, which was fully confirmed by Corbo's excavations. The diameter of the whole church was about 25 meters. In the excavations, a dedicatory inscription was found mentioning Modestus, the patriarch who restored the church after its destruction by the Persians in 614. The restoration seems to have followed the original plan. Corbo's excavations showed that there is no evidence for the previous assumption that the Byzantine structure was octagonal. The octagonal form of church — also found today — is to be ascribed to the Crusader period.

GETHSEMANE. In A.D. 385, Emperor Theodosius I erected a church in Gethsemane, the site, according to Christian tradition, where Jesus and his disciples spent the night before his arrest. From 1909 to 1920, the Franciscan Fathers, under the direction of the architect Barluzzi and G. Orfali, excavated the remains of the Byzantine church and of the Crusader church on the site, at the foot of the Mount of Olives. The Byzantine church is a basilica (22.5 by 16.5 meters) with a large external apse and two internal, lateral apses. Remains of a mosaic pavement were found in the nave in a pattern of wave and wreath and in the intercolumnar spaces in geometric patterns. A Corinthian capital belonging to the lower row of columns was also found.

The Period of Empress Eudocia. Eudocia was the wife, and afterward the widow, of the emperor Theodosius II. She visited Jerusalem for the first time in 437–439. After her separation from her husband in 443–444, she returned to Jerusalem and remained there until her death in 460. Eudocia dedicated considerable funds to the restoration of Jerusalem and its surroundings. She repaired and enlarged the city wall (see below) and founded a church dedicated to Saint Stephen in the northern part of the town, outside the Damascus Gate. This church, consecrated on the fifteenth of June, 460, was cleared in 1885–93 by the Dominican Fathers, who erected on the site their church and monastery, which also houses the Dominican Bible School. In the excavations, a basilical church (33 by 20 meters) with a projecting polygonal apse was discovered. The northern aisle of the church has been largely preserved. For the construction of the colonnades around the atrium, they seem to have re-used columns, capitals, and the epistyle of the Victory Arch, which stood not far away. Eudocia included the whole central valley in the walled area and built a church near the Siloam Pool, which she also included within the wall. Bliss excavated this church in 1896. Due to the special conditions prevailing at this site, it differed from the other churches of the town. The entrance is through a narrow atrium in the north. The basilica (35 by 16 meters) is divided into aisles and a nave, the latter terminating in an interior apse with a bench for the clergy running along its inner wall. The center of the church was roofed by a dome resting on four pillars. One of the aisles probably opened onto the pool, like a loggia. In the southern wall of the church, a door opened onto the stepped street. Beyond the pool on the south, a columned structure was erected along the length of the pool. According to literary sources, the Church of Siloam was consecrated in 438/39.

THE ASYLUM IN GIVAT RAM. According to literary sources, Eudocia also founded a home for aged people *(gerontocomium)* "before" (πρό) the Holy City, with a chapel dedicated to Saint George. In 1949, a group of buildings was discovered in Giv'at Ram, which was excavated by M. Avi-Yonah on behalf of the Department of Antiquities. A basilical church (17.5 by 14 meters) was cleared and south of it several rooms, including a chapel with an apse and a mosaic pavement in which was set the

inscription: "O Lord, God of Saint George, remember the donor!" West of the church were remains of monastic cells, and among them an underground burial chamber. It may be assumed that these are the remains of the monastery and of the home for the aged founded by Eudocia. The mosaics all show geometric and floral patterns.

The Period of Justinian. After Eudocia's death, the construction of churches in Jerusalem slowed down considerably, since the existing buildings satisfied the needs of the local population and of the visitors. Other causes were the bitter conflicts

Below: A Byzantine period house as excavated in the area south of the Temple Mount. Left: Mosaic pavement from the house. Opposite page: The Church of the Holy Sepulcher at the time of Constantine. Plan as reconstructed by Vincent.

which broke out within the Christian Church and the Samaritan revolt. During the uprising of the Samaritans in 529, many churches around Jerusalem were destroyed, compelling Emperor Justinian to erect new ones. To his reign is ascribed the large New Church (Greek: Νέα) dedicated to Saint Mary. In 1914, during the enlargement of the Sephardi Hospital Porat Yosef in the Old City, foundations were discovered which Vincent ascribed to the pedestals of the arches upon which this church had been erected (as related by Procopius). But the remains of the massive foundation of this church were uncovered only in Avigad's recent excavations in the Jewish Quarter. The church was consecrated on the twentieth of November, 543. During excavations carried out in 1963 outside the wall of the Old City, Kathleen Kenyon discovered near the above site the remains of two large structures, one orientated east–west and the other south–north. These may have been the foundations of colonnades. To the east and south ran drains filled with black earth. The excavators tentatively assumed that these are the remains of the large hospital attached to the Nea Church.

After Justinian's death, the building of Christian holy places did not cease. At the site called Dominus Flevit on the slopes of the Mount of Olives, the remains of a small church (14 by 7 meters) were discovered in 1955. The site contains a mosaic floor laid in geometric patterns and a dedicatory inscription mentioning the priest of the Anastasis. The church has one apse, and the foundations of an altar and of a chancel screen in front of it were also found. T. Milik ascribed the building of the church to approximately A.D. 675 on the basis of the literary sources. Notwithstanding its clearly Byzantine style, it thus dates from the beginning of the Arab period.

In addition to the above churches, whose dates can be established, several buildings were discovered in Jerusalem which, although clearly belonging to the Byzantine period, cannot be dated with certainty. The Franciscans, under the direction of S. J. Saller, cleared two churches, situated one above the other in Beit Ḥanina on the eastern slope of the Mount of Olives. Of the first church, only the apse, the prothesis and the diaconicon, and some fragments of a mosaic floor with geometric decorations are preserved. The excavators ascribe this church to the fourth/fifth

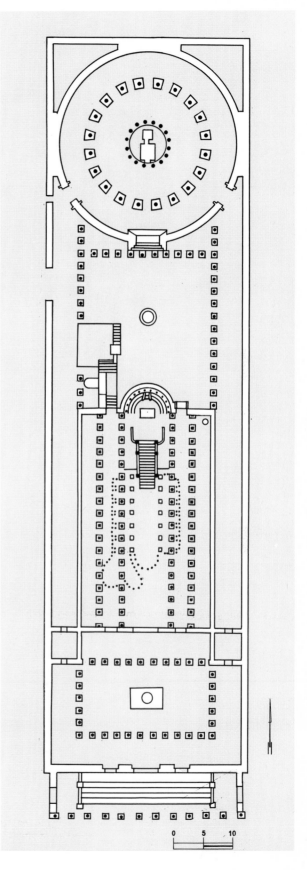

0   5   10

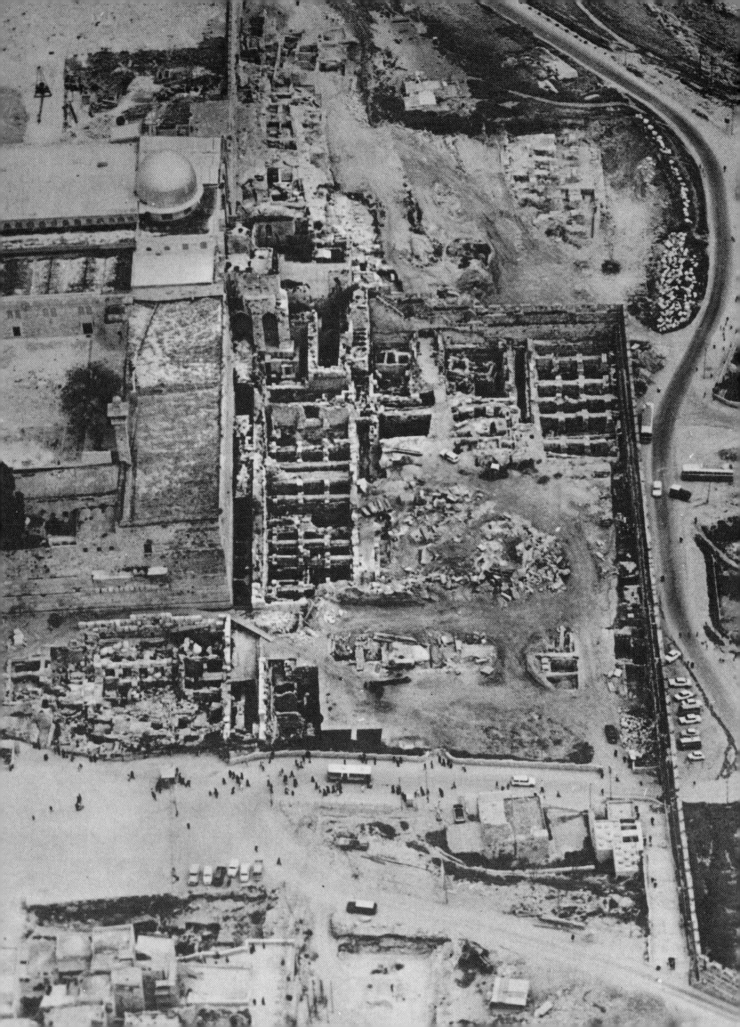

centuries. The later date seems to be correct. The second church is built atop the first one, except for the apse and the adjoining rooms, which were shifted 13 meters to the east. This church probably dates from the sixth century A.D.

The remains of another church were found south of the Russian Tower on the Mount of Olives. In a room to the west of the church proper was a mosaic pavement with a dedicatory inscription and a prayer for the salvation of Eusebius the priest, the deacon Theodosius, and three monks. Near the Sheep Pool, above the remains of the northern pool and the dam passing between the two pools, a church was probably erected in the seventh century. According to Vincent's reconstruction, the double row of columns on the dam served to divide the nave and the aisles, and the latter were therefore wider than customary (the church measures 28 by 20 meters).

In 1937, D. Baramki, on behalf of the Department of Antiquities, excavated a mosaic-paved chapel near the Third Wall. The chapel (6.1 by 3.05 meters) had formerly been part of a hall twice as long, which was afterward divided in two by the wall of the apse. West of the chapel was a narthex, and beyond the latter there were another two rooms. A long narrow corridor passes south of all the rooms. The excavator considers these the remains of a Byzantine monastery from the fifth century A.D., but judging from the style of the mosaics, a date in the seventh century seems more justified.

Besides the churches, a large number of chapels also served for Christian worship. Built above or near tombs, they can generally be identified by the mosaic floors still preserved and sometimes also by dedicatory inscriptions laid in the mosaics. Since dating these structures closely is difficult, they shall be described here in geographical order.

Mount of Olives. 1. Chapel built above a tomb (5.3 by 4.8 meters) near the Orthodox church Viri Galilaei. In the floor is an inscription in memory of a woman named Susannah. 2. A small chapel, with an apse and a mosaic floor ornamented with crosses but no inscription, is situated beneath the Pater Church. 3. Tomb chapels discovered north of the Russian Church on the Mount of Olives containing several pavements with Armenian inscriptions. One pavement is decorated with birds, fish, fruit, and the figure of a lamb in its

center. A dedicatory inscription mentions Susannah, mother of Artaban. 4. Another similar mosaic floor, also displaying in its center the figure of a lamb and an inscription mentioning the (Armenian) bishop Jacob. In a subterranean chapel in the same vicinity, there is an Armenian dedicatory inscription to "Saint Isaiah." 5. On the slopes of the Mount of Olives, there are numerous Christian tombs, the most famous of which is the so-called Tomb of the Prophets (in Arabic "Qubur el-Anbia"). It is entered though a flight of stairs which lead to a circular hall (8.5 meters in diameter), from which three rooms (9–12 meters long) extend spokelike and lead to a semicircular burial

The Umayyad structures adjacent to the Temple Mount. Opposite page: Aerial view of excavations. Below: Plan.

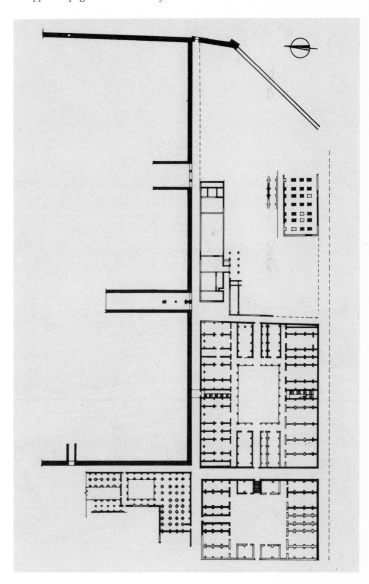

corridor in the outer wall of which there are twenty-six loculi. Another corridor, also rounded, connects the spokelike rooms but does not contain tombs. This tomb, which was explored by Clermont-Ganneau in 1870–74, contains numerous Greek-Christian inscriptions.

Area North of Damascus Gate. A vast burial site extended to the slopes of the Kidron Valley. Some of the tombs are noteworthy. 1. On the plot of the Swedish School, a Byzantine chapel, of which remains of two walls and a mosaic floor with geometric patterns have survived, was discovered during excavations of the Third Wall. The mosaic floor has an inscription naming the tomb as that of Anatolia of Arabissus, perhaps the sister of Emperor Mauricius (A.D. 587–602). 2. At a distance of 20 meters south of Saint Stephen's Church, two Byzantine chapels situated above Jewish tombs, re-used in the Byzantine period, were discovered during excavations of the church. 3. Near Damascus Gate two tomb chapels were found containing mosaics of outstanding workmanship: (a) one of the tomb chapels (6.3 by 3.9 meters), with a small apse on the east side, was found in 1894 on Prophets' Road. In the mosaic floor are depicted animals and various objects, probably offerings, such as baskets of fruit. An inscription accompanying these designs contains a dedication "to the memory and for the salvation of all the Armenians the names of whom the Lord alone knoweth." Judging by the similarities with the Shellal and Ma'on mosaic pavements, this mosaic can be dated to the beginning of the sixth century A.D. (b) At the entrance to the Damascus Gate another chapel (3.2 by 5.7 meters) with a mosaic floor was cleared in 1901. In the center of the mosaic there is a representation of Orpheus surrounded by animals with Pan and a centaur at his feet. Below this scene are two female figures, named Theodosia and Georgia, and below them the figure of a hunter. This mosaic is to be dated to the second half of the sixth century A.D.

The Valley of Hinnom. Most of the numerous tombs found here from the Byzantine period are re-used Jewish tombs. On the tombs it is stated that the persons buried there are from "Holy Zion" across the Valley. On Mount Zion itself, among the

Flight of steps leading to the western Huldah Gate from the excavations adjacent to the Temple Mount; Herodian period.

ruins of a Roman house above which Byzantine structures had been erected, was found a mosaic depicting animals and on its margins two sandals and the inscription: "Congratulations, Stephen."
In 1932, a cemetery from the fifth–seventh centuries was discovered near the YMCA building. It comprised very simple tombs dug into the rock and covered with stone slabs. Wherever the rock sloped, the tomb was completed by masonry. All the tombs are oriented east–west. Not far from the tombs are the remains of walls, perhaps of a monastery. An inscription in a building near the monastery states that this is the private tomb of "S[amuel] bishop of the Georgians and of the monastery who purchased it in the tower of David." (See also Monasteries, Jerusalem.)
In the village of Beit Safafa, on the outskirts of Jerusalem, J. Landau discovered a stone-built Byzantine tomb, which he cleared in 1953 on behalf of the Department of Antiquities. It consists of an underground chamber divided into eight cubicles — some containing lead coffins — and a chapel (8 by 7 meters) with a mosaic floor and a square apse in the west wall. Near the apse was an inscription mentioning the founder Samuel. It also gives a date (the year 206 of an unknown era). A similar tomb was found in 1932 on the grounds of the American School of Oriental Research. Judging from the more than one hundred bodies buried there, this was a common grave dug in time of war or epidemic.

Other Byzantine Buildings. The churches and tombs attest to the religious spirit characteristic of the period, but at the same time, buildings for lay purposes were also erected. The empress Eudocia restored an ancient wall enclosing Mount Zion and the eastern hill (Ophel) together with the valley between them. This wall ran above the remains of the Hasmonaean wall and was discovered during excavations conducted by Bliss in 1894–97. Bliss deduced that the walls he excavated were from two different periods, since in one of the cuts, a 2.5-meter high accumulation of debris separated the lower wall from the foundation of rough stones of the upper wall. In distinction to the earlier wall — built of ashlars with flat bosses and sunken margins, and laid without mortar — the upper wall is built (with partial use of the ashlars of the lower wall) of smooth, comb-dressed stones, but without margins, as well as of stones with flat

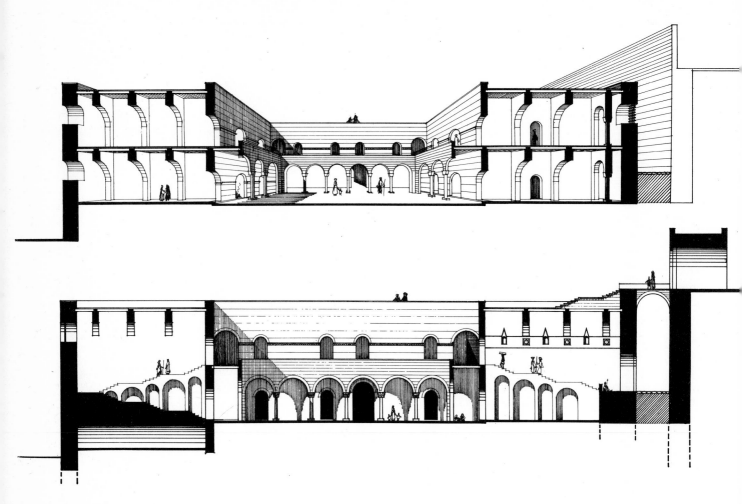

Umayyad building II. Above: Sectional view through center. Below: Sectional view through western part, looking west. Opposite page: Haram esh-Sharif (Temple Mount); plan.

bosses and sunken margins, but made with a claw chisel. The builders used mortar between the courses. The wall is about 2 meters wide, the width of the towers 10.5 meters; the distance between them is up to 30 meters, and they project about 3 meters from the wall. The wall was in existence a very long time.

Houses from the Byzantine period were cleared mainly in excavations on the hill of Ophel. In 1923–25, R. A. S. Macalister and J. G. Duncan found, in field 5 on the Ophel, a street and an adjacent private house which was named, from a stamp on earthenware drainpipes, the House of Eusebius. The house is square in plan, with an inner court in its center, surrounded by several rooms. The rooms are paved with mosaics laid in geometric patterns. One room, which probably served as the kitchen, is built partly against a cistern. On the walls of the cistern were found nine frescoes depicting fish. Above this house were the remains of walls and mosaics from the Late Byzantine or Early Arab periods. The excavators dated the House of Eusebius to the Roman period, but it is clear that it was not erected before Eudocia included the area inside the wall. The style of building and of the mosaics suggest a date in the fifth century, an opinion fully confirmed by Crowfoot's excavations (see below).

In 1927, Crowfoot, excavating in field 10 on the hill of Ophel, found a Byzantine street (about 40 meters long, 5 meters wide), its pavement completely preserved in a 20-meter section, with the remains of a row of shops and of houses behind them. The plan of the houses closely resembles that discovered in Macalister's excavations: square with rooms disposed around a central court. Rainwater drains passed under the pavement. Crowfoot dated the street to the sixth century. A

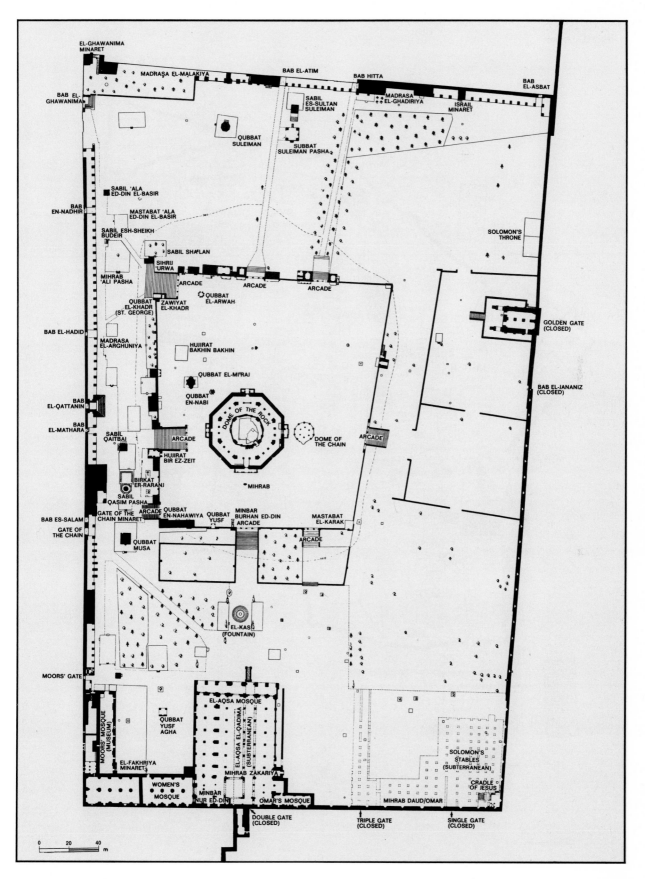

EL-GHAWANIMA
MINARET

MADRASA EL-MALAKIYA

BAB EL-ATIM

BAB HITTA

BAB
EL-ASBAT

BAB EL-
GHAWANIMA

SABIL
ES-SULTAN
SULEIMAN

MADRASA
EL-GHADIRIYA

ISRAIL
MINARET

QUBBAT
SULEIMAN

SUBBAT SULEIMAN PASHA

SABIL 'ALA
ED-DIN EL-BASIR

SOLOMON'S
THRONE

BAB
EN-NADHIR

MASTABAT 'ALA
ED-DIN EL-BASIR

SABIL ESH-SHEIKH
BUDEIR

SABIL SHA'LAN

SIHRIJ
'URWA

MIHRAB
'ALI PASHA

ARCADE

ARCADE

ARCADE

QUBBAT
EL-KHADR
(ST. GEORGE)

ZAWIYAT
EL-KHADR

QUBBAT
EL-ARWAH

BAB EL-HADID

MADRASA
EL-ARGHUNIYA

HUJIRAT
BAKHIN BAKHIN

GOLDEN GATE
(CLOSED)

QUBBAT EL-MI'RAJ

BAB EL-JANANIZ
(CLOSED)

QUBBAT
EN-NABI

BAB
EL-QATTANIN

SABIL
QAITBAI

ARCADE

DOME OF THE ROCK

DOME OF
THE CHAIN

ARCADE

BAB
EL-MATHARA

HUJIRAT
BIR EZ-ZEIT

BIRKAT
ER-RARANJ

MIHRAB

SABIL
QASIM PASHA

QUBBAT
EN-NAHAWIYA

QUBBAT
YUSF

MINBAR
BURHAN ED-DIN
ARCADE

MASTABAT
EL-KARAK

BAB ES-SALAM

GATE OF THE
CHAIN MINARET

ARCADE

ARCADE

GATE OF
THE CHAIN

QUBBAT
MUSA

MOORS' GATE

EL-KAS
(FOUNTAIN)

MOORS' MOSQUE
(MUSEUM)

QUBBAT
YUSF
AGHA

EL-AQSA MOSQUE

SOLOMON'S
STABLES
(SUBTERRANEAN)

EL-FAKHRIYA
MINARET

EL-AQSA EL-QADIMA (SUBTERRANEAN)

CRADLE
OF JESUS

MIHRAB ZAKARIYA

WOMEN'S
MOSQUE

MINBAR
NUR ED-DIN

OMAR'S MOSQUE

MIHRAB DAUD/OMAR

DOUBLE GATE
(CLOSED)

TRIPLE GATE
(CLOSED)

SINGLE GATE
(CLOSED)

0   20   40
m

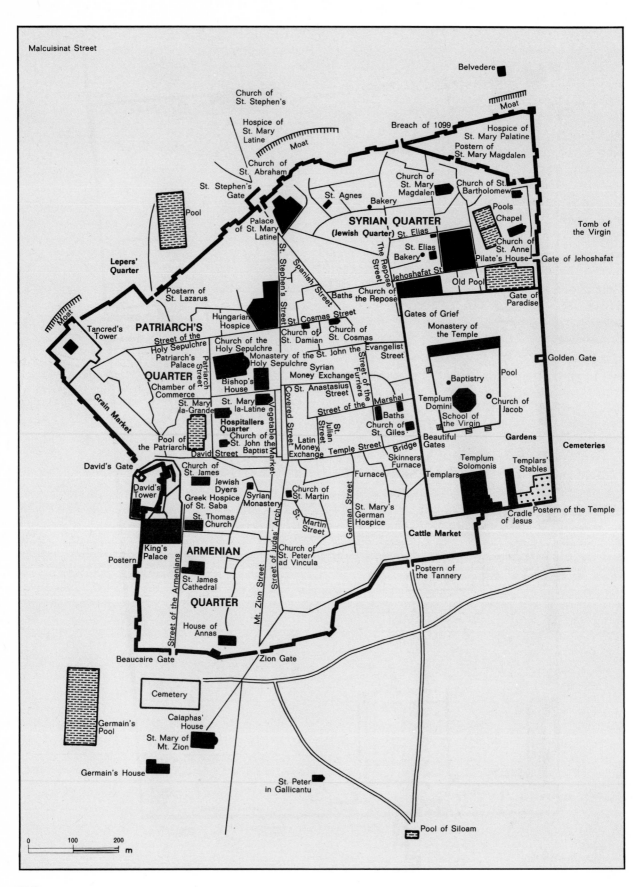

Malcuisinat Street

Belvedere

Church of
St. Stephen's

Moat

Hospice of
St. Mary
Latine

Breach of 1099

Moat

Hospice of
St. Mary
Palatine

Postern of
St. Mary Magdalen

Church of
St. Abraham

St. Stephen's
Gate

St. Agnes

Bakery

Church of
St. Mary
Magdalen

Church of St.
Bartholomew

Pool

Palace
of St. Mary
Latine

SYRIAN QUARTER
(Jewish Quarter)

St. Elias

Pools
Chapel

Tomb of
the Virgin

Lepers'
Quarter

St. Elias
Bakery

Church of
St. Anne

Postern of
St. Lazarus

The Repose Street

Pilate's House

Gate of Jehoshafat

Jehoshafat St

Old Pool

Gate of
Paradise

Moat

Tancred's
Tower

PATRIARCH'S

Street of the
Holy Sepulchre

Hungarian
Hospice

St. Cosmas Street

Church of
St. Damian

Church of
St. Cosmas

Baths of
the Repose

Gates of Grief

Monastery of
the Temple

Golden Gate

Church of the
Holy Sepulchre

Monastery of the
Holy Sepulchre

St. John the
Evangelist
Street

QUARTER

Patriarch's
Palace

Patriarch Street

Bishop's
House

Syrian
Money Exchange

St. Anastasius
Street

Street of the Furriers

Baptistry

Pool

Church of
Jacob

Chamber of
Commerce

St. Mary
la-Grande

St. Mary
la-Latine

Street of the

Marshal

Templum
Domini

Hospitallers
Quarter

Covered Street

Baths

School of
the Virgin

Pool of
the Patriarch

Church of
St. John the
Baptist

Vegetable Market

St. Julian
Street

Latin
Money
Exchange

Church of
St. Giles

Gardens

Cemeteries

David Street

Temple Street

Beautiful
Gates

David's Gate

Church of
St. James

Jewish
Dyers

Syrian
Monastery

Church of
St. Martin

Bridge
Skinners'
Furnace

Templum
Solomonis

Templars'
Stables

David's
Tower

German Street

Templars

Greek Hospice
of St. Saba

St. Thomas
Church

St. Martin
Street

Furnace

St. Mary's
German
Hospice

Cradle
of Jesus

Postern of the Temple

Street of Judas' Arch

King's
Palace

ARMENIAN

Church of
St. Peter
ad Vincula

Cattle Market

Postern

Street of the Armenians

St. James
Cathedral

QUARTER

Mt. Zion Street

Postern of
the Tannery

House of
Annas

Beaucaire Gate

Zion Gate

Cemetery

Germain's
Pool

Caiaphas'
House

St. Mary of
Mt. Zion

Germain's House

St. Peter
in Gallicantu

Pool of Siloam

0   100   200
m

bowl with the name "Anastasius" engraved on the lid was found in one of the houses, which is, therefore, known as the House of Anastasius. In one of its rooms, stairs were found leading to the roof or an upper story.

Not far from the site of Crowfoot's excavations, Kathleen Kenyon found in 1963 Byzantine houses, built inside Roman quarries and cisterns with stairs. The houses are large and well built.

The only remains attesting to the existence of a non-Christian settlement in Byzantine Jerusalem is the wall behind the Tomb of David on Mount Zion. This wall had two (or perhaps three) niches oriented to the north. In the excavations of J. Pinkerfeld, two superimposed mosaic floors were found. From the direction of the building, it may perhaps be deduced that these are the remains of a synagogue (mentioned in Christian writings) where in the fourth century the worshippers prayed facing the direction of the Temple Mount.

Excavations made after 1968 show that the Byzantine city was more densely settled than Roman Aelia, as could be assumed from its special status in this period as the Holy City of Christianity. In this period, Justinian erected the splendid New Church (see above), the discovery of which has solved an important topographical problem of Byzantine Jerusalem. The current restoration work in the Church of the Holy Sepulcher (then called the "Church of the Anastasis [Resurrection])", a joint effort of various Christian bodies, has gone far to clarify several controversial points: Thus, it was found that around the traditional tomb there had been a row of columns and piers supporting the dome, with open spaces between the piers. The architect Oekonomopoulos was able to expose the edge of the apse of the basilica which had stood to the east of the tomb and part of the stylobate of the eastern row of columns in the court surrounding Golgotha.

Byzantine remains were uncovered in almost all areas of the recent excavations. Noteworthy is the section of the Church of Mount Zion found in the excavations of M. Broshi. A large bathhouse was uncovered in the Jewish Quarter, and an important Byzantine complex was found near the Third Wall

Opposite page: Crusader Jerusalem. Below: Church of the Holy Sepulcher; Crusader western lintel with reliefs of the Last Supper and Jesus' entry into Jerusalem, second half of the twelfth century A.D.

during the excavations of Sara Ben-Arieh.

Of special importance are the building complexes found in Mazar's excavations near the Temple Mount. Some of these buildings were amazingly well preserved to a height of three stories. One group was found near the southwestern corner of the Temple Mount, a second group somewhat more to the west, opposite the western Huldah Gate near the Turkish wall, and a third group opposite the eastern Huldah Gate.

Two phases of building were distinguished by the excavator. In the first phase, the western quarter was erected in the time of Constantine. It was destroyed during the reign of Julian and rebuilt in the Late Byzantine period, at which time the eastern quarter was added. In a building in the western quarter, a menorah was found engraved on a stone, indicating that Jews had lived there in that period.

UMAYYAD PERIOD

An unexpected find of great importance was uncovered in 1968–74 in the excavations at the Temple Mount. A building complex from the Umayyad period, consisting of six structures of large proportions, was discovered in the area south and west of the Temple Mount. According to the excavator, one of the buildings was a palace. In that period the supporting walls of the Temple Mount were repaired, and on them were erected the Mosque of el-Aqsa and the Dome of the Rock.

THE CRUSADER PERIOD

The time of Crusader rule in Jerusalem (1099–1187) was a period of intensive building activity. Most of the buildings erected then have not been excavated. Some of them are still standing, some have been restored without excavations or have been demolished without prior scientific examination. Thus only those buildings which have been uncovered in archaeological excavations shall be dealt with here. As a rule the new buildings were erected on the foundations of older buildings, which can no longer be examined.

The Monastery near Mary's Tomb. The remains of the monastery were discovered during the digging of a sewer in the Kidron Valley near the Crusader church of the same name. It was excavated in 1937 by Johns, on behalf of the Department of Antiquities. From literary sources it is known that the monastery was erected at the beginning of the twelfth century by the Benedict-

ine Fathers and that Saladin destroyed it in 1187. The remains uncovered in two trenches show that, on the south side, there was a court surrounded by porticoes. Beyond the court were two narrow halls (an assembly hall and a hall for archives) flanking a wide hall (10 meters). In the center of the latter was a row of Early Gothic columns and pillars, which supported the vaults, as was customary in Crusader buildings. The walls were decorated with frescoes painted in red on a green background.

The Monastery near the Church of Beit Ḥanina. This monastery, discovered by Saller on the Mount of Olives, was founded by Queen Melisande (1131–43). An area of 62.5 by 50 meters was excavated. On the west side a corridor ran along the whole building, and behind it was a row of halls. In the central part there was a group of structures, probably the administrative block, and to its north a large refectory(?) and nearby a tower and a pen for cattle. A large court surrounded the monastery on the east and south.

The Citadel. During John's excavations, several Crusader buildings were discovered on top of the eastern, southwestern, and northwestern towers of the Citadel. These buildings were erected in the eleventh century when the Arab citadel became the palace of the King of Jerusalem. The later period of Crusader rule in Jerusalem, from 1229 to 1239, witnessed minor building activity. Most of Crusader buildings were included in the fortifications of the later Mameluke fortress.

Three churches in Jerusalem were examined in excavations or surveys:

The Church of the Holy Sepulcher (Anastasis), in its present-day form, which is that of a Romanesque church, with a circular passage along its eastern side and a dome resting on four pillars and remains of the Crusader belfry. The foundations of the Crusader parts were examined by W. Harvey in 1935 and by an inter-denominational committee of architects, which studied the building in 1960–63.

Chapel near Saint Stephen's Church (22 by 9 meters) consists of one hall, a curved raised bench for the clergy, and an altar in the single apse. Near the chapel were the stables of the Hospitalers.

Church near Gethsemane. During excavations of the Church of Gethsemane, another church, from the twelfth century (31 by 22 meters), was also discovered. It has a triple apse and vaults and arches in Romanesque style. Remains of colored frescoes from the same period, depicting angels, were also found. Two other Crusader churches, standing close together south of the Church of the Holy Sepulcher, were also discovered, one in 1893–98 when the foundations of the German Church in the Old City were laid, the other in 1900–01 during restoration work in the area under Greek ownership situated farther east. Both churches are built on the usual Romanesque plan with triple apses and vaults resting on arches. The first church is named Saint Mary of the Latins (German) and the second Saint Mary the Great (Greek).

The Church of Saint Thomas (a Jacobite church) and the Church of Saint Anne are Crusader buildings which have been examined but not excavated. The former is a church consisting of one hall only. The latter was reconstructed by Mauss according to its original plan as far as was possible.

In 1968–74, excavations were also undertaken at Crusader sites. In the Jewish Quarter, a church identified as that of Saint Mary of the Germans was re-examined together with an adjoining section of a street. On Mount Zion, the Church of Saint Mary of Mount Zion was excavated by M. Broshi. He also investigated a very large structure in the area of the Armenian Garden, which he identified as the palace of the kings of Jerusalem. In the area of Tancred's tower, a section of the wall, fosse, and aqueduct were excavated.　　　　M. AVI-YONAH

BIBLIOGRAPHY

For excavations in Jerusalem, see L. A. Mayer and M. Avi-Yonah, QDAP-1, with supplementary information in QDAP 2–14 and later in 'Atiqot, ADAJ and the annual archaeological reports in RB.
Roman, Byzantine, and Crusader remains discovered up to 1926 were published mostly in: L. H. Vincent–F. M. Abel, Jérusalem nouvelle, 1–4, Paris, 1914–26.
See also: M. Avi-Yonah, IEJ 18 (1968), 98–125; 21 (1971), 168–69 • B. Mazar, EI 9 (1969), 161–74; 10 (1971), 1–33 (Hebrew) • M. Ben-Dov, ibid. 10, 97–101 • N. Avigad, IEJ 20 (1970), 1–8, 129–40; 22 (1972), 193–200 • Ruth Amiran and A. Eitan, IEJ 20 (1970), 9–17; 22 (1972), 50–51 • Ruth Amiran, IEJ 21 (1971), 166–67 • J. B. Hennessy, Levant 2 (1970), 22–27 • P. Benoît, Harvard Theological Review 64 (1971), 135–67 • Nurith Kenaan, IEJ 23 (1973), 167–75, 221–29 • A. Obadiah, EI 11 (1973), 208–12 (Hebrew) • Sara Ben-Arieh and E. Netzer, IEJ 24 (1974), 97–107 • C. Caüasnon, The Church of the Holy Sepulchre, London, 1974 • Y. Yadin (ed.), Jerusalem Revealed, Jerusalem, 1975.

THE TOMBS IN JERUSALEM
The First Temple Period. All excavators of the remains of the First Temple period in Jerusalem (on the southeastern spur, the hill of Ophel) were eager to find the tombs of the kings of Judah which, according to the Bible, were located in the City of David. In his excavations on the Ophel, R. Weill discovered three rock-cut tombs, which are of special interest because of their size and form.

The best preserved of these tombs has the form of a vaulted tunnel, resembling a huge loculus, reached by several steps. Its length is 16 meters, width 2.5 meters, and height 4 meters in the front and 1.8 meters in the rear, where the floor level is elevated to form a shelf. In this shelf a shallow rectangular pit was cut, probably to hold a coffin. Slots in the walls indicate that the tomb was divided by beams into two stories.

Weill ascribed these tombs to the kings of Judah, and at the time his opinion was shared by other scholars. Today, however, it is no longer accepted, especially since no other evidence has been found to confirm that they belong to the Israelite period.

Across the Kidron Valley in the Siloam (Silwan) village are the remains of a necropolis from the period of the First Temple. The most outstanding and best known of these tombs is the so-called "Tomb of Pharaoh's Daughter," situated on a rock scarp, at the northern end of the village. It is hewn from the rock in the form of a cube (5 by 5.8 by 4 meters). At the top, the tomb terminates in an Egyptian cornice (a large cavetto with torus), which is surmounted by a pyramid of which very little remains. Its general aspect is that of a small Egyptian chapel. Inside the tomb is a small corridor and a single chamber with a gabled ceiling. An inscription was cut above the entrance in ancient Hebrew characters, of which only the last letter and part of another letter have been preserved.

In the rock scarp — which continues along the Kidron Valley — several burial chambers are cut, which have gabled roofs like that of the "Tomb of Pharaoh's Daughter." Within the village another rock-cut tomb, consisting of two chambers, was found above ground level. On its facade were carved two inscriptions in ancient Hebrew characters. This is the tomb of an official of the royal court whose title was "Steward of the House" and his maidservant (amah). The inscription contains a curse against any one who dare open the tomb. It is dated to the beginning of the seventh century B.C. The fragment of a similar inscription was found on a monumental rock-cut tomb nearby.

Outside the environs of the City of David, two tombs from this period have been discovered at the beginning of the Valley of Hinnom, the present-day Mamilla Road. There are no exact details on the form of these tombs. Potsherds from the period of the kings of Judah were found there.

In 1967–1974, additional tombs were explored in the Siloam village, among them a monumental tomb and small finely dressed burial chambers.

Another group of tombs was uncovered in the excavations of B. Mazar on the eastern slope of the western hill opposite the Temple Mount. These were shaft tombs hewn in the rock from the eighth–seventh centuries B.C. Two more contemporary groups of tombs were recently found, one opposite Damascus Gate and the other on the slope of the Valley of Hinnom, opposite the Armenian Garden. Neither of the latter two groups have been published yet.

BIBLIOGRAPHY

R. Weill, *La cité de David*, 1–2, Paris, 1920–1947 • Vincent–Stève, *Jérusalem*, 313 ff. • N. Avigad, *Ancient Monuments in the Kidron Valley*, Jerusalem, 1954, 36–39 (Hebrew) • Ruth Amiran, in: *Judah and Jerusalem*, Jerusalem, 1958, 65–72 (Hebrew) • S. Lofredda, *Studii Biblici* 16 (1965–66), 85–126 • D. Ussishkin, *BA* 33 (1970), 34–46 • B. Mazar, *Excavations in the Old City Near the Temple Mount*, Jerusalem, 1971; *idem*, in: *Jerusalem Revealed* (Y. Yadin, ed.), Jerusalem, 1975, 38–39 • D. Ussishkin, *ibid.*, 63–65 • G. Barkai et alii, *Qadmoniot* 30–31 (1975), 71–76 (Hebrew).

The Second Temple Period. The necropolis of Jerusalem in the Second Temple period spread over an extensive area surrounding the town on all sides. Only a few tombs have been discovered west of the town. The burials are concentrated in three main centers, in the north, east, and south. In the north, the burial area begins north of the Sanhedria Quarter in the Scopus Valley (Wadi 'Umm el-'Amed) and extends southward to the tomb of Queen Helena near the Third Wall of Jerusalem. In the east, the tombs are scattered over the slopes of the Mount of Olives and of Mount Scopus, and in the south, they are cut along the Kidron Valley and its tributaries, including the Hinnom Valley.

BURIAL FORMS. It can be assumed that the com-mon people were buried in simple graves dug in the earth. These have since disappeared, leaving no trace. The tombs which have survived and which have been exposed are family tombs consisting of underground chambers hewn in the rock. The most frequent type of small family tomb consists as a rule of a square room (length of a side 3–4 meters) with loculi cut into its walls (and sometimes also arcosolia). The room is entered through a small opening (about .5 meter). Since this chamber is less than the height of a man, a long pit, about .9 meter deep, was cut in the floor at the entrance in order to enable persons in charge of the burials or visitors to stand upright. In this manner shelves were formed along three sides of the room. In chambers high enough to allow a man to stand upright such pits were not necessary, and only low shelves — or none at all — were dug out.

The bodies of the deceased were placed in the loculi, and later, after the flesh had decayed, the bones were collected and put into ossuaries, thus making room in the cave for another member of the family. The ossuaries were usually placed on the shelves inside the chamber or were stored in a special compartment, but ossuaries are often found also within the loculi.

The custom of re-interment of the bones was widespread among Jews at the end of the Second Temple period and for several centuries afterward. Numerous laws in the Mishnah and Talmud deal with the modes of burial and the form and size of tombs. On the custom of gathering the bones, it is said: "At first they used to bury them in arcosolia; when the flesh withered, they used to gather the bones and bury them in cedar-wood" (Palestinian Talmud, *Mo'ed Qatan*, 81, 3–4). "Thus said my father at the time of his death: Bury me first in a field. Afterward gather my bones and put them in a cedar-wood ossuary" (*Semahot*, 12, 9). There also existed the custom of burial without re-interment, and some people used coffins (sarcophagi) in which the whole body was buried. Large and prominent families had their own large tomb caves cut for them with several chambers with loculi. Thus a series of chambers was formed which branch out horizontally and vertically on several levels.

Only the facade of such burial caves was visible from the outside. As a rule, the facade was plain and had only a small opening. If a porch stood in front of the cave, the entrance was large and wide. In some caves, the entrance is decorated with a pediment carved with plant motifs, such as vine leaves and fruit, acanthus leaves, etc., characteristic of Jewish decorative art. Some tombs have facades with architectural features characterized by two columns placed in the wide entrance between pilasters (distyle in antis) and generally supporting a decorative frieze in Doric style.

A special group of tombs consists of entire structures carved out of the rock and free standing above ground. In this group, the rock-hewn architecture of the tombs reaches its summit of perfection and splendor. Only two monuments of this kind are preserved from the Second Temple period: "Absalom's Tomb" and "Zechariah's Tomb."

Hundreds of cave tombs from the Second Temple period have been uncovered in Jerusalem. Isolated tombs, such as those in the Kidron Valley, have been visible for a considerable time, and other tombs, including some of the most impressive, were discovered generations ago. All these were cleared in their entirety and re-explored in modern times. Many simple tomb caves were pillaged long ago in unknown circumstances. Numerous tombs discovered in the twentieth century have been

systematically excavated and explored. For lack of space only selected examples are discussed here. These include most of the monumental tombs, which are of outstanding architecture, and those tombs in which ossuaries or inscriptions of interest have been found.

SEPULCHRAL MONUMENTS IN THE KIDRON VALLEY. In the section of the valley known as the Valley of Jehoshaphat, the slope of the Mount of Olives terminates in a high rock scarp in which four tomb monuments are cut: the Tomb of Bene Hezir, the "Tomb of Zechariah," the "Tomb of Jehoshaphat," and the "Tomb of Absalom." These monuments have been visible for a long time and were described by many travelers. In modern times they were cleared and re-explored.

THE TOMB OF BENE HEZIR is characterized by a pure Doric facade: two Doric columns between pilasters supporting a Doric frieze. On the architrave is a Hebrew inscription stating that it is the tomb and the *nefesh* ("funerary monument") of several persons referred to by name who were priests of the Bene Hezir family. The *nefesh* probably stood beside the facade. The burial cave consists of a porch, chambers with loculi, a flight of stairs leading up to ground level, and a passage

Tomb of the "Royal Steward." Plan and reconstruction of facade. At bottom, facsimile of the inscription.

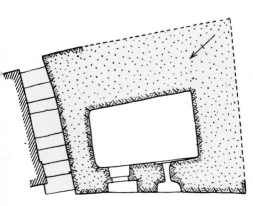

connecting the cave with the area to the south, where the "Tomb of Zechariah" stands. The Tomb of Bene Hezir is dated to the end of the Hasmonaean period and the inscription to the beginning of Herod's reign.

Avigad, *Ancient Monuments*, 37–78.

THE "TOMB OF ZECHARIAH." This monumental tomb is free standing. It is carved out of the surrounding rock in the form of a cube (length of a side 5 meters) crowned by a pyramid. The four sides of the monument are decorated with Ionic

Rock-cut tomb of the First Temple period, west of Western Wall. Above entrance, breach made by tomb robbers. In the ceiling, note the "nefesh."

columns and an Egyptian cavetto cornice. The monument served as the *nefesh* for a tomb. A small chamber was recently discovered in its lower part. It is not clear when this chamber was cut.

Avigad, *Ancient Monuments*, 79–90 • H. E. Stutchbury, *PEQ*, 1961, 101–13.

THE "CAVE OF JEHOSHAPHAT" consists of eight chambers. It has a large entrance surmounted by a pediment which is adorned with a relief of vine leaves and fruit.

Avigad, *Ancient Monuments*, 134–38.

THE "TOMB OF ABSALOM." In front of the "Tomb of Jehoshaphat" stands the so-called "Tomb (Pillar) of Absalom," the highest (20 meters) and most complete tomb monument found in Israel. It consists of two main parts. A lower square structure, most of which is rock cut, contains a small burial chamber with arcosolia. The four walls of the square structure are ornamented with Ionic columns, a Doric frieze, and an Egyptian cornice—an unusual combination of styles. The upper part of the tomb consists of a round structure built of stones in the form of a circular pedestal (tholos) topped by a concave conical roof. This round structure served as the monument or *nefesh* for the tomb below and perhaps also for the "Tomb of Jehoshaphat." The "Tomb of Absalom" is dated to the first century A.D.

Avigad, *Ancient Monuments*, 91–133.

THE TOMB OF JASON was discovered in 1956 in Alfasi Street in Jerusalem. It consists of two courts, a porch, a burial chamber with loculi, and an ossuary chamber. The overall length of the structure is 22 meters, and the length of the facade is 4.5 meters. In the wide entrance to the porch, a single Doric column stood between two pilasters. The column is built of stone drums. This is the only tomb found in Israel with only one column instead of the usual two columns in the classical style. Above the porch rose a pyramid. Some of its stones have been found in the rubble.
On the walls of the porch are charcoal drawings of ships, a Greek inscription, and several Aramaic inscriptions, the longest of which consists of three lines lamenting Jason, the deceased. In the tomb chamber were found much pottery and coins, mostly of the Hasmonaean period and some from

the reign of Herod. The tomb is consequently dated to the beginning of the first century B.C., and it continued in use up to the beginning of the first century A.D.

L. Y. Rahmani, *IEJ* 17 (1967), 61–100 • N. Avigad, *ibid.,* 101–11 • P. Benoît, *ibid.,* 112–13.

THE TOMB OF QUEEN HELENA OF ADIABENE is the largest and most magnificent tomb found in Jerusalem. It is mentioned in ancient sources and in reports of travelers from the sixteenth century onward. In 1863, F. de Saulcy excavated the tomb and mistakenly attributed it to the kings of Judah and named it the ''Tombs of the Kings.''

In front of the tomb, there is a 30-meter-long forecourt with a staircase, 9 meters wide, leading down to the main court. This court, 26 by 27 meters, was hewn into the rock to a depth of 8.5 meters. The facade of the tomb, which was 27.5 meters long and partly destroyed, was built in the style of two columns in antis. A decorative band of carved leaves adorned the architrave, which supported a Doric frieze. Instead of continuing the triglyphs and metopes in the center of the frieze, a bunch of grapes, wreaths, and acanthus leaves were carved there. Above the facade, there were originally three pyramids, as reported by Josephus. The tomb cave consists of a porch, a main chamber, and eight burial chambers with loculi and arcosolia. The entrance was closed by a rolling stone, accessible through a depression in the floor of the porch. The stone was apparently moved by some secret mechanism. The cave contained several decorated sarcophagi, one of which bore the inscription ''Queen Saddan.''

The tomb is ascribed to Helena, Queen of Adiabene (in northern Mesopotamia), a convert to Judaism who—as related by Josephus—was brought to Jerusalem for burial together with two members of her family, sometime after A.D. 50.

M. Kon, *The Tombs of the Kings,* Tel Aviv, 1947 (Hebrew).

THE TOMB OF NICANOR was discovered in 1902 on Mount Scopus on land occupied now by the Hebrew University. The plan of the tomb cave, which is one of the largest in Jerusalem, consists of a court, a porch, and four branches of burial chambers with loculi radiating from the center and descending to form several ''stories.'' In the entrance to the porch stood two pillars built of stone. The length of the facade is 17 meters. The cave contained several decorated ossuaries, one of them bearing an inscription in Greek, which relates that the ossuary contained the bones of the sons of Nicanor of Alexandria, who had donated one of the gates (of the Temple). Below the names of his two sons (Nicanor and Alexa) are written in Hebrew. The tomb is to be dated to the first century A.D.

N. Avigad, *EI* 8 (1967), 119–25 (Hebrew).

THE CAVE OF 'UMM EL-'AMED lies at the northern extremity of the necropolis of Jerusalem in Wadi el-'Amud. This cave, which has been visible for a long time, was re-explored recently. It consists of a court, a porch, and two burial chambers with loculi. Although the facade is mostly destroyed, its remains indicate that it had a distyle in antis facade with pilasters at the two extremities of the facade (7.5 meters long). Above the Doric frieze, extending along the entire length of the facade, is a row of dentils and a cornice with Doric guttae. This is the only place in Israel where

Tombstone with Aramaic inscription recording the reburial in the Herodian period of Uzziah, King of Judah. Found on the Mount of Olives.

guttae have been found underneath a cornice. The tomb had a most impressive facade. The walls of the facade and the porch are hewn in the rock in courses of drafted masonry.

N. Avigad, *Qedem* 2 (1945), 73–82 (Hebrew).

THE TWO-COLUMNED TOMB in the Sanhedria Quarter is a cave tomb containing loculi. It had two columns in the entrance to the porch (one of them is missing). The architrave is undecorated. Benches are found in the court.

N. Avigad, *PEQ* 1947, 119–22 • L. Y. Rahmani, *'Atiqot* 3 (1961), 96.

THE TWO-STORIED TOMB, a burial cave in Shmuel Hanavi Street, has two columns between pilasters (distyle in antis) and a Doric frieze. The

"Absalom's" tomb. Section, looking west.

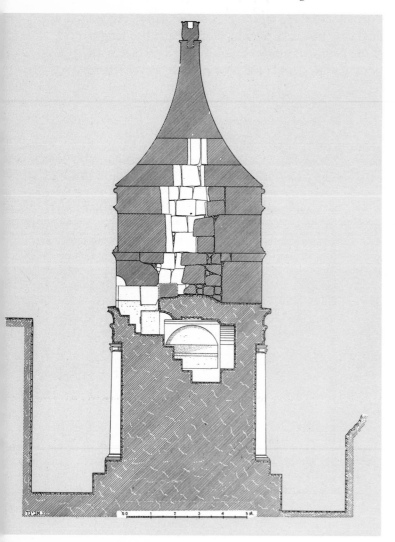

facade of the tomb was hewn out of the rock in the form of two stories, that is, above the usual facade, a second row of pilasters was carved in the rock wall. This tomb has been totally destroyed.

K. Galling, *ZDPV* 59 (1936), 111–23.

THE TOMB OF THE GRAPES lies northeast of the "Sanhedrin Tombs." Above the entrance is a pediment ornamented with vine tendrils and bunches of grapes. Decorative reliefs in floral and geometrical patterns are also found inside the porch. The tomb consists of a porch, a central chamber, three rooms with loculi, and one chamber with arcosolia.

L. H. Vincent, *RB* 8 (1899), 297 ff. • R. A. S. Macalister, *PEF QSt* 1900, 54 ff.

THE "SANHEDRIN TOMBS." This tomb cave, situated near the Sanhedria Quarter, is popularly known by this name because of the great number of burials it contains, which approximate the number of the members of the Sanhedrin. In front of the cave is a spacious court. The entrance to the porch is crowned by a pediment with acroteria. This is the finest tomb pediment uncovered in Jerusalem. Stylized acanthus leaves fill the entire area of the pediment, and pomegranates and other fruit are scattered among them. The style and workmanship are characteristic of Jewish decorative art at the end of the Second Temple period. Another smaller pediment, decorated with acanthus leaves, surmounts the entrance to the cave itself.

The large central hall (6 by 5.5 meters) is unique in having two rows of loculi, one above the other. Openings lead to two other rooms with loculi. Stairs in two corners of the floor lead down to other burial rooms. One of these rooms was not completely hewn out, so that the method of rock-cutting such tombs is illustrated clearly here.

J. Jotham Rothschild, *PEQ* 1952, 23–38; 1954, 16–22 (tomb 14) • L. Y. Rahmani *'Atiqot* 3 (1961), 93 ff.

THE TOMB OF THE FRIEZE is located in Shmuel Hanavi Street. The entrance is ornamented with a Doric frieze and an elaborate Corinthian cornice. The tomb consists of a porch and a burial chamber with loculi.

L. H. Vincent, *RB* 10 (1901), 448 • R. A. S. Macalister, *PEF QSt* 1902, 118.

THE TOMB OF HEROD'S FAMILY was discovered in 1892 near the King David Hotel. The entrance is sealed by an unusually large rolling stone. The tomb cave differs in plan from the other tombs, consisting of four chambers arranged around a small central hall. The walls of the chambers are faced with ashlars of excellent workmanship. Several stone sarcophagi decorated with floral patterns were found in the tomb. This was apparently the tomb monument of Herod referred to by Josephus. Near the cave were found the foundations of a structure which had probably served as a *nefesh* for the tomb.

C. Schick, *PEF QSt* 1892, 115–20 • R. A. S. Macalister, *ibid.*, 1901, 397–402 • Vincent–Stève, *Jérusalem*, 342–46.

MISCELLANEOUS TOMBS

1. Tomb cave situated in the Schneller area, discovered in 1906. It belongs to a Jewish family from Beth-Shean (Scythopolis), as attested by the bilingual Greek and Hebrew inscriptions incised on ossuaries found in the cave.

AMMIA	Ammia	'myh
ΣΚΥΘΟΠΟΛΙΤΙΣΣΑ	from Beth-Shean	hbšnyt
ΑΝΙΝ	Hannin from	hnyn
ΣΚΥΘΟΠΟΛΕΙΤΗΣ	Beth-Shean	hbšny
ΠΑΠΙΑΣ ΚΑΙ	Papias and	ppws
ΣΑΛΩΜΗ	Salome from	hbšny
ΣΚΥΘΟΠΟΛΕΙΤΑΙ	Beth-Shean	

Lidzbarski, *Ephemeris* 2 (1906), 191–99 • Frey, *Corpus* 2, 314 f.

2. Tomb cave in the Katamon Quarter, discovered in 1912. It contained six ossuaries with inscriptions which indicated that all the burials belonged to the Qallon family. This family was very likely related to the priestly family of Bene Jeshebab from the time of the Second Temple. The names on the inscriptions included Jeho'ezer, son of Simeon, son of Qallon; Shelomzion, wife of Jeho'ezer, son of Qallon, daughter of Gamala (= Gamaliel); Miriam and Jo'ezer and Simeon, children of Jehezaq, son of Qallon of the Bene Jeshebab family: ΙΩΣΗΠΟΣ ΚΑΛΛΩΝ.

H. Haensler, *Das Heilige Land* 57 (1913), 85–95; 124–44 • Frey, *Corpus* 2, 303 f.

3. Tomb in the Kidron Valley, discovered in 1924. This is a small cave with ossuaries bearing numerous inscriptions. These include Jehoseph, son of Simeon; Shallon, daughter of Li'ezer; Salome, wife of Eleazar; our father Simeon the Elder, Jehoseph his son; etc.

L. A. Mayer, *BBSAJ* 1 (1924), 56–60.

4. Tomb cave in the German Colony, discovered in 1926. It contains one room. A pit in the floor led down to another room containing twelve ossuaries. Most of them bear incised inscriptions such as Shalom and Mattiah her son; the wife of Mattiah and her son; Shelamzion, our mother; the children of Eleazar; and others. One of the ossuaries belonging to the head of the family bears the inscription "Father Dositheus." On its lid is a warning against opening it: "Dositheus our father, and do not open it."

E. L. Sukenik, *JPOS* 8, 1928 (113–21); 9 (1929), 45–49.

"Jason's" tomb: Drawing of warship; loculi in chamber 1.

Above: "Tombs of the Kings"; fragment of the facade.
Opposite page from top to bottom: "Tombs of the Kings";

Vincent's restoration of the facade; steps leading to the court.
Umm el-'Amed tomb; Avigad's restoration of the facade.

5. Cave on the Mount of Olives, discovered in 1928. In its single room were found thirteen ossuaries. Some of the ossuaries are ornamented and some bear Hebrew and Greek inscriptions, as, for example, "Daughter of Theodotion," ΘΕΟΔΟ - ΤΙΩΝΟΣ, ΣΑΠΙΡΑ.
One of the ossuaries has the inscription Theodotion on one side and ΔΙΔΑΣΚΑΛΟΥ, *i.e.,* "of the teacher," on the other side.

E. L. Sukenik, *Tarbiz* 1 (1930), 137–43 (Hebrew).

6. Tomb near Sheikh Badr, discovered in 1929. It consists of a small cave with one chamber, a loculus, and a niche. The objects found in the cave are of special interest. This is the only tomb in which a pottery ossuary was found together with a stone one. Iron nails were also found, indicating that there also had been a wooden ossuary. Also found were glass vessels, a bronze mirror, and round pottery lamps, attesting that the cave was used for burial after the destruction of the Second Temple, in the second century A.D.

E. L. Sukenik, *Tarbiz* 1 (1930), 122–24 (Hebrew).

7. Tomb cave on the western slope of Mount Scopus, discovered in 1932. It consists of a court, a chamber with loculi, and another room. Twenty-three decorated ossuaries and pottery vessels were found in the cave. The pottery included a group of lamps of the three most common types found in pre-Herodian and Herodian cave tombs. The ossuaries are inscribed with names such as Gerida, Mattatiah, Simeon, Boton, and Martha. The excavator believed this cave to be the tomb of the Baithos family, a priestly family at the end of the Second Temple.

E. L. Sukenik, *Qoveṣ*, Jew. Palest. Explor. Soc. 3 (1935), 62–73 (Hebrew).

8. Tomb cave in Wadi Ṣal'aḥ in the Kidron Valley, discovered in 1934. It consists of a spacious porch and a chamber with nine loculi. Five ossuaries were found here. One of them bears the inscription "Judah son of Johanan, son of Jethra." One of the loculi was found blocked with plastered stones and above it the warning written in Aramaic: "This loculus has been made for the bones of our fathers; it is two cubits long, and do not open it."

E. L. Sukenik, *Tarbiz* 6 (1935), 190–96 (Hebrew).

9. Tomb south of the Siloam Village, discovered in 1941. It consists of a single chamber with a large pit sunk in the floor. Ossuaries with Greek and Hebrew inscriptions were found as well as a group of complete pottery vessels from the Herodian

period. Among the numerous inscriptions is one mentioning Alexandros *Qrnyt* ("from Cyrene"), and it may be assumed that this tomb belonged to a Jewish family from Cyrene.

N. Avigad, *IEJ* 12 (1962), 1–12.

10. Cave south of Karem e-Sheikh in the Kidron Valley, discovered in 1941. It consists of two chambers and two loculi. Eighteen ossuaries were found. One of them is of special interest because of its unusual motif of four Ionic columns with three Greek inscriptions set between them in *tabulae ansatae*: ΣΑΛΩ ΙΩΣΗΦ

ΜΑΡΙΑ ΚΟΡΑΣΙΟΝ ("the maiden")
ΙΩΣΗΦ ΚΑΙ ΕΛΙΕΖΕΡ ΔΙΔΥΜΟΙ
("the twins")

E. L. Sukenik, *Qedem* 2 (1945), 26–31 (Hebrew).

11. Tomb cave in the Talpiot Quarter, discovered in 1945. It has one chamber with five loculi in which eleven ossuaries were found, most of them decorated with rosettes. Pottery typical of the Herodian period was found, as well as a coin of Agrippa I. The tomb is dated to the beginning of the first century A.D. On the walls of one of the ossuaries were charcoal drawings of large crosses, and two other ossuaries had Greek inscriptions reading Ἰησοῦς ἰού, Ἰησοῦς ἀλώθ.
The excavator interpreted the crosses and the inscriptions as expressions of sorrow at the crucifixion of Jesus, an interpretation not accepted by other scholars.

E. L. Sukenik, *AJA* 51 (1947), 5–30.

12. Tomb on Jebel Khalet e-Turi, south of the Siloam Village, discovered in 1955. The cave contains two chambers with loculi. In one of the rooms were found thirty ossuaries as well as a group of pottery vessels, including lamps of the three common types (pre-Herodian and Herodian). The ossuaries are of varied decoration. Some of them bear short inscriptions, and on one of the lids is a curse written in Aramaic: "Whatever a man may find for his benefit in this ossuary is an offering to God from him who is within it." This curse is unique for tombs from the period of the Second Temple, which have, as a rule, only the short warning: "Do not open."

J. T. Milik, *Liber Annuus* 7 (1956–57), 232–62.

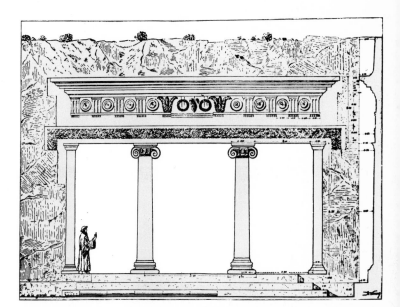

Both pages, counterclockwise: Ossuary found in the German colony, bearing the Aramaic inscription: "Dositheus our father and do not open it." The tomb of Herod's family: the entrance viewed from within; note rolling stone. Nicanor's tomb on Mount Scopus. "Sanhedrin tombs"; the pediment on the facade.

13. **Tombs at Dominus Flevit.** A huge necropolis from the Roman period, stretching over an area of about 6 dunams, was discovered in the early 1950's at the site known as Dominus Flevit on the Mount of Olives. This was the largest discovery of its kind in Jerusalem. Some twenty tomb caves of the arcosolium type were cleared, as well as about thirty-eight tombs of the pit type. These date from the third and fourth centuries A.D. and continued in use during the Byzantine period.

The tombs with loculi from the Second Temple period all belong to the usual type with one or two chambers and loculi cut into the walls. The floors of the main hall have a pit in the center. The entrances are small. Some of the small rooms were used for storing ossuaries. A rich collection of ossuaries, sarcophagi, and pottery was found here.

Seven sarcophagi of hard limestone were found, some adorned with elaborate reliefs of rosettes, wreaths, leaves, and vine tendrils.

The tombs contained 122 ossuaries of the usual type. Most of them were adorned with the common rosette pattern, with slight variations and in some the changes were more pronounced.

On the ossuaries were found forty-three inscriptions in Aramaic, Hebrew, and Greek, some of which are of considerable interest for onomastics and palaeography. Common names are: Zechariah, Jeshua, Maria, Azariah, Shelomzion, Simeon, Shapira. Inscriptions include: Martha, our mother; Salome and her son; Salome, the wife of Shapir (the masculine form of Shapira); Jehoni, the artisan; Menahem of the family of Jakhin, the priest; Φίλων Κυρηναῖος (Philon the Cyrenean); Διογένης Προσήλυτος Ζηνᾶ (Diogenes, the proselyte, the son of Zenas). On one of the ossuaries appears the monogram XP. The excavators attribute it to the burial of a Judeo-Christian, a claim which is doubtful.

P. B. Bagatti — J. T. Milik, *Gli scavi del Dominus Flevit*, Jerusalem, 1958 • M. Avi-Yonah, *IEJ* 11 (1961), 91–94.

During the years 1967–1974, additional tomb caves were excavated from the Second Temple and later periods. The tombs were found during construction work in two areas in Jerusalem: Giv'at Hamivtar and Mount Scopus.

The tombs found on Giv'at Hamivtar include:

1. **Tomb of Simon the Temple Builder.** This tomb is one of a group of four tomb caves with loculi

*Giv'at Hamivtar. Right:
The "Abba" inscription
above loculus in tomb cave.
Below: Ossuary of Simon
the Temple Builder.*

638

Nazirite tomb on Mount Scopus. Left: Chamber with sarcophagi and ossuaries in situ. Below: Stone sarcophagus with floral ornamentation.

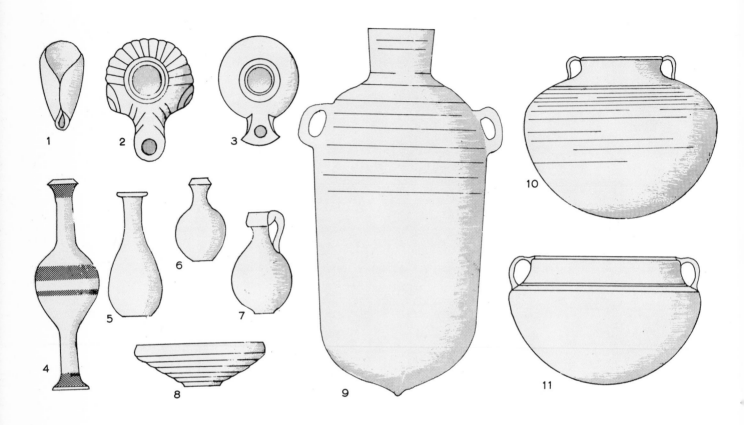

Above: Selection of pottery from tombs of the Second Temple period; see text for description of vessels. Below: Decorated ossuaries.

from the end of the Second Temple period. Ossuaries were found in three of the caves, some of them bearing inscriptions of the names of the deceased. Notable among these is the ossuary inscribed twice with the name of Simon the Temple Builder.

V. Tsaferis, *IEJ* 20 (1970), 18–32 • J. Naveh, *ibid.*, 33–37 • N. Haas, *ibid.*, 38–59 • Y. Yadin, *IEJ* 23 (1973), 18–22.

2. Another tomb cave in Giv'at Hamivtar, from the period of the Second Temple, is of great interest because of a long burial inscription incised above a loculus. The inscription, of several lines, is written in Paleo-Hebrew script. No parallel has been found as yet for this inscription which is unusual in form, content, and script. It is still under study. It reads: "I, Abba, son of the priest Eleaz(ar), son of Aaron the high (priest), I, Abba, the oppressed and the persecuted, who was born in Jerusalem, and went into exile into Babylonia and brought (back to Jerusalem) Mattathi(ah)."

E. Rosenthal, *IEJ* 23 (1973), 72–81 • J. Naveh, *ibid.* 23 (1973), 82–91; *idem*, in: *Jerusalem Revealed*, 73–74 • V. Tsaferis, *'Atiqot* 7 (1974), 61–64 (Hebrew).

Tomb of a Nazirite, on Mount Scopus. The tomb contains four chambers in which were found a number of ossuaries. Two inscriptions found on the ossuaries concerning a man and his wife are of interest: "Ḥanania son of Jonathan the Nazirite" and "Salome wife of Ḥanania son of the Nazirite." Also found in this tomb were two limestone sarcophagi, one plain and the other elaborately ornamented with reliefs which resemble the decoration on a sarcophagus from Herod's family tomb (see above).

N. Avigad, *IEJ* 21 (1971), 192–94; *idem*, in: *Jerusalem Revealed*, 66–67.

OSSUARIES. In the Talmud the small stone chests in which the bones were collected after the flesh had decayed are called *gluskamaot* (from the Greek γλοσσόκομον). They were made for the most part of soft limestone, and their length was sufficient to hold the femur — man's longest bone. Their length varied from about 45 to 75 centimeters, the width from 25 to 30 centimeters, and the height from 25 to 40 centimeters. The lids are flat, rounded, or gabled. Some of the ossuaries are plain, but generally one of the long sides, and sometimes more than one, is decorated. The most common ornamentation is a motif of two rosettes of six petals made with a compass in a border of wavy lines. There are numerous variations, such as a large number of rosettes or petals, the addition of floral patterns (acanthus or palm leaves), geometrical designs, or amphorae between the rosettes, borders of stylized leaves, etc. Architectural decorations columns, gates, or courses of hewn stones, are also used. Some of the ossuaries were painted red or yellow before the decorations were incised. A broad chisel was used for the incising in a technique borrowed from wood carving. On ossuaries of hard limestone, the ornamentation is sculptured in relief.

See bibliography of tombs with ossuaries above, and especially of Dominus Flevit and also E. L. Sukenik, *Jüdische Gräber Jerusalems um Christi Geburt*, Jerusalem, 1931 • N. Avigad, in: *Sefer Yerushalayim* (M. Avi-Yonah, ed.), Jerusalem, 1956 (Hebrew) • L. Y. Rahmani, *IEJ* 18 (1968), 220–25.

POTTERY. The pottery found in the burial caves is limited in range, comprising, as a rule, fixed types. The most frequent types are lamps, bottles, juglets, and cooking pots. Occasionally bowls and store jars are also found. The pottery is generally found scattered in the chambers and not in the tombs with the bones. It is therefore evident that the pottery was for the use of the gravediggers and visitors, for illuminating the cave, and for oil and water. In some cases, however, cooking pots and other vessels are found in the loculi, and these were probably funerary offerings.

The most common types of vessels are: (see illustration): 1. open lamp, with side walls folded together; 2. closed lamp with a grooved body, Hellenistic; 3. Herodian lamp with spatulated nozzle; 4. spindle bottle; 5. pyriform juglet (bottle); 6. pyriform juglet; 7. globular juglet; 8. cooking pot, with narrow mouth and rounded shoulder; 9. cooking pot, with wide mouth and carinated shoulder; 10. small bowl; 11. store jar.

The lamps of types 1 and 2 date from the Late Hellenistic period (second and first centuries B.C.), and the lamp of type 3 dates from the Herodian period (first century A.D.). In some cases, all three types of lamps were found in the same burial cave, indicating that it was used during both periods. The bottle (number 5) is a Hellenistic type, while the other vessels are characteristic of tombs from the Herodian period.   N. AVIGAD

P. Kahane, *IEJ* 2 (1952), 125–39, 176–82; 3 (1953), 48–54.

TABLES OF MAJOR ARCHAEOLOGICAL ACTIVITIES IN JERUSALEM SINCE 1863

Y. SHILOH

The tables and maps are intended to present briefly the archaeological-historical investigations in Jerusalem in the last 112 years. Only the major activities could be included, outlining the results concerning the various remains and monuments. The data are provided in a generally chronological order by region, with the excavator's conclusions as to dating and identification (occasionally modified in the light of more recent research).

LEGEND OF PERIODS

EB   = Early Bronze Age (32nd–23rd cent. B.C.)

MB   = Middle Bronze Age (22nd–16th cent. B.C.)

LB   = Late Bronze Age (16th–13th cent. B.C.)

1T   = First Temple period (10th–6th cent. B.C.)

2T   = Second Temple period (6th cent. B.C.–70 A.D.)

Hel. = Hellenistic period (Late 4th cent.–37 B.C.)

Her. = Herodian period (37 B.C.–70 A.D.)

Rom. = Roman period (70–324 A.D.)

Byz. = Byzantine period (324–638 A.D.)

(Dates approximate)

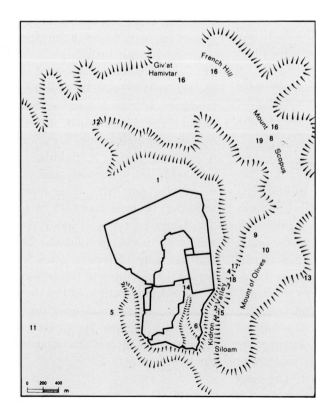

Tombs of the Jerusalem Necropolis.
1. "Tombs of the Kings."
2. "Tomb of Pharaoh's Daughter."
3. "Royal Steward's" tomb.
4. "Absalom's" tomb.
5. Herod's family tomb.
6. Tomb of Davidic Dynasty.
7. "Zechariah's tomb."
8. Nicanor's tomb.
9. Dominus Flevit.
10. Mount of Olives, western slope.
11. "Jason's" tomb.
12. "Sanhedrin tombs."
13. Mount of Olives, southeastern slope.
14. Western hill, eastern slope.
15. Siloam village.
16. Northern ridge group.
17. Cave of Jehoshaphat.
18. Bene Hezir tomb.
19. Nazirite tomb.

A. Tombs; Water Systems

	Tombs	*Water Installations*
F. de Saulcy 1863, 1865	1863, partial clearance of *Tomb of the Kings*, 1st cent.A.D.; 1865, *Tomb of Pharaoh's Daughter* in Silwan, 1T.	
Ch. W. Warren 1867–70		Discovered *Warren's Shaft*, LB(?); examination of *Gihon Spring*, Bronze Age on; *Siloam Tunnel* and *Pool*, 8th cent. B.C. on; *Strouthion Pool* (with Clermont-Ganneau, 1870); Birket Israin (both latter, 2T).
Ch. Clermont-Ganneau 1869–1871	1869, *Tomb of the Kings*, Her.; 1870, examined *Royal Steward's Tomb*, Silwan village, 1T; 1871, cleared facade of *Absalom's Tomb*, Her.	
White Friars and K. Mauss 1871		Cleared *Bethesda (Probatica) Pool*, 2T till Byz.
H. Guthe 1881		Thorough investigation of *Siloam Tunnel* and *Pool*, 1T.
C. Schick 1886–1901	1891, cleared *Herod's Family Tomb*.	1886, 1901, cleared *Gihon Spring*; examined external channels southward, 2T on; 1880, published *Siloam Tunnel Inscription*, 8th cent. B.C.
M. Parker (and L. H. Vincent) 1909–11		Cleared *Warren's Shaft*, LB(?); investigated water supply in *Gihon Spring* and *Siloam Tunnel*.
R. Weill 1913–14, 1923–24	Excavated *Tomb of Davidic Dynasty* in southern part of City of David, 1T (area used as quarry, Her.)	
N. Slouschz 1924	Final clearance of *Absalom's Tomb*; partially cleared *Zachariah's Tomb*.	
E. L. Sukenik 1925–46	1928–29, cleared *Nicanor's Tomb* on Mt. Scopus, Her.; 1926–46, cleared 38 tombs in around city, 2T.	
N. Avigad 1945–47, 1967; 1968–	Tomb monuments in *Kidron brook*: *Tomb of Pharaoh's Daughter*, *Tomb of Royal Steward*, 1T; *Absalom's Tomb*, *Cave of Jehoshaphath*, *Tomb of Bene Hezir*, *Zachariah's Tomb*, Hel.–Her.; 1967, *Mt. Scopus*: *Tomb of Nazirite Family*, 1st cent. A.D.	*Jewish Quarter*: cisterns, baths, drainage channels, Her.
P. Bagatti and G. Milik 1953–55	*Dominus Flevit* — western slope of *Mount of Olives*: clearance of rich cemetery, Hel.–Byz., mainly Her.	
P. Saller and P. Lamer 1954	Western slope of *Mount of Olives*: cleared cemeteries, MB–LB.	
L. Y. Rahmani 1954	*Jason's Tomb*, Rehavia, Hel.; tombs in *Sanhedria* area, 2T.	
H. Statchbury 1960	Final clearance of *Zachariah's Tomb*.	
K. M. Kenyon 1961–67	South-eastern slope of *Mount of Olives*: shaft-tombs, MB I.	*Area F*: examination of walls damming lower Tyropoeon valley (nothing earlier than Hel. — mostly Her. and Byz. — of dams and pools).
B. Mazar 1968–	Tombs on lower eastern slope of *Western Hill*, 8th–7th cent. B.C.	South-western corner of *Temple Mount*: aqueduct and cisterns, Her.; cisterns, 1T
D. Ussishkin 1968	Survey of tomb-caves in *Silwan village*, 1T	
Various 1968–	Tomb-caves with ossuaries: *Mount Scopus, French Hill* and other sites	
A. Mazar 1969		Survey of aqueducts from *Hebron–Bethlehem region*, 2T and later
J. Margovski 1970–71		Turkish aqueduct near *Burj Kabrit*.
D. Bahat and M. Ben-Ari 1971–72		*Zahal Square*: Crusader aqueduct

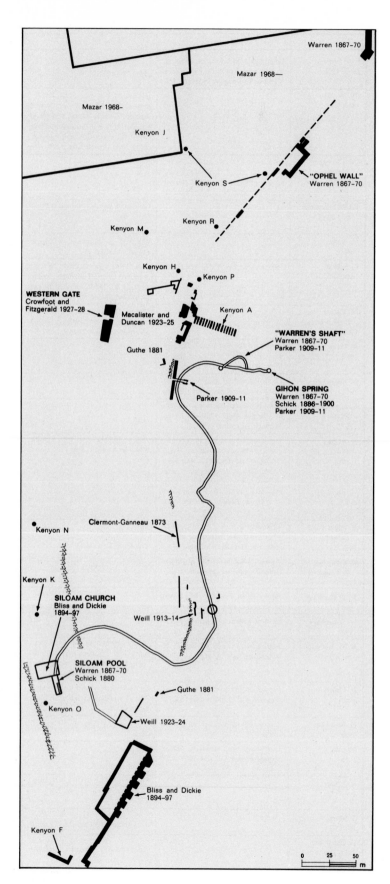

*Excavations in the City of David
(see table, opposite page).*

B. The City

	Old City and Vicinity	Temple Mount; City of David, North and West	City of David, East	Jewish Quarter and Mount Zion
Ch. Wilson 1867–68	Examination of facade of *Holy Sepulchre*, Crusader.	Discovery of *Wilson's Arch*, Her.		
Ch. W. Warren 1867–70	Trial excavations in *Muristan*; *Qal'at Jalud* (city-wall and tower fragment), late 2T (?); *David Street* (city-wall fragments and two towers of *First Wall*).	Trial shafts to bedrock around walls of *Temple Mount*, Her. on; base of pier of *Robinson's Arch*, Her; examination of *Wilson's Arch* and structures to west (with Ch. Wilson); examination of *Solomon's Stables*, Her. (?) on.	*Ophel Wall* and tower, probably no earlier than Her., reused in Byz. (Eudocia's wall, 5th cent A.D.?).	
H. Modsley 1871–75				Remains on line of *First Wall* at southwest corner of *Upper City* (Bishop Gobat's School); traces of quarrying and fosse.
Ch. Clermont-Ganneau 1873–74		Examination of *Antonia region* (Her.) and *Ecce Homo Arch* (Rom.); discovery of *Temple Inscription* forbidding entry of Gentiles.	*City-wall* fragment (20 m long), 2T.	
White Friars and K. Mauss 1863–76, 1888–1900	Discovery of church remains overlying *Probatica Pool*, St. Anne's (1879), Byz.			
H. Guthe 1881			*City-wall* fragments and dwellings, 2T.	
C. Schick 1886–1901		1891: Report on clearance of *Golden Gate* by Ottoman authorities.		
F. J. Bliss and A. C. Dickie 1894–97		*Siloam Church* over Siloam Pool, mid-5th cent. A.D.	City-wall fragments at SE corner of *Eastern Hill*, at end of Tyropoeon valley, 1T to Byz.	City-wall fragments and towers on S slope of *Mt. Zion*, 2T and Byz.; city-wall fragments, quarrying and fosse forming line to NE above *Tyropoeon valley* (apparently inner wall protecting E flank of Upper City), Hel.–Her. (?); dwellings and street fragments, Byz.
M. Parker (and L. H. Vincent) 1909–11			Building and fortification fragments, on E slope.	
L. H. Vincent 1910–13	Examination of city-wall fragments (*Third Wall*) at *Qal'at Jalud* (1912); Mt. of Olives: 1910, *Eleona Church*; 1913, *Church of Ascension*, Byz.			
P. G. Orfali 1909, 1919–20	*Gethsemane Church*, Byz.			
R. Weill 1913–14, 1923–24			*City-wall* fragments (20 m long); southern gate (?); square guard-tower; all 1T. Round tower, Hel.; discovery of *Theodotos Inscription*, 1st cent. B.C.	
R.A.S. Macalister and J. G. Duncan 1923–25		City-wall fragments in N, ascribed to Jebusite and earliest Israelite cities; apparently no earlier than Rom.–Byz.	*Jebusite wall*, two towers and glacis, held to be of Jebusite and earliest Israelite cities. Kenyon (see below) ascribes them to early 2T, mainly Hel. *Ophel Ostracon* discovered.	
E.L. Sukenik (with L. A. Mayer) 1925–27, 1940	Excavation of parts of wall and towers on line of *Third Wall* on N of city, between "Italian Hospital" and northern extremity of Kidron brook, mid-1st cent. A.D.			
J. Germer-Durand 1889–				Byz. church on premises of *Church of St. Pierre in Gallicantu*; dwellings and stepped street in same area, 2T and Byz.
J. W. Crowfoot and G. M. Fitzgerald 1927–28		City-wall and *western gate*, ascribed to Israelite through Hel. Kenyon (see below) ascribes them to no earlier than Hel.		
R. W. Hamilton 1931, 1937–38	1937–38, excavation of foundations of *Damascus Gate*: Her. remains; gate of *Second Wall*; gate of Rom. and later periods. Trench E of *Herod's Gate*, foundations of N face of Old City Wall — fragments of city-wall of Aelia Capitolina, Rom.			1931, *Tyropoeon valley*, paved street, drainage channels, Her. on.

Excavations in Jerusalem (see table, opposite page).

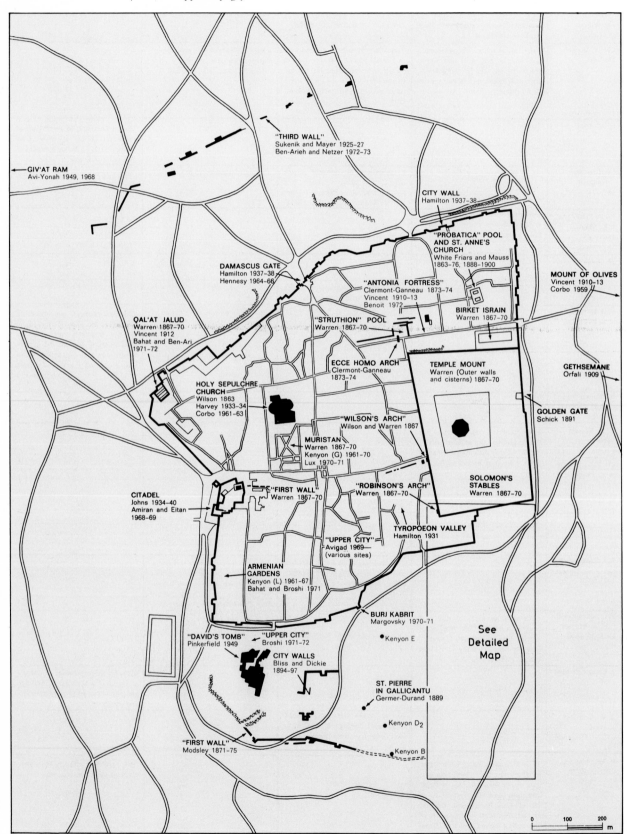

GIV'AT RAM
Avi-Yonah 1949, 1968

"THIRD WALL"
Sukenik and Mayer 1925–27
Ben-Arieh and Netzer 1972–73

CITY WALL
Hamilton 1937–38

**"PROBATICA" POOL
AND ST. ANNE'S
CHURCH**
White Friars and Mauss
1863–76, 1888–1900

DAMASCUS GATE
Hamilton 1937–38
Hennesy 1964–66

MOUNT OF OLIVES
Vincent 1910–13
Corbo 1959

"ANTONIA FORTRESS"
Clermont-Ganneau 1873–74
Vincent 1910–13
Benoit 1972

BIRKET ISRAIN
Warren 1867–70

QAL'AT JALUD
Warren 1867–70
Vincent 1912
Bahat and Ben-Ari
1971–72

"STRUTHION" POOL
Warren 1867–70

ECCE HOMO ARCH
Clermont-Ganneau
1873–74

TEMPLE MOUNT
Warren (Outer walls
and cisterns) 1867–70

GETHSEMANE
Orfali 1909

**HOLY SEPULCHRE
CHURCH**
Wilson 1863
Harvey 1933–34
Corbo 1961–63

GOLDEN GATE
Schick 1891

"WILSON'S ARCH"
Wilson and Warren 1867

MURISTAN
Warren 1867–70
Kenyon (G) 1961–70
Lux 1970–71

"ROBINSON'S ARCH"
Warren 1867–70

**SOLOMON'S
STABLES**
Warren 1867–70

CITADEL
Johns 1934–40
Amiran and Eitan
1968–69

"FIRST WALL"
Warren 1867–70

"UPPER CITY"
Avigad 1969
(various sites)

TYROPOEON VALLEY
Hamilton 1931

**ARMENIAN
GARDENS**
Kenyon (L) 1961–67
Bahat and Broshi 1971

BURJ KABRIT
Margovsky 1970–71

See
Detailed
Map

● Kenyon E

"DAVID'S TOMB"
Pinkerfield 1949

"UPPER CITY"
Broshi 1971–72

CITY WALLS
Bliss and Dickie
1894–97

**ST. PIERRE
IN GALLICANTU**
Germer-Durand 1889

● Kenyon D₂

"FIRST WALL"
Modsley 1871–75

● Kenyon B

0   100   200
m

646

	Old City and Vicinity	Temple Mount; City of David, North and West	City of David, East	Jewish Quarter and Mount Zion
W. Harvey 1933–34	Examinations of *Church of Holy Sepulchre*, remains from Byz. on.			
C. N. Johns 1934–40	Excavations in *Citadel*: wall and towers, Hel.; Herodian repairs and construction of *Phasael Tower* ("David's Tower"); remains of camp of Roman Tenth Legion overlying Herod's Palace; part of W city-wall of Aelia Capitolina, Rom.			
J. Pinkerfeld 1949				Trial-excavation of foundations in *David's Tomb*, Mt. Zion; apse discovered, possibly of synagogue Rom.
M. Avi-Yonah 1947, 1968	*Giv'at Ram*, W Jerusalem: remains of camp of Roman Tenth Legion; church and monastery, Byz.			
V. Corbo 1959, 1961–63	1959, summit of *Mt. of Olives*: *Church of Ascension*, Byz. 1961–63, examinations in *Church of Holy Sepulchre*.			
K. M. Kenyon 1961–67	*Area C* (*Muristan*): 2T, in excavator's opinion, outside line of "Second Wall"(?), traces of fosse of which were found; in Rom., area filled and levelled, being included within Aelia Capitolina; dwellings, Byz.	*Area G* (*Ḥakuret el-Khatuniyye*, S of SW corner of Temple Mount): remains of splendid public building, Early Arab (but ascribed to Rom. Byz. by excavators; with R. de Vaux). *Areas K, M, N*: Israelite construction at top of hill; Hel. dwellings, cut by city-wall of late 2T; paved area of street; Her.; overlying remains of destruction of 70 A.D., Byz. settlement. Further evidence of gap in settlement of area of "City of David" in Rom. and early Byz. till 5th cent. A.D. (Excavator suggests N line of defences of "City of David", through areas A-P-H-M).	*Area S*: Thick wall of ashlar masonry, 8th cent. B.C. — S line of wall on S of Temple Mount (?). *Area A*: pottery from EB on; remains of city fortifications at lower end of sectional trench, from 18th cent. B.C. till end of 2T; supporting terrace walls of city on slope ("Millo" ?), from LB till destruction of 1T; remains of dwellings of above periods, on abovenoted terraces; above, fortifications of 5th cent. B.C. on, mainly Hel. (the "Jebusite wall"). *Areas A, H, R*: Clear evidence of absolute destruction of city in 70 A.D; above, Byz. dwellings.	*Areas B, D₁, D₂, E* (on slope of *Mt. Zion*): In excavator's opinion, no remains earlier than period of Agrippa I found; thus, earliest settlement on Mt. Zion and its fortifications no earlier than mid-1st cent. A.D; traces of dense settlement, especially in Byz. *Area L* (in *Armenian Quarter*): Pottery of 8th-6th cents. B.C.; remains of walls, Persian period (?); objects from camp of Roman Tenth Legion; dwellings, Byz.; remains of Mameluke market.
J. Hennessy 1964–66	Revealing of early gate beneath *Damascus Gate* (ascribed to *Third Wall*, with repair and use in Rom.–Byz.).			
B. Mazar 1968–		S and SW of *Temple Mount*: remains from Her. on		
R. Amiran and A. Eitan 1968–69	Excavations in *Citadel*: Iron II, Hel. Her. Rom.–Byz. remains			
N. Avigad 1969–				*Jewish Quarter*, various sites: Israelite settlement, 8th cent. B.C. on; Hel., Her., Byz., Arab remains
U. Lux 1970–71	Investigations beneath *Erlöser Kirche*; segment of wall and fill, 1st cent. A.D.			
J. Margovsky 1970–71				Excavation adjacent to *Burj Kabrit*: Base of tower, prior to 12th cent. A.D; Byz. street segment; part of paved street, Her.
D. Bahat and M. Broshi 1971				Excavations in *Armenian Garden*: Her. and Crusader remains
M. Broshi 1971–	Excavations adjacent to SW segment of Turkish city-wall; segment of *First Wall*, Hel. on.			Excavations on *Mt. Zion* (*Armenian churchyard*): Iron II, Her., Rom., Byz., early Arab, Crusader remains
P. Benoit 1972	Investigation of *Lithostrotos*, 2T, Rom.			
D. Bahat and M. Ben-Ari 1971–72	*Zahal Square*: Crusader remains			
S. Ben-Arieh and E. Netzer 1972–73	Excavation near American Consulate on N of city: Remains ascribed to *Third Wall* (late 2T); remains of monastery (?), Byz.			

CHRONOLOGICAL TABLES

The Prehistoric Periods in Palestine

PERIOD	CULTURE	ICE AGE IN EUROPE	GEOLOGICAL EPOCH	APPROXIMATE DATES
Lower Paleolithic	Abbevillian	Mindel	Middle Pleistocene (Quaternary)	500,000
	Lower and Middle Acheulian	Mindel-Riss		to
	Upper Acheulian	Riss		120,000
Middle Paleolithic	Micoquian, "pre-Aurignacian"	Riss-Würm	Upper Pleistocene (Quaternary)	80,000
	Yabrudian	Würm I		
		Würm II		
Upper Paleolithic	Phase I "Emireh"	Würm III		35,000
	Phase II			
	Phase III–V Aurignacian			
Epipaleolithic (Mesolithic)	Phase VI Kebaran			15,000
		Würm IV		
	Natufian	Post glacial	Holocene	8,000
Pre-pottery Neolithic	Phase A			
	Phase B			
Pottery Neolithic				5,500
Chalcolithic	Early phase			4,000 to
	Ghassulian phase			3,150

The Archaeological Periods in Palestine

Paleolithic (Old Stone Age)   25,000–10,000 BC
Mesolithic (Middle Stone Age)   10,000–7500
Neolithic (New Stone Age)   7500–4000
Chalcolithic   4000–3150

Bronze Age
Early Bronze Age I A–C   3150–2850
Early Bronze Age II   2850–2650
Early Bronze Age III   2650–2350
Early Bronze Age IV (IIIA)   2350–2200
Middle Bronze Age I   2200–2000
Middle Bronze Age IIA   2000–1750
Middle Bronze Age IIIB   1750–1550
Late Bronze Age I   1550–1400
Late Bronze Age IIA   1400–1300
Late Bronze Age IIB   1300–1200

Iron Age
Iron Age IA   1200–1150
Iron Age IB   1150–1000

Iron Age IIA   1000–900
Iron Age IIB   900–800
Iron Age IIC   800–586

Babylonian and Persian Periods   586–332

Hellenistic Period
Hellenistic I   332–152
Hellenistic II (Hasmonaean)   152–37

Roman Period
Roman I (Herodian)   37 BC–AD 70
Roman II   AD 70–180
Roman III   180–324

Byzantine Period
Byzantine I   324–451
Byzantine II   451–640

Early Arab Period   640–1099

Crusader Period   1099–1291

Selected List of Kings

Egypt

Pre-Dynastic Period		
4th and 3rd millennium		
Proto-Dynastic Period		
Ist Dynasty	*c.* 3100–2890 BC Narmer	
IInd Dynasty	*c.* 2890–2686	
IIIrd Dynasty	*c.* 2686–2613	
Old Kingdom		
IVth Dynasty	*c.* 2613–2494	
	Snefru	
	Khufu	
	Khafre	
Vth Dynasty	*c.* 2494–2345	
VIth Dynasty	*c.* 2345–2181	
	Pepi I	
First Intermediate Period		
VIIth Dynasty–Xth Dynasty		
Middle Kingdom		
XIth Dynasty	*c.* 2133–1991	
XIIth Dynasty	*c.* 1991–1786	
Amenemhet I	1991–1962	
Senusert I	1971–1928	
Amenemhet II	1929–1895	
Senusert II	1897–1878	
Senusert III	1878–1843	
Amenemhet III	1842–1797	
Amenemhet IV	1798–1970	
Sebeknefrure	1789–1786	
Second Intermediate Period — the Hyksos Period		
XIII–XVIIth Dynasties		
New Kingdom		
XVIIIth Dynasty	1567–1320	
Ahmose	1570–1546	
Amenhotep I	1546–1526	
Thutmose I	1525–1512	
Thutmose II	*c.* 1512–1504	
Hatshepsut	1503–1482	
Thutmose III	1504–1450	
Amenhotep II	1450–1425	
Thutmose IV	1425–1417	
Amenhotep III	1417–1379	

Amenhotep IV (Akhenaton)	1379–1362 BC
Smenkhkere	1364–1361
Tutankhamon	1361–1352
Eye	1352–1348
Haremhab	1348–1320
XIXth Dynasty	1320–1200
Ramses I	1320–1318
Seti I	1318–1304
Ramses II	1304–1237
Merneptah	1236–1223
Seti II	1216–1210
XXth Dynasty	1200–1085
Ramses III	1198–1166
Ramses IV–XI	1166–1085
End of New Kingdom	
XXIst Dynasty	1085–935
XXIInd Dynasty	935–730
Shishak I	935–914
Osorkon II	914–874
XXIIIrd Dynasty	817–740
XXIVth Dynasty	730–709
XXVth Dynasty (Nubian or Ethiopian)	750–656
Shabaka	716–695
Taharka	689–664
XXVIth Dynasty	664–525
Psamtik I	664–610
Necho II	610–595
Psamtik II	595–589
Psamtik III	526–525
XXVIIth Dynasty (Persian)	505–404
Cambyses	525–522
Darius I	521–486
Xerxes	486–466
Artaxerxes	465–424
Darius II	424–404
XXVIIIth–XXXth Dynasties	404–343

Assyria

Shalmaneser I	1274–1245 BC
Tiglath-Pileser I	1115–1077
Ashurnasirpal I	1049–1031
Shalmaneser II	1030–1019
Tiglath-Pileser II	966–935
Adadnirari II	911–891
Ashurnasirpal II	883–859
Shalmaneser III	858–824
Adadnirari III	810–783
Shalmaneser IV	782–772
Tiglath-Pileser III	745–727
Shalmaneser V	726–722
Sargon II	721–705
Sennacherib	704–681
Esarhaddon	680–669
Ashurbanipal	668–631

Neo-Babylonian Kingdom

Nabopolassar	626–605 BC
Nebuchadnezzar II	605–562
Amel-Marduk	562–560
Nabunaid	556–539
Nergal Sarussur	560–556

Persia

Cyrus	559–530 BC
Cambyses	530–522
Darius I	522–486
Xerxes	486–464
Artaxerxes I	464–423
Darius II	423–404
Artaxerxes II	404–359
Artaxerxes III	359–338
Arses (Xerxes II)	338–336
Darius III	336–331

The Kings of Judah and Israel

THE UNITED KINGDOM

Saul	ca. 1020–1004 BC
David	1004–965
Solomon	965–928

JUDAH		ISRAEL	
Rehoboam	928–911	Jeroboam	928–907
Abijam	911–908	Nadab	907–906
Asa	908–867	Baasha	906–883
Jehoshaphat	867–846	Elah	883–882
Jehoram	846–843	Zimri	882
Ahaziah	843–842	Omri	882–871
Athaliah	842–836	Ahab	871–852
Joash	836–798	Ahaziah	852–851
Amaziah	798–769	Jehoram	851–842
Uzziah	769–733	Jehu	842–814
Jotham	758–743	Jehoahaz	814–800
Ahaz	733–727	Jehoash	800–784
Hezekiah	727–698	Jeroboam	784–748
Manasseh	698–642	Zechariah	748
Amon	641–640	Shallum	748
Josiah	640–609	Menahem	747–737
Jehoahaz	609	Pekahiah	737–735
Jehoiakim	609–598	Pekah	735–733
Jehoiachin	597	Hoshea	733–724
Zedekiah	596–586		

The Hasmoneans

Jonathan	152–142 BC
Simeon	142–134
John Hyrcanus	134–104
Aristobulus	104–103
Alexander Jannaeus	103–76
Salome Alexandra	76–67
Aristobulus II	67–63
Hyrcanus II	63–40
Matthias Antigonus	40–37

The Herodians

Herod (the Elder)	37–4 BC
Archelaus	4 BC–AD 6
Herod Antipas	4 BC–AD 39
Philip	4 BC–AD 34
Herod Agrippa I	AD 37–44
Agrippa II	53–100(?)

The Procurators

Coponius	*c.* AD 6–9
M. Ambibulus	9–12
Annius Rufus	12–15
Valerius Gratus	15–26
Pontius Pilatus	26–36
Marcellus	36–37
Cuspius Fadus	41–46
Tiberius Alexander	46–48
Ventidius Cumanus	48–52
Antonius Felix	52–60
Porcius Festus	60–62
Albinus	62–64
Gessius Florus	64–66

Seleucid Kings

Seleucus I Nicator	311–281 BC	Antiochus VII Grypus	121–96
Antiochus I Soter	281–261	Antiochus IX Cyzicenus	115–95
Antiochus II Theos	261–246	Seleucus VI Epiphanes Nicator	96–95
Seleucus II Callinicus	246–225	Demetrius III Philopator	95–88
Seleucus III Soter	225–223	Antiochus X Eusebes	95–83
Antiochus III the Great	223–187	Antiochus XI Philadelphus	94
Seleucus IV Philopator	187–175	Philip I Philadelphus	94–83
Antiochus IV Epiphanes	175–164	Antiochus XII Dionysus	87–84
Antiochus V Eupator	163–162	Antiochus XIII	69–64
Demetrius I Soter	162–150	Philip II	67–65
Alexander Balas	150–145		
Demetrius II Nicator	145–140		
Antiochus VI Epiphanes	145–138		
Antiochus VII Sidetes	138–129		
Demetrius II Nicator	129–125		
Cleopatra Thea	126		
Cleopatra Thea and Antiochus VIII Grypus	125–121		
Seleucus V	125		

The Ptolemies

Ptolemy I Soter	304–282 BC
Ptolemy II Philadelphus	285–246
Ptolemy III Euergetes	246–221
Ptolemy IV Philopator	221–204
Ptolemy V Epiphanes	204–180
Ptolemy VI Philometor	180–145
Ptolemy VII Neos Philopator	145–144
Ptolemy VIII Euergetes II	145–116
Ptolemy IX Soter II	116–107
Ptolemy X Alexander I	107–88
Ptolemy IX Soter II (restored)	88–81
Ptolemy XI Alexander II	80 BC
Ptolemy XII Neos Dionysos	80–51
Cleopatra VII Philopator	51–30
Ptolemy XIII	51–47
Ptolemy XIV	47–44
Ptolemy XV	44–30

Overlapping dates usually indicate co-regencies.

Roman and Byzantine Emperors

Augustus	27 BC–AD 14	Septimius Severus	193–211	Gallienus	253–268	Theodosius	379–383
Tiberius	AD 14–37	Clodius Albinus	193–197	Aurelian	270–275	Honorius	393–423
Caligula	37–41	Pescennius Niger	193–194	Probus	276–282	Arcadius	383–408
Claudius	41–54	Caracalla	198–217	Diocletian	284–305	Theodosius II	408–450
Nero	54–68	Geta	209–212	Maximianus	286–305	Marcian	450–457
Galba	68–69	Macrinus	217–218	Constantinus I	293–306	Leon I	457–474
Vespasian	69–79	Diadumenianus	218	Galerius	293–311	Zenon	474–491
Titus	79–81	Elagabalus	218–222	Constantine I	306–337	Anastasius I	491–518
Domitian	81–96	Severus Alexander	222–235	Magnentius	337–353	Justin I	518–527
Nerva	96–98	Maximinus	235–238	Constans I	337–350	Justinian I	527–565
Trajan	98–117	Philip the Arab	244–249	Constantius II	353–362	Justin II	565–578
Hadrian	117–138	Decius	249–251	Julian	361–363	Tiberius II	578–582
Antoninus Pius	138–161	Trebonianus Gallus	251–253	Valens	364–378	Focas	602–610
Lucius Verus	161–169	Valerian	253–260	Valentinian	364–375	Heraclius	610–641
Commodus	176–192					Constans II	641–668